OBSERVING VATICAN II: THE CONFIDENTIAL REPORTS OF THE ARCHBISHOP OF CANTERBURY'S REPRESENTATIVE, BERNARD PAWLEY, 1961–1964

OBSERVING VATICAN II: THE CONFIDENTIAL REPORTS OF THE ARCHBISHOP OF CANTERBURY'S REPRESENTATIVE, BERNARD PAWLEY, 1961–1964

edited by
ANDREW CHANDLER and CHARLOTTE HANSEN

CAMDEN FIFTH SERIES
Volume 43

CAMBRIDGE
UNIVERSITY PRESS

FOR THE ROYAL HISTORICAL SOCIETY
University College London, Gower Street, London WC1 6BT
2013

Published by the Press Syndicate of the University of Cambridge
The Edinburgh Building, Cambridge CB2 8RU, United Kingdom
32 Avenue of the Americas, New York, NY 10013-2473, USA
477 Williamstown Road, Port Melbourne, VIC 3207, Australia
C/Orense, 4, Planta 13, 28020 Madrid, Spain
Lower Ground Floor, Nautica Building, The Water Club,
Beach Road, Granger Bay, 8005 Cape Town, South Africa

First published 2013

A catalogue record for this book is available from the British Library

ISBN 9781107052949 hardback

SUBSCRIPTIONS. The serial publications of the Royal Historical Society, *Royal Historical Society Transactions* (ISSN 0080-4401) and Camden Fifth Series (ISSN 0960-1163) volumes, may be purchased together on annual subscription. The 2013 subscription price, which includes print and electronic access (but not VAT), is £142 (US $237 in the USA, Canada, and Mexico) and includes Camden Fifth Series, volumes 43 and 44 and Transactions Sixth Series, volume 23 (published in December). Japanese prices are available from Kinokuniya Company Ltd, P.O. Box 55, Chitose, Tokyo 156, Japan. EU subscribers (outside the UK) who are not registered for VAT should add VAT at their country's rate. VAT registered subscribers should provide their VAT registration number. Prices include delivery by air.

Subscription orders, which must be accompanied by payment, may be sent to a bookseller, subscription agent, or direct to the publisher: Cambridge University Press, The Edinburgh Building, Shaftesbury Road, Cambridge CB2 8RU, UK; or in the USA, Canada, and Mexico: Cambridge University Press, Journals Fulfillment Department, 100 Brook Hill Drive, West Nyack, New York, 10994-2133, USA.

SINGLE VOLUMES AND BACK VOLUMES. A list of Royal Historical Society volumes available from Cambridge University Press may be obtained from the Humanities Marketing Department at the address above.

Printed and bound by CPI Group (UK) Ltd, Croydon, CR0 4YY

For Margaret Pawley and Virginia Johnstone

CONTENTS

ACKNOWLEDGEMENTS

The editors acknowledge with gratitude the guidance of Cressida Williams at Canterbury Cathedral Library and staff at Lambeth Palace Library in London. The work has been much encouraged by Margaret Pawley and by Virginia Johnstone, who typed most of the reports in Rome. It has also been greatly assisted by many conversations with other scholars and thinkers, particularly those who came to discuss Vatican II in its ecumenical context at a colloquium in George Bell House, Chichester Cathedral, in June 2013. The editors take full responsibility for any errors or omissions.

The book has essentially been made possible by a generous research grant from the University of Chichester. We would like to thank staff at the library of the University of Chichester and our colleagues in the Department of History there.

We owe a great debt to Hester Higton for her meticulous copy-editing and for her fundamental contribution to the creation of a credible index. Much is also owed to Alice Petersen for her patient work on the intricacies of the text.

Andrew Chandler and Charlotte Hansen
Chichester, June 2013

INTRODUCTION

Charles de Gaulle famously called the Second Vatican Council the most important event in modern history.[1] Many commentators at the time saw the Council as nothing short of revolutionary, and the later judgements of historians have upheld this view. The astonishing enterprise of a man who became, quite unexpectedly, Pope John XXIII in 1958, this purposeful *aggiornamento* of the Roman Catholic Church was almost at once a leviathan of papers, committees, commissions, and meetings. Scholars have been left to confront no less than twelve volumes of 'ante-preparatory' papers, seven volumes of preparatory papers, and thirty-two volumes of documents generated by the Council itself. A lasting impression of the impressiveness of the affair is often conveyed by photographs of the 2,200-odd bishops of the Church, drawn from around the world, sitting in the basilica of St Peter, a vast, orchestrated theatre of ecclesiastical intent. For this was the council to bring the Church into a new relationship with the modern world, one that was more creative and less defiant; a council to reconsider much – if not quite all – of the theological, liturgical, and ethical infrastructure in which Catholicism lived and breathed and had its being.

Integral to these ecclesiological reconsiderations was the question of how Rome should begin to acknowledge the new realities of the ecumenical age and the possibilities of open, even official, relationships with other churches. A defining dimension of Vatican II was the presence of a number of Observers invited by John XXIII to represent other traditions and to report the workings of the Council to their own leaders. As the Council unfolded, however, it was perceived that those who came simply to 'observe' eventually came to exert at least a modest influence, too. Vatican II was not merely a succession of formal sessions which occurred to revise and adopt a series of statements: it

[1] Books on Vatican II are not difficult to come by but, for a solid historical overview, John O'Malley's *What Happened at Vatican II* (Cambridge, MA, 2008) currently leads the field. See, too, Massimo Faggioli, *Vatican II: the battle for meaning* (Mahwah, NJ, 2012). Peter Hebblethwaite's fine *John XXIII: Pope of the Council* (London, 1984) is followed by his equally imposing *Paul VI: the first modern Pope* (London, 1993).

was an immense conversation, of which the Observers were clearly a significant part.

Between 1961 and 1964 the Archbishop of Canterbury – first Geoffrey Fisher, then Arthur Michael Ramsey – employed a representative in Rome at the Vatican Council. This was Bernard Pawley. During the Council itself Pawley was joined by other Anglican Observers, particularly the Bishop of Ripon, John Moorman. Pawley's achievement was to open a regular channel of information and opinion which created an important new dimension in the long, and often difficult, history of the relations of the two communions. This soon found a striking place in the new age of ecumenical diplomacy which the twentieth century brought, first to the Protestant world and then, by degrees, to the Roman Catholic and Orthodox churches too. But Pawley also created a vivid record of the Council at large as he watched and interpreted it from his own particular position. He certainly had his own view and he was unafraid to indulge it. Accordingly, he teaches us almost as much about the attitudes of his own Church as he does about those of Rome in the days of the Council. He also shows the extent to which Roman Catholicism, Anglicanism, and Protestantism at large continued to negotiate with the claims of a disputatious history.

Long after the tumult of the sixteenth and seventeenth centuries the place of Roman Catholics in the United Kingdom remained a question of public politics across national society. In 1701 the Act of Settlement not only precluded a Catholic from becoming king of England but also effectively ended any hope of a reunion of Rome and Canterbury. Although there were stray encounters, eloquent friendships, and even committed private exchanges (as took place between Archbishop Wake and the French Church in 1718–1719[2]), it was not until the middle of the long nineteenth century that both Rome and Canterbury again gave serious thought to a reunion. A number of pivotal events were to mark the relationship between the two and even point towards the coming of the Second Vatican Council. The English Catholic Church experienced a reawakened self-awareness (which was part of a wider Catholic crusade, fought on a number of fronts), while the Anglican Church was in turmoil, not least because of the intellectual challenges issued by strikingly gifted members who it saw defecting to Rome.

In a century of reform in which the British state sought to consolidate its authority by incorporating those hitherto excluded from government, it was the need to conserve the union of Britain

---

[2] The most extensive treatment of this remains Norman Sykes, *William Wake: Archbishop of Canterbury 1657–1737* (2 vols, Cambridge, 1957); see esp. vol. 1, chapters 1 and 4.

and Ireland that in 1829 brought the Catholic Emancipation Act. At a stroke this repealed laws that imposed civil disabilities on Catholics and allowed them to hold parliamentary office. Twenty-one years later Pope Pius IX (1846–1878) decided to restore the Catholic hierarchy in England as Rome had become increasingly aware that there was an upsurge in Catholicism in the country, much of it the consequence of a swelling migration across the Irish Sea. On the 29 September 1850 Nicholas Wiseman was appointed Archbishop of Westminster and became the first English cardinal since the Reformation.[3] His well-known pastoral letter from October of that year, *Without the Flaminian Gate of Rome*,[4] signalled the beginnings of a halcyon period for English Catholicism. On the one hand Catholic emancipation and the restoration of the hierarchy showed a degree of tolerance of the foreign Catholic faith; on the other hand it unleashed fierce 'no popery' agitation and cries of 'Papal Aggression'. Evidently, the old fear of this foreign religion was still deeply entrenched in parts of the national psyche. When they looked back upon 400 years of Anglo-Catholic relations Bernard and Margaret Pawley saw the restoration to have had fatal consequences for ecumenical relations as it signalled 'the triumph in the Roman Catholic community for a policy of dependence on Rome'.[5]

As the restoration gathered formidable momentum, the Established Church in England was dealing with problems of its own. The travails of the Oxford Movement represented something more than a crisis of sensitive consciences. Even before they took off for Rome, Tractarians had begun to envision unity with Rome (or in some cases with Eastern Orthodoxy). The converts themselves were far from easy to dismiss; a vigorous assortment, they included the familiar names of John Henry Newman, one day to be a cardinal, and Henry Edward Manning, later Archbishop of Westminster. Other luminaries such as the theologian and mathematician William George Ward and the co-editor of the *Rambler*, Richard Simpson, now contributed immensely to the richness of the English Roman Catholic tapestry. But if conversion for these individuals possessed the quality of resolution, such a leap of faith had not landed them in a situation in which everything was easy or obvious. The breach with Rome had not quite evaporated. Some English-speaking Catholics sometimes found having to follow Vatican

[3]Wilfrid Ward, *The Life and Times of Cardinal Wiseman* (London, 1897).
[4]Published by Hooker, 7 October 1850.
[5]Bernard Pawley and Margaret Pawley, *Rome and Canterbury through Four Centuries: a study of the relations between the Church of Rome and the Anglican Churches, 1530–1981* (London, 1981), p. 203.

directives that bore no direct relevance to their own understandings or circumstances perplexing.

Nobody in the nineteenth century would have allowed that politics and religion were in any way separable matters, least of all when it came to Rome. Nor was the place of Roman Catholics in the United Kingdom simply a matter of constitutional amendments or native prejudice.[6] Roman policy did not stay still. The question of loyalty – to the Pope or to the Crown – was now perpetuated by the general victory of Ultramontanism in Rome during the lengthy pontificate of Pius IX (1846–1878). In order to compensate for its weakened diplomatic and political position in relation to national governments throughout the nineteenth century, the Holy See began to play a more direct and aggressive role in the political and intellectual life of the individual national churches than it had done under *l'ancien régime*. Rome increasingly became a dominant force in the international direction of Catholic theology, led by a revival of Neo-Thomistic philosophy and theology, and intervened in virtually every theological controversy that arose. The devotion to the Holy See and to the figure of the Pope in particular also grew among ordinary Catholics, who for the first time in history could see depictions of their Pope, thanks to modern mass media. Such popular devotion was cleverly utilized by a resurrected scholastic body. This development of curial bureaucracy and the elevation of the teaching authority, the *Magisterium*, would have consequences for the Second Vatican Council. The increase in papal prestige also caused strong reactions from opponents of papal centralism both within the Church itself and externally, as notable Liberal Catholics and, later, so-called Modernists lamented the lack of such development as seen outside the Church. If anything, a rapprochement with the Anglicans had become more difficult.

On the 8 December 1854 the Dogma of the Immaculate Conception of the Virgin Mary was solemnly proclaimed in Rome. Although the observance of the Conception appeared in the Book of Common Prayer for this December day, no provisions were made for its observance. Anglican theologians had long pointed out that the dogma was not contained in scripture, that it was unlikely to be deduced from scripture or defined by an ecumenical council, and that the definition of it as a dogma was unnecessary. But it was the fact that it was the Pope alone who had promulgated the dogma which ruffled Anglican (and some Catholic) feathers. By now, signs of what was to come were clearly discernible. The historian Patrick Allitt has observed, 'The later nineteenth and early twentieth centuries showed unmistakably

---

[6] For an extensive recent treatment of this, see Michael Wheeler, *The Old Enemies: Catholic and Protestant in nineteenth-century English culture* (Cambridge, 2011).

that the Catholic Church had decided to climb out of the river of contemporary intellectual life rather than swim along in midstream, despite the hopes of Newman, Brownson, Hecker, and many other converts.[7]

Most efforts to 'modernize' Catholic thinking were met with the crushing iron fist of papal power. In 1864 Pius IX issued his *Quanta Cura*, which denounced the separation of church and state, repudiated freedom of religious worship, and decried freedom of expression and the press as false and pernicious ideas. Attached to it was the *Syllabus of Errors*, which listed eighty propositions relating to topics including rationalism, socialism, the abrogation of Church privileges, the supremacy of civil authority over legislation, and the liberties and rights associated with liberalism, as these were considered part of a broad secular attack against the Church. The *Syllabus* condemned many of the principles which contemporary social scientists and biblical critics outside the Catholic Church were by now freely applying in their studies. It concluded by condemning the proposition that 'the Roman Pontiff can and ought to reconcile himself, and come to terms with progress, liberalism, and modern civilization'.[8]

The *Syllabus* was a heavy blow to both Newman and the Catholic layman John Acton. Although the latter remained within the Catholic fold he increasingly came to see the 'Roman world' through the eyes of the Anglican politician William Gladstone, who published furiously on Roman matters, trying to reconcile what he found to be the best of both the Catholic and the Anglican worlds. But all three of them must have known that they were now swimming against a very stiff tide indeed. In 1870, Ultramontanism reached its zenith with the promulgation of papal infallibility at the First Vatican Council. Despite the insistence of such towering figures as Newman and the German church historian Ignaz von Döllinger that the historical evidence supporting the promulgation was insufficient, a majority of the bishops present voted for elevating the Pope's authority. Manning, too, supported papal infallibility: Ultramontanism actually equalled liberty and religious freedom from the civil state. One of the main reasons for his conversion in 1851 had been the *Gorham* case, in which the judgement of the state had overruled the verdict of an Anglican bishop.

The First Vatican Council crushed any ecumenical hopes that might once have been harboured. Already in 1857 a small group

---

[7]Patrick Allitt, *Catholic Converts: British and American intellectuals turn to Rome* (Ithaca, NY, 1997), p. 8.

[8]*The Syllabus of Errors Condemned by Pius IX*, available at http://www.papalencyclicals.net/Pius09/p9syll.htm (accessed 5 June 2013).

of Anglicans, Catholics, and Orthodox, under the leadership of the prominent convert Ambrose de Lisle, had founded the Association for the Promotion of the Unity of Christendom with Cardinal Wiseman's blessing. The purpose of the Association was to pray and work for the reunion of churches and church bodies in the East as well as in the West. When Manning succeeded Wiseman, the Association found itself condemned by the Holy Office in 1864 and the Catholic participants were forced to withdraw. Without the oxygen of official patronage, other schemes working for partial union, such as the Order of Corporate Re-union, eventually floundered.

Anglicans interpreted all of this with severity. To Mandell Creighton, Bishop of London between 1897 and 1901, the Roman Church was built on an autocratic power of clergy while the English Church was founded upon learning and liberty. He wrote,

> The function of the Church of England is to be the Church of free men. [. . .] Its enemy is the Church of Rome, but it ought not to treat its foe with fear, but with kindly regard. The Church of Rome is the Church of decadent peoples: it lives only on its past, and has no future.[9]

A kindly regard for decadence seldom serves as a very robust basis for a rapprochement.

Though the conversions from the Church of England to Rome were luminous, many who were touched by the Oxford Movement stayed within the Anglican Church. To this they brought a rich vision of the universal Church, a vivid argument of history, a lively neo-Gothic imagination, and a certain amount of local trouble. Ritualism was a problem for those who sought order in the Church of England, at least in part because its rise was a part of that flourishing of Victorian religion which simultaneously saw the emergence of a more vigorously Protestant evangelicalism. Both had their patrons, apologists, activists and campaigners, pamphlets, sermons, and hymns. There was even a broad symmetry in their patterns: the Anglo-Catholic Lord Halifax was nicely matched by the ultra-Protestant Sir William Harcourt. Naturally, neither of these movements had any love for the other. Often they were virtually at war.

A certain amount of this could be tolerated, even smiled upon, without undue fuss. Creighton himself sought to take a large view and to frame a broad policy, though he maintained a firm conviction that Protestantism offered a necessary simplicity in religion. 'The more I see the working of the Church of Rome', he remarked, 'the less I believe in its elaborate machinery. The Anglican plan of laying down a minimum, and leaving room for more as each individual thinks

---

[9] W.G. Fallows, *Mandell Creighton and the English Church* (Oxford, 1964), p. 45.

fit, is certainly more invigorating.'¹⁰ He did not much like incense in church but he would eventually shrug it off: 'If they want to make a smell', he remarked blithely, 'let them.'¹¹ He thought an Italian could carry it off well enough, but not an authentic Englishman. However, even Creighton bristled and fumed at the increasing adoption of the word 'Mass'. He did not want altars washed, crosses adored, or the benediction of paschal candles. Congregations holding palms could properly be blessed, but not the palms themselves. Holy water was, he maintained, something the English Church knew nothing about. When some London clergy began to require personal confession from their parishioners before Communion he drew a line: this intruded on the proper realm of Christian liberty. Then there were new services – benediction, the Rosary of the Virgin, services for the dead – which revolted openly against all the principles of the Church of England. This, in short, was a matter of doctrine – and doctrine was what bishops were meant to defend, not tamely with words but with actual discipline. That Creighton never prosecuted anyone under the Clergy Discipline Measure of 1840 was hardly noticed by Ritualists but deplored by Evangelicals. Little wonder that he should come close to despair; little wonder that his friends saw his life shortened by it all.

For all its querulousness, Anglo-Catholicism created a new basis within the Church of England for Anglican–Roman understanding. Furthermore, by the end of the nineteenth century a new encyclical by Leo XIII, *Ad Anglos*, seemed to strike a more generous note in Rome. Should an attempt be made to cultivate this? Perhaps it was a territory best navigated not by a senior cleric under authority but a layman free to work under his own steam? Charles Wood, second Viscount Halifax, was rooted firmly in Ritualism. It was at the invitation of Edward Bouverie Pusey, one of the leaders of the Oxford Movement, that he had become President of the English Church Union (the Anglo-Catholic lobby), a position which he retained for much of the rest of his life. At least a part of the significance of his new 'Italian Mission' lay in that it showed how direct communication with Rome might circumvent the English Catholics entirely and instead trace an elegant line to Rome through France, for that was where Halifax found his greatest collaborator and ally, in the Abbé Ferdinand Portal.

Halifax had his admirers but he often looked as though he was merely a quixotic enthusiast who could always be devastated by the faint praise that he was, of course, well-meaning. But the little canoe that he so often paddled alone was robust, and Halifax evidently

---

¹⁰ *Ibid.*, p. 94.
¹¹ *Ibid.*, p. 91.

knew the value of persevering. Bishop Creighton was one of those who watched him, not unsympathetically but from a distance. 'You may go on well enough for a distance', he mused, 'and then comes the blank wall of the papal monarchy.' Anglican Orders were entirely valid. It was not because of a sixteenth-century secession but because the Roman Church had denied them that a breach between them had arisen. Creighton added to this: 'The restoration of the unity of Christendom will be – not by affirming any one of the existing systems as universal, but by a federation.'[12]

For a time Anglo-Catholics were hopeful, but in 1896 Pope Leo XIII (1878–1903) made a categorical declaration in the papal bull *Apostolicae Curae* that Anglican orders were 'absolutely null and utterly void'.[13] When this appeared, Creighton pressed that there must be a reply. He, with Bishops Stubbs of Oxford and Wordsworth of Salisbury, was put to work by the Archbishop of Canterbury, Edward Benson, and a predictable defence was mounted. It all came to very little. A modest number of Anglican clergymen who saw themselves as members of the worldwide Catholic communion felt that they had no choice but to resign from their livings and convert to Catholicism. Others merely took a dismal view of the whole business and continued to shelter behind the usual barricades. A leading article in *The Times* announced the publication of the Bull as follows:

> The long and exhaustive study under the Pope's direction declaring the orders conferred by the English Church absolutely invalid, will be a shock to well-meaning members of the Anglican communion and puts an end to all hope that the Pope will smooth the road for reunion of the two churches by at least recognising that the Anglican Church exists as a Church.[14]

Creighton had hit a nerve when he wrote of Rome as an oppression to those who cherished liberty. Under Pius X (1903–1914) the Biblical Commission sternly set its face against the discoveries of the historians and exegetes to whom Protestantism turned for new understanding and wisdom. Stray clusters of Catholic Modernists who sought to stir a new openness to critical theological thought at the onset of the twentieth century were cruelly suppressed by papal policy. The reign of Benedict XV saw something of a thaw, and it was indeed in these years that a British Legation to the Vatican was established, in 1915. But the thaw was a very slow one and many sensed no change at all.

It was increasingly the case that Anglican–Roman Catholic discussions would find a new place within the ecumenical movements

---

[12] Fallows, *Mandell Creighton*, p. 47.

[13] Quoted in Pawley and Pawley, *Rome and Canterbury*, p. 253.

[14] See Charles Linley Wood Halifax, *Leo XIII and Anglican Orders* (London, 1912), pp. 355–356.

of the twentieth century. Ecumenism was, by and large, a Protestant enthusiasm but it enjoyed a widening dispensation across all the churches, sometimes in the realms of authority but more often still in the lives of the laity. Under Randall Davidson (Archbishop of Canterbury, 1903–1928) a quiet but increasingly purposeful view of ecumenical possibilities began to emerge across the Church of England. Davidson saw no embarrassment in worshipping with Baptists, Methodists, Congregationalists, or Presbyterians. For him all of this lay happily under the umbrella of the natural calling of the national Church. He also became cautiously alive to the emerging importance of ecumenical endeavours internationally, while many of his bishops were soon vigorous participants in these enterprises. The most striking innovation came at the 1920 Lambeth Conference, when a bold 'Appeal to all Christian people' was issued. With this the Anglican Church at large nailed its colours to the mast of union, albeit according to the terms of what had become known as the Lambeth–Chicago Quadrilateral.[15] Those who led the Free Churches in Britain recognized this to be a defining moment and set about their replies. An unsmiling Roman Catholic hierarchy steadfastly looked the other way.

If anything, English Roman Catholicism looked more intently towards a solid self-establishment on its own high ground than anything involving any other church. The new century had brought a new Archbishop of Westminster: in 1903 the Bishop of Southwark, Francis Bourne, succeeded Herbert Vaughan.[16] Bourne had no intention of maintaining a ghetto; he was resolved to present the Catholic faith openly in public. He defied the law on Eucharistic processions by giving the benediction from the loggia of Westminster Cathedral in 1908. By 1911 he wore a cardinal's hat. In issues of national politics Bourne was quietly accommodating. However, beyond occasional frigid civilities, in the relations of churches he was resolutely uninterested. Those who longed for some development in Anglican–Roman understanding looked long and hard, and found none.

The 1920 Lambeth Conference Appeal did provoke a gracious telegram from the Primate of Belgium, in May 1921. This was the Archbishop of Mechelen (Malines in French), Cardinal Mercier. Mercier had charm but he was no mere manager of Church affairs; possessed of a rich and generous mind, a Thomist and an intellectual, he knew too much of the world to lock himself away in an ecclesiastical

---

[15]In short, the Holy Scriptures, the Creeds, the two sacraments, and the historic episcopate.

[16]Fallows, *Mandell Creighton*, p. 47.

fourth dimension. He had lost much of his cathedral and thirteen priests during the German occupation in the war; after a vigorous pastoral letter in January 1915 he had been duly subjected to house arrest. Mercier was a man on the side of the angels. When the Catholic Modernist George Tyrrell was hounded by the Catholic Church in England, Mercier offered him a job in Belgium. In 1919 the archbishop had visited the United States and proven a palpable hit. To the Episcopal Church he affirmed 'we are brethren in the Christian faith', and was cheered to the rafters.[17] On the other hand, Mercier was sufficiently connected to Rome to know how to cultivate Pope Benedict XV and he evidently enjoyed the approval of the Papal Secretary of State, Pietro Gasparri. He was, in short, someone with whom venturesome English Anglicans might hope to do business.

The old roots set down in 1896 now yielded some new fruits. The friendship of Portal and Halifax was not yet played out. Lord Halifax travelled to Malines for the first time in 1921. Mercier was ready for more of this: friends of Halifax were cordially welcome. In December of the same year, three Catholics met three Anglicans there. None of this had concerned Archbishop Davidson.[18] But the glimmering of momentum in these conversations, and the hope that something of real value might be wrung out of them, began to call upon the sanction of higher authorities. With this came a growing seriousness and a deepening caution. Davidson was careful not to jump: he would acknowledge but not participate – and this, too, only if Rome did the same. On his side Mercier applied for due recognition and got what he wanted. In Westminster even Cardinal Bourne now seemed to Halifax 'very friendly and generally sympathetic'.[19]

The unfolding history of the three Malines Conversations was not without mishaps and melodrama.[20] The conferences grew weightier in turn but, however hard they worked, they could not find a way round papal jurisdiction. Though plenty were sketched, no literary formula would do. By now the Bishop of Oxford, Charles Gore, was a part of the enterprise. In Halifax's opinion, Gore was only a nuisance. Gore thought much the same of Halifax. Others thought that Gore, unlike Halifax, knew how to draw a firm line of principle – and when

---

[17] 'Minutes', *Journal of the General Convention of the Protestant Episcopal Church of the U.S.A.* (1919), pp. 375–378.

[18] For a detailed treatment see G.K.A. Bell, *Randall Davidson: Archbishop of Canterbury* (3rd edition, Oxford, 1952), pp. 1254–1302. It is the kind of extensive, intricate treatment that no academic publisher would now allow – and yet indispensable to scholars for all these reasons.

[19] G.L. Prestige, *The Life of Charles Gore: a great Englishman* (London, 1935), p. 480.

[20] See Bernard Barlow, *'A brother knocking at the door': the Malines Conversations 1921–1925* (Norwich, 1996).

he did so it was in elegant French. Meanwhile, Davidson did the best he could to keep the powers of the Church of England in the picture, going off to Convocation and giving a statement, which was duly approved. But Evangelicals were clearly twitching that too much was being done, while Anglo-Catholics were beginning to fret that it was not enough, and now the English Roman Catholics were growing restive too. They did not want some gentle scheme of integration. They wanted to see wholesale absorption into the Church of Rome, starting at Westminster itself. Mercier looked over his shoulder to Rome and found Gasparri still smiling at him. A further meeting was put off until May 1925. In this time some grew more eager and others lost all confidence. The gulf between the ardent Halifax and the deflated Gore widened.

Mercier now decided to confront squarely the question of whether there could be reunion without 'absorption'? He looked to the Uniate Church for evidence that there could. Was this the answer and the way forward at last? Might there be a Canterbury patriarchate? A paper by Gore, 'Unity with diversity', now argued that, if they could but distinguish between fundamental doctrines and others, agreeing on the former and allowing difference over the latter, there might yet be the reconciling of unity with order and freedom. Moreover, it was not only a matter of categorizing doctrines. Was there a difference between substance, which did not change, and language – which did? This third meeting at Malines was a landmark. But nothing would follow. Mercier was dead by the following January and with his passing the enemies of the conversations had their chance in Rome. There was a new archbishop at Malines, but the conversations ended.

The silence that followed was a long one, but it was not permanent. All such ventures rely more heavily on the fortunes of context than their advocates often care to admit. In the later 1930s the context altered dramatically. Time, too, brought new leaders into the foreground, some of them surprising. By now the leadership of the English Roman Catholic community had rested for over thirty years in the hands of capable Cardinal Bourne. But the impression left by those decades is something dour, brittle, dry, and introverted. This was a Catholic community still not quite at home in national society, one often defined by a deeply regional character, a particular sociology (Irish, working-class, aristocratic, and rather little in between), a rather petulant striving for legitimation, and a bristling grievance that the Establishment still refused to acknowledge its existence at state occasions. Nor was it a community always at peace with itself. The English bishops were notoriously querulous – and Rome knew about it. In 1935, when Cardinal Bourne died, Pius XI dispatched the long-term director of the Venerable English College in Rome and Apostolic Delegate in Africa, Arthur Hinsley, to replace him.

Hinsley was devoted to the papacy and this must have been at least one reason why Pius XI wanted him at Westminster. But the perspectives that he brought to his new job were generous ones. He disavowed purely clerical company and his view of the Roman Catholic Church was by conviction a laicizing one. The historian Adrian Hastings has observed, 'No archiepiscopate was effectively less ultramontane or clericalist.'[21] Hinsley was ardent in his support for Catholic Action. *The Tablet* had long ago been incarcerated by a defensive clerical caste; now he promptly turned it over to the laity and watched it prosper under Douglas Woodruff. He enjoyed G.K. Chesterton, looked up to Christopher Dawson and Arnold Toynbee, and fostered the work of the young Barbara Ward. A careful observer might have sensed that all of this could yield something significant. It did.

The experience of a desperate war altered almost everything. Hinsley found that he was a patriot and threw himself into the national effort with abandon. This was widely valued, not least by Churchill himself. It also reassured, because some – including the Bishop of Durham, Herbery Hensley Henson – bristled at the neutrality of the Vatican in a war waged against palpable evil. But one of Hinsley's greatest gifts lay in the personal rapport that he managed to achieve with the leaders of others churches. He got on well with the Archbishop of Canterbury, Cosmo Lang, with whom he met regularly to discuss the affairs of the world and the views of the churches. But he also came to admire the man who was by now the leading light of Anglican ecumenism, the Bishop of Chichester, George Bell. Bell was convinced that the churches must sink their differences over doctrines and questions of order and unite urgently against the new foe, dictatorship. Hinsley promptly agreed. For their part, Archbishops Lang and William Temple paraded their support for the Pope's Five Peace Points in 1939 and built upon them purposefully. Perhaps something of a united Christian front against the powers of totalitarianism was an actual possibility in the world? The British government, meanwhile, was unique in keeping a diplomatic envoy, Sir D'Arcy Osborne, at the Vatican throughout the war.[22] This remarkable mission was run on a shoestring from a little annexe attached to the convent of Santa Marta. Osborne found a priest who allowed him to use his bath and store his valuable possessions in his

---

[21] Adrian Hastings, *A History of English Christianity, 1920–1985* (London, 1985), p. 331.
[22] See Owen Chadwick, *Britain and the Vatican during the Second World War* (Cambridge, 1986).

own flat nearby. This was a hard-working member of the Secretariat of State called Giovanni Battista Montini.

In wartime Britain the definition of such hopes came with a new impulse, the Sword of the Spirit movement, and a glimmer of authentic ecumenical progress in wartime. A succession of meetings wore almost the aspect of rallies for idealists who were exhilarated by these new, bracing alliances. When, at a meeting of the movement in May 1941, Bell whispered to Hinsley that perhaps Protestants and Catholics might say the Lord's Prayer together, Hinsley was ready to lead it – a quiet revolution, no doubt, but an authentic one, even so. Hinsley's own bishops disagreed with most of this and yet they never squabbled with him. It was enough, after Hinsley died in 1943, to pretend that it had never happened. Indeed, without Hinsley the Sword of the Spirit had nowhere to go and it was soon only the pious memory of a few stranded progressives who could do nothing but return bleakly to their old bunkers and hope for the wind to change again.

Hinsley's successor was Bernard Griffin, whose qualities appeared solid, rather than inspirational. With Temple's successor at Canterbury, Archbishop Geoffrey Fisher, Griffin got along well. Even so, there was more than a whiff of retreat in the early post-war years. Observers may at first have found rather little in Fisher to excite hopes of a new rapprochement with Rome: he was, if anything, a 'broad' churchman who had no instinctive sympathy for Roman Catholicism and was more than faintly suspicious of it. But there were still murmurs of activity on the Continent, in Paris and in Strasbourg in 1950. And there were still figures who were capable of quietly navigating the vast grey area which divided the two churches. One was G.L. Prestige, editor of the *Church Times* and effective general secretary of the Archbishop of Canterbury's Council on Foreign Relations. Another was the approachable Bishop David Mathew, for many years a happy anomaly in English Catholicism. A third, in Italy, was D'Arcy Osborne's old benefactor, Mgr Montini. Both Prestige and Mathew saw clearly that Montini might come to matter a great deal. They were right. In November 1954 Montini became Archbishop of Milan. In the following May he was visited by the pre-eminent Anglican ecumenist and internationalist of his generation, George Bell, who confirmed the perception that Montini was a man who might do much for the cause of church unity.[23] Only two years later Montini played host to a little colloquium of Anglicans and Roman Catholics in Italy. One of

---

[23] See R.C.D. Jasper, *George Bell: Bishop of Chichester* (London, 1967), pp. 336–337.

his guests was Bernard Pawley. The impression left of the gathering was a wholly happy one.[24]

Few had foreseen the coming of Angelo Roncalli in 1958. Once he became Pope John XXIII a sense hung in the air that he was already too old to do much of note in the Church. But a declaration of intent came almost at once, with his creation of a new Secretariat for Christian Unity in 1959. Archbishop Fisher met its Secretary, the Dutch Monsignor Jan Willebrands, quietly present as an unofficial observer at a meeting of the Central Committee of the World Council of Churches. This conversation produced a revelation. On 2 December 1960 the Archbishop of Canterbury went to the Vatican to see the Pope. The Pope's own advisors twitched anxiously in the background; the Catholic press hardly knew what to say. Left to their own devices, Fisher and John settled down to enjoy each other's company. They were together for just over an hour. According to Fisher, John spoke of those 'separated brethren' who might one day 'return to the Church of Rome'. Fisher challenged this: 'Your Holiness, not *return*.' John asked him to elaborate. 'None of us', added Fisher, 'can go backwards, only forwards. Our two churches are advancing on parallel courses and we may look forward to their meeting one day.' John paused, then responded: 'You are quite right.'[25] This exchange became famous.

Even the sympathetic Cardinal Bea, President of the Secretariat for Christian Unity, was purposefully opaque about this meeting.[26] However, it proved sufficiently rich in symbolic power to conjure up a quite new atmosphere. It was now that Fisher took the decisive step of dispatching Bernard Pawley to Rome, to observe the coming of Pope John's great council and to provide information about the Church of England to his Secretariat for Unity.

Pawley was very much a man in Fisher's image. He was wary of the illusions on which enthusiasts thrive; he was proud of being both principled and pragmatic. He was interested in the world and its tumbling affairs. He was not put off by the reading of books, but was in no particular danger of intellectualism. He spoke Italian fluently and read Latin quite well: these may have been the decisive qualifications for the job. In churchmanship he was neither High nor Low. He was sure that the Church of England was neither Roman nor Protestant;

---

[24]The gathering is fully described by Peter Hebblethwaite in *Paul VI*, pp. 267–271. Hebblethwaite notes that Montini 'was already well on the way to becoming the Anglicans' favourite archbishop. There was no competition' (p. 270).

[25]Geoffrey Fisher, *Touching on Christian Truth: the kingdom of God, the Christian Church and the world* (London, 1971), pp. 187–188.

[26]See Augustin Cardinal Bea, *The Unity of Christians* (London, 1963), pp. 64–72.

he would have agreed firmly with Fisher that it was both catholic and reformed. In many ways he was very much an Anglican liberal of his time in disavowing clericalism and wanting to see more power in the hands of the laity. At the same time his outlook was Romanocentric: evidently he had little sense of what the Free Churches were about and the Lutheran World Federation might have been a distant continent to him. He viewed the World Council of Churches from a quizzical distance, anxious that it had turned ecumenical idealism into the unresponsive solidity of the ecclesiastical corporation: at times even its greatest names seemed oddly obscure to him.

Pawley was not at all at home with the Roman Catholic hierarchy in England. He did not care for Cardinal Godfrey, Archbishop of Westminster from 1956 to 1963; Godfrey's secretary thought Pawley charmless.[27] He could be frankly suspicious of Roman propaganda, which later commentators have found embarrassing.[28] He resented conversions and the teaching of the Roman Catholic Church on mixed marriages. He bristled when it canonized its own martyrs and ignored all the others who had died for their faith, often at the hands of Romanism. He cared about religious persecution and also feared the power of the Roman Catholic Church to persecute its own. Yet, like so many of his predecessors, Pawley found that he could view Catholics abroad amiably and even come to enjoy spending time with them.

The Rome to which Pawley came on 13 April 1961 might well have alienated him at once. It did not. Indeed, something in him seemed to relax. His soul did not rebel at the baroque poetry of the Catholic Reformation. He found the people pleasant and, in particular, enjoyed the company of the men who worked at the new Secretariat for Christian Unity. He judged Vatican affairs in the round with sympathetic curiosity but a nice degree of detachment. He also enjoyed being part of something that clearly mattered. Anglicans had recourse to two bastions of their own in Rome: St Paul's Within-the-Walls (consecrated in 1876, an essentially American concern, and the recipient of many benefactions) and All Saints (consecrated in 1887, a little spire which John XXIII used to enjoy viewing through binoculars; always strapped for cash).[29] The Pawley family moved into a flat belonging to the first of these.

The personal qualities of the new Pope were sufficiently powerful to eclipse his often conventional ideas. At his first meeting with John XXIII, Pawley was immediately struck by the kindly, pragmatic qualities which Fisher before him had known how to value:

---

[27] See Frederick Bliss, *Anglicans in Rome* (Norwich, 2006), p. 53.

[28] *Ibid.*, pp. 56–57.

[29] Frederick Bliss describes both elegantly: *ibid.*, pp. 20–28.

John: Are you married?

Pawley: Yes.

John: Well, that need not divide us. So was St. Peter. Parents still alive?

Pawley: Yes.

John: Are they very old?

Pawley: No, only in their seventies.

John: Are you a theologian? [. . .] Nor am I. It is theologians who have got us into the mess, and we have got to get ourselves out of it; it is practical men like you and me who will deliver us from it.[30]

This was a bracing presence, a mind in many ways wholly conventional and yet at the same time sharply observant of life at large and open and responsive to it. Anything might come of this.

As he saw the new councils and committees setting to work around him, Pawley rejoiced in the very fact of the new Vatican Council. For him it was undoubtedly an immense contest between liberals, who sought a new generosity which could yield progress in the relations of the different traditions and which could build a new relationship with the modern world at large, and conservatives, who repudiated the cause of change and clung doggedly to what was obsolete, obscurantist, or simply inoperable. His own sympathies were firmly committed to the former. He longed to see ecumenical relationships break out of the old impossibilities: that the Church of Rome was the only universal Church of Christ; that only a return to Rome would signal the achievement of unity. Fisher's insistence in 1961 that the churches must grow out of the rhetoric of return would have been his starting point. Roman Catholics and Anglicans must find a new understanding of one another and a new relationship together. But, above all, they must be honest to each other. When John XXIII was succeeded by the Anglophile Cardinal Montini, who became Pope Paul VI on 23 June 1963, Pawley knew at once that a great moment had come: Montini's claims on Anglican affections had long been unique. But he knew well that a careful Roman progressive was still a particular sort of Catholic and not necessarily one who was more nearly an Anglican like himself. These men were still citizens of a rather different world, grappling with a particular set of issues, a particular set of powers, and a particular vocabulary. At Lambeth Palace the Archbishop's secretary for ecumenical affairs, John Satterthwaite, began to suspect Pawley of something like fraternization. Like his

---

[30]Recounted in *ibid.*, p. 44.

Anglican predecessors in these things, Pawley admired and enjoyed the company of Continental Catholics, but he still viewed English ones with some suspicion. In Rome he could not quite conquer his dislike of John Heenan, the Archbishop of Westminster, and at times was almost too ready to indulge it.

Although he was breezily open about his own opinions and commitments, Pawley knew that his first obligation to his masters in London was to provide information while he cultivated connections. However makeshift, the Rome flat became an embassy of a sort. Pawley was fortunate in a supportive and creative marriage: his wife, Margaret, had worked for the Special Operations Executive in Italy during the war and in Rome she proved a superb ally. He was also able to find a highly efficient secretary in a young English woman then living in Rome: Virginia Johnstone. Pawley enjoyed a sense of public history but also relished private conversation. One of his great virtues was that he was ready to be led a good way by personal qualities rather than dogmatic postulations or party lines. In short, all kinds of curious people now turned up for all kinds of reasons in the reports, to make conversation and then disappear back into the hurly-burly of the world. Pawley thoroughly enjoyed meeting the great majority of them and wrote even more vividly of those whom he disliked. There is more than a hint of the manners and mores of the political Cold War in all of this: Anglican priests are 'turned' and converts cross to another side; there is a fear of Roman Catholic propaganda and a suspicion of Roman Catholic motives and manoeuvres.

When the little army of Observers from the various churches came to the Council, Pawley remained a representative and guest there, supporting Bishop Moorman, the American Frederick C. Grant, and the Archdeacon of Colombo, Charles Harold de Soysa. He now watched intently both the Council in its sessions and the Observers in theirs. It was Pawley who suggested that the Observers meet together weekly. He remained very much at the heart of these affairs until the end of the third session in November 1964. Perhaps it was as well. Bishop Moorman, who stayed on until the end, later remarked, 'By 1964 the fun of the Council was beginning to wear off'; it was 'the same grind all over again'.[31] In December 1965 it finally closed with two vast masses in St Peter's. Here, certain Observers were invited to participate in the reading of the lessons. They were publicly acknowledged, and thanked, by Paul VI. 'The work for Christian

---

[31] Recounted in Bliss, *Anglicans in Rome*, p. 44.

unity', he pronounced, 'is but beginning.'[32] Historians and theologians will continue to tussle with the significance of the Council's many revisions and redefinitions. Few can deny the measure of redefinition which it so purposefully realized.

Bernard Pawley had served the Anglican Church well in Rome, particularly in publishing a succession of little books which brought the importance of the whole occasion home to a Western, Protestant audience.[33] There is at least a sense that Pawley himself knew the value of his work to posterity. His confidential reports to London matter to the historian for a number of reasons. They present a careful record of the actual, painstaking, and even dreary business of church reform as it went on at the Council, day by day. In general, he is a thorough recorder: the essential debates which characterized the three sessions which he attended are captured succinctly, and sometimes suffused with vivid experience. His working methods were themselves observed closely by Virginia Johnstone:

> Each morning during the week Canon Pawley set off on the 64 bus to attend the general congregation. [...] He took with him a notebook and sat with other observers in seats reserved for them in the tribunal of S. Longinus that became known as the Observers' Box, writing notes on the more important speeches in English as they were delivered in Latin, a task often made more difficult by the local accent of the speaker. It was not always possible to catch the name of the bishop and so sometimes the notes were preceded by 'German after the South American' or some such description. The next day he took a second notebook while I typed the notes from the first, looking in the Vatican newspaper, L'Osservatore Romano, then the Annuario Pontificio, the Vatican Who's Who, in order to check the name and see of the bishop. During the later session [...] more accurate press reports were issued by the Vatican, but to begin with these were inadequate and often edited to suit the official curial view, so there was no short cut to making notes if the Archbishop and his Council on Foreign Relations were to be kept informed.[34]

The extent to which Pawley invested his own views in his reports reveals not merely a personality engaging with the subject before him but a good deal about the attitudes of his own Church in general. We can understand more clearly how the enduring problems of division continued to work in the mind and see what distinct forms they

---

[32] Quoted by Michael Manktelow, *John Moorman: Anglican, Franciscan, Independent* (Norwich, 1999), p. 107. For much more detail, see John Moorman, *Vatican Observed: an Anglican impression of Vatican II* (London, 1967).

[33] Manktelow, *John Moorman*, p. 105. See also Bernard Pawley, *Looking at the Vatican Council* (London, 1962), *An Anglican View of the Vatican Council* (London, 1962), and *Anglican–Roman Relations and the Second Vatican Council* (London, 1964).

[34] Virginia Johnstone, 'Separated brethren', article for the magazine of St Paul's, Knightsbridge, April 1982. Typescript kindly provided to the editors by Miss Johnstone.

assumed. More than this, the reports allow us to glimpse not simply the great machinery of the Vatican Council but also the eager, busy fringes of the occasion – the intricate connections of ecumenical diplomacy across many quarters of the world. This opens a window onto the world of the later twentieth century, with its political divisions, its fears of totalitarianism and nuclear warfare, the disputes of Church and state in many countries, the waning of the old Eurocentricism, and the gathering confidence of the post-colonial world.

Unlike so many earlier ventures, the Pawley mission did not prove to be an isolated moment. It inaugurated a new era in Anglican–Roman relations, one that was most visibly present in the establishment of a new Anglican Centre in Rome in 1966.[35] Although the precariousness of the Centre's history has echoed the fragilities of the Pawleys' own conditions during the Council, it has endured, notched up a string of directors, created a fine library, and made a visible contribution. The relations of the two churches have in the same period been defined by the meetings of the Anglican–Roman Catholic International Commission, which was first convened in 1969. Reports on authority and the Virgin Mary have become important to aficionados. Relating these ideals and enterprises to the wider currents of ecclesiastical policy has not always been straightforward. Meanwhile, the international ecumenical movement, in which so many progressive hopes were vested in the middle years of the twentieth century, had by the beginning of the twenty-first lost much of its charismatic force and dwindled. By this time the future of the Roman Catholic Church itself was a much debated theme. Some of the thorny questions unacknowledged, quietly avoided, or buried by Vatican II would come to haunt the Church. Others, new in their way, and unforeseen, would break out and defy the requirements of conventional understanding. It is not difficult to see a great deal of wriggling going on inside the paradigm which Vatican II created. But at some point the adjustment of what was the new wisdom of 1962–1965 will no longer seem to work. Ninety years divided the First Vatican Council from the Second. When will a third follow?

---

[35] See Bliss, *Anglicans in Rome*, p. 89.

EDITORIAL NOTE

The 167 reports which Bernard Pawley sent to London between 1962 and 1964 present an editor with a sum of almost 240,000 words. This length lies beyond the scope of the present series. Accordingly, fairly extensive cutting has been necessary and the criteria which have been applied by the editors should be clearly stated at the outset.

Sections of the text which simply present material available to the scholar in other printed editions have been excised. There are obscurities which lead nowhere in particular and which amount to digressions in the overall argument at work across the reports. There are also repetitions: views which, once set down, need not reappear. A good deal has been removed from the reports of the Council in session, particularly speeches which concern intricacies in the draft documents, rather than broad (and recognizable) matters of substance, voting statistics, and the like. Pawley's interest in Greek Orthodoxy also receives lighter attention here. It must be acknowledged that a modest amount of material is workaday or simply dull. Pawley knew this himself and was prepared to give some of the speeches short shrift and disregard others altogether. Freed from his obligations to report at great length to church authorities at home, the editors have held in mind a different audience and simply extended his own principles.

To present these debates without the reader having recourse to the actual schemata which the Council debated in turn represents an obvious liability. How well do the reports stand up without them? The brief commentaries at the beginning of each section offer a broad picture of the substance of these debates. But for Pawley himself the arguments at stake were often clearly visible to the informed, but unfurnished, outsider. In this edition the editors have chosen the contributions which define and illuminate the terms of the debates at large and which are not dependent upon a close parallel reading of the schemata themselves.

The editors have sought to achieve a balance between a minimal apparatus and a cluttering of the text with unnecessary footnotes. The *dramatis personae* offers biographical information about those who become the leading, or recurrent, figures in the reports; significant others receive briefer attention in footnotes. The official position of many of those speaking at the Council is given in the text and we have often deemed that to be sufficient.

The presentation of the text varies little from the original and any editorial changes have been for the sake of consistency and to make the whole text more readable. Each document originally bore the title 'Rome Reports' and was marked confidential. The sections of the reports were numbered; in this edition, however, the numbers have been deleted because excisions have rendered them meaningless. Pawley was fortunate in the services of an excellent typist, leaving the editors with very little tidying up to do. Simple inconsistencies of style (for example, the use of upper-case letters) or typographical variations (the spelling of a word such as 'Secretariat') have been made consistent. Double inverted commas have been turned into single ones, and quotations within quotations have received double inverted commas. In the original reports the paragraphs were separated by a line and the first line of each paragraph was indented; here the separation of paragraphs has made the retention of the latter convention unnecessary. Words underlined in the original documents have been italicized. The spelling of names has been made consistent: an English typewriter had limited ways of handling continental spellings, so in this text diacritics of various kinds have been introduced (for example, 'Koenig' becomes 'König'). Occasional spelling errors, often of names, have been rectified.

Abbreviations

The text presents a number of often-repeated abbreviations, which are listed here for convenience:

BVM	Blessed Virgin Mary
CACTM	Central Advisory Council on Training for the Ministry
CFR	Archbishop of Canterbury's Council on Foreign Relations
CIR	Council on Inter-Church Relations
PECUSA	Protestant Episcopal Church of the United States of America
WCC	World Council of Churches

CHRONOLOGY, 1958–1966

1 January 1958	European Economic Community founded
9 October 1958	Death of Pope Pius XII
28 October 1958	Election of Pope John XXIII
25 January 1959	John XXIII announces the Second Vatican Council
17 May 1959	Ante-Preparatory Commission set up
30 June 1959	Pope John's first meeting with the Ante-Preparatory Commission
5 June 1960	Preparatory Commission set up
2 December 1960	Archbishop Fisher visits Pope John in Rome
13 April 1961	Bernard and Margaret Pawley arrive in Rome
5 May 1961	State visit by the Queen to the Vatican City
20 June 1961	John XXIII addresses the Central Commission, affirming that the purpose of the Council is an *aggiornamento* of the Church
19 November–5 December 1961	Third General Assembly of the World Council of Churches in New Delhi
17 January 1961	Archbishop Fisher announces his retirement
31 May 1961	Arthur Michael Ramsey becomes Archbishop of Canterbury
3 January 1962	John XXIII excommunicates Fidel Castro
25 May 1962	Consecration of Coventry Cathedral
11 October 1962	Second Vatican Council opens, inaugurated by Pope John's *Gaudet Mater Ecclesia*
14–28 October 1962	Cuban missile crisis
22 October 1962	John XXIII makes the Secretariat for Christian Unity into a Commission
6 December 1962	John XXIII announces the creation of a Co-ordinating Commission
8 December 1962	Close of the first session of the Council
March 1963	John XXIII sets up the Papal Commission on Birth Control
3 June 1963	Death of Pope John XXIII
21 June 1963	Election of Archbishop Montini as Pope; he becomes Paul VI
29 September 1963	Opening of the second session of the Council
4 December 1963	Close of the second session of the Council

14 September 1964	Opening of the third session of the Council
21 November 1964	Close of the third session of the Council
14 September 1965	Opening of the fourth session of the Council
4 December 1965	Paul VI leads a service for the Council Observers and guests at St Paul's-Outside-the-Walls
7 December 1965	Closing ceremonies of the Council
8 December 1965	Second Vatican Council closes
23/24 March 1966	Archbishop Ramsey visits Pope Paul VI in Rome and dedicates the new Anglican Centre there

VATICAN II – *DRAMATIS PERSONAE*

Alfrink, Jan Bernard (1900–1987), Cardinal-Archbishop of Utrecht. Member of the Central Preparatory Commission and member of the Council of Presidents.

Stephen F. Bayne (1908–1974), American Episcopalian and Bishop of the Diocese of Olympia, 1946–1959. In 1959 he was appointed the first Executive Officer of the Anglican Communion by the Archbishop of Canterbury. He was also made Bishop-in-Charge of the Episcopal Church's Convocation of American Churches in Europe.

Bea, Augustin (1881–1968), German Jesuit and former Rector of the Pontifical Biblical Institute (1930–1949). Member of the Central Preparatory Commission and in 1960 made President of the newly established Secretariat for Christian Unity. His interest in ecumenical matters was long-standing and he was held in high esteem by many of the observers.

Browne, Michael (1887–1971), Cardinal. Irish Dominican. Rector of the *Angelicum* (1932–1941) and Master General of the Dominicans (1955–1962). Member of the Preparatory Commission on Bishops and Vice-President of the Doctrinal Commission.

Butler, Christopher (1902–1986), English convert to Roman Catholicism and the seventh Abbot of Downside Abbey, home to Benedictine monks. He was present for all four sessions of the Council and was a member of its Commission for Doctrine. Butler also participated in the debate on war and peace, with particular reference to nuclear deterrence.

Cardinale, Igino Eugenio (1916–1983), Apostolic Delegate to Great Britain, 1963–1969.

Cicognani, Amleto Giovanni (1883–1973), Italian Cardinal. Secretary of State, 1961–1969. Prefect of the Congregation for the Oriental Churches and member of the Central Preparatory Commission. President of the Preparatory Commission on the Oriental Churches, President of the Council's Commission on the Oriental Churches, and President of the Coordinating Commission.

Congar, Yves-Marie (1904–1995), French Dominican and Professor of Theology at Le Saulchoir. He was consultant for the Preparatory Commission and served as *peritus* on several commissions. In 1950 he was censured after the encyclical *Humanis Generis* but was made a cardinal in 1994. His journal from the Council has recently been published in an English translation.

Cullmann, Oscar (1902–1999), German Lutheran theologian. Professor of New Testament Studies at Basel, Paris, and the Sorbonne. He was Pope John XXIII's personal guest at the Council. After the Council closed he co-founded the Ecumenical Institute of Tantur in Jerusalem.

De Smedt, Émile-Joseph (1909–1995), Bishop of Bruges. Vice-President of the Secretariat for Christian Unity and an important spokesman in the Council for the Secretariat. He presented the early draft supporting religious liberty to the Council.

Döpfner, Julius (1913–1976), Cardinal-Archbishop of Munich. Member of the Central Preparatory Commission and of the Coordinating Commission. One of the moderators at the Council.

Fisher, Geoffrey Francis (1887–1972), ordained an Anglican priest in 1913. In 1939 he was made Bishop of London and in 1945 he became Archbishop of Canterbury, a post that he retained until 1961. His visit to Pope John XXIII in December 1960 profoundly changed the relations between the Church of England and Rome.

Frings, Joseph (1887–1978), Archbishop of Cologne from 1942. Member of the Central Preparatory Commission and a member of the Council of Presidents. During the Council Joseph Ratzinger was his personal advisor.

Heenan, John (1905–1975), Archbishop of Westminster from 1963 until his death. Elevated to the Cardinalate in 1965. During the Council he famously launched an attack on the *periti* as he felt that they were undermining the faith ('timeo peritos et dona ferentes': 'I fear experts and those bearing gifts'). But even before the Council opened he had been appointed to the newly established Secretariat for Christian Unity.

John XXIII, Angelo Giuseppe Roncalli (1881–1963). In 1921 he was called to Rome to reorganize the Society for the Propagation of the Faith. Upon being nominated Titular Archbishop of Areopolis and Apostolic Visitor to Bulgaria (1925), he focused on the problems of the Eastern churches. In 1953 he became Cardinal-Patriarch of Venice, and expected to spend his last years there doing pastoral work. His election to Pope in 1958 came as a surprise to both himself and onlookers. Less than three months into his pontificate he announced that he would convoke an ecumenical council for the universal Church.

König, Franz (1905–2004), Cardinal-Archbishop of Vienna and a member of the Central Preparatory Commission. In 1962 he was elected to the Doctrinal Commission and was a wholehearted supporter of *Nostra Aetate*. He was convinced that the Roman Church should seek closer relations with the Orthodox churches and should take a clear stand against anti-Semitism. He named Karl Rahner his personal theologian for the Council.

Lefebvre, Marcel (1905–1991), missionary in Africa and Archbishop of Dakar (Senegal). In 1962 he was elected superior-general of the Holy Ghost Fathers and became a member of the Central Preparatory Commission. He was concerned about the direction that the Council was taking and became a member of the group of bishops known as *Coetus Internationalis Patrum*. He repudiated the Council and was excommunicated in 1988 for ordaining four bishops for his schismatic group – without papal approval. In 2009 Pope Benedict XVI lifted the excommunication of the four bishops, a move which caused much controversy.

Léger, Paul-Émile (1901–1994), Cardinal-Archbishop of Montreal and a member of the Preparatory Commission, the Doctrinal Commission, and the Commission on Canon Law.

Lercaro, Giacomo (1891–1976), Cardinal-Archbishop of Bologna. After the death of John XXIII he was regarded as *papabile* and was a member of the Liturgical Commission. Lercaro was active in the 'Church of the Poor Group'.

Liénart, Achille (1884–1973), Cardinal-Archbishop of Lille and President of the French Episcopal Conference. He was a member of the Central Preparatory Commission, sat on the Council of Presidents, and was also a member of the Coordinating Commission.

Maximos IV Saigh (1878–1967), Melchite Patriarch of Antioch (Syria) and leader of the Melchite bishops at the Council. He was a member of the Central Preparatory Commission and of the Commission on the Oriental Churches. Although the official language of the Council was Latin, Saigh was notorious for slipping into French most of the time. At the Council he advocated the use of vernacular languages at services and championed Eastern orthodoxy.

Moorman, John (1905–1989), Anglican clergyman and Bishop of Ripon (1959–1975). Archbishop Michael Ramsey appointed him chief Anglican Observer at the Second Vatican Council from 1962 to 1965. Moormann was fluent in Italian and enjoyed a personal friendship with Cardinal Montini (who was to become Pope in 1963). In 1967 he became the Anglican chairman of the Preparatory Commission which led to the setting up of the Anglican–Roman Catholic International Commission, of which he was a member from 1969 until 1981. He was also the driving force behind establishing the Anglican Centre in Rome.

Ottaviani, Alfredo (1890–1979), Italian cardinal and Secretary (head) of the Holy Office from 1959. Member of the Central Preparatory Commission and President of the Preparatory Theological Commission and of the Doctrinal Commission. Before and during the Vatican II years he resisted the development of doctrine which led the Council to approve the *Declaration on Religious Freedom*.

Paul VI, Giovanni Battista Enrico Antonio Maria Montini (1897–1978), Cardinal-Archbishop of Milan. He was appointed to the Central Preparatory Commission for the Second Vatican Council and also to the Technical-Organizational Commission. Upon his election as Pope in June 1963 he committed himself, in his first message to the world, to continue the work begun by his predecessor.

Pawley, Bernard Clinton (1911–1981), Anglican clergyman. Canon Residentiary of Ely Cathedral and from 1972 Archdeacon of Canterbury Cathedral. He was chosen by the Archbishop of Canterbury for the Anglican liaison in Rome as he spoke Italian and had many contacts with Christians in Germany, Belgium, Italy, and France.

Ramsey, (Arthur) Michael (1904–1988), ordained an Anglican priest in 1929. He served in parish and academic appointments until 1952, when he was appointed Bishop of Durham. He then served as Archbishop of York from 1956 until 1961 and Archbishop of Canterbury from 1961 until 1974. As a keen ecumenist Ramsey was bitterly disappointed when the Synod would not endorse a scheme for Anglican–Methodist unity. He was the first Archbishop of Canterbury in modern times to visit the Vatican formally, when he was received in the Sistine Chapel by Paul VI in 1966.

Ruffini, Ernesto (1888–1967), Cardinal-Archbishop of Palermo and a member of the Central Preparatory Commission and of the Council of Presidents.

Schlink, Bernhard (1903–1984), leading ecumenical theologian who observed the entire Council as a delegate of the Evangelical Church in Germany.

Siri, Giuseppe (1906–1989), Cardinal-Archbishop of Genoa and a member of the Central Preparatory Commission and of the Council of Presidents. In 1959 he was appointed the first President of the Italian Episcopal Conference by Pope John XXIII, a post which he held until 1965.

Skydsgaard, Kristen Ejner (1902–1990), Danish Lutheran theologian and Professor of Dogmatic Theology at the University of Copenhagen (1942–1972). On behalf of the Lutheran Council of Churches he was present at Vatican II as an Observer and contributed prolifically to the dialogue between the Catholic Church and the Lutheran churches.

Spellman, Francis (1889–1967), Cardinal-Archbishop of New York. He was the first American assistant to the Papal Secretariat of State (1925–1931). During the Council he was a member of the Central Preparatory Commission, of the Council of Presidents, and of the Coordinating Commission. Spellman lobbied for restored diplomatic relations between the United States and the Vatican and later supported American involvement in Vietnam.

Suenens, Léon-Joseph (1904–1996), Cardinal-Archbishop of Malines-Brussels and a member of the Central Preparatory Commission and of the Coordinating Commission. He recommended to Pope John XXIII that the Council should focus on a handful of key questions and should divide the work into internal church reform on the one hand and the Church's relations with the rest of the world on the other. In June 1963, Pope Paul VI made Suenens one of the four moderators of the Council who presided over it. He was in favour of the Church re-examining its condemnation of contraception and when Pope Paul took the question out of the hands of the Council Suenens warned of 'another Galileo case'.

Tardini, Domenico (1988–1961), named Secretary of State by the newly elected Pope John XXIII in 1958. Famously a conservative at the Council.

Tisserant, Eugène (1884–1972), French cardinal and Dean of the Sacred College of Cardinals. He was a member of the Central Preparatory Commission and then of the Doctrinal Commission.

Willebrands, Johannes (1909–2006), Dutch priest and later bishop and cardinal, whose frequent travelling to ecumenical gatherings earned him the name of 'the flying Dutchman'. In 1948 he founded the Catholic Conference on Ecumenical Questions; although it did not seek the Holy See's approval it kept the latter informed of its activities. The Conference was in informal contact with the World Council of Churches. Until he was made titular bishop in 1964, Willebrands was Council *peritus*. On the penultimate day of the Council it was he who read out the momentous declaration cancelling the mutual excommunication of the Catholic and Orthodox churches in 1054. Upon the death of Cardinal Bea in 1968 Willebrands succeeded him as President of the Secretariat for Christian Unity.

REPORTS OF THE REVEREND B.C. PAWLEY, CANON OF ELY CATHEDRAL, FROM ROME FOR THE INFORMATION OF THE ARCHBISHOPS OF CANTERBURY AND YORK THROUGH THE SECRETARY OF THE CHURCH OF ENGLAND COUNCIL ON INTER-CHURCH RELATIONS

THE COMING OF THE COUNCIL, APRIL 1961–OCTOBER 1962

Commentary: preparations for the Second Vatican Council

In October 1958 Cardinal Angelo Roncalli was elected Pope. He took the name John XXIII and in January of the following year he announced that he intended to convoke an ecumenical council. John XXIII pursued two aims in calling the council: first, he wished to promote 'the enlightenment, edification, and joy of the entire Christian people'; secondly, he wished to extend 'a renewed cordial invitation to the faithful of the separated communities'.[1] John XXIII died after the first session and his successor, Paul VI (1963–1978) continued the work of the Council and presided over the final three sessions held in 1963–1965.

During the period from the announcement of the Council until its opening in October 1962, the texts to be discussed were prepared by commissions, headed by prefects of the Curia. A Central Preparatory Commission oversaw the work of the others and in 1960 the Pope established a Pontifical Secretariat for Promoting Christian Unity, which was to communicate with other Christian bodies. The Commission was made up of members, who had the right to vote and freely express their opinions, and consultors (the *periti*), who did not.

Between 1962 and 1965 bishops and theologians from all over the world, as well as representatives from the media, gathered in Rome. Meetings were held in the central nave of St Peter's. Before the Council commenced, the Vatican had consulted the World Council of Churches in Geneva and sent invitations to the non-Catholic churches. These, with a few exceptions, accepted the invitation to 'observe' the Council. The ecumenical observers attended all four sessions from 1962 to 1965 and they sat in a tribune that had been especially reserved for them – in other words, they had good seats in the Basilica. Although they officially took part as observers sent by their respective churches, some of them also worked as theological advisers for the drafting of a number of conciliar documents.

---

[1]Quoted in John O'Malley, *What Happened at Vatican II* (Cambridge, MA, and London, 2008), p. 17.

The Anglican observers were the first to accept the invitation which came from Cardinal Augustin Bea. According to Massimo Faggioli, 'The representatives of the Anglican Church approached Vatican II with a history of dialogue and conversations with the Roman Catholic Church, even if the relationship between the two remained ambiguous in England because of the dominant attitude among Catholic bishops to "win back" England for the Catholic Church.'[2] The Communion was represented by John Moorman, Bishop of Ripon (England), Najib Atallah Cuba'in, Bishop of the Diocese of Jordan (Lebanon and Syria), Eugene R. Fairweather, Professor of Divinity, Trinity College, University of Toronto (Canada), and Clement W. Welsh, Canon-Theologian of Washington Cathedral and Director of Studies, College of Preachers, Washington, DC (USA). Moorman was the most active of the Anglican representatives in making a contribution to the Council, not least because he was fluent in Italian.

The Council Fathers debated, amended, voted on, and eventually approved and published sixteen documents that covered a wide variety of themes. The four largest and most important documents that resulted from the Council are called Constitutions, while the shorter documents that address more specific issues are either called Decrees or Declarations. Many point to three as being the most significant: *Lumen Gentium* (Dogmatic Constitution on the Church), *Gaudium et Spes* (Pastoral Constitution on the Church in the Modern World), and *Dignitatis Humanae* (Declaration on Religious Freedom).

Report No 1.   19 April 1961

ARRIVAL
I arrived here on Thursday April 13th, 1961.

ADDRESS
St. Paul's American Episcopal Church, Via Napoli 58, Rome.

PUBLICITY
A considerable amount of publicity surrounded my arrival. A photographer was at the door of the American Church House when I arrived and the press had been alerted. I had much difficulty in evading

---

[2]Massimo Faggioli, *Vatican II: the battle for meaning* (New York and Mahwah, NJ, 2012), pp. 43–44.

their constant requests for information. Even so, several papers carried completely fictitious reports of my arrival (including the invention that I arrived by air) and intentions. Monsignor Willebrands was alarmed at first about this and requested me to go to the Secretariat on the first morning, which I did. He showed me a copy of the letter he had written to you. I was quickly able to persuade him that we were not responsible for this publicity and, in fact, hoped to avoid it. Nevertheless, I got the impression that he wished he had been officially informed of my arrival, so that a joint statement could have been put out. I also am inclined to think that we ought to make careful use of publicity, so that what is published is at least correct. I told Colonel Hornby[3] of my date of departure at least six weeks previously. When so many people must necessarily know of an event, it is not possible that it can remain secret. The lack of information has made some sections of the press speculate as to whether my arrival has anything to do with the Queen's visit. The first Secretary of the British Legation to the Holy See also hinted that he would have liked to have been officially informed of my arrival. I told him, as I also told Willebrands, that the Secretary of the C.I.R. was out of England at the time, and that might account for the omission; and that the Archbishop was in Africa.

I told Mons. Willebrands that it was the Archbishops' general intention that I should 'lie low' as much as possible in order not to embarrass them, and that I had in fact written to Fr. Boyer[4] privately a week previous to my arrival in order to inform him that I was coming. Willebrands was very soon satisfied about the whole matter. While I was in his office he was called three times by reporters to ask if I was there, so that I had either been followed or somebody had made a very lucky guess. The staff of the Secretariat, including Willebrands himself, are quite prepared for this affair to have better, but controlled, publicity. They complain about the bad press relations of the Vatican and get a certain amount of innocent delight from the discomfiture of their elders from their failure to be more adventurous.

I have reported this in some detail because I think that care should be taken at the time of my return etc. Perhaps the C.I.R. might like to take up the question of an occasional agreed statement with Willebrands. I will pursue it further with him.

---

[3] Colonel R.J.A. Hornby, Chief Information Officer, Church House, Westminster.
[4] Fr Charles Boyer of the Gregorian University (1884–1980), Thomist scholar and Director of the Foyer Unitas.

THE AMERICAN CHURCH

The flat put at my disposal is large and comfortable, and considering that the Americans call it 'make-shift', quite adequately furnished. I am having to provide some household utensils for myself, but all the main items of furniture are found.

The new American chaplain, the Reverend Wilbur C. Woodhams, has arrived and is very friendly. I gather that the chaplaincy here has had a difficult history for some time, but I should think that this era is at an end. The new chaplain has been brought from Bishop Bayne's own diocese of Olympia.

The leading American vestrymen etc. have been very friendly indeed and express themselves as very anxious to be associated with my work [. . .]. The same general current of feeling makes these generous people say repeatedly that they suppose I am 'representing the whole Anglican Communion'. I am disclaiming this as gently as I can, but I must obviously not appear to be rebuffing them. No doubt you will already be aware of this general situation, and I expect it can best be resolved through the good offices of Bishop Bayne. I am looking forward to my first talks with him when he comes at the end of the month to institute the new chaplain.

THE SECRETARIAT

My first visit was precipitated by the need to confer about publicity, referred to above. This whole discussion ended on a note of much cordiality. It was regarded as a great joke by all Willebrands' staff that the first Cosmonaut and I had caused the Italian press totally to ignore the arrival and meeting of the Liturgical Commission of the Council. This Commission is regarded as the most important and certainly has the heaviest weight of cardinals on it.

The Secretariat went into plenary session on Sunday, 16th, for ten days, at Castel Gandolfo.[5] This is very convenient for my purposes, as it leaves me free to get myself established here while they are deliberating. Presumably Archbishop Heenan will be returning to England about the 27th or 28th of this month and it might be a help if you could check whether there are any press reports of the Secretariat's work about that time.

The whole atmosphere of my reception was very pleasant indeed. They seemed genuinely pleased to see me and went out of their way

[5]The retreat and summer residence for the Pope, fifteen miles from Rome.

to say that they thought I could be useful. When I asked for some 'homework' while they were all away at Castel Gondolfo, I was given Volume I of the Acta et Documenta of the preparatory stage of the Council to study. It is a lengthy document.

I am now in possession of a full list of the members of all the Commissions and Secretariats and am able to say that the list of names of the Unity Secretariat I previously gave you is correct. The members of the office staff whom I met are as follows:-

Mons. J.F. Arrighi	(Affairs in France and Italy), a Corsican
Fr. Th. Stransky, C.S.P	(" England and U.S.A), an American
Fr. J. Salzmann	(" Germany), a Swiss

These men, who are all even younger than Willebrands, talk with misgiving of the senility of the senior cardinals and speak openly of Tardini etc. as reactionaries, but seem to think that their influence is on the wane. Mons. Willebrands said that he hoped that I should have an interview with Cardinal Bea in a fortnight's time, and perhaps eventually an audience with the Pope.

DATE OF THE COUNCIL

The general talk seems to be that the Pope would like the Council to be at the end of 1962, though everybody sees this to be impossible. Three responsible people have said to me that Easter 1963 is, in their view, the earliest possible date.

FREE ENQUIRY

At a lunch party today I had an opportunity of discussing this subject with a group which included Mons. Clark, Vice-Rector of the English College and Fr. [Tucai], S.J., Editor of *La Civilta Cattolica*.[6] They had been discussing the difficulties of a biblical scholar whose researches had caused him to be called to heel by his bishop. They said he had resigned from the teaching staff of a seminary and asked to be sent back to a parish. When I suggested that this might be the official version of the fact that he had been dismissed, they laughed and agreed that this might be so. They then asked how we dealt with independent theologians in our universities. I was able to explain the comparative independence of our university faculties from episcopal control and our reluctance to persecute heresy. They asked for information about

---

[6]Periodical founded by the Jesuits in 1850 to defend the cause of the Church and the papacy and to spread the teachings of Thomas Aquinas. Although Jesuit it carried the weight of formal approval by the Secretariat of State of the Holy See.

Bishop Barnes[7] and the affair of the Bishop of Woolwich and 'Lady Chatterley's Lover'.[8] I said that I supposed that the Archbishop only administered rebukes in both cases when he thought that the offenders were causing pastoral distress, and that one heretical bishop in half a century was not a dear price to pay for freedom of enquiry. The company gave me the impression that this issue was causing increasing disturbance in Roman seminaries.

Report No. 2   19th. April 1961

VATICAN PRESS CONFERENCE ABOUT THE COUNCIL

The General Secretary for the forthcoming Council, Monsignor Pericle Felici, Titular Archbishop of Samosata, held a press conference today at 12 Via Serristori, which was said to be the future press office for the Council. You might care to make a note of this address. I summarize the main points of his speech as follows:-

a) If the work of the Commission proceeds at its present rate, there is considerable hope that the Council will take place in the Autumn of 1962, as the Pope has often said he hopes it will.
b) The eleven Commissions and three Secretariats are hard at work.
c) The Central Commission has recently authorised the publication of fifteen volumes of documentation of the preparatory phase. These are not yet available to the public, for they are being carefully indexed.
d) It is not possible at the moment to say for certain what subjects will be before the Council, as this decision is in the hands of the Holy Father. But one thing is certain, which is that clerical celibacy will not be under discussion, as the Holy Father distinctly said at the time of the Synod of the diocese of Rome.
e) Journalists and the public in general must not expect too much of the press office of the Council. Although it is very desirable that all the faithful should take the keenest interest in the proceedings of the Council, it must be borne in mind that the Council is a solemn act of the highest authority and jurisdiction of the successors of

---

[7]E.W. Barnes (1874–1953), Bishop of Birmingham, 1924–1953. A purposeful rationalist, his controversial 1947 book, *The Rise of Christianity*, provoked calls for his resignation – or removal – as a bishop of the Church of England.

[8]The Bishop of Woolwich, John Robinson, had provoked public controversy by defending the publication of D.H. Lawrence's book, *Lady Chatterley's Lover*, in court. The book was regarded as sexually explicit.

the Apostles, with the successor of St. Peter at the head of them. They should therefore look up to them in reverent silence, praying that the Holy Spirit will illuminate and encourage them in the highest interests of the Church. The Commissions are working at the moment under conditions of the strictest secrecy.

The Secretary then answered certain questions as follows:-

a) Asked about the participation of the laity, he said that active participation was only possible for the 'ecclesia docens'.[9] This does not preclude the laity from making suggestions to their bishops if they feel so inclined.
b) Asked what language would be used, he said that it would certainly be Latin, though he did not exclude the possibility of certain · bishops asking to speak in their own native tongue.
c) The Secretary said, in answer to a question about non-Catholics, that he did not rule out the possibility of their being invited as observers, though this was still under consideration.

MY RELATION TO THE SECRETARIAT

Willebrands has said that he hopes to justify his willingness to accept me by the loophole which is given in the Encyclical Letter Ad Petri Cathedram, of the 29th June 1959, which the Pope quoted in his Motu Proprio[10] setting up the Council. In it he says that he trusts 'that those who are separated from the Holy See may accept his gentle invitation to speak and to obtain that unity which Christ Jesus asked from His heavenly Father in the most earnest prayers'.
[. . .]

Report No. 3   22nd. April 1961

SCOPE OF THE COUNCIL AND OF THE SECRETARIAT

I have been handed a cyclostyled document called 'BACKGROUND TO THE SECRETARIAT', copies of which I enclose. You may already have received one, for the document is not new.

---

[9] The Pope and the bishops of the Catholic Church.
[10] A document issued by the Pope on his own initiative and under his own name.

I draw special attention to Section 4 in which it speaks of 'obtaining suggestions from Catholic and non-Catholic sources by written, intermediate, and especially personal contacts.'

If it is the intention of the Church of England to put in any written representation, I imagine that this should be done as soon as possible, as whatever is submitted would have to be adjudicated upon by Commissions now sitting. The present Archbishop did mention one or two minor items that might go in in the way of suggestions. Perhaps you could be so kind as to let me have some comments on this matter.

BACKGROUND TO THE SECRETARIAT FOR PROMOTING CHRISTIAN UNITY (official English title)

(Official titles; Secretariatus ad Christianorum Unitatem fovenam Praepartorius Concilii Vaticani I; Segretariato per l'Unione dei Cristiani; Secretariat pour l'Unité des Chrétiens; Sekretariat fuer die Einheit der Christen')

I   *History of the Creation of the Secretariat (1960)*
On May 30, 1960, His Holiness Pope John XXIII announced his intention to erect a Secretariat in a semi-public meeting of all the cardinals.

On June 5, the Pope issued a 'Motu Proprio', called 'Sperno Dei nutu' (from the initial three words), which dealt with the setting up of ten commissions and two secretariats to prepare for the coming Ecumenical council.

On June 6, he appointed Augustin Cardinal Bea to be the president of the Secretariat

On June 24, Mons. J.G.M Willebrands was appointed the Secretary.

During September the members and consultors, along with the working staff, were appointed.

On October 24, the new offices opened at Via dei Corridori, 64.

On November 14–15, the first sessions of all the members and consultors were held in Rome.

II   *Purpose of the Secretariat*

1. In 'Superno Dei nutu',[11] His Holiness restated the *primary* purpose of the coming council, quoting his own words from his first encyclical Letter, 'Ad Petri cathedram', 29 June, 1959:

---

[11] A motu proprio promulgated 5 June 1960. The essential author was the Secretary of State, Tardini. This instituted the preparatory commissions for the Council.

'the development of the Catholic Faith and the renewal along the right lines of the habits of the Christian people, and the adapting of the Church's discipline to the needs and conditions of the present time. The event will surely be a wonderful manifestation of truth, unity, and charity; a manifestation, indeed, which we hope will be received by those who behold it but who are separated from this Apostolic See, as a gentle invitation to seek and find that unity for which Jesus Christ prayed so ardently to his heavenly Father'.

Referring to the Secretariat, the Pope said:

'As a token of our affection and goodwill towards those who bear the name of Christians but are separated from this Apostolic See, to enable them to follow the work of the Council and to find more easily the path by which they may arrive at that unity for which Jesus Christ prayed so ardently to his heavenly Father, we are establishing a special "Advisory Board" or Secretariat, presided over by a Cardinal whom we shall choose, and organised in the same manner as the Commissions.'

2. The Secretariat has a double purpose:

(a) Its *immediate* purpose is to inform accurately non-Catholic Christians on the work of the coming Council, to receive their wishes and suggestions relating to the Council, to weigh them, and, if needs be, to pass them on to other Commissions (e.g. Theological Commission, Commission for the Missions; Commission for the Eastern Churches; Liturgy Commission, etc.)

The Secretariat is not a mere Information Centre. It aims to help guide the Council in those theological and pastoral matters which directly or indirectly bear on the problem of Christian Unity.

(b) Its *larger* and *more general* end is to aid non-Catholic Christians to find 'that unity for which Jesus Christ prayed so ardently to his heavenly Father'; to establish, for example, the exact situation with its Unity problems in various countries: (1) what various non-Catholic Christians here and now have in common with the Roman Catholic Church in doctrine, discipline, and cult; and also how they differ from it; (2) what are the desires of these different groups touching on the Unity Problem, and what ways can the Catholic Church help them to true Unity.

The Secretariat, at the same time, does not want to be a substitute for the initiatives of qualified private individuals and, even less so, for those centres and institutes which for some years have been established to study ecumenical problems.

III   *Composition of the Secretariat*

1. The permanent working staff in Rome comprises:

   (a) The President, Augustin Cardinal Bea, 79 years, a German-born Jesuit. An internationally known biblical scholar who, especially in biblical studies, has had for many years personal and written contacts with non-Catholic Christians and non Christians. For years he was the head of the Pontifical Institute for Biblical Studies in Rome.

   (b) The Secretary, Monsignor J.G.M. Willebrands, 51 yrs., Dutch-born. Former professor of theology at the Major Seminary in Warmond, Holland. He is also Secretary for the Catholic Conference on Ecumenical Questions. Since 1951 this Conference has held at least annual meetings of Catholic theologians on ecumenical questions. Often the problems were common to those being considered by the World Council of Churches.

   (c) The assistants, Monsignor Jean-Francois Arrighi from Corsica and Father Thomas F Stransky, a Paulist Father from the United States.

2. With the Secretariat are members who have voting power in the Secretariat's general sessions, and those who are only consultors. The composition of both groups is very international; it represents especially those countries in which there is a large number of non-Catholic Christians;

   (Here follows a list of the voting members and consulting members, already despatched)

IV   *Mode of Operation of the Secretariat*

The Secretariat utilizes every means of obtaining suggestions from Catholic and non-Catholic sources by written, intermediate, and especially personal contacts. It also keeps abreast of the many pertinent articles appearing in periodicals.

According to their importance, the results of this research are studied more closely by the voting and consulting members, who work in small subcommissions and in general sessions. They evaluate the theological and practical implications. The voting members then decide, if and how the suggestions should be passed on to the other commissions of the Council, and what recommendations should be made.

V   *The Permanency of the Secretariat*

The Secretariat has been erected explicitly and immediately for the needs of the coming Ecumenical Council. The result of the Council's coming deliberations and their importance for Christian Unity will reveal in what way the Secretariat should be continued.

From the Secretariat
(25.1.1961)

Report No. 4   26 April 1961

[...]

OTHER COMMUNICATIONS AND THE VATICAN COUNCIL

In answer to my question as to what other Communions or bodies had made personal or written communications to the Secretariat for the Council, I was told that they had been in touch with the following:-

(a) *The World Council of Churches.* They had had a written statement from the General Secretary acknowledging the Pope's intentions with regard to unity and giving an assurance that member churches would be made aware of them. But of course it is recognised that the W.C.C. cannot act in this matter.

(b) *Federation Protestante de France.* This is an unofficial grouping of Lutheran and Calvinistic congregations in France. The theological sub-committee of their Commission for Ecumenical Studies under Pastor Herbert Roux wrote in about two points, though I have not been told what they were.

(c) *Lutherisches Kirchenamt* of Hanover. I imagine that this is one of the independent synods of the Lutheran organisation. Apparently they are in direct and active communication with the Archbishop of Paderborn,[12] who is a member of the Secretariat. This is the only other case at the present of there being a direct and recognised channel of communication between the Roman Church and some other body.

(d) *The Lutheran World Federation.* Professor Skydsgaard of Copenhagen, its President, has been in personal communication with the Secretary and has expressed his intention of persuading as many of the member churches as possible to send in an official statement later.

---

[12]Lorenz Jäger (1892–1975), Archbishop of Paderborn, 1941–1973.

THE ORTHODOX CHURCHES

It was explained to me that certain difficulties are being experienced in deciding who shall be the authority responsible for dealing with the Patriarch of Constantinople etc. as between the Secretariat and the Commission for the Oriental Churches (this latter is, of course, to be distinguished from the Congregation for the Oriental Rites). There is some hesitation, apparently, on the Commission about making the first approaches. But the Secretariat is very insistent that it should be done and done soon. They do not hold out any hope that the Patriarch will make the first move (is this so?). The Secretariat is going to propose to the Commission that immediate relationships, on the level of information only, be established with the Patriarchate at once [. . .]

OBSERVERS AT THE COUNCIL

This has been under discussion at the recent meeting of the Secretariat. It is therefore very confidential. The Secretariat intends to recommend that observers from non-Roman churches should be able to be present, although it is by no means certain that the recommendation will be endorsed. It is taken for granted that the decision about this will have to be made not later than the Autumn of 1961. The Secretariat is not clear to whom invitations would then be issued. They could clearly not go to all the hundreds of constituent members of the W.C.C. If a favourable decision is made by the Central Commission, approaches will be made to the main confessional groups only (Anglican Communion, Lutheran World Federation, Presbyterian Alliance etc.). Willebrands intends eventually to go to Germany to speak with Bishop Dibelius about this matter.[13]

MY OWN POSITION

The Secretary thanked me this morning for having 'lain low' as requested. Cardinal Bea will see me in a few days' time. He is said to be anxious to have seen me, and to have regularised my position, before the Queen comes (!).
[. . .]

---

[13]Otto Dibelius (1880–1967), Lutheran theologian. In 1925 he became General Superintendent of the Kurmark and took part in various early conferences of the Ecumenical Movement. He was dismissed from his post in 1933 and, although put under restraint by the Nazis, he collaborated with the Confessing Church. Bishop of Berlin, 1945; Presiding Bishop of the Evangelical Church in Germany, 1949; President of the World Council of Churches, 1954.

Report No. 5   1st May 1961

CONTACTS

ARCHBISHOP DAVID MATHEW. I met Archbishop Mathew at a lunch party at the British Legation to the Holy See. He was exceptionally friendly [. . .]. He is R.C. bishop to the forces in England and Secretary of the Commission on Missions. He had been Auxiliary to Cardinal Hinsley[14] and said openly that Hinsley's two successors, being lesser men, had not taken so satisfactory a view of the Church of England, and that he was sorry for it. He hoped for better things in the future. [. . .]

BISHOP DWYER OF LEEDS.[15] He is a member of the Commission on the government of dioceses etc. I met him at lunch at the English College. He said that he hoped that the Church of England had him down on their list of friends, and said that I could call on his help at any time. I had previously been told that this bishop was by no means friendly and I am glad to know that I was mistaken. I had a long talk with him for several hours at which I was able to explain our hopes about South India.[16] On the subject of Freedom of Enquiry, he said that there was much more liberty in the Roman Church than we supposed. But the Roman Church was much more sensitive of the danger done to the faith of simple people by allowing the ill-digested results of enquiry to be published unnecessarily. He thought that the Church of England had been much too easy-going about this and had lost much ground in consequence. I admitted that there was some truth in this though we were not masters in our own household. I said that I thought the Roman method stood to lose most in the long run, and that for them the run still had a long way to go.

He said that there could be no unity without theological agreement. I said that we thought the same, but that the difficulty was to decide what should be the limits of theological definition.

---

[14]Arthur Hinsley (1865–1943), Archbishop of Westminster, 1935–1943; created Cardinal, 1937.

[15]George Dwyer (1908–1987), Bishop of Leeds, 1957–1965.

[16]As archbishop, Fisher had overseen the work of the churches of south India to create a united church with other traditions. This had become controversial within the Anglican Communion because, in the eyes of 'High' church people, a priest who had not been ordained by a bishop could not be a priest at all. This was still a dispute when Pawley was in Rome. The hope was that in time the issue would simply recede and the Church of South India would be accepted as a full member of the Communion.

He spoke with great respect of the Bishop of Ripon[17] and said that he supposed that he would take a prominent part in any future relationships between us.

CARDINAL BEA

I had my first long official interview with the Cardinal this morning. It was very friendly and lasted for an hour and a quarter. He spoke with great warmth of the visit of the present Archbishop of Canterbury and asked me to convey greetings, which I have done in a separate letter. He expressed the hope that the Archbishop-designate would also visit Rome in due course.

He made many courteous offers of facilities for my work and expressed himself anxious to do all that was possible to help.

He said that he had told the Pope about my assignment and that His Holiness had been pleased about it. The Cardinal said that he thought that I would eventually be received in private audience. He said that my position was now perfectly well established and that there was no further need to be furtive about it; though now, as always, we should be careful about the press. He commented on a statement he had read in the paper that when, in a few days' time, the Queen holds a reception for the Roman Curia, there will be no Anglican clergy present. He seemed surprised that this should be so. I told him that the chaplain and I were going to be presented to the Queen at one of the civil receptions. I said further that with regard to my own case as far as the Holy See Legation was concerned, any decision would have been made before my position was as clear as it now seemed to be, and that probably the Minister would have wished to be careful. The Cardinal said that he did not think that there was any further need for this kind of care. I thanked him for this assurance. I hope he is right.

The Cardinal was pleased that the Moscow Patriarchate had in the last few days intimated its willingness to accept membership of the W.C.C. I had not known about this. He was also very pleased that the General Secretary of the W.C.C.[18] had written to tell him about it.

The Cardinal told me that the Lutheran World Federation was intending to send a representative to be in Rome eventually, and that the Secretariat were pleased about this.

When I asked the Cardinal whether the Secretariat was expecting written representations from us, he said that they would certainly be

---

[17] John Moorman (see *Dramatis personae*).
[18] Willem Visser 't Hooft (1900–1985), First General Secretary of the World Council of Churches.

gladly received. I am afraid I haven't yet got a clear impression as to whether they really want written representations or not. I told him what my present plan of working was and asked him what I might do when I had finished that. He said he thought I might start on drawing up the written representation. I told him that I was not authorised to do that. I said that the whole subject would have to be given careful consideration by experts in England and that it would take a long time, in which case it would not be ready in time for the Council. So I do not think that they can be seriously expecting the Church of England to be going to produce a detailed written statement of their position before the Council. What alternative the Cardinal could have in mind, I am not quite clear, and I shall have to bring the subject up in some other way. I thought that at this first interview I could not represent the Church of England as being very keen to submit such a document, because I have not yet been authorised to say so.

The Cardinal asked me whether I thought that liberal modernism had 'had its day' in England, as in Germany. I said that I thought that the movement in England had never taken quite the same shape that it had in Germany and that biblical scholarship in England had in the last 25 years taken on a more orthodox trend. He expressed himself as a great admirer of English biblical scholarship. He was examining the new English Bible[19] and so far had been quite pleased with it.

I told the Cardinal of my general plan of visits to Rome and he agreed that it would be convenient.

Report No. 6   7th May, 1961

OFFICIAL DOCUMENTS

I have now completed my reading of Volume 1 of the Acta et Documenta Concilio Oecumenico Vatican II Apparando (Official Pronouncement of the Pope on the subject). This is the only volume that I shall be able to see as the others are confidential to the members of the Central Commission of the Council. It was given to me as showing better than anything else the intentions and aspirations of the Roman Church for the Council [. . .]

---

[19] The New Testament of the New English Bible was published in 1961; the Old Testament would follow in 1970.

Report No. 7   18th May, 1961

QUEEN'S VISIT

You will know from other sources that the visit of the Queen and the Duke of Edinburgh was a very great success here. I was present at the Commonwealth Reception, at which there were over three thousand guests, and also at the much more select reception at the British Embassy.

I feel bound to report that there was very widespread comment on the fact that there was no Anglican clergyman present at the reception given at the British Legation to the Holy See by the Queen to meet the Curia and their Roman Catholic clergy, including the English Roman clergy in Rome; and that there were no members of her ecclesiastical household, or an Anglican cleric, in the suite which went to the Vatican. Cardinal Bea and other Roman clergy have commented on this to me, the Italian press was very keen to know about it, and there were comments on it in the papers here, and I gather also in the English press. I gave no interviews on the subject, though pressed to do so.

I should like to comment on the above situation as follows. Sir Peter Scarlett[20] was kind enough to ask me about it shortly before the Queen came. I had to say reluctantly that until my position was regularised with Cardinal Bea I thought it would be as well if I were not present. Had it been a week later my position would have been different, for I am now apparently under no obligation to lie low. Though I do not think it would have made much difference; I did, in fact, see Cardinal Bea on the Monday before the Queen's arrival. But since he asked for my comments I did venture to say to the Minister that I did think that some Anglican cleric, either the chaplain in Rome (who is an honorary Queen's Chaplain, anyhow), or the Archdeacon, or Bishop of Gibraltar should be there, but nothing was done about this. I don't know what the protocol about this sort of thing is, and I don't suppose the occasion will arise for a long time again, but I should like to place on record that the reaction in Roman circles and among the British and American communities was one of considerable surprise. I am, of course, a tyro in all these matters and quite anxious to learn. Since I have ventured the above comments I might as well go the full length and record my surprise that with the exception of the Minister, the staff of the Legation seems to consist of such intense Romans. I have

[20] Sir Peter Scarlett (1905–1987), British Minister to the Holy See, 1960–1965.

had one or two occasions to wish it were otherwise. That does not in any way modify the fact that they have all been very kind, hospitable and cooperative.

ENTERTAINMENT

There are two very stately rooms in this house which the Americans have very kindly put at my disposal for the purposes of entertainment and I have given a few lunch parties [. . .]. Thanks to having my wife here, the cost of entertainment is considerably less than it might have been otherwise. We are looking forward to a series of meetings with Bishop Bayne next week-end, who will be here for Pentecost (Whitsun you call it) and to institute the new American Chaplain.

LA CIVILTA CATTOLICA

I have made contact with the Jesuit Editor of the right-wing periodical, who appears to be very friendly. He has very kindly given me a long series of off-prints of articles to do with the preparations for the Council. I have completed an examination of them and append a series of notes, extracts, etc. You will easily believe that the longer I am here the less there is, proportionately, to report. I have to wade through pages of themes which I have already reported to you and which there is no need to repeat. Some of this is old history by now, but I thought you might care to have it for the purposes of record:-

(a) 1960 December number 'The Courtesy Visit of Dr. Fisher to His Holiness John XXIII'

The first paragraph describes Dr. Fisher as Anglican Archbishop of Canterbury 'and so in a certain manner the most authentic representative of the Anglican communion in England, and of the communion throughout the world.' After saying that this is only one of a long series of visits of Dr. Fisher to 'other churches', the article quotes from the Canterbury Diocesan Gazette in which the Archbishop is alleged to have said that there had been a rapid change of attitude on the part of Rome from ignorance and suspicion to a growing interest and sympathy and even, in certain quarters, to a manifest desire to enter into the spirit of the Ecumenical Movement. Dr. Fisher had said that the constitution of the new Secretariat was a clear indication of this change of front. The article comments that the Archbishop did not give due weight in his article to the fact that there has been a considerable change of attitude also among non-Catholic bodies towards the Church of Rome.

Although the Italian electoral campaign was working up to a pitch of considerable excitement, and the American Presidential campaign was in full swing, the international press gave a very great deal of publicity to this visit. The review then indulges in a lot of verbiage to show that this degree of publicity was out of proportion to the importance of the visit. It makes very heavy weather of this and quotes English, Italian, French and German newspapers in defence of its thesis. Some papers saw in the visit 'the first steps towards a future pact for united action in social matters', and the left-wing paper 'il Paese' thought that the visit would represent 'the creation of a united religious front of a political character against Marxism and the powers behind the curtain.' The *Stuttgarter Zeitung* on the other hand, thought this line of interpretation constituted 'Latin exaggeration'. Then there follow quotations from Dr. Fisher's address to his Diocesan Conference and to the Church Assembly. The next long paragraph labours the fact that the Holy Father quite frequently receives very important personages and that Dr. Fisher's visit was nothing special. In fact in the previous twelve months he had received Bishop Dibelius, Mervyn Stockwood and Canon Donald Rea. This section is rather distasteful. The writer then turns on the heat about the change of front in the Church of England, quoting the way in which the establishment of the Roman Hierarchy in England in 1850 was received by the English bishops [. . .]

In a paragraph headed 'fundamental doctrinal divergences' the articles refers to 'the primacy and infallibility of the Pope, validity of Anglican orders, concessions and ambiguities in the matter of birth control in Lambeth 1958, and compromise in the precise meaning of episcopal ordination as witnessed in South India. A section on 'Anglo-Catholics' says that they are unrepresentative, though influential out of all proportion to their numbers. The article continues: 'the Anglican Reformation has nevertheless preserved, to a greater degree than have the Lutherans or the Calvinists, certain positive elements, which make it a little less distant from the Catholic religion. Among these elements we can name a considerable consciousness of the visible Church, an ecclesiastical structure based on the episcopate, a reasonably rich liturgical piety and a theology which on the whole preserves the traditions of antiquity in such a way as to avoid the grosser excesses of the application of the principle of the free examination of the scriptures. But of course that is not sufficient to make up for the other serious doctrinal divergences.'

The concluding paragraph says that no one in their senses thinks that this visit of courtesy is even the beginning of negotiations for reunion. Nor is it the 'Canossa' of Anglicanism. The most realistic attitude will in the long run be the most helpful. It then quotes from AD PETRI CATHEDRAM,[21] in particular the phrase that 'the love of the truth will in the end dissipate all hesitancy and disunity'. And ends, as these things always do, with a eulogy of His Holiness.

[. . .]

Report No. 8   May 22nd, 1961

[. . .]

BISHOP BAYNE

The Bishop was here yesterday and instituted the Chaplain. I had a long and very useful talk with him. He said openly, as I had been warned he would, that he hoped my whole mission would be regarded eventually as being on a wider basis than it is at present. I explained the reason for it being on its present basis, and he seemed to understand; there was no trace of criticism in what he said. He made an offer of financial help, for which I thanked him, though I said that due to their kindness, expenses were at the moment proving less than might have been expected and that all was well so far. When he asked what other help he could give, I said that I should appreciate as much information as possible on the relations between the Roman Church and other churches in the various continents, particularly where there would seem to be infringements of religious liberty. I presume there is no need for me to record the various things that he told me on the Roman question in general, as they will be available to you direct. The thing that surprised me most was to hear that objection had been raised to my mission in Canada. That there had been grumblings in Sydney was, of course, no surprise.[22]

[. . .]

---

[21] The first encyclical promulgated by John XXIII, 29 June 1959.
[22] The Anglican diocese of Sydney was famously – or notoriously – conservative evangelical in its Protestantism.

RERUM NOVARUM 1891–1961

I was present in the large square outside St. Peter's when the Pope gave a discourse on the 70th anniversary of the great sociological Encyclical. There was a very large crowd present, estimated variously as 19,000 and 70,000 in different newspapers. The Pope promised a new Encyclical in a week or two's time elaborating the doctrines of RERUM NOVARUM in a way that QUADRAGESIMO ANNO did in 1931.

There is no doubt in my mind that the Roman Church in Italy is too conscious of the communists as the source of all their troubles, both political and religious. I think the political influence of communists is exceedingly strong in Italy, and a menace to them and to the whole of Europe. But I think the Roman Church deceives itself if it thinks that opposition or misunderstanding in the case of religion comes only from them. There is a very large body of ordinary lay people who are disaffected and anti-clerical who are also very anti-communist. A considerable amount of this kind of opinion thinks that the last three dogmatic pronouncements went too far. In fact I have often heard laymen say that 'no one believes them here, except priests and women'.

Similarly the Roman Church, in its analysis of the political situation, eventually seems to find the communists, East or West of the iron curtain, at the root of all evil. This tendency is even more noticeable when it is indirect, as for example in the standard declaration that 'the objective of political life must be the safeguarding of the free expression of opinion among workers.' In my view the Church's invective should be directed also, if not primarily, against all those sources of corruption and injustice in Italian political and economic life which make the path of the communists so easy. And to achieve this the aim would have to be much more to the right than it is at present. Quite a number of the more objective clerics with whom I have discussed this question would agree with the foregoing.

[. . .]

DOM CUTHBERT McCANN[23]

Dom Cuthbert arrived as you said. He confirmed that Downside had been entrusted with work for unity, but in a different sense from what we might suppose. They have been given this assignment, as within

---

[23] A leading participant in Roman Catholic ecumenical work, McCann (1904–1989) was ordained in 1944. Much of his commitment to the cause took root in 1960–1961, when he studied at Louvain.

the Benedictine Order as a whole, and not specifically for work in England. They regard their chief work as being towards the Orthodox, such as they carry on at Chevetogne²⁴ in Belgium. It does not mean that they are the proper channel of communication in England. That would be the episcopal committee to which reference will be made later.

CARDINAL BEA

I had another long interview with Cardinal Bea last Wednesday the 17th. Whenever I go to see him, or the Secretariat, I am rung up by the press afterwards. There can be no doubt that there are people in the pay of the press in both places. They might be doorkeepers or liftmen.

The Cardinal had noticed that Archbishop Fisher had drawn attention to the novena of Prayer for unity, and he asked me to thank him for doing so. He told me that His Holiness had heard about this and was pleased. It is hoped that I shall have an audience with the Pope in the first weeks of June.

I tried out a new line with the Cardinal, of good humoured protest about the activities of the 'Foyer Unitas' which I have been observing for a long time, which sees unity mainly in terms of propaganda and conversions. I took with me the current number of UNITAS, Fr. Boyer's paper. In it there was an article on 'Tendencies in the Church of England towards Rome'. I said that it was now being said in England that if you wanted to have fair conversation about reunion you had to turn to the Benedictines or Dominicans, and that Fr. Boyer's association was becoming suspect. The paper in question was open to criticism on two grounds, first that the thesis was not in fact true. Dr. Pusey was dead and the influence of the Oxford Movement had broadened out, leaving the Church of England with a thirst for Catholicism, though not for Rome, between which conceptions it was now able to draw a broad distinction. Secondly, the paper was controversial in an unfriendly way; it made unnecessary reference to individual conversions. The Church of England could do the same [. . .]. The Cardinal said that he was in agreement with what I said [. . .]. Controversy should not appear, as such, in a paper called UNITAS. The Cardinal agreed.

---

²⁴The monastery at Chevetogne was founded by Dom Lambert Beaudoin in 1924. For some years, annual meetings of theologians and scholars from across the churches had taken place there. McCann was closely associated with its work and sought to make Downside comparable in certain strains.

FR. BOYER AND 'UNITAS'

On the same morning I had to lunch the said Fr. Boyer, S.J. and Mons. Arrighi, a Corsican, an administrative member of the Secretariat for Unity, and Fr. Augustine Hoey, of the Community of the Resurrection. Fr. Hoey spoke no languages other than English, but I was glad for them to meet another member of an English community. They both seemed to have met Fr. Curtis. Mons. Arrighi has always struck me as a brilliant man. He evidently has a good reputation, and it is a pity that he speaks no English. I told Fr. Boyer all that I had said to the Cardinal, in front of Mgr. Arrighi. He was, of course, impenitent, though he looked serious when I said that we were more inclined to turn to the Dominicans and Benedictines. He said that he was interested in individual conversations. I agreed that he had every right to be, but that he should not make so much capital of them in a magazine entitled UNITAS. The whole conversation was very amicable and conducted with much leg-pulling.
[. . .]

Report No. 9   26th May, 1961

MY RETURN

I have received the notice of dates of meetings of the C.I.R. Provisionally I had already arranged to leave here on Tuesday the 13th June and shall therefore be able to attend the R.C. Committee[25] on Friday 16th.

HOUSE OF LORDS' DEBATE ON UNITY[26]

I have had to try and explain this to quite a number of contacts. I have been put at a disadvantage by the fact that they (Willebrands, Fr Corr, the Benedictines of St. Anselm's) have been in possession of offprints of Hansard, while I have not. I have had other occasions than this to admire their information service. I suppose in future tours I ought to

---

[25] The Anglican–Roman Catholic Committee chaired by J.N.D. Kelly (see p. 347, n. 21).
[26] For this debate of 10 May 1961, see Hansard, Debates of the House of Lords, Fifth Series, vol. 231, cols 230–336. The motion was proposed by the Earl of Arran and included a waspish exchange between Lord Alexander of Hillsborough, very firmly a Protestant, and the Archbishop of Canterbury, who insisted on being both Catholic and Protestant. Arran ended up wondering if the debate had done more harm than good for the cause of Christian unity.

ask somebody at home (Secretary of C.I.R.? or whom?) to send me any vital material of this sort which comes to hand. I did my very best to explain away the harmful conclusions they might have drawn from this debate. In my view the Archbishop's speech at the end saved what from this angle would have been a total wreck. Apart from the speeches of the bishops, the two outstanding speeches were by Roman Catholic laymen [. . .]. What the Archbishop said towards the end of his speech about the treatment of the Reformation happens to have come in very usefully on an occasion referred to below.
[. . .]

FURTHER IMPENDING CANONISATIONS

Mons. Willebrands said that his main reason for asking me to come to the office was to tell me from Cardinal Bea that the Holy Office was proceeding to canonise a large group of English Reformation martyrs and that the Cardinal was himself the 'penens' of the question. The Cardinal particularly wanted it to be understood that this process had been planned a long time previously (the candidates concerned had now been beatified some years), and it was not intended in any way as anti-Anglican propaganda. I thanked him for his courtesy in informing me and assured him that I would pass the information on to the appropriate authority. I said that I did not think it would be advisable to issue any statement about this, or any disclaimer, for it would come under the general rule that 'Qui s'excuse s'accuse'[27] [. . .]

THE ENGLISH ROMAN HIERARCHY AND UNITY

I told Willebrands that I had received invitations to speak in England on 'the Roman Catholic conception of Unity' and that when the occasions were to have been public I naturally refused them, saying that the organisers should ask Roman Catholics. I explained that in some parts of England they would only get a rebuff to this request. To whom should they then turn if they wanted to pursue the matter? He then told me of the existence of a Committee of the hierarchy for these matters to whom I should address the question. The members were:-

The Archbishop of Liverpool, Mons. Heenan, Chairman
The Bishop of Shrewsbury, Mons. Murphy
The Bishop of Clifton, Mons. Rudderham
The Aux. Bishop of Portsmouth, Mons. Holland

---

[27] 'He who apologizes condemns himself.'

Bishop Cashman, St. Mary's Cadogan St., Chelsea[28]
Had you heard of this Committee, and are you in touch with them?

THE ROTARY CLUB

I consulted Bishop Bayne on the advisability of attending the meetings of this Club here, of which I am the member representing the cathedral in Ely. It seemed to be a good way of making contacts with Italian laymen. I am very pleased that I have done so as the contacts are invariably interesting and the membership of the central Rome club which I attend is distinguished, I should say more so than a corresponding club in England.

I have enquired why the Roman clergy do not seem to be represented. Nobody seems to know why this is and there is no prohibition. Cardinals are frequently guests, and the members to whom I have spoken so far all seem to be practising Romans. I was involved in an interesting conversation with a group dominated by a professor of chemistry in the University of Rome. He was talking about the increase of theoretical communism among the intelligentsia. Not only were the workers sold on it, but 15% of the university teaching staffs and 20% of the schoolteachers held a party ticket. But more than this, the ecumenists were the effective minority. When I asked if the Italians realised that the corollary of dialectical materialism was totalitarian occupation by Russian troops, he said that they did not think that possible – 'it couldn't happen here'. They envisaged an independent communist state, such as that of Tito in Jugoslavia. I said that that took extreme moral and physical courage which, with respect, the Italians did not possess. The speaker agreed. He reckoned to be a loyal Catholic. He said further that they were unfortunate in Italy in not having a strong phalanx of Protestantism to set between the two dogmatisms of Catholicism on one hand and Communism on the other. I questioned him at this point and elicited the fact that he meant what I hoped he meant, that as a result of the reforms of the 16th century we (i.e. England, Germany and the Scandinavian countries) had found a place for true humanism and freedom which gave us a sturdy independence and reliability, enabling us to think for ourselves, and to see the fallacies, as well as the attractions, of the communist

---

[28]John Heenan (see *Dramatis personae*). John Murphy (1905–1995), Bishop of Shrewsbury, 1949–1961; Archbishop of Cardiff, 1961–1983. Joseph Rudderham (1899–1979), Bishop of Clifton, 1949–1979. Thomas Holland (1908–1999), Coadjutor Bishop of Portsmouth, 1960; Titular Bishop of Etenna, 1960–1964; Bishop of Salford, 1964–1983. David Cashman (1912–1971), Auxiliary Bishop of Westminster, 1958; Titular Bishop of Cantanus, 1958–1965; Bishop of Arundel and Brighton, 1965–1971.

ideology. Their difficulty in Italian universities was that people came to them from the Church schools or state schools (indifferently) taught how to assimilate information, but not how to think. This was traceable to the whole Jesuit pattern of education, which had been taken over by the state without question, which ministered continually to this defect. What they wanted was new educational methods in the schools. These were not forthcoming.

I asked what they intended to do about it (there was now a group of 5 listening and approving). They said 'What can we do; we must wait.' I said that that wouldn't do. If it was too late to have a Protestant reformation, they should at least have one on the pattern of the French, which, though it had started by being liturgical was now thoroughgoing in some parts. When they asked what it comprised, I said the discovery of the Bible and the priesthood of the laity. There were nods of approval, but the opinion was expressed that the Curia was too strong for that to happen in Italy, at least for the present.

CARDINAL TISSERANT

I had a short interview with the Cardinal on Wednesday last and to my astonishment and pleasure he immediately accepted an invitation to come to dinner here in the near future. He joked openly against Cardinal Tardini several times. His next visitor after me was the Israeli Ambassador to Italy, a Jewish scholar of some distinction. Tisserant said that Cardinal Tardini didn't like having Jews in the Vatican under any circumstances 'because they killed Jesus'.

Report No. 10   31st May, 1961

CARDINAL TISSERANT'S VISIT

The Dean of the Sacred College[29] came to dinner as arranged, together with Dr. Bolshakoff[30] who first effected the introduction. I presented the English Chaplain after dinner. The old man talked almost incessantly for nearly two hours and a half, chiefly about himself; but as his life, work and views are all interesting, nobody

---

[29] Eugène Tisserant (1884–1972), French Cardinal and Dean of the Sacred College of Cardinals.
[30] Sergius Nikolaevich Bolshakoff (1901–1990), much-travelled Russian Orthodox scholar and ecumenist.

noticed the passage of time. Among the things of direct interest to my work which he spoke about were the following:-

(a) In talking of the political situation in Italy, he gave a description of it almost identical with that reported in my Report No. 9. He always gives his voice against the habit in the Curia of condemning communism out of hand instead of trying to understand it, interpret it and convert it. He also deplores the failure of the Curia to launch criticism in any other direction.

(b) As the effective bishop of a 'suburbicarian diocese' he lamented his failure to bring about any reforms at all in popular piety. He laughed at my suggestion that the Church in Italy could do with a reform on the French pattern. He agreed heartily, but said 'You try'. There were the first indications of attempts in the North (Milan, Bologna etc.), but he thought the rest of Italy would have to wait another 60 years.

(c) The Synod of Rome. The old man was in particularly good form about this, and was enjoying being indiscreet. The whole thing had been 'a flop'. The synodical rules were openly flouted, and no single reform had been effected, this in the Pope's own diocese. The chief reason for this was that the people on whose advice the Pope chiefly relies (Tardini, Ottaviani, etc.) were out of touch with the situation. He himself was, of course, a dangerous liberal.

He made no reference to my work at table, or in the conversation afterwards, and I didn't feel inclined to force it on his attention. Dr. Bolshakoff told me that the Cardinal knew about it and was very interested. He preferred to stand off and observe people at first acquaintance and disliked being 'got at'. I was pleased when at the end he said 'We haven't talked about your work tonight, but I know all about it and am very interested. Don't hesitate to let me know if I can do anything for you.' He was insistent that the dinner party should be small, and I was wondering whether he was a little bit nervous about coming. But I was glad to hear from the Secretariat today that he himself had told them that he had been and had enjoyed himself.

THE IMPENDING CANONISATIONS

I enclose a copy of my letter to Willebrands.[31] When I get their reaction, I will send it. I should then value comments from someone about procedure. If I feel you are in general favour of continuing with the subject I shall send my letter to some historian. It would have been the Dean of Winchester, who had promised to help.[32] Who is now

[31] This is absent from the sequence of reports.
[32] Oswin Harvard Gibbs-Smith (1901–1969), Dean of Winchester, 1961–1969.

our best Reformation historian? I don't get the impression that either Greenslade or Owen Chadwick[33] have made a special study of it. I wish Gordon Rupp[34] were one of us.
[. . .]

| Report No. 11. | 9th June, 1961 |

MY RETURN AND PUBLICITY

Attached hereto is a draft agreed with Cardinal Bea of a press statement to cover my return. They are not going to put anything in the Italian press, though I think they would be better advised to do so. A large number of people know of my departure from here; and if a journalist happens to get interested, his conjectures could lead anywhere. I do hope our Central Office will put this message out to forestall the kind of misrepresentation which resulted in England and Italy, in my opinion, from too little information at the time of my arrival out here. As you may imagine, I am also anxious to avoid another press attack on my home.
[. . .]

THE CARDINAL SECRETARY OF STATE'S DEPARTMENT

I went this week by appointment to see the Sostituto of the Cardinal Secretary of State, Mons. Dell'Acqua (Tit. Archbishop of Chalcedon),[35] via his secretary Mons. Cardinale. I was asked by them not to mention to the Unity Secretary that I had been in their department. Dell'Acqua said that a message of greeting to the Cardinal might be a good idea. After much negotiation to-and-fro with Cardinal Bea etc. this was agreed as per enclosed and eventually sent through the Unity Secretariat to the Secretary of State. Dell'Acqua was very effusive, and thanked me when I said that at least half my work here had been in reporting to England objectively what the Roman Church was saying about the forthcoming Council. I thanked him for what he was known to have done for Anglicans in Rome. He thought that a visit of respect to the Cardinal might be arranged on

---

[33]Michael Washington Greenslade (1929–), historian. William Owen Chadwick (1916–), British historian; Dixie Professor of Ecclesiastical History, Cambridge, 1958–1968; Regius Professor of Modern History, Cambridge, 1968–1983.

[34]Gordon Rupp (1910–1986), Methodist scholar and historian, later to be Dixie Professor of Ecclesiastical History at Cambridge, 1968–1977.

[35]Angelo Dell'Acqua (1903–1972), staff member of the Secretariat of State, 1938–1950; elected Titular Archbishop of Chalcedonia, 1958; created Cardinal, 1967.

my next visit in October. I was presented with a very large bound volume of essays published in honour of Pius XII by various persons extolling his work in all parts of his Pontificate.

I cannot report that I learned anything new or useful in this interview except that the atmosphere of intrigue and suspicion between the various Vatican departments is even deeper than I supposed it was, though I should think both Dell'Acqua and Cardinale are honest enough in themselves.

[. . .]

MGR. HÖFER

I have seen a good deal of this eminent man. He is a full member of the Secretariat, professor of Theology at Paderborn and Ecclesiastical Counsellor to the West Germany Embassy to the Holy See. When we met recently he spoke of:-

(a) the Italian pastoral situation. He said that Italian priests, especially in Rome, had almost no right, or even the possibility, of entry into people's homes, except on formal occasions. Their only pastoral ministry, therefore, was in the administration of the Sacraments. He said this wasn't fatal to the practice of religion, because faith was a family affair. The Italian had from his Roman ancestors a sense of an other world than this, now expressed in the culture of the Saints which was a good, even a necessary background to religion in this world.

(b) the Council. His hopes for the Council were confined almost entirely to internal reforms. The Curia, he thought, was still too strong and reactionary for the great progress which the Church would make in some areas (Germany, Austria, France) if there were more decentralisation.

SACRED MUSIC

A contact on this subject led to some interesting exchanges from an unusual quarter. At the Assoc. Italiana S. Cecilia per Musica Sacra, I had an interview with the (clerical) Secretary, Don Olivieri, because he wanted to collect some compositions for a Marian festival at Lourdes, and wondered if I could name any good contemporary English composers. I said gladly I would, having in mind Benjamin Britten, Francis Jackson, Arthur Wills and one or two others. He would supply the texts. I said that we should be a little selective about the degree of 'Mariolatry' in them, though I told him that we sang Byrd's 'Beata Virgo' and such things, without blenching, at Ely. This brought out the astonishing revelation that he had not heard of

Byrd, Gibbons, Tallis etc. After a broader discussion I was asked, in ingenuous honesty, 'have you the Eucharist?', which made me insist on a further meeting the following morning. At this meeting I played my tape-recording, which I had brought from England, of the canticles at Matins (Vaughan Williams Te Deum in F) and the whole of the Sung Eucharist (Wills' Missa Eliensis) on Easter Day 1961 in Ely Cathedral. This was a very good performance and did great credit. I was able to explain the Eucharist in detail. Several members of the neighbouring Institute Pontificio per la Musica Sacra (Direttore Mgr. Angles) came in and were obviously very impressed. He, the Director, is not well informed, not having heard of Vaughan Williams, or of Benjamin Britten! Hindemith, a German Protestant (or Jew) had declined to contribute to the series. The Secretary was anxious that I should get the Archbishop of Canterbury's approval to this scheme!

I hope to develop this contact in future visits. It has considerable, if unexpected possibilities. I shall, for instance, bring some records of our best music. It is a remarkable thing that in this country which is renowned for its tradition of secular and sacred music, there is today almost no normal performance of Church music in acts of worship. The Sistine Chapel Choir, for instance, though it is quite good (not up to the standards of a good English cathedral), only performs, when summoned, at large papal functions, not in the daily performance of the offices.

This might be a convenient point at which to relate an interesting episode at which I was present. On Ascension Day the Pope canonised S. Maria Bertilla Boscardin, a member of an order which has since spread into France, and many French people were present. When the Sistine Chapel choir started an elaborate Credo in the Papal Mass, a great roar of French voices started up the common Creed and drowned them. This was widely commented upon in Rome and people said 'This is a great day; the liturgical revival has reached St. Peter's'.

FOYER UNITAS

You will remember from previous references that I have been trying to bring about a change for the better in this organisation, which is entirely under Fr. Boyer's control and which suffers from his well-intentioned but limited attitude (see my Report No. 8).

[. . .] When we arrived Boyer asked me to speak also. I took a chance on this and spoke as follows:-

There were many people speaking and working for reunion who did not seriously believe that there was any hope of eventually coming to terms with the Roman Church. Their conception of future developments was limited to the hope of a peaceful co-existence similar to that in the political world. The Archbishops of Canterbury and York, on the other hand, wanted to make it clear to all that their eventual aim was not duality or peaceful co-existence, but unity, which was an absolute term. We hoped that the Roman Church would consider the same distinction. By too rigid an insistence on their claims, the Roman Church could in fact force us all into this difficult position, which was obviously not according to the will of God. I said frankly also that one of the hopes of the Church of England was that the Roman Church at the forthcoming Council would not resist the will of God by making further dogmatic definitions, particularly with regard to the Blessed Virgin Mary, which would drive a deeper wedge between us.

I said that the Archbishop of Canterbury had asked the Church of England to join in the Novena of prayer called by His Holiness for the Council from Ascension to Whitsun. I hoped that all present would reciprocate by asking God's blessing on the plenary meeting of the W.C.C. in New Delhi in November of this year.

There was much enthusiasm expressed, and I suspected that Fr. Boyer jumped up to propose the vote of thanks slightly sooner than he would have done had the applause been less lively. I was also slightly irritated that Fr. Boyer had seen fit to invite an ex-Anglican priest called Davies (formerly of the diocese of St. Albans and editor of a particularly stupid paper called the 'Dome') to this meeting. Boyer has made much of this particular conversion in his writings in 'Unitas', but I have heard since that Davies has now left (or been asked to leave) the Beda College.[36] So his presence at the Foyer was all the more extraordinary. He is apparently now without means of support.

Report No. 12   11th June, 1961

UNITY IN BRITAIN

[. . .] I have exchanged letters with Archbishop Heenan who replied in a very friendly manner. He says that the Committee of the hierarchy

---

[36]The Pontifical Beda College in Rome. In 1852 Pius IX approved a plan to accommodate in the city a number of clergymen from England who had converted to Roman Catholicism and who wished to prepare for the priesthood. In 1898 Leo XIII decided that the college should be placed under the patronage of the Venerable Bede. The college has developed its own system of priestly formation, with the studies being conducted in English.

to which I referred has not yet met. We can refer all such matters direct to him at present.

[...]

ANGLICAN ORDERS

These have recently been under discussion in the Secretariat. The line seems to be that although the matter is closed officially, it might be possible to ask for further investigation of the historical background. Though there are those who think that this might do more harm than good (see below). Others ask why we don't short-circuit the whole matter by arranging for consecrations always to have present bishops of whose place in the succession there could be no doubt. I have been asked if it could be ascertained from Lambeth what consecrations have been so 'regularised'. I said I was sure that a detailed register was kept at Lambeth.

DOM GRIBOMONT, O.S.B.

Dom Gribomont, Prior of S. Girolamo, came to see me. He is a patristic and biblical scholar, friend of Fr. Dalby etc. He is engaged on work in connection with the text of the Vulgate. He is very objective about unity. He hoped that the Church of England would not hesitate to send written representations to the Council. Subjects which he would like to see treated were:-

(a) objectivity of truth, especially in regard to history. Here we might even be a help to liberal elements in the Roman Church. Texts available to students are all 'doctored' in the interests of Roman dogma, and it would be better if they were not so. I asked if the various Denzinger Handbooks would be regarded as cases in point. He agreed;

(b) certainly religious liberty;

(c) perhaps the sufficiency of the present ordinal, and e.g. the ordinal of South India, which he regarded as excellent. He was against the idea of opening up the question of Anglican orders, for fear of making the situation worse than it is.

(d) Asking particularly for no further dogmatic definitions which would drive the wedge deeper.

Speaking about the last he said that he thought the dogma of Maria co-redemptrix and Maria Mediatrix would come eventually, though not through the Council, or at all soon. But they were already in the liturgy implicitly, and the step to dogmatic definition was not a long one. I protested at this, and said that the declaring of them divinitus revelata was a big step, as was the anathematising and consequent excommunication of those who did not feel able to accept them. To my surprise he said he would himself accept the doctrines; though he thought we should not worry unduly about them, because they did not change the situation, from one point of view, much from what it was at present. He quite recognised that we drew a distinction between papal and conciliar definitions, but since the infallibility decision was itself a conciliar one, he did not now think there was much in the distinction.

Speaking of the Liturgical Commission, he said that he thought that the normal work of the Congregation of Rites was very much swallowed up in the activities of the Commission for the present. He himself particularly hoped to see secured a wide use of the vernacular, and 'concelebration' in convents and monasteries. He hoped for great measures of decentralisation, to the disadvantage of the Curia, and felt sure they would come. He said there could be no hope of progress in the Church until the Holy Office was radically altered or abolished.

THE CENTRAL COMMISSION OF THE COUNCIL

Willebrands told me that the Commission was to meet on Monday 12th for a week and would be of the greatest importance. It would have before it much of the collected work of the subordinate Councils, Commissions and Secretariats, though they had by no means yet reported in full. The Unity Secretariat had prepared four reports. Three of them were going to be presented that very day both to the Central Commission and to the Theological Commission. They were on:-

(a) the nature of the Church,
(b) the hierarchical structure of the Church,
(c) the priesthood of the laity

all as they concerned oecumenical matters. The fourth was a liturgical report, to be presented to the Liturgical Commission. Further reports were being prepared on Religious Liberty and Mixed Marriages.

I asked if he thought that the Central Commission would be in a position to fix the date, or the agenda, of the Council. He thought it unlikely. It was said that their time would mostly be occupied by consideration of the intensely complicated questions of procedure which must arise. Is each of 3,000 bishops to be able to speak on any motion, and on any footing and at any lengths, in any language? The main language must certainly be Latin, but there was much difficulty in the national pronunciations. Willebrands thought that the question of observers might come up, and hoped it would, for even if a single affirmative decision were given about them, immense administrative problems would still be left over to solve. I asked if it would be essential

for observers to be able to speak Latin. He said he thought not, for he supposed that observers would probably not be able to observe the actual proceedings, but would be invited daily to meetings which would report, in the manner of a press conference, the daily progress and decisions. This was only his private opinion.
[. . .]

Report No. 13   12th June, 1961

PATRONAGE OF S. JOSEPH

I have been reading further past files of *La Civilta Cattolica*[37] concerning the preparations for the Council. On March 15th last the Pope, in a public audience, announced that he had just put the whole Council under the auspices of S. Joseph. He then made a very florid discourse on Our Lady's Most Chaste spouse which I will forebear to translate because it is couched in language so foreign and excessive that it would seem ridiculous to our ears. But it is evident that the Pope was most devout in the dedication. I mention this because it is, in my view, essential background to the understanding of the Council. So strong is the belief in the efficacy of the prayers of the Saints that, not to mention the Holy Ghost (who isn't mentioned as often as He should be!), they alone guarantee the success, and the inerrancy, of the Council; and its decisions. I remember reading somewhere that at the 1st Vatican Council, Bishop Dupanloup and others made a last effort to dissuade the Pope from declaring infallibility, only to be met with the response that 'Our Lady is with me; I cannot resist her'.

THE LAITY AND THE COUNCIL

Cardinal Cento[38] gave a television interview in France in February on the above subject. He was bowled some very fast balls by the interviewer, some of which he found rather difficult to play. Asked if the creation of a Commission of the laity did not create a precedent, the Cardinal said that of course the laity had always been there and had always been a part of the Church, but now they were waking up and realising that they are the Church.

---

[37]Jesuit periodical (see p. 37, n. 6).
[38]Fernando Cento (1883–1973), ordained Titular Archbishop of Seleucia Peiria, 1926; Apostolic Nuncio in Venezuela, Peru, Belgium, Luxembourg, and Portugal. Created Cardinal Priest of Sant'Eustachio by John XXIII, 1958; appointed Major Penitentiary of the Apostolic Penitentiary, 1962.

Asked if the laity were now going to be given a voice in the government of the Church, the Cardinal said that the direction of the Church must of course always rest with the ecclesia docens, the hierarchy, but the hierarchy welcomed every possible suggestion and help from the laity. It did not fall to the laity to participate in the Council itself. Asked then what was the chief duty of the laity, the Cardinal said that it lay in the matter of active apostolate under the general direction of the hierarchy of the clergy.

THE COUNCIL AND PROTESTANTS

(a) Cardinal Bea, speaking at Genoa in January, said:-
    What are the possibilities for Protestants from the forthcoming Council? The first seems to be the possibility that some of the dogmas previously declared could perhaps be explained in a way which should be more satisfactory to them. Difficulties often come from the fact that a dogma is not understood, or is even perverted. Methods of thought are changed in the course of centuries. Our separated brethren, cut off now for centuries from the Mother Church have since then been under the influence of many secular systems of thought which have made it impossible for them to understand the fullness of Catholic truth without it being totally re-expressed.
    [. . .]

RELIGIOUS LIBERTY

In an interview with Willebrands I asked openly about a book called 'Roman Catholicism and Religious Liberty', by Dr A.F. Carrillo de Albornoz. No secret has been made of its existence or contents, nor of the circumstances of the author, who is an ex-Jesuit from Spain, at present working on the staff of the W.C.C. in Geneva. The book is known about and is acknowledged as objective by the Secretary. It is true that there is a great variety of opinion and practice in the Roman Church in this matter. The Church had to keep the faith alive and fulfil her mission in many different places and ages. It was realised that the Church was accused of being opportunist in these matters and as having no fixed policy. It was hard to say if there was any 'official teaching' of the Church on this subject. There were no conciliar decisions; no papal infallible pronouncements; there were few references in the third category (of Encyclicals sent to Bishops not being ex-cathedra); and the only reference one could point to with any authority was the speech of Pope Pius XII to the Italian lawyers in December 1953. This speech can almost certainly be taken as a rebuke to Cardinal Ottaviani for his speech at the Pontificio Ateneo Lateranense on 3rd March 1953. Even so this speech is only in the fourth category of authoritative importance.

Willebrands said that there is admittedly divergence of belief among Roman theologians and difference of behaviour by the Church over against changing situations in different places and ages. How could it be otherwise? It would be difficult for the Church to behave in the same way in the 15th century in France and the 19th century in Ireland. But it was now admitted by many (and should be admitted by more) that many mistakes had been made and that greater consistency of policy and practice should be aimed at.

In the course of further discussion, the Secretary mentioned discrimination against R.C.s in Sweden. I said that we should admit that the principle of 'cuis regio cuis religio'[39] at the Reformation was itself in essence a cynical and intolerant principle. None of us were in very good shape for casting stones at the others. We agreed that all concerned should pray for God's guidance on the situation and on the Council, that it may be guided to bring new light and understanding.

The technical answer to the question whether the subject will be under discussion at the Council is that the agenda has not yet been drawn up. But the Secretariat for Unity is preparing a report on Religious Liberty which will be submitted to the Central Commission with the proposition that it be considered at the Council for discussion (see my Report No. 12 item 5).

My own additional thoughts on the matter were as follows[:] that the non-Roman Catholic world itself holds such a variety of opinions about the proper relations between Church and State that it should not be surprised if there is this variety of opinion among the Romans in the matter of religious liberty; second, that whatever the practice of the Roman Church with regard to the liberties of others, they have in recent years a very good record in resisting unto blood for the faith itself; third, that it would be ironical if pressure were brought on the Roman Church from non-Roman sources, to make official pronouncements on a matter on which there is apparently liberty of opinion. But of course what we want them to do is to remove obvious inconsistencies and contradictions.

---

[39] 'Who governs the realm dictates its religion.'

AUDIENCE WITH THE POPE

On my last day, Monday June 12th, I had a long private audience with the Pope, quite alone. His Holiness said he had heard of my mission and was pleased I had come. What was my exact relationship to the Archbishop? He had supposed I was a member of his personal staff. He asked in detail about my work at Ely, my family and past career. He spoke with much warmth about Archbishop Fisher and said 'There is a straightforward man, of high ideals, and great sincerity. I see many people here from kings to the least of men: but I knew at once that here was a great man of God.' I agreed, and said that I was sure he would find the same qualities in the new Archbishop.

His Holiness had just come from the first meeting of the Central Commission of the Council. He said it had gone well, but was mainly concerned with organisation. An analysis of his published speech will appear in my next report. He was doing all the talking, very vigorous and at high speed, but very scintillating and vivid.

He then told me his views on unity which were identical, of course, with those already expressed in speeches reported previously. We were in a very much better position than our forefathers were in 1893 (?) when Leo XIII issued invitations to the other churches and was met with rebuffs on all sides, and even insults.[40] Now there had been a most friendly reception on all sides of the announcement of the Council and of the invitation to unity. It was no use discussing unity problems now while the Council was putting the Roman Church in order. Afterwards, when that was accomplished, they would say to all, particularly to us, 'Here is your mother Church, all resplendent and beautiful: now surely you will want to find your way back.' I said that I hoped in that case that such changes as would be made at the Council would make it easier, rather than more difficult for us to contemplate approaches. He said Yes, he hoped so. We had been together for 16 centuries: what a shame it was that we ever parted. He then gave me a hasty sketch of English Church history, starting of course in 597. I thought it inadvisable to argue the point.

His Holiness then relaxed and told me to tell him 'all that was in my heart'. I had prepared points, one of which had been made above. So I said that most of his visitors from the Church of England so far had been from the 'High Church' wing. Archbishop Fisher, and now I following him up, represented the whole generality of opinion in the C of E. who were indeed friendly towards the Church of Rome, but

---

[40]The year in which Leo XIII promulgated the encyclical *Providentissimus Dei*.

who also, in thinking of Union, had to have in mind the Orthodox and the many Protestant sects. Reunion must eventually include them all. I said that was not an easy position. The Pope agreed. I then said we welcomed the opportunity to exchange information. So much harm had been done by misrepresentation in the past, particularly in manipulating history to suit dogmatic needs. Thirdly I was so glad to be able to state our views direct to Rome because, as His Holiness knew, contacts in England and America were not as friendly as we should like them to be. He said, Yes, he knew, but they were getting better. Did I know Archbishop Heenan? I said I did indeed, and how grateful we were for his attitude.

The Pope said 'Your principal difficulty is the Primacy of the Holy See.' I said 'Yes, and the new Marian definitions'. He: 'Yes, but they derive from the former.' I said they had their separate difficulties about the nature of truth and the place of dogma. He then gave me a rapid statement of the Primatus Petri,[41] beginning with the Acts. He said 'You accept the Scriptures?' I said 'Of course, but it depends on the interpretation.'

The Pope then went off on the matter of first and second grade questions. The question of the Anglican rite, which was good, offered no difficulty. Nor did clerical celibacy. He mentioned S. Peter (!) and the Uniates. He said 'I'm very fond of Anglicans: you're friendly, you're sincere. I like the English character, its robustness. I am trying hard to speak English well. I read it easily. Fr. Faber's writings have had a great influence on me.[42] I wish the Orthodox were more approachable, like your Archbishop Fisher. They're afraid, they're resentful of past political glories lost, and the great days of the Byzantine Empire.' He then reminisced, touchingly, about his days in Constantinople, Bucharest, etc.

The whole interview was exceedingly cordial and animated. Much good humour. He was complimentary at the end and said Cardinal Bea had reported well of me and my mission and Cardinal Montini had also spoken of me. He invited me to come and see him again. I was to be careful of the press. The interview was a secret. But he said I could say when I got back to England that I'd been received by the Pope, and what a jolly old fellow the Pope was!

---

[41] The primacy of Peter and the Petrine succession.
[42] Fr Frederick William Faber (1814–1853), hymn-writer, scholar, and translator of devotional literature; a priest in the Church of England who converted to Roman Catholicism in 1845 and was ordained two years later; a leading Oratorian.

His Holiness presented me with a medal and 2 large volumes, one of his speeches and the other the Acta Synodus Romanie. At the end he made me kneel for a blessing (!), though he prefaced it by saying that it was not a sacramental matter.

I talked in the anticamera with two domestic chaplains, Mgr. Pocci and Mgr. Capovilla. The audience lasted 25 minutes.
[. . .]

RETURN

I leave Rome on Tuesday June 13th, 1961, by train.

Report No. 14   23rd September, 1961

This report is submitted from ELY.

GENERAL

[. . .]
It has been a surprise to come across the considerable number of foreign visitors to Ely Cathedral who have asked if this was the cathedral from which a canon was 'assigned to Rome'. Sometimes I have owned up and the result has always been most warm and friendly.

READING

I have taken and digested the Acta Apostolicae Sedis,[43] the 'Civilta Cattolica',[44] Documentations Catholiques,[45] the Osservatore Romano (daily!),[46] and the Tablet.[47] The news items which follow are extracted principally from them.

---

[43]*Acta Apostolicae Sedis* (*Acts of the Apostolic See*), often quoted as A.A.S.; the official gazette of the Holy See, established in 1908 by Pope Pius X.

[44]Jesuit periodical (see p. 37, n. 6).

[45]*Documentations Catholiques*, a bi-monthly periodical founded in 1919 to provide information on the thoughts and writings of the Church, the message of the Pope, etc.

[46]*Osservatore Romano*, a daily newspaper which carries the Pope's discourses and reports on the activities of the Holy See as well as on the main events taking place in the Church both in Italy and around the world. A weekly edition is available in various languages.

[47]*The Tablet*, a British Catholic weekly journal which has been published since 1840. It reports on religion current affairs, politics, social issues, literature, and the arts, with a special emphasis on Roman Catholicism while remaining ecumenical.

[...]

THE POPE ON THE SAINTS

In a general audience the Pope said 'Many accuse us of exaggerating the cultus of the Saints. That is not so. We *adore* the persons of the Holy Trinity; we *venerate* Our Lady and we *honour* the Saints.'

The fact is, though, that a very large proportion of celebrations, discourses and exhortations are centred upon the cultus of the saints and involve supplications to them for their aid without mention, except incidentally, of the persons of the Trinity. The whole thing is a matter of proportion.
[...]

CZECHO-SLOVAKIA

On July 6th the Pope published a message of condolence to Abp. Beran of Prague on the occasion of his 50th anniversary of ordination to the priesthood. He paints a doleful picture of the state of the Church in that country which, he says, is as bad as anywhere in the world. It is the victim of full systematic persecution.

THE B.V.M.

In a radio message to the people of France on July 11th, the Pope used the extreme words of his predecessor in which he spoke of the B.V.M as 'omnium memborum Christi Sanctissima Genetrix'[48] (Enc. Mystici Corporis).
[...]

July 30th
Death of the Secretary of State (Cardinal Tardini)
[...]

NEW SECRETARY OF STATE

On Aug 15th the O.R. carried the news of the appointment of Cardinal Amleto Cicognani (to distinguish him from his brother Gastano) as S[ecretary] of S[tate] in place of the late Tardini.

---

[48]'The most holy Mother of all the members of Christ.'

NATURE OF THE CHURCH. A Report from Spain

The Archbishop of Barcelona, in a pastoral letter gives a very rigid interpretation of the doctrine of the Church in order to bolster up a programme of caution towards 'precipitate hopes of reunion'. He lays particular emphasis on the idea that although all the baptised are thereby made members of Christ and of the Church, when they consciously adhere to a separated body they 'put themselves outside the real Church of Christ'.

[...]

PROCEDURE OF THE COUNCIL

[...]
It is expected that the work of the Council will be done partly in plenary sessions and partly in Commissions. These are not to be confused with the preparatory Commissions. The Commissions will consist only of Fathers of the Council.

[...]

Report No. 15   25th September, 1961

This report is submitted from Ely.

THE NEW SECRETARY OF STATE

The R.C. papers have been trying hard to find something good to say about Cardinal Cicognani. He has at least lived a long time in America, and is bound to be an improvement on his predecessor. The *Tablet* starts its notice ruefully by saying 'Cardinal Cicognani is not 79 until next February.'

[...]

THE CATHOLIC INFORMATION CENTRE

in London is reported to have had an increase in enquiries of 5% in 1960, with 6,500 conversions to its credit, bringing the total since 1954 up to 100,000.

MGR. HEENAN

I went at Abp. Heenan's invitation to stay with him in Liverpool. I was shown round some very powerful and impressive institutions, schools and churches in new suburbs, and the pre-cathedral in its crypt. I tried not to be too depressed by the comparison between that and the Liverpool Cathedral. In the latter there seem to be almost no weekday services: in the Roman pre-cathedral there are mid-day masses on several weekdays and at the one I attended there were not less than 400 young people present.

We covered a lot of familiar ground, but the main points of conversation which were new to me were as follows:- There is to be a meeting of the *Central Commission* of the Council in the middle of October, which will probably fix the main shape of the Council itself, date, agenda, etc. The October meeting of the Secretariat has been postponed till after this meeting. That is because it will wish to know in what form, if any, the matter of unity will be before the Council. I shall be in Rome by then and the Abp. promised to call on me after the Secretariat meeting if possible.

He apologised at some length for the appointment of *Fr. Ripley* as Secretary of the R.C. Hierarchy's unity committee in England. He is a known reactionary. But he had been the very able Director of the C.M.S.(!),[49] and after a serious illness which has caused his resignation, is in need of a job. Heenan, who was his predecessor but one, has a high regard for him, but does not intend to let him have any say in the direction of the committee. He is to be a post-bag and minute-man only.

He spoke of the new Secretary of State, *Cardinal Cicognani*, whom he knew personally. He would be a great improvement on Tardini, and (for an Italian Cardinal) had quite broad views. He had been in America and had met a large number of people. But he was old.

I asked for clarification of the phrase 'receiving the wishes and suggestions of non-Catholics regarding the Council' in the aims of the Secretariat, and whether the secretariat would really like the Church of England to send in a formal statement on these lines. He was very strongly in favour of it in principle, and asked me what I thought such a letter might contain. I said that I had discussed this with no one and was only guessing, as follows:-

1. A message congratulating the Pope on setting up the Secretariat, thanking him for his good wishes and high hopes expressed

---

[49] Congregation of the Mission. Not to be confused with the Anglican Church Missionary Society, with which it shares its initials.

therein: telling how we had already used it most profitably and hoped to continue to do so.

2. A message of goodwill to the Pope and the fathers of the Vatican Council, assuring them of our prayers for their guidance.

3. A sentence saying that while, as was known, we, in common with a large proportion of Christendom, were unable to accept the Vatican Council as oecumenical, we should nevertheless await its decisions with interest and would hope that they would make [it] more easy, rather than more difficult, for us to advance towards unity.

4. A sentence telling the Pope of the blessings we had already found in seeking unity with other Christian bodies and how without the sacrifice of principles we had been able to achieve a unity which already bore signs of most abundant fruits.

5. Perhaps a suggestion that theological continuation committees should be set up after the Council.

6. Expression of the hope that all parties would feel able publicly and frankly to confess that their own failures had contributed to the present estrangements.

7. Perhaps something on religious Liberty.

8. And mixed marriages.

He said that such a document would do much good, perhaps more than we thought, and as he would be the person who would have to introduce it, he spoke with some authority.

I repeated that these headings were only my impromptu suggestions so far, and that great difficulties might face us even in considering such a course. I asked if any other bodies had considered sending representations. He said that the Orthodox would undoubtedly reply to the message already sent to them and that the World Lutheran Federation were likely to send in something.

I asked whether in his view it would appear discourteous if we sent nothing written. He said not, because the Church of England had in a way responded to the 'invitation' by sending me, though he thought it would be more satisfactory if we committed ourselves to at least something in writing.

DR BOLSHAKOFF

This character is well known to C.I.R and they know that his opinions are to be treated with reserve. My experience is that they come direct from Cardinal Tisserant, and in so far as they do so, are reliable. I send an analysis of a recent letter.

1. *Belgium.* The death of Cardinal Van Roey will enable the Consistory to reconstitute the Belgian hierarchy, subdividing the huge archdiocese of Malines, setting up new Bishoprics of Brussels and Antwerp.

2. *Russia.* 53 Russian Bishops met at Zagorsk on July 19th and discussed the situation created by the intensification of persecution. Plans to complete the introduction of communism by 1980 mean that new religious persecution must be expected. In the last two years 29 monasteries out of 69 were closed and 3 seminaries out of 8 and literally thousands of churches. Taxation of the clergy has become such that only the largest town churches can pay it. Those who cannot are struck off the 'register of cult' and lose the right to celebrate. Those who violate this are sent to prison for years, the bishops at Zagorsk have either ordained many 'worker-priests' or have given laymen wide powers in order to forestall the sudden disappearance of the clergy.

Report No. 16   29th September, 1961

MONS WILLEBRANDS

paid me a long day's visit on September 15th. He was staying with the friars of the Atonement, Westminster. He had been the previous day to see the Abp. of Canterbury and had called at West Malling Abbey on the way back. Much of this report will therefore probably be familiar, but I submit it for record.

He was as usual anxious for there to be no publicity, though much easier than he has been in Rome. He gave as his reasons (a) dangers of misrepresentation of his motives in Rome. It might be supposed that he was trying to pre-empt the decisions of the Central Council in favour of the Secretariat's policy by his frequent tours abroad. The Holy Office and the Secretariat of State are both jealous of the Secretariat for Unity inasmuch as their fields might overlap; the Holy Office in the matter of theology and the Secretariat of State in questions of local relationships with the hierarchy. (b) possible misunderstandings with the hierarchy in England. But he said that the position was getting better here all the time, and Heenan was established, entrenched with full papal support and able to flourish his membership of the Secretariat in the face of gainsayers.

He said that the new Secretary of State, Cardinal Amleto *Cicognani*, was an improvement on his predecessor from our point of view, though he was of course too old.

He spoke about the observers at the *W.C.C. 3rd Assembly* at *New Delhi*, though he added nothing to what has already been in the papers.[50]

He had already had a meeting with Cardinal Godfrey[51] who had been quite affable. But he considered it necessary to have a further interview with Mgr. Worlock,[52] his private secretary, who needed further conversion. He, Worlock, was worried about rumours that Anglican priests had been touring France with bogus 'celebrets'[53] and obtaining entrance to French altars. He was going to tell Worlock that he must not give credence to rumours and that he was sure the Anglican authorities would be severe on any priest who committed this indiscretion. I assured him that this was so. Worlock could produce no names.

He mentioned discussions he had had with *English secular (R.C.) clergy* who had said that 'you are flirting with the very episcopate which our Blessed Martyrs gave their lives rather than accept'. He had said that 'you are wasting everybody's time keeping alive the bitterness of the 16th century. The Blessed Martyrs are undoubtedly throwing their prayers in on the side of peace and reconciliation.'
[. . .]
Speaking of the forthcoming *Council* he said, in spite of what the General Secretary is reported as having said, that 1963 is more likely than Autumn 1962. The Central Committee will meet in the middle of this Oct., when it will probably make the decision. The meeting of the Unity Secretariat, which was to have been in the middle of Oct., is postponed to November. The Pope will probably issue a Bull. He thinks it is likely there will be observers. When I asked what they could really expect to do more than receive bulletins at the end of sessions, he said that if observers were allowed, they would clearly have to be something more than journalists and would be real observers of part at least of the proceedings. They would therefore *have* to be Latinists. 60% of the proceedings of the Unity Secretariat were in Latin. Heenan, e.g. was quite fluent. He thought the Council might conceivably have

---

[50]The World Council of Churches Assembly at New Delhi had taken place from 19 November to 5 December 1961.

[51]William Godfrey (1889–1963), Archbishop of Liverpool, 1953–1956; Archbishop of Westminster, 1956–1963; created Cardinal, 1958.

[52]Mgr Derek Worlock (1920–1996), Bishop of Portsmouth, 1965–1976; Archbishop of Liverpool, 1976–1996.

[53]A letter of approval given by a bishop to a priest so that he may say Mass when travelling.

more than one session (i.e. might disband and go home for months and then reassemble).

It was fairly certain that one of the outcomes of the Council would be *theological continuation conferences*, especially with us. He spoke of the catholic body already in being which, he hoped, would extend itself by invitation, and start by trying to convert the Roman clergy where necessary especially the seculars. They would meet at Oscott[54] rather than at Downside to emphasise the appeal to the secular clergy.
[...]
I pressed Willebrands as to whether they really expected the Church of England to send *written representations to the Council*. He said that they did so expect, and that he understood that the Archbishop of Canterbury was already contemplating submitting statements with regard to Religious Liberty and Mixed Marriages. But he did not seem clear as to whether this was in direct connection with the Council or not. I asked further whether he thought a general statement of our hopes (and fears) would be acceptable. He thought it certainly would be, and handed me the latest version [...] of the 'Background to the Secretariat', copies of which I believe are already in the possession of the Archbishop and of the C.I.R. [...]

His response was immediately that he thought we ought to send such a note. I am bound to report that my own opinion is that we ought to profit by the occasion, and that to be cautious or hesitant would be to miss a real opportunity. Notwithstanding the considerable difficulty of sanctioning such a statement.

Russia
He spoke of Russia in terms identical with those of Dr. Bolshakoff, already reported.

Report No. 17.   September 30th, 1961

The enclosed report is submitted from Ely.

MIXED MARRIAGES AND THE SECRETARIAT

Mgr. Willebrands seems to think that the Archbishops intended to submit something on this subject to the Secretariat. If this is so could

---

[54] St Mary's College, Oscott: the Roman Catholic seminary in Birmingham.

I please be kept informed? [*Handwritten note: 'This was written before my last interview with the Archbishop, who answered the question.'*]

RETURN TO ROME

I propose to return to Rome on October 19th, arriving 20th. I have already told Willebrands, but I get the impression that he would like to be informed officially by C.I.R. When I got out there last time it looked as though the Minister to the Holy See would also have liked to be informed [. . .]

Report No. 18   12th October, 1961

This report is submitted from ELY
[. . .]

PASTORAL THEOLOGY

August and September were the season for summer schools and conferences all over Roman Catholic Europe. I read at length the themes and findings at a 'Pastoral refreshment Course' for the diocese of Turin. They were very disappointing, hopelessly behind anything that would be achieved on a similar occasion in France or in Germany. The chief enemies of the Gospel are 'communism' and 'laicism'. The latter was defined as 'a systematic and hysterical tendency to oppose any influence of religion or the hierarchy upon human institutions'; i.e. what we should call anti-clericalism. There is a total absence of self-criticism in the speeches and comments, no trace of a search for the possible causes of the phenomenon. The only remedies proposed seem to be an intensification of methods at present in use. This whole conference seems very reactionary and not up to the standard even of Milan or Bologna. But I imagine it is typical of much of the pastoral attitude in Italy.
[. . .]

THE LAITY AND THE COUNCIL

In a recent speech the Pope said that in the great mass of opinions, suggestions and requests which had been sent in to the Central Commission by the bishops we could be quite sure that the wishes of the clergy and the laity were fully represented. He wished to thank the laity, particularly those who had worked in close cooperation with the hierarchy, for their help and interest. He hoped that they would continue to exercise to the full their proper, and important, function in the Church, which was to pray and to cooperate with the hierarchy in the apostolate.

This, and similar utterances, are a clear indication, in my view, that there has been uneasiness among Roman laity in some circles that they had in fact no say whatever in the deliberations of the Council. [...]

MGR. HEENAN'S COMMITTEE OF THE HIERARCHY

The *Universe* of 4.8.61 published an article of Mgr. Heenan about his new Secretariat. No doubt it will have reached you. It follows the lines which would be expected and seems to be eminently reasonable. He even puts the Anglican doctrinal point of view fairly, except that he quotes us as believing that whereas we've preserved the faith which S. Augustine brought, we think they've lost it. In fact we should say that they have added to it in those 1300 years things which were not there.

Report No. 19   28th October, 1961

This report comes from Rome again, where I arrived on October 20th.
[...]

DATE OF VATICAN COUNCIL

The excitement is increasing here because of the realisation that the Pope must soon announce the date of the Council and publish the Bull convening it.

The Central Committee will meet from Nov. 7th–20th. It is likely that the announcement will be made soon after that. But Willebrands says that there are strong rumours that the Pope may 'jump the gun' and make an announcement on Nov. 4th. There is no doubt that there is considerable tension about this. Professor Witte, who is a member of the Theological commission, says that there is no question of their being adequately prepared by the autumn of 1962.[55] On the other

[55]Johannes (Jan) Witte, Dutch Jesuit, Professor of Ecumenical Theology at the Gregorian University in Rome; appointed Council expert in 1962.

hand he agrees that if they had to get ready by then they would do so, though it would be at the sacrifice of thoroughness.

The Pope is at the moment indisposed (with 'flu) and it is thought that this will give him an additional inclination to want to hurry the Council through.
[. . .]

OBSERVERS AT THE COUNCIL

This will certainly be on the agenda of the Central Commission soon to meet, referred to above. Willebrands is hopeful about the matter. He says that the Unity Secretariat has presented quite a strong recommendation in favour of it, and that it was well received. He hopes for a decision in favour in principle, and that details will then be left to the Secretariat to work out.
[. . .]

DATE OF THE COUNCIL

Since writing [the] above, I have read in one newspaper: 'It is reported from well-informed Vatican sources that in his address at the Mass in S. Peter's on Christmas Day, the Pope will probably announce the date of the forthcoming Council'. I have not so far been able to check this rumour against other information. The most likely explanation is that nobody knows and many are guessing.

Report No. 20.   November 4th, 1961

PROFESSOR KILPATRICK[56]

I had the good fortune on arrival here to find the Dean Ireland's Professor of Exegesis doing research in the Vatican Library. He was well acquainted with my mission and immediately allowed me to use him. I invited him to meet Professor Witte, S.J. Professor of Protestant Theology at the Gregorianum, (a Dutchman). Kilpatrick had seen the

[56] George Dunbar Kilpatrick (1910–1989), Dean Ireland's Professor of the Exegesis of Holy Scripture at the University of Oxford, 1949–1977.

correspondence in the *Tablet* about 'Extra ecclesiam nulla salus' and Ratcliff's[57] and Vidler's[58] comments on it.

The two professors exchanged a lot of information about personnel. Witte expressed admiration of Kilpatrick's knowledge of theological faculties on the continent. They talked about Catholic faculties in State universities, e.g. Munich and Strasbourg, and their comparative independence of the hierarchy.

We eventually turned the conversation on to the nature of the Church. Witte admitted that there were differences of opinion among Roman theologians. His way of expressing this (it is quite common here) is to say that 'there were certain things about the doctrine (e.g. of Mystici corporis) which needed further definition'. When pressed he admitted that all were made members of Christ's body the Church at baptism, but that there were grades of membership. 'Grace unto salvation' could undoubtedly be given outside the Catholic Church, but the full attainment of it (i.e. salvation) demanded in this world full use of the sacraments.

A ROMAN RUMOUR ABOUT ANGLICAN CANONISATIONS

The illustrated paper *Tempo* (rather like *Picture Post*) carries an alarming heading 'George VI on the altars'.

The main points of the text are as follows:-

(1) There are rumours not only in England but in other parts of the Anglican communion that George VI would be the sort of person who would be qualified to be canonised according to the ideas of the Church of England.

(2) Dr. Fisher, Archbishop of Westminster (sic) arranged at the last Lambeth Conference that a committee should investigate the question of canonisation in general.

(3) It was the Bishop of Rockhampton (McCall) who started the idea about George VI, in a published sermon.

(4) Anglican opinion is by no means unanimous about this. The whole question was discussed in the press. One of the leading figures in the discussion was Canon E.C. Ratcliff, Titular Professor (sic) of Divinity in Cambridge who said that 'it was not outside the realm of possibility that George VI might be canonised'.

[57] Edward Craddock Ratcliff (1896–1967), liturgist; Regius Professor of Divinity at the University of Cambridge, 1958–1964.

[58] Alec Vidler (1899–1991), Anglican priest, historian, scholar, and writer; editor of the journal *Theology*.

I have sent the text of the article to Professor Ratcliff, and look forward to hearing his reaction.
[. . .]

DOWNSIDE AND UNITY

I asked Mgr. Willebrands what was the exact position of Downside with regard to unity. They had been said to have a special responsibility in England and I wondered if that had been superseded by Archbishop Heenan's committee.

The answer was that Leo XIII had asked the Benedictine order to have a special interest in problems of unity, in the encyclical Equidem verba. They were the oldest of the orders and dated from the days of the undivided Church. Their chief responsibility was to be to the Orthodox east. The foundation of Chevetogne in Belgium was their chief response to this request.

At a meeting of abbots in 1960 it was suggested that the order was now doing little in this interest and that the matter should be revived. Accordingly it was decided to appoint one abbey in each country to have an eye to this matter, and Downside was appointed in England. The effort still doesn't amount to much, and is in any case directed mainly towards the Orthodox.
[. . .]

THE BRITISH LEGATION

I have had much help, as previously, from the British Minister to the Holy See, Sir Peter Scarlett.

I attended a reception given by Brian McDermott, the First Secretary, and at it met, among other people, Canon Curtin, the new Principal of the Beda, Fr. Tindal-Atkinson, O.P., of St Mary Major (one of the Roman members of the Vidler theological group), Archbishop David Mathew, Mgr. Lamb Vice-Principal of the Beda, Mgr. Tickell and Mgr. Clarke, Rector and Vice-Rector of the English College, Mgr. Ryan, an enormous Irishman who translates into English (!) for the Pope. All friendly.
[. . .]

CARDINAL BEA

I have had a further long interview with the Cardinal, which was chiefly an exchange of courtesies. He spoke about the Council and seemed to know nothing new about the dates or agenda, though he repeated that there was every intention of 'clarifying' the doctrine about the Church. He asked for a great deal of information about P.E.C.U.S.A. and the Presiding Bishop. He told me that he had received a communication from the Archbishop of Canterbury, which was presumably the Archbishop's message to the Pope on the occasion of his official 80th birthday.

Report No. 21   8th November, 1961

[...]

MGR. WILLEBRANDS and C.I.R.

Willebrands has asked me about C.I.R., etc., and how it is constituted, how it works. He imagined that the R.C. section of it was in fairly frequent session these days considering the relationships of the Church of England in view of the forthcoming council. I was able to hide the gruesome truth by saying that the Council was being reconstituted by the new Archbishop and said that I was sure that a strong panel would be recruited to deal with this situation.

[...]

CORONATION ANNIVERSARY AND 80TH BIRTHDAY NOV. 4TH.

I was present in S. Peter's in a first class seat, just behind the cardinals, and in among the diamond tiaras of the Italian noble families, thanks to the kindness of the Secretariat. The spectacle was most moving, and the 80-year-old Pope was in good form. The allocution had three main points:-

(1) S. Carlo Borromeo (whose day it was) was effective for the Church in the days of the Council of Trent, which is a good omen for us and our Council.

(2) S. Leo the Great is one of the most important Popes and should be more closely studied. The Pope intends to issue an encyclical specially about him soon.

(3) Some leg-pulling about the longevity of the Roncalli family, with the consequent implication that the Church may have John XXIII for a long time yet.

The Pope made no reference to the date of the Council. Afterwards I met Cardinal Montini, with whom I stayed in Milan in 1956, for a few minutes. I hope to see more of him in the next weeks.

[...]

THE CENTRAL COMMISSION OF THE COUNCIL

The Central Commission started its meetings on Tuesday last in the Vatican Palace. The session was presided over by the Pope himself who delivered the opening speech. According to my information the meetings of the Central Commission will last nearly a fortnight, so my next few reports will be concerned mainly with the press announcements about it.

THE POPE'S INAUGURAL SPEECH

The Pope announced the formation of three Sub-Committees. The work of the Commission itself will be to correlate their reports. His Holiness said that the preparations for the Council were going ahead in an atmosphere charged with much prayer and goodwill in every corner of the Church. Moreover, it was a matter of much satisfaction to him to note how much attention the separated brethren, and even those who had no Christian allegiances at all, had been giving to their work. A torn and distracted world looked to the Church for guidance and comfort. What he had seen of the preparatory work so far encouraged him to hope that the work could be carried to a successful conclusion.

[...]

THE NEW CONFESSION OF FAITH

The Second Meeting of the Central Commission was held on Wednesday November 8th. The opening speech was made by Cardinal Ottaviani, the Grand Inquisitor, Prefect of the Holy Office, as President of the Theological Commission, on the question of the new formula for confession of faith to be administered to the Fathers of the Council. In all Councils it is usual after the solemn opening for such a declaration to be administered. A fusion will be effected between the present formula and the anti-modernist oath. This will be brought up to date as necessary and will then be a standard profession of faith. The Cardinal explained that there would be no question of re-stating old dogmas or of adding new ones. The formula at present in use is that prescribed by Pius IV and modified by Pius IX in 1877 to include the dogma of the Immaculate Conception and the definitions of Vatican I. It was Pius X in 1910 who ordered that the oath, as well as being read, should be subscribed and accompanied by the anti-modernist oath.

THE SOURCES OF REVELATION

The third day of the proceedings of the Central Commission was taken up with the preparation of a 'Constitutio' on the above subject. The subject was introduced again by Cardinal Ottaviani. It is a pity that this character seems to play so much part in the proceedings, but unfortunately he is President of the Theological Commission. He represents the extreme right wing, both in theology and in politics. He has an insensate hatred of communism and is often referred to as a fascist.

He said that in the proceedings of the Commission and eventually at the Council, the word 'Constitutio' would be used for proposals concerning doctrinal themes and 'decretum' for the text of findings of disciplinary matters. The theme of this 'Constitutio' is exactly what it would be expected to be. The two twin sources of revelation are Holy Scripture and Tradition. Holy Scripture can roughly be described as that part of God's revelation which He wished to be written down; Tradition was at least at the beginning passed on by word of mouth, though now, of course, its truths are enshrined in the documents of the magisterial ecclesiae and in the writings of the Fathers and Doctors of the Church. There are two fountains, but one source. Holy Scripture, although it is the word of God is enshrined in human language, which, because of all the imperfections and limitations of human modes of expression, is often in need of exact interpretation and authoritative explanation. These cannot come from mere man, but only through a body which has upon it the promise of the continued assistance of the Holy Spirit.
[. . .]

OBSERVERS AT THE COUNCIL

There is another heavy-footed warning in the 'Osservatore Romano'[59] that rumours about the above are premature. But it does also say that Cardinal Bea and Cardinal Amleto Cicognani made their recommendations to the Commission today.

[59] See p. 70, n. 46.

Report No 23   21st November, 1961

THE CENTRAL COMMISSION CONTINUED: DISTRIBUTION OF CLERGY

The last day of the first week of the Commission's meetings was concerned with the distribution of the clergy. Cardinal Ciriaci, as President of the Commission on 'The discipline of the clergy and Christian people' introduced the theme. On the practical side this discussion was bound to turn at once to the principle of 'incardination' of clergy in the dioceses, i.e. the principle whereby clergy can only move from one diocese to another by permission of the bishop, and whereby, in effect, they are anchored in the same diocese for life. The principle is an extension of the one whereby we are unable to ordain men except to a 'title'. The difficulties of our system were felt at their worst, in my opinion, at the end of the war when the returning chaplains to the forces were nobody's particular responsibility, and are felt still to a certain extent by returning missionaries. But the inelasticity of the Roman system is now obviously causing them trouble. They also have to reckon with the fact that as an increasing proportion of vocations are to the religious life their distribution is out of the control of the diocesan bishops.

The Roman Church is obviously scared of having presbyteri vagantes. They traced a long history of these back to the Council of Nicaea. Statistics show that the density of clergy varies from 1 priest to 500 to 1 priest to 11,000. In the 1,100 dioceses which have returned statistics, there are approximately 200,000 priests for 400 million Catholics among a population in the same area of 700 million. In order to obtain a distribution of 1 priest to every thousand Catholics, they would need 190,000 more priests: and to achieve a ratio of 1 priest to every thousand of the overall population of the world, they would need half a million more priests.

THREE CHARACTERISTICS OF THE MEETINGS

The Press service has put out a line of propaganda under the above heading. The three characteristics of the meetings of the Central Commission are: a. Universality b. Historical Continuity and c. Liberty of Expression – this last, of course, in the limited sense in which the Romans understand it.
[...]

MIXED MARRIAGES

I was interested to hear from the Secretary of C.I.R. that a memorandum is being prepared on this subject for presentation to the Secretariat. In his letter he also states that 'our own Roman Catholic Committee is also to provide another memorandum on other causes of friction between the Church of England and the Roman Catholic Church in this country [. . .] After they have received the approval of the Archbishop of Canterbury they will eventually find their way to you to be presented to Monsignor Willebrands.'

I am pleased to hear that we are to start communication of a more formal kind with the Secretariat. But I beg leave to express the hope that our communication will not consist only, or even mainly, of complaints. I feel sure that there is a great opportunity open to us to make general observations of a positive kind on some of the matters which we now know will be before the Council.

Report No. 24   27th November, 1961

[. . .]

THE CENTRAL COMMISSION: THE DUTIES OF THE CLERGY

This discussion centred round proposals for the reform of the canon law. This also was mainly concerned with the distribution of the clergy as over against the pastoral situation. It was interesting to see that there is evidently a problem parallel to what we call 'the freehold of the clergy', although it takes a different form in the Roman Church. The discussion grouped under three main heads (a) the duty of residence of a priest upon his cure, (b) the duty of the 'application of the mass'; that means the current duty of reviewing the circumstances under which the mass is celebrated in order to see that its benefits are available to as many people as possible; (c) the duties of the administration of the other sacraments and of religious instruction.

The report spoke of the increasing and more variegated responsibilities of the parish priest confronted with his situation in the modern world; and a lot was made of his need for continual spiritual renewal. It speaks of the constant danger of overwork, with its consequences of actual illness if it is persisted in, or of superficiality. There is also the danger of discouragement. As far as I could see the discussion ran along more or less the same lines as it would in the

Church of England except that perhaps more emphasis was given to the need for meditation, spiritual retreat (at least once a month) and study than would be the case in our more activist circles. The word 'holiness' is used more than any other to describe the excellence at which the clergy should aim [. . .]. There is a certain preoccupation about 'modernism' in its effect on the clergy as well as upon the laity, though it is admitted at the end of the discussion that the problem is a chronic one.

THE CENTRAL COMMISSION: ECCLESIASTICAL OFFICES AND BENEFICES AND THE ADMINISTRATION OF CHURCH PROPERTY

The last-named subject is described as 'not being of interest to the public' and so is not reported upon. I sometimes feel that the Church Assembly gets itself a bad reputation in the public mind by allowing too much of its administrative business to be reported.

The report distinguishes two classes of ecclesiastical offices: one of direct divine institution such as that of the papacy (!) and the three orders of ministry; and others which are of human expediency. There was apparently a lot of discussion about the provision of benefices, i.e. about our old friend the stipends of the clergy. Although I have read through all the available reports I am not sure that I have got hold of the whole of the story here, and I will make further enquiries. The situation with regard to the payment of the clergy, I imagine, varies from country to country. I understand that there are some lucrative tied benefices in Italy which stand in the way of progress, and there the problem is similar to that of our endowments. But in other cases and places the problem is that of lack of adequate provision for livelihood. The question of 'worker-priests'[60] obviously came up for discussion at this point, though in what sense it is not easy to tell. The only idea which seems clear from the press reports is that no priest should be obliged to earn his living in a secular occupation for lack of means of support. Cardinal Ciriaci, who seemed to be in charge of this discussion, was obviously against the whole principle of worker-priests because their secular occupation took up too much of their time. But he is a known reactionary and his views should not be taken as typical.

[60]The inspiration of Fr Jacques Loew (1908–1999), this was a post-war movement within French Catholicism which affirmed the importance of the secular workplace and sought to place priests in factories and other places of employment for working-class people. The movement spread to other countries but never quite took root there. Pius XII was never much at ease with it and even sought its suppression. Many, but not all, returned to parochial duties. The movement withered for lack of official patronage but did not quite disappear.

UNITY SECRETARIAT

This began its further session on Monday November 27th at Ariccia, near Rome. Mgr. Heenan was here on Nov. 25th and came to see me. The visit was mainly social, though we did talk about observers. I gather from him that though still unofficial these are extremely probable. He sympathised with us over the open letter to the Archbishops about intercommunion which is to him an incomprehensible and badly-timed act of indiscipline, calculated to cause dissension inside the Church and mistrust outside it.

THE CENTRAL COMMISSION: END OF SESSION

The Central Commission has now dispersed and gone home. It will meet again in January. It is now supposed that the Commission has covered sufficient ground and made sufficient recommendations for the Pope to be able to announce the date of the Council and the general outline of its business before the end of the year. Certain statistics concerning the number of people who could be present at the Council have now been published [. . .]

THE CENTRAL COMMISSION: A RUMOUR

A reliable source told me that the meetings of the Central Commission have been very lively and that there had been much opposition, in particular to Ottaviani's extreme right wing theories about the Papacy and the Curia. It was reported that the Northern European bishops in particular are going to make a very strong bid for more discretionary powers.

A SPEECH BY CARDINAL BEA

Speaking in an interview with the review *France Catholique* the Cardinal said:-

'We Catholics owe a duty to the Protestants to help them find their way back to the Catholic faith. We failed them badly in the 19th century when they fell a prey to many secularist ideas; to their great impoverishment. Works of charity undertaken together should be a great help to this as Cullmann has often suggested. The Protestants, who are not alone responsible for the splitting up of the Church, can also aspire to salvation on a level footing with the Catholics. In a certain manner they are also united to the Church, and we Catholics should do all we can to foster that unity.'

CARDINAL BEA IN SWIITZERLAND

The Minister to the Holy See[61] entertained the Cardinal to lunch and I had a long talk with him there. [. . .] I asked him for further clarification of his reported statement that the 'Council was not primarily one for union'. He had said that it was to be regarded as being concerned with the necessary preliminaries to union. In particular he hoped that the embodiment of ecclesiastical authority would undergo such a revision as to make it more acceptable both to the Orthodox and the Protestants. When I asked if this meant curtailing the powers of the Curia he said he hoped so!

Report No. 25   7th December, 1961

CARDINAL BEA ON DOGMA

In an article entitled 'The Council as viewed by the Protestants', the Cardinal reviews again the difficulties as Protestants see them. He says that we should be thankful that old propagandist cries, the cause of so much hatred in the past, such as 'popery', 'papalism', 'lust for power' are dying out but many difficulties remain, the chief of which is of course a totally different conception of dogma. Professor Schnell, a Lutheran teacher in one of the German universities, said that 'Anybody who shuts himself up in a dogmatic prison will not be able to do any service to the cause of unity'. [. . .] Cardinal Bea comments that no well-instructed Catholic could ever suppose that the Council, the Supreme Pontiff and the Church, could or would change a single dogma. It is their unchanging duty to preserve entire the inheritance of doctrine and tradition, and no love for our separated brethren could persuade us to change a single item of it. Any ironical attempt to level down doctrine would be infidelity to the Church's commission received from Our Lord. The more serious and respectable of the separated brethren would not wish to have unity at the expense of truth. He quotes Asmussen as saying that 'The great possibility that Rome and Wittenberg may meet peacefully at the Council will not be helped by making unlawful concessions' and Professor Bornkamm, President of the German Evangelical Federation, has said that 'The way to unity should never ask of anybody the sacrifice of conscientious conviction'.

[61] Sir Peter Scarlett (see p. 48, n. 20).

The only possibility is that the Council should be able to demonstrate the internal harmonies and the religious and moral elevation of Catholic doctrine as a whole: to clarify the sense of individual dogmas and to remove common false interpretations such as the confusion between infallibility and impeccability, and the difference between ex cathedra and other pontifical pronouncements.

PUBLICITY

I confess to wondering whether the Church of England is doing as much as it could or ought to answer the immense blast of propaganda that the Roman Church is putting out about the Council. I get the impression that this is being very effective in England. [. . .] Is any agency in the Church, to your knowledge, putting out any literature or taking any steps to instruct the people of the Church of England about the issues involved? The Roman reviews here have been careful to see that their readers are given the proper 'slant' about the World Council of Churches, what it is all about, and why it is 'safe' for Roman observers to be there. I am inclined to think that if and when we are invited to send observers, at the latest, we should be ready to put out some explanations.
[. . .]
Incidentally I do not think it will be necessary to take any steps about preventing publicity about my return home this time. I've had no trouble from journalists since October and the hue and cry seems to have died down [. . .]

WORLD LUTHERAN FEDERATION

The W.L.F. set up an ecumenical institute in Copenhagen after Evanston. Professor Skydsgaard is the President of it, and Pastor Petersen, of the Danish State Lutheran Church, is its permanent secretary. He called on me in Rome. He explained the position of the Church in Denmark, which is in considerable bondage to the State, according to him, to a degree even worse than Sweden. He also tried to explain the exceedingly complicated organisation of the W.L.F. throughout the world. He thought it likely that the W.L.F. would send written representations to the Council, and that some office similar to my own might be created nearer to the Council itself.

FR. BECKER, ORATORIAN

Fr. Becker, R.C. chaplain at Leipzig University in the Eastern zone, whom I had met previously, called again. He had been allowed out for a second time to attend the meetings of the Secretariat. He gave me much interesting information about 'the Church in silence' which is not relevant to this report. He referred again to the tendency of Lutherans to sell out to the communists, mentioning especially Emil Fuchs.[62] He repeated that the R.C.s had actually gained in persecution more than they had so far lost. He said that of students from African and Asian countries coming to Germany to study $\frac{1}{2}$ are usually sent to West German and $\frac{1}{2}$ to East German universities indiscriminately. He believes that this is turning out very much to the benefit of democracy and the Christian Church when comparisons are made by the returning students.

THE UNITY SECRETARIAT

At the meetings of the Secretariat concluded last week, the question of 'guests' at the Council was discussed. At every meeting with Willebrands he refers to this subject first as though it is the subject I am most interested in. I have had to try to play this down and give the impression that though we should most probably accept invitations we are not consumed with desire to be present.

Willebrands asked me at length about our attitude to intercommunion. I made it clear that our action at New Delhi was entirely canonical and that express permission for extension of the moral regulations was being written into the new canon law.
[. . .]

Report No. 26   28th December, 1961

This Report is submitted from Ely.

WORLD COUNCIL OF CHURCHES

Cardinal Bea showed great interest in the W.C.C. and asked for my comments, particularly on the speeches of Sittler[63] and Franklin Fry.[64]

[62] Emil Fuchs (1874–1971), Lutheran pastor, socialist, and pacifist; by this time actively involved in the work of a commission which sought a rapprochement between Church and State in the German Democratic Republic.

[63] Joseph A. Sittler (1904–1987), American Lutheran and professor of theology at the University of Chicago.

[64] Franklin Clark Fry (1900–1968), leading American Lutheran much involved in the creation of the American Lutheran Church; head of the Lutheran World Federation, 1957; Chairman of the Policy and Executive Committees of the World Council of Churches.

There was no point in hiding that I thought, as he did, that they were unbelievably verbose, and we agreed that Lutherans were inclined to be that way (I was going to say Germans, but remembered in time that Cardinal Bea is a German – though most untypical). I was able to present him and Willebrands with the discourse of the Archbishop of Canterbury which was greatly praised by both. Cardinal Bea said 'This is why your Church has so much to contribute: you always have such level-headed people at the top. I wish all our leaders could always be the same.'

OBSERVERS AT THE COUNCIL

When I took leave of Cardinal Bea before returning he referred once more to the above subject and said that it was now morally certain that 'guests' would be invited. It had been recommended to the Pope that they should be known by that title. He said that the Unity Secretariat had been discussing details. I might inform the Archbishop of Canterbury (though this would please remain confidential for the moment) that the Anglican Communion would probably be invited to send three 'guests'. The Secretariat hoped that the guests taken all together would represent Christian opinion throughout the world. They had decided that the invitations would have to be confessional rather than regional. How did I suppose the Archbishop would allot three places to the Anglican Communion? I replied that it was difficult for me to say, though when the Cardinal seemed anxious for me to guess, I ventured (with appropriate safeguards) to say that the Archbishop might, for example, allot one place to the Church of England, one to the Church in America and one to one of the new provinces in Africa or Asia. The Cardinal said that I would be invited privately, and would be an addition to any delegation which the Anglican Communion sent. He hoped that those chosen would be theologians, and preferably 'Latinists'. I put in a caveat about this last and said that although we had many men who were both theologians and fluent Latin scholars, even our most eminent men would not necessarily be able to follow a discourse in 'church Latin' as pronounced in Italy, France, etc. without some practice. And it was very unlikely that a suitable e.g. African Anglican delegate would be able to follow Latin. He said it was not essential, only preferable, that he should. I said that in all these matters I imagined that the Archbishop would make use of the consultative committee of the Lambeth Conference.
[. . .]

THE WALDENSIANS[65] AND THE COUNCIL

I attended a series of 3 lectures at the Waldensian seminary by Prof. SIBILIA (the successor in office to the late Giovanni Miegge) on the forthcoming council. The lectures were very critical, and I thought rather bitter. People to whom I spoke afterwards said that the late Professor would have been more understanding. The main points of the lecture were:-

a. The Council is not ecumenical in any Catholic sense of the word.
b. The papacy since Vatican I is in such a position as to be able to impose the will of a minority on the Church.
c. The Council will have no idea of the fallibility of councils (though history should teach them about it), and so cannot approach the issues in penitence and humility, which is a sine qua non of God's blessing on any assembly.
d. The attitude to unity is preposterous. They are hoping to set the Church in order. It will then be presented to the world 'sine macula et sine ruga'[66] for the amazed contemplation of the rest of Christendom, who will then be scarce able to resist its blandishments. This conception offends the sensibilities of reasonable men.
e. Only persecution can purify the Roman Church.

DATE OF THE COUNCIL

The Pope's broadcast of Christmas Day was according to our predictions, though it failed to include a date for the Council. But it can now reasonably be inferred that the Council will start in the autumn of 1962 and will be adjourned at least once and go into 1963. [...]

COUNCIL ON INTER-CHURCH RELATIONS

Willebrands has twice asked for information on how the Church of England decides its policy. Who in fact decides what will be the relation of the Church of England to the Vatican Council? I replied in terms of the new constitution of the C.I.R. as sent to me, and repeated that the Council had been reconstituted. He has the impression that

---

[65] The Waldensians came from a Christian movement with roots in twelfth-century France, whose devotees sought to follow Christ in poverty and simplicity. They suffered centuries of persecution in Italy and ultimately came to represent a reformed and Protestant identity there. Their place in a united Italy was far from easy.

[66] 'Without spot or wrinkle'.

Archbishop Fisher liked to keep the reins of government solely in his own hands. I said that he should not make too many deductions from the fact that Archbishop Fisher's visit was indeed an individual gesture on his own responsibility. I added that although the Church of England valued democratic methods it tried not to be the slave of any constitutional theory and was quite content to see its prelates take their own line occasionally. In this case there was no doubt that Archbishop Fisher's action had been strongly endorsed ex post facto in all responsible quarters. I told him I did not know what the present Archbishop's policy would be in these matters.

[. . .]

Report No 27.   10th January, 1962

This Report comes from Ely.

LIBERTY OF OPINION

On December 12th, the English press reported that a Spanish Baptist and an American companion were stopped on the frontiers of Spain and 5,000 copies of St. John's Gospel were confiscated as subversive literature. I expect that the various Protestant agencies which are concerned with this subject will have taken notice of this extraordinary event and that the defence which will be offered from official Roman sources is that they cannot be responsible for acts of the Spanish government. It is always difficult to establish the complicity of the Spanish hierarchy even where it is morally certain.

[. . .]

THE BULL 'HUMANAE SALUTIS'

With the signing of this 'apostolic constitution' on Christmas Day, the Pope solemnly convened the forthcoming Vatican Council. The important passages are the following:

a. 'The Council will be held in the year 1962 at a convenient date to be announced later.'
b. 'We invite all Christians separated from the Church of Rome to join us in prayer that the Council may turn out to their advantage as well as to ours . . .'
c. 'Several of these communities have already promised to send representatives (legates), so that they can follow the proceedings of the Council at first hand.'

THE CHURCH IN POLAND

Cardinal Wyszynaki has written a letter to the Polish government, protesting against the new restrictive legislation perpetrated by the Polish government. The restrictions of which he complains are the usual ones, including crippling taxation, which had been made retrospective. The Polish government does more than most to keep up the fiction of being democratic. In this case it has 'suspended' the action of the new decrees 'for investigation', though there is no doubt of the end of the affair. The 'investigation' is merely to see what is the will of the People's Party.

[. . .]

Report No 28.   24th January, 1962

This Report comes from Ely.

THE CENTRAL COMMISSION OF THE COUNCIL: THIRD MEETING

The press reports of the sessions say, that the main preoccupation of the Commission will be Moral Law. The main object seems to be to assert the opposition of the Christian Moral Law to all opportunist and expedient systems of morality as now adopted in many political circles. They are an offence against the dignity of man and the law of God. The Press, the Stage, and Radio will come under special review. Some of the principles of psycho-analysis will also be considered.

[. . .]

Report No 29   6th February, 1962

This Report comes from Ely.

CENTRAL COMMISSION OF THE COUNCIL

A full session of the Commission took place on the 18th of January and the following days. The Commission considered certain matters sent up to it by the Commission of the Discipline of the Sacraments, particularly that of Holy Order. In the reports on these matters from official sources, stress is always laid on the fact that neither the substance nor the divine institutions of the Sacraments, which were adequately defined, once and for all, at the Council of Trent, were discussed. Discussions only concern particular adaptations to meet present circumstances.

Particular attention was paid to the Diaconate. The functions of this order, according to canon law, are to distribute Holy Communion, to baptise, and to catechise. The idea of a married diaconate in the mission field, which would not lead on to the order of priesthood, is one that must be very seriously considered. Consideration will also be given to the revival of the order of Reader. Experiments have been made with this in the Diocese of Rome. It consists mainly of young men, trained to read the Epistle at Mass, and functions rather like a Fellowship of Vocation in an English diocese. The whole of the discussion is contained under the sub-heading 'Helps for the Priesthood'.

Consideration was also given to the multiplicity of Oriental rites. The Roman Church sees no harm in an infinite variety in ways of worshipping, or of the invention of new rites, so long as they are sound in form and matter. There is no intention of forcing uniformity on the Church. On the other hand, there are too many rites current in the East and there should be some reform. It must first of all be made clear that the Oriental patriarchs have no independent jus liturgicum.[67] The only orders which have this right are the Supreme Pontiff and the episcopate. This will have to be the first point of discussion in any matters concerning the Oriental churches.

After this unpromising start the report goes on to say that it is too soon yet to talk of a 'thaw' in the relations with the Eastern churches which are always referred to as 'Non-Catholic Oriental Christians'.

The Central Commission have also dealt with the report submitted to them by the Theological Commission, but as this was presented to them, by Cardinal Ottaviani, it contains nothing but a record of the well-worn phrases of right-wing Roman Theology.

The Pope himself presided over the last session of the Commission on January 23rd. In very florid language, he described the assembly of the 'teaching church' as likely to constitute a 'new Pentecost'. [...]

DATE OF THE COUNCIL

On the Feast of the Purification, Pope John XXIII announced the date of the beginning of the Council as the 11th of October, of this

[67]Liturgical jurisdiction.

year. The appropriateness of this date is said to be, that it was on this very day that the priest Philip left the Church of St. Peter-in-Chains in Rome to represent Pope Leo at the Council of Ephesus.

GUESTS AT THE COUNCIL

Now that the date of the Council is known, I hope that the Archbishop will be selecting his three nominees. May I report that if the number is to be three, they will most probably be one Englishman, one American, and one national from one of the new churches? [...] It will be remembered that Cardinal Bea suggested that guests should if possible have a knowledge of Latin.

RETURN TO ROME

I plan to return on Thursday, 15th February, I shall be at the Church Assembly for the previous two days if required for anything.

THE CHURCH IN EAST GERMANY

[...]
My Roman Catholic informants say with apparent (and I believe real) sorrow that many of the Lutheran clergy are 'selling out' to the Communist Regime. See my report, no.25. Others interpret the same phenomenon as 'a real attempt to adapt the Christian faith to life under the new conditions, and to avoid unnecessary provocation'.
[...]
My informants all say that anti-church repression is more severe than under the Nazi regime. There is a compulsory youth organisation called the 'Pioneers'. Nevertheless, a lot of religious education for the young has been attempted even in state schools. Ironically enough, freedom of religion is guaranteed, by articles 42–45 of the constitution. But sadistic difficulties are always put in the way of its implementation. The Church puts a certain amount of hope in the fact that the government are at present over-reaching themselves. They seem to do more than anybody else in the matter of secular ceremonial ritual
[...]

Report No 30.   27th February, 1962

This report is written from ROME. I returned here on Friday, February 16th and propose to remain until March 29th. I have to do the month of April in residence in Ely and shall then return here immediately.

[. . .]

THE BISHOP OF SOUTHWARK[68]

The Bishop of Southwark is coming here in April and is contemplating fixing himself up with a private audience. [. . .] He was kind enough to ask me whether I thought this was a good thing. This was before the Archbishop's circular went round. I am inclined to think that the Bishop of Southwark is one for whom an exception might well be made. There is no doubt that his warm personality made a very great impression here when he last saw the Pope. At my first interview with His Holiness he made special mention of Mervyn Stockwood, who had been to see him just before his consecration. They have exchanged Christmas cards regularly ever since and I think this whole exchange has served to wear down the aloofness of the R.C. Bishop of Southwark (Cowderoy)[69] who is one of the least co-operative.

CARDINAL BEA

I have had my first interview with Cardinal Bea. His Eminence explained that the Secretariat are having much perplexity in deciding how far to scatter their invitations to guests at the Council. They are particularly anxious not to run the risk of having any rebuffs. He realises that there is no question of that from Canterbury. He asked if I knew whether the Archbishop had in mind what sort of people he was going to nominate. I said that I did not know whether the Archbishop had sounded any individuals, but it seemed to me that the Archbishop would want fairly exact details as to what was the proposed programme for the guests before he was able to decide as to whom to send. The Cardinal said that he hoped that the matter would be cleared up at the meetings of the Secretariat between the 6th and 10th of March. Willebrands was away in Athens and Constantinople (this is said to be *very* secret) sorting out the question of the Orthodox representation. They are wondering whether the Russians will come or not.

I told the Cardinal about the proposal for me to write a book about the Council from the Anglican point of view. He said he was very pleased to hear that this was so and that they had always assumed that

<hr />

[68] Mervyn Stockwood (1913–1995), Bishop of Southwark, 1959–1980.
[69] Cyril Cowderoy (1905–1976), appointed Roman Catholic Bishop of Southwark in 1949; Archbishop of Southwark, 1965–1976.

I would. He was sure that Willebrands would read the proofs of what I wrote, at least as far as it concerned the facts of the Roman situation.

FR. STRANSKY, O.S.P.[70]

The American chaplain had Bishop Emrich[71] and me to lunch with Fr. Stransky who is an American Paulist and one of the permanent officials of the Unity Secretariat. We had a long conversation on the Council and the NATURE OF THE EPISCOPATE. We pressed Stransky about the dangers to Catholic order involved in an elaboration of the Pope-in-Curia. He argued that much of the episcopate was now in remote and undeveloped countries and could not adequately look after itself and not only needed but wanted central direction. We agreed that this might be so, but that the central control required ought to be more frequent councils or sub-committees of the Council which were international and which were composed of bishops. He agreed that the Curia was becoming too large and hoped that the Council would bring about a reform in this matter.

Bishop Emrich asked whether there might be any new alignment on the matter of BIRTH CONTROL or population control. Stransky said he thought it was very unlikely. So far scientists seemed to differ so much in what the basic problems were behind population control and the problems were not understood. It would not be reasonable to ask Christendom to limit itself voluntarily while the non-Christian world was proliferating ad lib:. The Bishop said that the East would not expect the West to go on indefinitely feeding its multiplying populations unless they undertook some form of population control. The American government would have to face up to this issue fairly soon and the Roman Catholic community in America would not be able to contract out of a decision.

THE POPE

It is rumoured that the Pope is to have an operation of the prostate gland in July.

---

[70] Fr Thomas Stransky (1930–), American Catholic who was one of the original staff members of the Secretariat for the Promotion of Christian Unity. He began his service in 1960 soon after the Secretariat was formed and served with Cardinals Bea and Willebrands, the first two Secretariat Presidents. In October 1960, Stransky was given the file on a proposal for the Council to address the Church's relationship with the Jewish people. In 1986 he became Director of the Tantur Ecumenical Institute in Jerusalem.

[71] Richard Emrich (1910–1997), Bishop of the Episcopal Diocese of Michigan, 1948–1973.

THE 'CHURCH TIMES'

I have now written and accepted the offer of the *Church Times* to be their correspondent, anonymously, during the Council.

THE SECRETARIAT

I visited the office of the Secretariat on the 21 February and had a long time with Mgr. Arrighi, Willebrands' first assistant. We spoke at length about infallibility. He said he thought much could be done to 'explain' it. He places much hope in the Roman Canon 228 which says that supreme authority in the Church is vested in the universal episcopate acting in union with the Pope. The second phrase of it, which gives the Pope a veto, even against a unanimous decision of a Council, is 'unthinkable', and has in fact never been invoked. He had been present at the declaration of the Assumption in 1950. When the Pope made a declaration he wore a mitre, and the assisting Bishops all put on their mitres while the Pope read the decree. All the bishops in the world had been consulted in writing, and a very large majority had agreed. The decision was certainly not unanimous.

There were many spirits who had been anxious lest there should never be another council, since the Infallibility decree. To remove this anxiety was one of the present Pope's chief motives in calling the Council.

[. . .]

THE COUNCIL AND THE RECITATION OF THE BREVIARY

In an 'Epistula ad clerum universum'[72] the Pope makes a strong appeal to all members of the order of priesthood to be diligent in offering their daily round of prayer for the forthcoming Council. This seems very natural to us, but there is beneath it an undertone of reminder that the place of the order of priests in the forthcoming Council is to pray rather than to think, or to express their opinions too loudly.

THE COMMISSION FOR THE APOSTLESHIP OF THE LAITY

An official press notice has appeared about the work of this Commission. It gives very little information, but seems at pains to suggest that the work of the laity is to carry out loyally the decisions of the hierarchy when they are known. The work of this Commission

---

[72] Letter to the universal clergy.

is divided into three departments: (a) Catholic action and direct apostolate, (b) charitable work, (c) social action.

Report No. 31	1st March, 1962

OBSERVERS AT THE COUNCIL

The Secretariat have still not been able to make final arrangements because of difficulties which are continually arising, though it is hoped that matters will advance considerably at the ensuing meetings (March 6th–10th).

There will be three types of session at the Council, Solemn, plenary and study. Observers will be able to be present at the first two. In addition special meetings will be arranged at which 'explanations' will be given to observers by experts and at which questions will be possible. Willebrands said that the sessions will probably be prorogued in December and reassemble the following February or March. It would on the whole be desirable to have observers who could stay through the time of the whole Council. But it was recognised that if the people appointed were of consequence, this would not be possible. Perhaps 'alternates' could be appointed for the subsequent sessions as required. He confirmed that he was hoping to come and see the Archbishop in Canterbury or London at some date between March 12th and 24th and will be writing soon to ask for an appointment.

ORTHODOX PATRIARCH OF CONSTANTINOPLE

Willebrands has just been to Istanbul. He saw the Oecumenical Patriarch[73] and his foreign relations committee. This appeared to be stiff with Metropolitans, chiefly of places now depopulated and under Turkish rule, such as Ephesus and Chalcedon. I observed that then it must have been like a Vatican congregation – and he agreed. Speaking of the conference at Rhodes he said that the R.C.s there were not strictly observers, but press agents etc. The Orthodox had not wanted to ask Roman observers because they were afraid of the behaviour of the Russians. Had the Russian delegations suddenly sprung an anti-Vatican tirade in the middle of proceedings that might have been awkward.

---

[73]Aristocles Spyrou (1886–1972), Patriarch Athenegoras of Constantinople, 1948–1972.

Willebrands had been to discuss the question of observers at the Vatican Council. He had been very pleased indeed with the manner of his reception, not only by the Oecumenical Patriarch but by all concerned, even more so because, although the conclusions were far from satisfactory, yet there was complete understanding.

The Oecumenical Patriarch and all the committees said that there was no doubt at all but that all the Patriarchs wanted to send observers. But the brethren behind the Iron Curtain were a great problem. If they wanted to come and were not allowed to they would have to say to the world that they did not want to – and they hoped the Romans would understand this necessary prevarication. By Orthodox custom they should either all come or none at all. The committee were not very ready to say what they would do if the churches behind the Iron Curtain were unable to come. There was a further complication, which was that the patriarchates were autocephalous, and the Committee was not in a position to speak for all the others. It was decided that invitations, if they were sent at all, were to be sent to the Oecumenical Patriarch and his committee for distribution, though this would not imply any recognition of the Oecumenical Patriarch's claim to jurisdiction.

Willebrands was further asked to consider what would be the Vatican line about communism at the Council. It was possible that Khrushchev,[74] for example, would allow his delegation to come in the hope that it might be an embarrassment to the Council. Would the Council be able to denounce atheism without denouncing communism? If they did the latter the Russian delegation would have to walk out, and the rest of the Orthodox delegations, for reasons of ecumenical solidarity, would have to do the same. Willebrands said that the Secretariat would be considering these questions at their meeting next week. I observed that the Vatican seemed to me now to be in a dilemma with regard to the Russian delegation, if it came. If it made any move to denounce communism, that would have the consequences adumbrated above. If they didn't it would look like a change of front, and as if they had drawn in their horns and were afraid. Perhaps they had been too ready to confuse communism and atheism in the past. Willebrands said that he had always thought that this was so.

---

[74] Nikita Khrushchev (1894–1971), First Secretary of the Communist Party of the USSR, 1953–1964.

THE THEOLOGICAL COMMISSION

I said to Willebrands that I thought that some of the press reports of the meetings of the Central Commission, particularly the reports of the Theological Commission, already made disappointing reading for us. In days when the key-word of the Council was 'aggiornamento' (bringing-up-to-date) were we going to have no let-up about the philosophy of S. Thomas Aquinas? Were S. Thomas' five proofs to be stuck to as the only possible expression of the doctrine of God in philosophical terms? S. Thomas himself represented a bold attempt to restate the doctrines of the Christian faith, in their philosophical implications, in terms of the philosophy then current, viz. Aristotelianism. Was it not advisable at least to leave open the possibility that that could be done in our day? Willebrands hoped that it might, but said that the Theological Commission had very reactionary members on it. Yet the Central Commission had referred back a very great proportion of the Theological Commission's work to be recast. This had been widely reported and commented on as one of the most significant developments of the preparations for the Council.

[. . .]

THE LATIN LANGUAGE

The Pope has just issued a 'Constitutio Apostolica'[75] which will be known by the title 'VETERUM SAPIENTIA'[76] on the use of Latin, not only in the liturgy but in the life and studies of the Church. The main points of the document seem to be as follows:

a. Latin is a priceless and irreplaceable inheritance from the past.
b. It is an actual vehicle of unity.
c. It is the only certain way of expressing theological truths accurately without danger of misunderstanding.
d. The decline of the use of Latin in the Church would be an irreparable loss and would be bound to lead to division and confusion.

In order to safeguard the position of the Latin language in the life of the Church, the Pope then made the following provisions in the strongest language, saying for example, 'We, with full regard to our office and authority, do ordain and decree as follows [. . .]':

[75]The highest level of papal decree.
[76]'The wisdom of the ancient world'.

a. All bishops and generals of religious orders in charge of seminaries are to observe our wishes in this matter most scrupulously.
b. They are not to allow anybody to write or speak against the use of Latin in seminaries.
c. All seminary courses are to begin with a thorough grounding in Latin. Moreover students advancing to higher studies are not to be allowed to lose their familiarity with the Latin tongue.
d. If in any country the study of Latin has been relaxed under pressure from misguided modernistic ideas, it is to be reinstated immediately.
e. The principal sacred subjects are to be taught in Latin. No excuses are to be allowed or evasions tolerated.
f. There is to be founded by the Sacred Congregation of Seminaries and Universities an Academical Institute of Latin studies.
g. The Academical Institute is to be concerned also to see that students proceeding to degrees in Theology are conversant with Greek.

There is no doubt that this has given a very severe shock to all the people with whom I usually consort. They regard it as very ill-timed, coming just before the Council, and therefore being obviously calculated to limit discussion. It is apparently intended, among other things, to check the enthusiasm of those who hope for liturgies in the vernacular, though it does not actually mention liturgical matters. It represents a victory for the old guard, though, as a German Monsignor said to me this evening, 'It is a victory of Pyrrhus'.[77] It is expected that the whole thing will be shelved and immediately forgotten as soon as possible. But I think it has shaken all of them to think that it could have happened at all.
[. . .]

Report No 32.   2nd March, 1962

[. . .]
THE CENTRAL COMMISSION OF THE COUNCIL

The Central Commission had another session from the 20th–28th February. It has now appointed three further Sub-Commissions for Procedure, Mixed Questions, (i.e. to decide how to regulate

---

[77]Pyrrhus was king of the Hellenistic kingdom of Epirus, whose costly military successes against Rome in 280–279 BC gave rise to the phrase 'Pyrrhic victory'.

questions which could come under three or four heads at once) and Amendments.

In his opening address to the Commission, the Pope stressed that the Church was an army on the march and should beware of settling down in any one place for long. He was very lyrical about the presence of Cardinal Zyszynski from Warsaw,[78] representing the 'Church in Silence'.

The first report received was that of the *Commission on Bishops and the Government of Dioceses*. The report contains a preamble on the history, nature and organisation of dioceses, which would be quite acceptable to us. The rest of the report tries to hide the signs of struggles that are likely to go on at the Council. The missionary bishops are clearly complaining that there are too many dioceses in Italy, complete with curias. There has obviously been some murmuring about the large number of titular bishoprics and non-episcopal ordinary jurisdictions (abbacies Nullius[79] – situations equivalent to what would happen if the Dean of Windsor had the whole of a rural deanery as a 'peculiar'). There is the further struggle going on about national episcopal conferences. As I have reported before, the bishops e.g. of France and Germany want a good deal of independence from the curia. The curia counter by recommending regional conferences such as that now operating in Latin America. They would evidently prefer an occasional European episcopal conference, in which Italians and Spaniards could outvote the French and Germans.

The concluding part of this report, however, is cast in a very conventional mould. It emphasises that the authority of the Pope and of the curia is there for the help, and not for the hindrance, of the bishops. The relationship as it is works very well. That is what the official report says, but there are many people here who would not agree. [. . .]

The report of the *Commission on the Discipline of the Clergy and People* was next considered. The Commission examined the five precepts of the Church. The tone of the official reports about these is again one of alarming satisfaction. [. . .]

The *Commission on Vocations and Seminaries* (C.A.C.T.M., as it were) presented the report which has already been referred to (Report No.

[78] Cardinal Stefan Zyszynski (1901–1981), Archbishop of Warsaw and Gniezno, 1948–1981; created Cardinal and Primate of Poland by Pius XII, 1953.

[79] A territory which is set apart from any diocese and in which the clergy and the people are subject to an abbot as their local ordinary. The prelate who presides over abbacy *nullius* is called an abbot *nullius*.

23. I). It repeats the alarming statistics there given, and adds that of 43,000 clergy in Italy, 10,000 are over the age of 60. It seeks out Latin Americans for special reference as a place where priests are very thin on the ground. It advocates intense fostering of some vocations (it does not use the word 'recruitment'). It recommends the grouping of seminaries. Some of the dioceses of Italy are certainly very small and they all have their own independent seminaries. The report urges very strongly the continuing of separate Catholic universities.

[. . .]

In his closing speech the Pope used the words 'Restauratio et renovatio universali ecclesiae'.[80] This is now a stock phrase used for this type of occasion. It deliberately avoids use of the word 'reformatio'. He hoped that the whole Church would use Lent as a 'vigil for the Council'.

[. . .]

THE GERMAN AMBASSADOR TO THE HOLY SEE

I was asked to dinner with Mgr. Höfer specially to meet Dr. von Scherpenberg,[81] who had expressed an interest in my mission. I did not realise that Western Germany is one of the countries which has an Ambassador at the Vatican, as opposed to a Minister. He is alternately an R.C. or an Evangelical. This Ambassador is a Lutheran. [. . .]

The German Ambassador seemed pleased to make my acquaintance and said that he could let me know confidentially that I should 'have a companion before long'. I was to take that to mean that the Lutherans would be sending a representative to Rome. I said that I was pleased to hear it, though I would rather know what sort of Lutheran he was and what his briefing would be before I said any more. I asked the Ambassador if he knew of Prof. Skydsgaard's symposium on the Council, 'The Gospel and the Papal Church', but though he seemed to be well instructed in other matters, he didn't know of it, though he knew of Skydsgaard. Mgr. Höfer didn't seem to know of the book either. The Ambassador seemed very interested when I expressed disappointment, and pressed for my reasons. I said it seemed so disappointing that the Church seemed to be still so bound to Luther and his teachings, as though they were all divinely inspired. I hoped the Church would have advanced in 400 years. He said that he didn't think they had learned much, or advanced. There were ways in which the Evangelische Kirche was further back than it was at the

---

[80] 'Restoration and renovation of the whole Church'.
[81] Albert Hilger von Scherpenberg (1899–1969), German diplomat; German ambassador to the Holy See, 1961–1964.

Reformation. The Aufklaerung[82] had done it much harm. He said he was not disappointed to hear that the Evangelische Kirche still stood by Luther and his Protest. I said I had no objection to the protest, most of which was no doubt still valid, but I deplored the total lack of self-criticism, (except in one essay), in the book. The Ambassador said he wished that the Romans were back at the Council of Trent: it would be easier for us all if they were. He continually spoke of 'Protestantism' as if it were a whole, and I had to say how difficult it was for us to decide whether to allow ourselves to come under that description, especially when in Italy.

The Ambassador said he thought that the great wave of liberalism with regard to unity etc. in the Vatican had now passed over and that the tide was running in the other direction. I said that I would never have described what had happened as 'a great wave of liberalism'. There never had been any immediate prospect of e.g. doctrinal concessions. He agreed that perhaps this was so. In that case what hope was there from the Council? I said that we must wait and see what Cardinal Bea means by the 'explanation of difficult doctrines'. In any case this Council was only ever given out to be a beginning of new things. We might at least hope for the establishment of permanent relationships on the present unofficial footing. I also ventured to say that if we expected a great reformation from the Roman Church we must undertake the same ourselves, e.g. the Lutheran Federation was a loose and rather chaotic assembly of discordant bodies. Could they not improve upon that? He agreed that they could and should.
[. . .]

Report No.33   12th March, 1962

LUTHERANS AND THE COUNCIL

The Secretariat now confirm that the Lutherans are about to send a representative to Rome with roughly the same duties as myself. It is to be Professor Schlink of Heidelberg. Can I be told what is known about him, please?

[82]The Enlightenment.

[...]

THE LAITY

The insistent comments of the press on the total absences of the laity from the Council has led to the Pope again, in an audience to journalists, to say that the exclusion of the laity from the deliberations of the Council is a matter of doctrine. The government of the Church was entrusted by Christ to the 'sacred hierarchy' and to no one else. The Council is not a debating society or a parliament. The communist paper *L'Unita* suggests that the Council should give a definition of the position of the laity and such as will 'liberate them from the yoke of the hierarchy'.

[...]

CLERGY DISCIPLINE

If any reader of these reports feels occasionally depressed about clerical scandals in the Church of England he might like to be encouraged by the thought that at the moment there are current in the Italian papers glaring headlines and reports of the following cases:

  a. A Monsignor from the diocese of Naples charged with being a leader of a gang organising a slot-machine racket under the late 'Lucky Luciano' of Chicago!
  b. Four Capuchin friars in Sicily being tried for homicide and blackmail, in the dock with leaders of the 'Mafia'.
  c. A priest in the North of Italy has resigned his orders and is trying to get married. Certain people, including his mother, probably instigated by the local bishop, are trying to get him certified. This is holding up the marriage. A neighbouring priest, asked for his opinion, cynically told the press: 'I don't see why he had to go to all these lengths: the same objects are usually accomplished by much simpler methods'.

[...]

Report No 34.   12th March, 1962

[...]
GRADES OF DOCTRINE

I had a visit from Mgr. H.F. Davis, R.C. lecturer in the faculty of Theology at Birmingham, Consultor of the Unity Secretariat, in

Rome for that purpose.[83] He forms part of the theological team which treats with us. [...]

I said that the reactionary views about the Catholic universities seemed to have prevailed in the pre-Council commissions, particularly 'Studies and seminaries'. He agreed that this was so, and that it was to be regretted. He thought that from every point of view they did better to go in to the secular universities as far as they could. I said that there seemed to be a frightening anti-clerical attitude abroad in the secular universities in Italy, and that that might be due to the segregationalist policy. He agreed that that was so.

We talked of the Council, and he asked me what I would like to see the Council do for unity. I said that we hoped for signs of a real change of attitude. Friendliness was a pleasant change, but by itself did not constitute a desire for union. We hoped, for their sakes, as well as ours, to see that the Catholic conception of the episcopate was not any further compromised than it had been by the infallibility decree, and that what was done in 1870 might generally be recognised as very dangerous. I then hoped for further clarification, which had been all but promised, in the matter of the doctrine of the Church. Was Cardinal Bea's view to be the official doctrine? What was, then, the status of the baptised non-R.C. who in good faith believed he was receiving the sacraments, was in full communion with Catholic Christendom, but who was bound in conscience to repudiate as de fide the last unilateral decree of Roman councils etc.

I pressed him further about the relative importance of dogmas. Was it true that the Assumption article was de fide in exactly the same way (and with the same consequences for the non-believer) as the Incarnation? He said that the formula 'anathema sit'[84] applied only to 'catholics' who failed to receive the doctrine. I answered that if that was what it meant it was not what it said, 'quis non credit ...'.[85] He then said that there was a 'certain difference' in this respect between the 'fundamental doctrines' and the others. I said that in that case there was a difference between scholars in this matter, for others (I was thinking of Witte for one) had said otherwise. I asked whether the question of 'fundamental doctrines' could not be further clarified at this Council (i.e. what we call 'catholic' doctrine), or whether perhaps he would think it better to let it alone for the present. He became rigid

---

[83] H. Francis Davis, Newman scholar and Lecturer in the Department of Theology at the University of Birmingham. Davis became the Vice-Postulator to the Cause for Newman's canonization.

[84] A formal ecclesiastical curse of excommunication or a formal denunciation of a doctrine.

[85] 'He who does not believe ...'.

about this and said that S. Thomas (Aquinas) held both views together, and said that they were not inconsistent, i.e. that in rejecting one you rejected all and that some doctrines were more 'important' than others. Mgr. Davis defined the difference by saying that by rejecting one (e.g. the corporal Assumption) you only ceased to be a 'catholic', but that by rejecting the incarnation you ceased to be a Christian. I said that we took some comfort from thinking that they did not hold the terms to be synonymous. There is clearly a little room for manoeuvre here if only they would exploit it.

BISHOP BECK of SALFORD[86]

I have just come across a report, in a French review (Documentations Catholiques)[87] of a sermon preached in the Roman Cathedral at Westminster by the above-named prelate of a very contentious kind, giving a contemptuous, one-sided, ill-instructed view of Reformation history. 'Englishmen are not historians: if they read history, they would become Catholics.' 'The national churches being formed now behind the iron curtain under the heel of communist governments can be compared in their origins to the State Church in England. If they have to survive 400 years in that condition they too may become venerable, but that will not make their origin any more respectable.' [. . .]

PROFESSOR SCHLINK

The Professor has arrived in Rome. I heard this news from Cardinal Bea, to whom he went to present his credentials. I have sent a note of welcome to Schlink and invited him to a meal. [. . .]

CARDINAL BEA IN ENGLAND

The Cardinal honoured us with his presence at lunch here today. In the course of it he told me that he is coming to Heythrop in the middle of August to address a conference of R.C. clergy (2 from each diocese), organised by Archbishop Heenan, on the new attitude to ecumenical matters. He said 'They can certainly do with some new ideas in England'.

---

[86] George Andrew Beck (1904–1978), Bishop of Salford, 1955–1964; Archbishop of Liverpool, 1964–1976.

[87] See p. 70, n. 45.

He hoped to see Cardinal Godfrey.[88] I naturally asked whether he was planning to see the Archbishop of Canterbury. He said he would certainly like to do so, but that it might be better if they met on neutral ground. Could I be told, please, whether this will be possible? I should have thought that there ought now to be no difficulty in the Cardinal coming to Lambeth, but he evidently does not want to offend Godfrey.

Report No 35.	15th March, 1962

OBSERVERS AT THE COUNCIL

Willebrands asked me to his office this morning and gave me particulars of the decision of the Unity Secretariat at their meetings last week. I have communicated the substance of them previously, as I have heard guesses from other members of the Secretariat, and Willebrands will no doubt be communicating them to the Archbishop at his visit on Monday. The five points were:-

a. a formal administrative resolution that observers will be admitted if invited;

b. that observers will be admitted to solemn and to plenary sessions; Willebrands asked me at this point my opinion as to how far I thought they could trust the discretion of invited observers not to reveal details of intimate 'scandals' that might come to light. Who could tell what might be said? Did I think they could extract a 'parole d'honneur'?

I said that I thought they could not do this, but that in the written notes for guidance of observers, and indeed in the preliminary invitations, the point could be made as a strong request. They could then do no more than leave it to the discretion of invited guests not to take advantage of their privileged position. Perhaps the presence of observers might make the fathers of the Council careful? They could reserve the right to exclude guests at any difficult point. Willebrands thought that would not be easy. I reminded Willebrands that Tardini had said 'We have no secrets';

c. observers will not have the right either to speak or to vote.

d. The Secretariat will organise special sessions for observers, at which explanations will be given and at which questions may be asked;

---

[88]William Godfrey (1889–1963), Archbishop of Liverpool, 1953–1956; Archbishop of Westminster, 1956–1963; created Cardinal, 1958.

e. The Secretariat will act as an intermediary for any communications which the invited guests may wish to make to the Council, either before or during it. I asked about this and elicited that if, e.g. an inaccurate report about the Church of England was made by a father of the Council, we could hand in at once a written correction (as I believe was done once by the Roman observers at New Delhi).

SPOKEN LATIN

The importance of being able to understand spoken Latin becomes more evident. I wish it weren't. Fr. Corr comes to me twice a week to speak Latin at me, and I go to an occasional lecture. Although I read Latin fluently the accent comes slowly, and, as has often been stated, the great difficulty will be the pronunciation.

Incidentally, the encyclical Veterum Sapientia has caused great misgivings. Even Cardinal Bea said yesterday that 'it has been much misunderstood: the Pope did not intend it to have the effect it has had'. I couldn't embarrass him by any further questions, but I suspect that he really means that the whole Church is conspiring to see that it is forgotten as soon as possible.

ANGLICAN ORDERS

Willebrands (who introduced the subject) said that many of them would like to reopen the question. But there was no point in doing so until both sides could say that 'We believe we are right, but are quite prepared to be proved wrong'. There were not yet sufficient R.C.s who could honestly say that. Were there Anglicans? I ventured to say that I thought there was a very large number of Anglicans indeed who would not have a closed mind on the subject, and would welcome a renewed enquiry.

Willebrands said he, and many others with him, drew an immense distinction between ourselves and e.g. Lutherans. They deliberately repudiated the succession of the Apostolic ministry and wanted a new start. We as deliberately intended to continue it, and in good faith believed we had succeeded in doing so. Even if it were proved that through an accident of history we had failed to do so, there was our faith to work on. The present Archbishop was reported as having said to the R.C.s 'According to you I am a "laicus vagans extra ecclesiam".[89] If you honestly believe that[,] I am prepared for you to

---

[89] 'A layman-vagrant outside the Church'.

say so, if you must. But much then depends on the spirit in which you say it.' Willebrands commended this saying. For his part he would not so describe an Anglican cleric.

Were we really teaching orders as a matter of faith? I said that many of us were, but not all. He asked how the actions of the Church of England in South India, Ceylon etc. were to be interpreted with regard to the above. Did they represent a weakening of faith in the sacramental effectiveness of Holy Orders? (I still don't know whether he knows about the Open Letter or not – I suppose Heenan or Leeming must have told him). I said that on the contrary it could be taken as showing how much importance the Church of England attached to the place of the apostolic ministry in the Church – we valued it so much that we were prepared to tolerate a period of possible disciplinary irregularity in order to secure its eventual wider availability. Were they prepared to make a similar sacrifice?

Willebrands asked if I thought the Archbishop of Canterbury would mind if he brought up this subject (orders in general) when he was at Lambeth. I said I was sure he was free to mention any subject.

He asked how strong was the movement for the ordination of women in the Church of England. I said it had very little support indeed. Unfortunately he asked if there were any bishops who supported it, and I said I thought only one (Birmingham).

Report No 36.   21st March, 1962

RETURN

I return from here on March 29th, arriving in Ely March 30th. I should like to be able to visit Lambeth, and if possible to see the Archbishop, some time during April. Could I be given a date, please?
[. . .]

THE CURIA AND THE EPISCOPATE

A very interesting development has taken place in the above relationship. The Pope has created 10 new cardinals, bringing the number up to 87. At the Secret Consistory at which the names were announced, the Pope revealed that it was his intention to give episcopal consecration to all the cardinals (old and new) who were not already in that order. It will be remembered that there are three 'grades' of cardinals,

Cardinal Bishops, who are bishops of the old suburban sees (Palestrina, Ostia etc.)

Cardinal priests, who are all in episcopal orders before appointment, and

Cardinal deacons who are in priests' orders on appointment and usually stay in that condition.

The last two grades hold titles as incumbents of the old parishes of Rome.

The new announcement, made on the Pope's own initiative, has given rise to much speculation. It could represent a move either to the right or to the left. The status of the cardinals not in episcopal orders has already been a subject of criticism by 'liberal' commentators, and I have always made it clear that their existence is very puzzling to us. In particular, commentators have attacked the status of Cardinal Ottaviani who, being head of the Theological Commission and therefore in a very important position in respect of the forthcoming Council, is only in priests' orders – with a loud voice and a vote in the Council of Bishops. It is as if we were to wake up one day and find that Cardinal Satterthwaite,[90] still in priests' orders, had a voice and vote at the Lambeth Conference!
[. . .]
I am now on sufficiently good terms with the Secretariat staff to be able to make jokes about this sort of thing, such as suggesting that the new move represents the Pope taking notice of, and acting upon, Pawley's often-voiced suggestions for streamlining the Roman Church. But I have now told them that, although this is a good beginning, it is still not nearly enough, even in the matter of restoring catholic order in the Roman hierarchy. I have always said that we have no objection to the status of cardinals as such, providing that the primacy of episcopal order is in no way compromised. But now there remains the question of the titular bishoprics. These 'cardinal deacons' will be consecrated to the title of some place which is a heap of stones in Turkey. (e.g. Archbishop Mathew is Archbishop of Apamea in Bithynia, which is in fact Hissarlik hill, the site of Troy). Thus they are given status and order without jurisdiction or cure of souls, almost as if they were being made a 'conte' or a 'marchese' or as if, in our case, a man were being

---

[90]John Satterthwaite (1925–1980), head of the Archbishop of Canterbury's Council on Foreign Relations and later Bishop of the Diocese of Europe.

consecrated bishop in vacuo just to give him a seat in the House of Lords.

[...]

There is no doubt that the more liberal men here are very dissatisfied about the titular non-pastoral consecrations. Pope Pius XII, e.g., never held a pastoral cure until he became Bishop of Rome. Can we declare his consecration irregular?

Report No 37.   28th March, 1962

CARDINAL TISSERANT

The Cardinal did us the honour of coming to dinner again. We also had Stewart Perowne, archaeologist,[91] so that the conversation was mainly archaeological. But the Cardinal did seem to think that observers at the Council would be well advised to brush up their Latin. He also said that the atmosphere in the Curia was improving all the time towards reunion and said with a smile that certain recent deaths had contributed to the change.

[...]

MGR. WILLEBRANDS AT LAMBETH

Mgr. Willebrands has told me of the substance of his visit to Lambeth, with which he seems to have been very pleased. I am glad about Cardinal Bea's visit in August and hope that a visit to Canterbury will mature. Willebrands is quite clear that Cardinal Bea will be welcome, though it is not yet certain about the attitude of the Roman hierarchy in England.

[...]

DR. SCHLINK

I invited Professor Schlink, who has recently arrived in Rome, to a meal, together with his secretary, Herr Jung, a layman, a theological research student in Heidelberg. I received him very warmly and said how pleased I was to have a colleague in the work. He immediately started to ask how far I had access to the documents which were to be before the Council, and seemed very disappointed when I revealed

---

[91] Stewart Perowne (1901–1989), archaeologist, diplomat, authority on the antiquities of the Mediterranean, and scion of a deeply Anglican family.

that I had no access to any others than had already been entrusted to him by the Secretariat. I said it was not reasonable to expect access to the confidential documents. Had he read the literature put out by the Romans about the Council? He had, very widely. Had he digested the press hand-outs from the Vatican Office? And the *Osservatore Romano* ad loc.?[92] He had done these things, and of course is already widely read on the theological points at issue. He then asked, I thought naively, what I thought there would be for him to do in view of the fact that there were no documents to study, and seemed to imply that there would not be much. I said that there was first 400 years of prejudice and mischievous ignorance, and even adverse propaganda, to be cleared away. He made a modest answer but I imagine he was thinking that that might not be the right work for a professor of dogmatics. The whole discussion seemed to me to throw up in a high light two aspects of this whole situation. First, it is perhaps typical of the Lutherans to send a high-powered theologian for this work, as it is typical of us to send a man who, if he has any qualifications at all, has those of a general man of ecclesiastical affairs; and second, it perhaps shows up a difference between the German ecumenical scene and ours. They have been in constant contact for four hundred years of a mainly ecclesiastical kind in Germany. Our national antipathy to Roman Catholicism (it is surely that) is racial. I heard from Schlink again how much has been amicably discussed between the two sides in the past quarter-century. Very great strides in the clarification of the problems of justification and sanctification have been made, so that, as Schlink says, they can no longer be said to constitute a major obstacle, at least at the academic level.

I suggested that it was up to all of us, if we expected great things from the Romans at the Council, to be able to show tokens of reform ourselves. What programme of domestic reform, with the ultimate union of Christendom in mind, had the Evangelische Kirche? Schlink did not seem to understand the question. [. . .]

He commented on the ignorance of the Curia cardinals of the main issues in oecumenical discussion. It was a tragedy that the primacy of Peter had been made juridical as well as pastoral, otherwise it might have been a rallying point for divided Christendom. He is a very stimulating and friendly man, and it is a great pleasure to have his companionship here. He paid high tribute to the speech of the

---

[92] See p. 70, n. 46.

Archbishop of Canterbury at New Delhi[93] and asked me to convey his respects and good wishes to him, which I hereby do.

OLD CATHOLICS

I was sorry to hear Willebrands say that they might have difficulty in inviting Observers from the Old Catholics. [. . .] I suggested that they might ask an observer from the Old Catholics and could reasonably stipulate in the invitation that the observer would not be a priest who had been under the Roman obedience. I should hope they would have the tact to choose such a one in any case.

CARDINAL MONTINI[94] ON THE COUNCIL

What this Cardinal says is always news. The speech indicates the limits of what we may expect from the Council, as Montini is on the left wing. His points were, inter alia:-

a. To understand the Council you must have a clear doctrine of the Church as a divine institution.
b. A full understanding of Peter's position among the Apostles, as revealed, is also essential. The Church is one, and essentially hierarchical in structure, grouped round Peter.
c. The decisions of the Council will show God the Holy Ghost in action in this generation.
d. The main object of the Council is to cleanse the bright robe of the Church from everything which defiles it.
e. The 1st Vatican Council dissolved in a hurry and its findings are incomplete. There have been those who have doubted whether another council would ever be necessary. Now they have had their answer.
f. When the Council is over it will be clear to all the world that Christ's promise to the Church to be with her always, is still coming true.

With the exception of para (e) this is disappointing, but his friends say that Montini feels obliged to make a 'safe' speech from time to time. [. . .]

---

[93] At the third General Assembly of the World Council of Churches.
[94] See *Dramatis personae*, under Paul VI.

Report No 38.   May 20th, 1962

MY BOOK

I mention this item first as being the cause of, and the occasion of an apology for, the long gap in these reports. This has been written in about six weeks in between attempts to do my two usual jobs, and must therefore show signs of haste. But the 36,000 word MS went off to David Edwards three days ago. It will appear in September. It is to be published in the British Commonwealth by S.C.M.[95] and the U.S. by Morehouse, and is to be called 'Looking at the Vatican Council'. It carefully disclaims any official status.

[. . .]

THE COUNCIL

[. . .]

There has been much speculation about the length of the Council. The majority opinion in Rome seems to believe that there will be two sessions, the first Oct–Dec 1962 and the second after Easter 1963, not before it as previously conjectured. But these prognostications may prove to be 'famous last words'. There are undoubtedly forces in various parts of the world who want to do battle in this matter and to keep the Council (or sub-Commissions) sitting until its work is done, however long this may be.

One slightly disturbing rumour (coming straight from Cardinal Cicognani) is that the first (pre-Christmas) session will be quite considerably occupied with ceremonial sessions, canonisations etc. and that this more important work will be done at the second. This seems to me to bear on the question of observers, which is still difficult. If this is true it is clearly not going to be worth the while of an eminent delegate to sit through a lot of such things, when his presence would be more important at later sessions, when weightier matters were being transacted. Willebrands is away at the moment, and I shall have to discuss this carefully with him and with Cardinal Bea as soon as possible.

[. . .]

---

[95] SCM (Student Christian Movement) Press in London, arguably the leading publisher of general theology in Britain. David Edwards was its editor.

Report No. 39   31st May, 1962

[...]
CUBA

I was surprised to find that communist Cuba sends an Ambassador to the Holy See. It was said of him that the only thing he knows is that he doesn't know which leg he is standing on.
[...]

Report No. 40   3rd June, 1962

[...]
COLLEGIO BELLARMINO

This is the Jesuit post-graduate house of studies. The former principal was Fr. C. Boyer, head of the Foyer Unitas. He has now retired and has been replaced by Fr. Furlong, a young Irish-American Jesuit who is a great improvement on his predecessor.

I was asked to lunch and to address the students afterwards. This was one of the most rewarding experiences of the whole expedition. They were very frank and open accepting all my thrusts with apparent good humour, asking interesting questions and openly criticising the Vatican on many of the same lines as we should. The most remarkable thing was the keenness about 'grades of doctrine'. They seemed to be for conciliar government of the Church.
[...]

Report No 41.   6th June, 1962

CENTRAL COMMISSION

[...]
Technical and Organisation
The Council will be held in the nave of S. Peter's, in front of the Confessional in a special structure called the 'Aula Conciliaris'. 100 yds x 22 yds. The basilica will still be in use for public functions. The Aula will be surrounded by wooden walls some 12 feet high. The Pope's desk etc. will be under the baldachino. There will be a portable

altar. And on the altar will be a copy of 'the Gospel' (presumably the New Testament), the same copy as was used at Vatican I. There are two 'tribunes' (rather like small stands at a football match) one behind the main seats at each side, giving a view of the whole assembly. Is this for the guests? Or perhaps the press?

CENTRAL COMMISSION MAY 3RD–12TH.

The commission had a further 'group of sessions' at the beginning of May, of the proceedings of which the following are the chief points:

Theological

The important 'schemata' on the doctrine of the Church were examined. The necessary role of the Church in human salvation was defined as being that 'a man cannot be saved without belonging to the Church, ether in fact, or in implicit intention (ex voto implicito), that is by desire'.

A letter of the present Pope to the Chinese cardinal Tien-Chen-Sin, 1961, has now become a locus classicus, in which he states that you cannot belong to the Church except through the bishops, successors to the Apostles, united to the Supreme Pontiff, successor of S. Peter. The text of the report defines 'in voto' as covering those who would form part of the Church if they could, but who are out of reach of its actual ministrations, but also those who 'through actual grace make an act of sincere love towards God. In such an act there is implicit a desire to belong to the Church if they know of it'. But in that case where do we come in!

Liturgical

There is no doubt that much consideration has been given to proposals for a fixed liturgical and calendar year, including of course a fixed date for Easter, though how far the proposals are likely to prevail in the Council it is impossible to tell. It was said that no step would be taken without 'full consideration of the separated brethren'.

I regret that that is all which has so far come across to me from the May meeting of the Central Commission. Willebrands confirms that there is not much more to know. His comment on the last paragraph of 2 as above was that 'you don't depend on the votum sacramenti at all, because you have the res. Yours is an altogether different, and better, case'.

The Commission meets again June 12th–20th.

SOCIETY OF THE HOLY CROSS[96]

The visit of the Society to the Pope in March got a lot of publicity in the R.C. press in England. The head, Fr. Simmons, delivered an unwise discourse at Pusey House which had headlines in the *Catholic Herald* and the *Universe*.

I asked these people to be careful before they went, but it is difficult to anticipate how undiplomatic people can be. They are open to censure on at least four points.

a. They represented us here as being very keen to open up again the question of Anglican Orders. I have always understood it to be my duty to represent a certain indifference in this matter.
b. They asked Willebrands, Cardinal Bea and the Pope 'what they ought to do in their situation' (i.e. for the most part as being Papists inside the Church of England). Willebrands told them it was not his duty to resolve their personal conflicts and certainly not to give them advice about their priestly lives, for which they should look to their own hierarchy.
c. They asked what 'condition' would be required for a 'uniate' church.[97] They were told that the question of a 'uniate' church did not arise. I wish such people would tell Rome what we expect them to do, rather than ask vice-versa.
d. They gave a general impression of ineptitude, confusion and indiscipline.

All this is a pity. I do hope we can discourage unofficial conversations as much as possible.

JEWS AT THE COUNCIL

The *Observer* of 27.5.62 said that there is 'a chance that Jewish observers might be present at the Council'. There is of course no truth in this. [...]

---

[96] An Anglo-Catholic organization from priests within the Church of England. Founded in London in 1855 by Charles Lowder, its popular fortunes were in decline by this time, but it remained a striking and significant presence in bastions of Anglo-Catholic faith and worship.

[97] Uniate Church: any of several churches in Eastern Europe or the Middle East which acknowledge papal authority but retain their own liturgy.

Report No 42.   20th June, 1962

[. . .]

THE WALDENSIANS

At a lunch party yesterday I overheard a remark which implied what I had already heard rumoured, that of 42–5 students in the Waldensian seminary in Rome some $\frac{1}{3}$ are ex R.C. priests. I have not had time to verify this.

[. . .]

MESSAGE TO THE COUNCIL

Professor Schlink was anxious to know if the Archbishop of Canterbury is going to send any kind of formal greeting with the observers to the Council. If so, could he give some indication of whether it will be formal, or have some content? I said I thought that if any went at all it would be formal. We were sending a memorandum on Mixed Marriages. Schlink never seems to know what the Lutherans will do.

[. . .]

CARDINAL GODFREY

I had a conversation with this prelate a few days ago. The exchanges were courteous but formal, but in answer to his question I was able to say that my reception everywhere here had been most friendly, leaving him to infer, if he wished, that it was not entirely so in England.

[. . .]

OBSERVERS

You will have received the invitations. The Secretariat regret that they can give no information about the duration of the Council, or about the nature of the Sessions. Italian papers carry the rumour that the Russian observers will not come. Willebrands knows nothing about this. What about the expenses of the other English observer? I hope adequate provision is being made for these. Ought we to start the ball rolling on June 25th at the R.C. Committee of C.I.R.? No doubt this has been thought of. Willebrands says that the observers will come at their own expense, though the Secretariat will help them find accommodation if required.

[. . .]

THE CENTRAL COMMISSION

The final meetings are now being held and Schemes for the regulation of Clerical Manpower and Toleration have been under further discussion. The news bulletins give no information whatever, and it is now a common joke that 'never before in the history of the Church have so many words of so many people said so little'. Willebrands was at dinner last night and asked if I had picked up any crumbs of information. I said none, except that I was able to quote the epoch-making first sentence of the Report on Studies and Seminaries, which was that 'The word seminary derives from the Latin word seminarium', which, for what it is worth, I hand on to you.

It is said, however, that there is a great struggle ensuing on the issue of Toleration and Freedom. They seem mainly preoccupied under this head with the freedom of scholars from the restrictions of the Holy Office.

Report No 43.   28th June, 1962

[. . .]
THE EASTERN CHURCHES

Father Thijssen,[98] a Dutch ecumenist of very wide sympathies, and a member of the Unity Secretariat, came to see me here a few days ago. He said that the Patriarch of the Melchites had recently given his opinion that if the Roman Church meant business about unity, it should withdraw the Latin Patriarch from Jerusalem and leave the field to the Orthodox.

[. . .]

---

[98] Fr Frans Thijssen (1904–1990), Dutch priest. Together with his fellow Dutchman Cardinal Willebrands, he was a member of the Board of the Catholic Association of St Willibrord, which, since its creation in 1948, had been involved in promoting a *rapprochement* between the various Christian denominations in the Netherlands.

Report No 44.   4th August, 1962

THE CENTRAL COMMISSION AND UNITY

The Commission was finishing its work as I left Rome at the end of June. Its sessions were wound up as usual by a visit from the Pope himself. His Holiness congratulated the Commission on their work and said that their work was completed. It now remained to the bishops throughout the world to read and pray over their findings, and to be ready to translate them into workable guidance for the life of the Church. The gospel of S. John should continue to show the pattern of high priestly activity which it was the Church's age-long role to fulfil in the world. This activity led up to the high-priestly prayer for unity.

THE COUNCIL PRESS OFFICE

At the end of the meetings the Press Office issued a statement which was widely commented on in the press, as follows:

> On the question of the union of all believers in Christ, there is need for great caution in order to avoid giving way to impulses which may be generous without being enlightened and to avoid the dangers of religious indifference, inter-confessionalism and compromise.
>
> The result of such errors would be the possible aggravation rather than the cure of the present state of things.
>
> The so-called ecumenical irenicism (peaceful relations between the churches) is, in fact, something quite different from the real unity desired and recommended by Christ.
>
> The word ecumenicalism, as normally used today by non-Catholics and particularly by Protestants, indicates a form of understanding – almost a federation with equal rights – of all Christian churches.
>
> According to this theory the churches must consider themselves equally guilty as regards divisions and no Church can presume to be the only true Church of Christ, but only a part of it.
>
> The future Church, which would thus be the result of the union of the different churches of today, would not be the same as any Church now existing, but would be a completely new Church.

This is not a statement of the Central Commission but a scholium[99] or midrash[100] stuck in by the reactionary people who are in charge of the office. The international press reports regarded it as a sign that the forces of reaction were really on top all the time.

My reaction is that we must expect the die-hards to show their hand from time to time and must never forget that they are always in a majority. But it is a dwindling majority and the fact that they have to use these sudden methods to assert their opinions shows that they realise they are under heavy fire.

I have never let it be supposed that the Church of England thinks there will be radical changes in the Roman Catholic ecumenical attitude at the Council. I tend to say, perhaps rather patronisingly, that we are pleased with the progress they have made though we are under no illusions about the further distance still to be travelled.
[. . .]

THE POPE: PERSONAL

It was confidently reported in Rome that the Pope was not going to Castel Gandolfo,[101] but they have proved false and he is now up there. But he has had an old tower on the top of the Vatican Hill renovated with a view to living there during the summer for longer periods than his predecessors.

It was also reported (and I have heard it again in this country) that the Pope was to have an operation in July, though I have seen no press reports of it.

Report No 45.   11th August, 1962

THE BISHOP OF RIPON[102]

The Bishop came to stay with me here last week and we had a very pleasant time discussing the prospects. He had read my reports and most of the published literature concerning the Council. I am glad that the Bishop feels able to put a good deal of time in at the Council,

---

[99] An explanatory note or commentary, as on a Greek or Latin text.
[100] Midrash is commonly defined as the process of interpretation by which the rabbis filled in 'gaps' found in the Torah.
[101] See p. 36, n. 5.
[102] John Moorman (see *Dramatis Personae*).

and if necessary to do a good deal of to-ing and fro-ing. Even so it is not going to be easy to ensure that he is there if required at short notice if a vital question should come up suddenly. He will be there for most of the first session. It is a great relief to think I shall be no longer alone on this assignment. I am informed that Dr. Grant,[103] the American observer, is a New Testament scholar, largely responsible for the New Testament in the R.S.V.[104] It is difficult to predict how the Council will work out in practice for us. I imagine that our team would need to be able to spot an error, if one were made, e.g. in their statement of what was the Anglican belief about the sacrifice of the Eucharist, or to give a quick definition of it if called for! Perhaps we had better take Cross's Dictionary into the observers' box with us daily and hope for the best!

OBSERVERS AT THE COUNCIL

In a recent letter Willebrands refers to my position at the Council. He says it would be best to regard me as 'a fourth Anglican observer, if the Archbishop agrees'. May I say that he does?
[. . .]

ROMAN SLACKNESS

A reliable source recently quoted said that 'in the archdiocese of Liverpool, where there is a great tradition of home visiting, only 54% of the Catholic population made their Easter duties last year'.

THE AGENDA FOR THE COUNCIL

This has now been circulated to R.C. bishops throughout the world. There are 119 booklets with 2,060 pages – which makes even a Church Assembly agenda look small.[105]
[. . .]

At the First Vatican Council, there were only four preparatory commissions, and the projects of two of them, on religious orders and on Eastern churches and missions, never came up for debate. Papal infallibility, the outstanding topic then, was not submitted originally by

---

[103] Frederick Clifton Grant (1891–1974), American scholar; Edwin Robinson Professor of Biblical Theology at Union Theological Seminary, New York, and President of Seabury-Western Theological Seminary, Evanston, Illinois; member of the Revision Committee for the Revised Standard Version of the Bible; observer delegate for the Anglican Communion at Vatican II.

[104] Revised Standard Version.

[105] The Church Assembly of the Church of England, founded in 1921 and very much in its prime by this time.

a preparatory commission but was introduced by a group of bishops when the Council was already in session.
[...]

JEWISH OBSERVER

In spite of Willebrands' firm denial of this possibility to me, R.C. papers carry news of the appointment of a Jewish observer.

Report No 46.   31st August, 1962

MY RETURN

I propose to return to Rome on Sept. 17th and then have an opportunity to go on to Greece, which is irresistible [...]

ECUMENICAL ACTIVITY IN HOLLAND

In January of this year the Dutch R.C. episcopate issued a directive concerning the limits of fraternisation. The main points were:-

a. There should be many more meetings for mutual study
b. There should be meetings from time to time for lectures on neutral territory which can be addressed by authorised agents of both parties
c. There can be no objection to occasional use of churches for this kind of function, or for elementary mutual prayer. This should always be plainly shown to be exceptional rather than normal
d. There should be much more common activity in social matters.

I am told that this encyclical was being translated into Italian, but was withdrawn.

HANS KÜNG

This man's book[106] has swept the world and made the deepest impression. It is believed to have made a major contribution to the preparations for the Council. In a recent article in a German magazine

---

[106] Hans Küng, *Konzil und Wiedervereinigung* (Vienna, Freiburg, and Basel, 1960), published in English as *The Council and Reunion* (London and New York, 1961), was a phenomenon that was soon available in eight languages.

he said that it would be 'morally irresponsible' for the Council to define any further Marian dogmas.

CARDINAL BEA AT HEYTHROP

Fr. Corr came here to give a (confidential) report of the meeting. He said that those who were of a more 'liberal' mind were very pleased with it. It was obviously staged to give the Cardinal a chance to say that the Pope wanted a more liberal spirit in these matters. There was no message from Cardinal Godfrey, but a specially intimate one from the Pope was read. The Cardinal said that the 'polemic mentality must be played down'. Admittedly the bishops must be careful. Too precipitate action would arouse the mistrust of clergy and laity. More objective study of non-Catholic points of view must be undertaken in seminaries. There is no time later. To refuse all discussion of Catholic truth with others suggests that it will not stand up to closer examination. There should be much more cooperation in matters where the faith is not affected.

Fr. Corr said that the meeting was by no means entirely behind the Cardinal. There were those who said openly in discussion that 'it is impossible for those who work outside England to know the situation we have to face here'. But Fr. Corr said that the number of sympathisers was very much greater than he would have thought possible. There is no doubt that much progress has been made.

Bishop Rudderham of Clifton[107] is said to have melted considerably in the last few years. The Heythrop talks are to be published.

MIXED MARRIAGES

Fr. Corr, at my request, put the Roman case about mixed marriages after reading the relevant passage in my book. It was based on the Israelite duty to preserve their people from marrying 'outlandish women' and their being pulled away to strange gods, and on S. Paul's advice of caution in the case of New Testament marriages.

I argued very strongly indeed against their basing any case on the comparison of us with Phoenician women or Corinthian debauchees. I think he saw the force of this. It was very surprising that he could have been so naïf as to mention this, even if he thought it. I must find out how far this is prevalent in manuals of instruction.
[...]

---

[107]Joseph Rudderham (1899–1979), Bishop of Clifton, 1949–1974.

PREPARATIONS FOR THE COUNCIL

There is to be a world-wide novena for the Council from Oct. 1st–8th and Cardinal Godfrey has suggested Sept. 21 as a special day of penitence in England. When Cardinal Bea was in England he made two television films which will be put out just before the Council. This is no doubt part of the carefully arranged propaganda programme being staged by the Romans as a build-up for the Council. Are steps being taken to see that they don't have the field to themselves? I know that Guthrie Moir of Associated Television has asked for a copy of my book for review purposes, but what about the B.B.C.?
[...]

Report No 47.   2nd October, 1962

ARRIVAL

This report is sent from Rome, at which I arrived from Athens on Oct. 1st. I expect to be here until the first session of the Council dismisses, about December 10th.
[...]

Report No. 48   6th October, 1962

THE APOSTOLIC LETTER 'MOTU PROPRIO, APPROPINQUANTE CONCILIO' OF SEPT 14TH

The Church's mission to the world is three-fold, to teach, to sanctify and to govern (the text quoted is Matt.28.19). With this end in view the following regulations are announced:-

   a. *Public Sessions* The Pope will preside at these and the fathers of the Council will vote. These will be of a formal kind and will be sessions to which all business will eventually be submitted.
   b. *General Congregations.* It is in these that most of the work will be done and the general business of the Council transacted.
   c. *Conciliar Commissions.* These are departmental, specialist commissions to which people will be nominated according to their competence. They will only meet ad hoc and will consider questions referred to them. They correspond to the

ten preparatory Commissions, except that the Secretariat for means of publicity has been fused with the Commission for the laity.

d. *The Secretariats*
   1. for the Union of Christians
   2. for technical matters
   3. For organisation

   continue as before, except that of course only bishops are now members.

e. *Ten Cardinal Presidents* have been nominated to take the chair at various meetings. They represent a good selection from our point of view. Only one Italian and a very good sprinkling of liberals.

f. *The Observers*

   They will be able to be present at Public Sessions and General Congregations except in special cases which, in the opinion of the Council of Presidents, would be better held in camera. They could sometimes be present at the Special Commissions, by permission of the respective presidents. They may report to their respective communities on the work of the Council, but are under secrecy as regards any other communication.

g. *Language*

   Latin only in the public sessions and general congregations. 'Readers, interpreters and translators will be at the disposal of the Fathers to facilitate their use of the Latin tongue'. In the Commissions vernacular is permitted. A current joke in Roman circles is that an amiable American bishop, tackled by his clergy about the severe encyclical 'Veterum Sapientia' on the use of Latin said, 'Ah, well, you know, Summus Pontifex locuta est;[108] so we must obey.'

h. *Voting.* A two thirds majority is necessary in all voting. But the Pope has a complete veto.

1. PREPARATIONS FOR THE COUNCIL

The fever of expectation, as may be imagined, is steadily mounting. The press delegates and publicity hounds are moving in and the tempo is increasing. The observers are arriving. Dr. Grant and the Archdeacon of Colombo[109] arrived on the 4th and the Bishop of Ripon on the 8th. Arrangements have been made for our preliminary meetings as a team of observers. In this we

---

[108] 'The Highest Pontifex has spoken'.
[109] Charles Harold Wilfred de Soysa (died 1971), Archdeacon of Colombo; Bishop of Colombo, 1964–1971.

have the very ready help of the Minister to the Holy See and of the English and American chaplains.

A little light relief has been afforded by the discovery in S. Peter's of two time-bombs, near the specially constructed Aula conciliaris. They were rendered harmless, and S. Peter's has now been sealed off.

2. The rest of the items of this report are the result of my first visit to Mgr. Willebrands on returning.

[. . .]

THE ORTHODOX

I gave an account of as much of my visit to Athens as seemed discreet. Willebrands did not seem to question that the Orthodox position was difficult. But he said they were always hard to deal with. They had still not replied officially to his approaches [. . .].

He was very keen that I and everyone else should know that the Roman Church had never received invitations to Rhodes[110] and therefore had not refused them. It was widely rumoured that they had, but that was not true. I suppose he must be right about this?

THE BAPTISTS

The Baptist World Alliance had declined invitations. But Dr. Jackson,[111] the negro president of the Southern Baptists, U.S.A., had decided he would come, on the strength of a casual invitation issued by the Pope in a private interview. He had held a great press conference, disassociating himself from the decision of the Baptist World Alliance and had left America. Since writing this we learn that Dr. Jackson has arrived and has been received as a guest but not as an observer.

---

[110] The Central Committee of the World Councils of Churches held a meeting in Rhodes in August 1956. Pawley had visited a number of Greek Orthodox Church leaders in the summer of 1962.

[111] Joseph Harrison Jackson (1905–1990), American pastor and the longest-serving President of the National Baptist Convention.

THE FIRST SESSION AND AFTER, OCTOBER 1962–SEPTEMBER 1963

Commentary: October–December 1962 – the first period of the Council

Sacrosanctum Concilium

The first document that emerged from the Council, in December 1963, was *Sacrosanctum Concilium* (Constitution on Sacred Liturgy) and it set the tone for the rest of the Council's work. The initial document still insisted on the primacy of Latin in the liturgy and the priest continuing to turn his back to the worshippers.

Some bishops began to question how people could be involved if the priest had his back to them and said Mass in Latin. Maximos IV Saigh, the Melchite Patriarch of Antioch (Syria) and leader of the Melchite bishops at the Council (who was known for his outspoken comments, delivered in French), reminded his brothers at the Council that Latin was a language of the Roman rite and not of the Universal Church. Christ had spoken the language of his contemporaries.

The final constitution left it to the Episcopal conferences in different parts of the world to propose to the Holy See the degree and modes to which the vernacular language could be admitted into the liturgy. According to John O'Malley, the Council 'set in motion a programmatic reshaping of virtually every aspect of Roman Catholic liturgy unlike anything that had ever been attempted before'.[1]

Lumen Gentium

The first draft of *De Ecclesia* (the later *Lumen Gentium*, Dogmatic Constitution of the Church) was rejected as it was considered to be triumphalistic, clerical, and too judicial, referring to its members as 'subjects'. Among the most notable emphases in the Constitution was that the Church was conceived as being the People of God, an earthy, tangible image as opposed to the spiritual image that had been dominant, the Mystical Body of Christ. The longest chapter of *Lumen Gentium* (chapter three), focused on the hierarchy, in particular the

---

[1] John O'Malley, *What Happened at Vatican II* (Cambridge, MA, and London, 2008), p. 139.

episcopate, but was preceded by an elaboration of the meaning of the Church as the People of God in chapter two.

The main issue that was under discussion in the document was the relationship between Vatican I and Vatican II, specifically the relationship between the Pope and the bishops. It explained how the doctrine of papal infallibility functioned alongside the increased emphasis on collegiality among the bishops. The theme of collegiality, which was introduced by Cardinal Suenens, became *the* diversifying subject of the Council. The Belgian Cardinal-Archbishop encouraged the Council to view collegiality both within the Church and in regard to its relations to other churches.

The document also clarified that the realm of political and social change was the domain of the laity: 'the laity, by their vocation, seek the kingdom of God by engaging in temporal affairs and ordering them [. . .] [I]t is therefore his [the layman's] special task to illumine and organise these affairs [. . .] according to Christ's mind.'

Some critics have pointed out that, while bishops were authorized to meet at national levels, there were no clear mechanisms for broad episcopal influence on the Vatican. While the national councils approved local modifications of the liturgy, the changes still had to be approved by the Roman Curia.

Dei Verbum

The *Dei Verbum* (Dogmatic Constitution on Divine Revelation) essentially addressed the roles in the Church of scripture, tradition, and the *Magisterium* (the teaching authority) and of their relationship to each other. The original document, which spoke of two sources of revelation – tradition and scripture – was rejected and had to be revised. Initially tradition was considered to be more important than scripture, a notion which was met with immediate opposition. The Council of Trent had spoken of the Gospel of Christ as the one source to which both scripture and tradition gave witness; the *periti* were strongly opposed to the initial document and Bishop De Smedt and others vehemently criticized the lack of ecumenical awareness. Although 60% voted against the text, the Doctrinal Commission managed to find a technical loophole which said that a two-thirds majority was needed in order to approve/reject a document and that the same text should be used as basis for discussion. The Pope intervened and declared that a two-thirds majority was only needed for acceptance not rejection; the document was therefore to be re-assessed by both the Doctrinal Commission and the Secretariat for Christian Unity. It is ironic that papal overruling was accepted in the same session where collegiality had been so fervently discussed.

Report No 49.   15th October, 1962

THESE REPORTS

I am continuing to send reports in this same form until further notice. The Observers have had a preliminary consultation as to what form their reporting should take. So far we have had no instructions from Lambeth. [...]

Whatever form we decide upon will have to take account of the fact that Dr. Grant and I will be the only permanent members of the team. I have suggested that Dr. Grant be asked to submit reports on theological issues as they arise and that I continue my series, concentrating on matters of Roman Catholic organisation etc. The Bishop of Ripon would in that case add a chairman's summary and comments from time to time. This system is in force until we get guidance from Lambeth.

THE OBSERVERS

This extraordinary body has now assembled. We are a motley crew and are not a good representation of non-Roman Christendom. The Orthodox, to begin with, are not properly represented, as you know. Two very fine-looking, intelligent Russians appeared a day late and strode straight into the limelight. One is an Archimandrite, speaking (or saying he speaks) no language other than Russian – it is difficult to see what use he can be. The other is an Archpriest from Leningrad, whose name I have not yet learnt. Syrian and Armenian and Ethiopian Orthodox as well as representatives of the 'Russian Church outside Russia'. These last have been speaking amicably to the representatives of the Patriarchate of Moscow.

There are Copts, Old Catholics, Lutherans (Skydsgaard and Lindbeck), Reformed (French Reformed, Shaw the Scots Presbyterian and Nichols a divinity professor from U.S.A.), Schlink representing German Evangelical Churches, Disciples of Christ, Quakers, Congregational (Norton and Caird), Methodist (an American Methodist Bishop and Dr. Harold Roberts), Lukas Vischer, representing W.C.C. and two Unitarians (!!). As guests there are two brothers of Taizé, Oscar Cullmann, Archpriest Schmemann of an

Orthodox seminary in New York. Hildebrandt (the one who used to be in England) is in as an alternate. Dr. Jackson, the Southern Baptist chief, has turned up, and has been received as a guest.[2]

The main objection to the Observers is that they are nearly all German, British and American. The almost total non-representation of Africa and Asia is lamentable. The Secretariat have commented favourably on the Archbishop of Canterbury's action in appointing de Soysa. This leads me to wonder whether it wouldn't be a good thing to appoint an African alternate to de Soysa if one can possibly be found.

TELEVISION

On the eve of the Council I took part in a performance of *Panorama*, an evening television programme. The two dramatic personae were Cardinal Gilroy of Sydney[3] and myself, and we spoke from the nave of S. Peter's. They had of course intended to have the Bishop of Ripon had he arrived in time. The main point I made, in answer to the usual questions, was that the Council had certainly achieved a good deal before it started. A few years ago it would have been unthinkable that an Anglican could be televised in the nave of S. Peter's discussing these issues amicably with a Roman Cardinal.

OPENING CEREMONY

You will have seen full reports in the press and perhaps on television. We had most advantageous seats, on special chairs put in front of the diplomatic corps. It is said that the Pope, touring the basilica the previous evening to see that all was in order, saw that the observers were high in a remote gallery. He ordered this to be changed.
[. . .]

OBSERVERS' FIRST MEETINGS

Dr. Schlink and I, as the 'oldest inhabitants' called a first meeting of the Observers, at the American Church. It was a social occasion.

---

[2] One of the most eminent observers was George Lindbeck (1923–), American Lutheran theologian, professor at Yale Divinity School, and from 1968 to 1987 member of the Joint Commission between the Vatican and the Lutheran World Federation. He became widely acknowledged as one of the leading lights in the development of a 'post-liberal' theology in the United States.

[3] Norman Thomas Gilroy (1896–1977), nominated as Bishop of Port Augusta in South Australia, 1934, despite little pastoral experience; Archbishop of Sydney, 1940–1971; created Cardinal, 1946. At the Council Gilroy was appointed to the Council of Presidency.

The Secretariat called us together on Friday 12th for a briefing. There will be regular meetings at which themes will be explained and question can be asked. The Associated Press, we are told, circulated a news item to the effect that 'a secret meeting, behind closed doors has been held between Anglicans and Roman Catholics to begin negotiations'. This again is totally untrue and we hope that Col. Hornby[4] will trace it to its source and deny it. There is no doubt that there are considerable sections of the press who are out to cause trouble, and if possible, even where no difficulties exist, to invent them maliciously.

AUDIENCE WITH THE POPE

On Saturday 13th, the Secretariat suddenly announced that the Pope would receive the observers at 11 a.m. the following day, Sunday 14th. The Anglican delegation immediately said firmly but politely that they regretted they could not attend, as they would be observing the Lord's Day in a Catholic manner. All the Protestants agreed and the time of the audience was rearranged.

The audience was held in the Sala del Concistorio. Two features of it were notable. There is a magnificent raised throne in this hall, but the Pope had ordered an ordinary chair to be set on the floor level. Also, he made the whole of the Secretariat of State's department and the Papal Household turn out for the event, which is the usual protocol for royal visits.

1ST GENERAL ASSEMBLY

This was held in the Basilica of S. Peter's on Saturday October 13th. After the Mass the first business was the election of the departmental commissions. The Bishops had been provided with three documents, a list of all the 'Fathers of the Council', a blank voting paper and a list of those who had formed the preparatory commissions. Had the elections happened that first day it is likely that the bishops would have had to elect more or less the same people who had formed the preparatory commissions, having no alternative. This is what the conservatives thought that they would do.

Cardinal Liénart (of Lille) and Frings (of Cologne) immediately suggested a postponement until Tuesday so that in the meanwhile they could meet and decide who were the most suitable candidates.

[4]See p. 35, n. 3.

This was carried with acclamation.[5] During the weekend nominations have been prepared by national or regional councils of bishops. This can be regarded as an initial triumph for the liberals.

CARDINAL BEA'S RECEPTION

The Cardinal received the delegated observers (and wives!) on Monday Oct. 15th. Practically all the members of the Secretariat were present. In his speech the Cardinal addressed the observers as 'My brothers in Christ' and spoke of the grace of Baptism which had established bonds that are indestructible, stronger than all the divisions. These bonds had prompted the Pope to create the Secretariat for Promoting Christian Unity and the presence of the observers at the Council. The Cardinal referred to the painful fact that a 'good number of venerable Orthodox churches of the East' were not represented, and the necessity to continue to pray for the removal of obstacles which prevented closer relationship. He offered to the observers as much help as they cared to ask for, from himself and members of the Secretariat and asked for positive criticism. He regarded the occasion as a family gathering, a spiritual feast, a kind of 'agape' in the One Lord.

Professor Schlink replied on behalf of the observers.

2ND GENERAL ASSEMBLY

This took place on Tuesday October 16th. Cardinals Ottaviani and Roberti moved that the elections take place without further delay and that the procedure be by 'relative majority', as distinct from 'absolute majority'. This would shorten the campaign considerably. The argument was fortified by the fact that this was the method recommended in the Standing Orders. The motion was carried, and although this represents a slight triumph for the 'old guard', the postponement even for three days was a very important development.

We were given a new place this day, in one of the tribunes, facing the confessional. It was announced that the first meeting for 'disputations' would be on Monday 22nd. The first subject to be dealt with will be the Liturgy. This is regarded as a good piece of news, representing a determination to get down to practical matters first and making theology take its place in the queue, and perhaps even take its shape according to the needs of liturgy.

[5] This was at once regarded as a crucial action to gain some control over the proceedings by the men of the liberal majority.

We have been provided with a first volume of 'Schemata' or motions for debate. I was very pleased to find that I can follow the Latin of the debates very much better that I had feared. But in any case the members of the Secretariat sit with us and interpret liberally. Cardinal Cushing, Archbishop of Boston, who seems to fulfil a role in the Council rather parallel to that of the last Bishop of London in the Church Assembly,[6] asked the group of Anglicans afterwards: 'Say, can any of you guys tell me what language that was they were talking in this morning?' And also 'See if you can find out who the two guys are who are sitting on either side of me. I suppose they're cardinals from some place, but I daren't ask them who they are after all this time.'
[. . .]

Report No 50.   29th October, 1962

GENERAL

Life here is really rather exhausting at the moment. We quite often have a service somewhere before breakfast (often involving travelling, e.g. to All Saints' or to some place where the Observers meet for prayer), long sessions listening in Latin till 12.30. Then there is correspondence, business, interviews in the afternoon and quite often official junketings at noon and at night, to say nothing of our own entertainment here. In addition there are meetings called by the Secretariat. There is no meeting of the Council on Thursdays, but even then we have social functions.
[. . .]

THE FIRST THREE SESSIONS OF THE COUNCIL

These were concerned with elections, and the general issues are referred to in the last report. The main result is, I think, good for us, though time must show. Most of the names are unknown to us: but there is a welcome absence of Irish and Italians, and those who are otherwise our friends seem to be very satisfied with the results.

COUNCIL SESSIONS IN GENERAL

These begin at 9 a.m. with a Mass. There is then the solemn 'enthronement' of the Bible at the altar, which is I think a pleasant surprise to the Protestants. The session is presided over by a council

---

[6]Presumably Henry Montgomery Campbell (1887–1970), Bishop of London, 1956–1961.

of 10 cardinals, taking it in turn to be the Chairman. We sit in a very advantageous position right opposite the cardinals. The loud speaker system is excellent and we have the help of translators as required.

4TH GENERAL ASSEMBLY OF THE COUNCIL

On Monday October 22nd, as previously announced, the Fathers of the Council began their discussion of the agenda according to the prepared 'Schemata', with the section dealing with the Liturgy. Owing to the difficulties of speaking in Latin, the proceedings could not possibly be considered to constitute a debate as we understand it, as in the Convocation or even in Parliament, and consisted of a series of carefully prepared written speeches.

For the most part, the suggestions in the 'Schemata' for bringing up-to-date the Liturgy of the Roman Church are eminently reasonable and acceptable by us. As the Bishop of Ripon remarked, 'If they go on like this, they'll find they've invented the Church of England.' We often comment that the general principles are similar to those of the Preface to the Book of Common Prayer.

[. . .]

Cardinal Montini, Archbishop of Milan suggested that the questions at issue be put to international commissions of bishops who have their finger on the pastoral points. On the matter of the use of the vernacular, he thought that Latin should be retained for countries where Latin was spoken, but that other languages should be permitted elsewhere. Liturgy was made for man, not man for liturgy. He advocated the avoidance of long ceremonies with meaningless repetitions, but that monastic peculiarities should be allowed.

Cardinal Spellman, Archbishop of New York was cautious. He would like to see careful experiments before anything new was adopted. He was not anxious to see independent action and said that the unity of the Church must be evident, especially in worship. He defended the use of Latin generally, with some exceptions as in the case of Marriage.

Cardinal Döpfner, Archbishop of Munich wished for the deliberations of the Preparatory Central Commission to be duplicated and distributed. He also asked for a Commission to be set up after the Council for the revision of service books. The language of the Liturgy should be the vernacular as far as possible. Salus populi[7] always the rule. Regional Commissions should discuss these questions.

[. . .]

---

[7] 'The health of the people'.

Cardinal Silva Henríquez, Archbishop of Santiago said that the participation of the faithful was most important, especially among some of his illiterate.
[...]
Archbishop Egidio Vagnozzi, Apostolic Delegate of the U.S. was very reactionary and asked the Fathers not to renew too much and keep an eye on 'Mediator Dei'. The 'Schemata' he felt, went as far as they ought to go.
[...]
An Italian Bishop made an unusually strong protest, for an old man, against spurious relics which in his opinion should all be collected and burned!

Bishop Kempf of Limburg near Cologne made the point that actions and gestures in the Liturgy should conform to present social conventions. He stressed the need to take the ecumenical view and watch parallel developments in other confessions.

Cardinal Rugambwa of Bukoba spoke on behalf of the African bishops and said they accepted the Schemata with joy.

A (to me) unknown Italian bishop said that if the vernacular were used it would make it easier for the Protestants to 'come over'!

THE ENGLISH HIERARCHY

We were entertained at lunch by the English College and found ourselves in the presence of the whole English hierarchy, including the Cardinal. The Bishop of Ripon and I sat on either side of Cardinal Godfrey at lunch. He spent most of the time asking me about the organisation of our cathedrals. Archbishop Heenan reckoned not to be disturbed by press misrepresentations.

MEETING FOR OBSERVERS

These are organised weekly: the first one started with an explanation of the Liturgical Schemata by a Swiss Jesuit from the Gregorianum, Fr. Schmidt. He gave a very objective account of the background. The Roman Church and the Protestant bodies had much to learn from one another in this matter. During discussion *Cullmann* asked if there was going to be any further explanation of the relation of the Mass to the sacrifice once-for-all on Calvary. The speaker said they hoped to work on the meanings of the word 'representative'. He admitted that there were differences in the Roman Catholic Church in the relationship.

Professor Berkouwer (Holland) asked what was to be the starting-point of discussion if we reject the dispute between 'symbolic' and 'realistic'. Schmidt said that they were not yet certain of the distinction between repetition and representation as applied to the sacrifice. The Orientals had the key to the theory of representation.

Max Thurian, Prior of Taizé,[8] said that they would like to see a more Trinitarian approach to the whole schemata on the Liturgy, though they were pleased it was so Christological. He wanted more mention especially of the Holy Spirit. I asked about the phrase in the prooemium that 'Liturgia, per quam, maxime in suo centro, opus Redemptionis exercetur . . .'.[9] We were a liturgical church and understood the meaning of this. Surely some indication ought to be given, for the sake of the Protestant brethren, that the work of redemption is accomplished by other means as well. The speaker accepted this comment.

In these meetings we find ourselves sometimes in embarrassing company. Two speakers at this meeting spoke of 'the Protestant Church'. We questioned this conception and it seemed to be agreed that there was no such thing. Am I right in thinking that there is a 'World Council of Churches' mentality growing up round the illusion that 'Protestants' are already a homogeneous body?

There is no doubt that most of the other delegates think of the future in terms of 'discussions' primarily, there being too large a proportion of academics among them.

Report No 51.   2 November 1962

PRIVATE MEETING OF OBSEVERS

At a private meeting presided over by Schlink two points were mentioned which the assembly thought should be handed on to the Secretariat. One was the matter of freedom of conscientious objection to war, which was severely limited in Roman Catholic countries. The

---

[8]Max Thurian (1921–1996), Sub-prior of the ecumenical monastic Taizé community in France. Invited as a non-Catholic observer to the Second Vatican Council. He converted to Roman Catholicism in 1988 and was ordained a priest.

[9]'For the liturgy, through which our redemption is accomplished, most of all in its centre'.

other was the hope that the observers would be able to meet groups of Bishops, not treat always through the Secretariat.

I said that although we were quite in agreement with the suggestions we must be aware of trying to function as a bloc of observers. Where that came naturally there was not necessarily any objection to it. But out prime duty was to represent our own confessions only; and any communiques to the Secretariat should normally be in that form. There was no objection to, and much to be said for, communal discussion of themes. Confessional groups should then decide separately to send, or not to send, representations to the Secretariat.
[. . .]

RECEPTIONS

These happen thick and fast. I have been to eight during the week ending Sat 27th Oct. and we have given two dinner parties ourselves. The Bishop of Ripon and I join as hosts in the handsome rooms in the American Church House and we share the expenses.
[. . .]

5TH GENERAL ASSEMBLY OCTOBER 23RD

Discussions in the Council began on the section of the Schemata which deals with the subject of the Liturgy, and was in general terms.

Cardinal Ottaviani said that the text should be revised by theologians. He did not think it was right to say baldly that 'the redeeming work of Christ is fulfilled in the Liturgy'. A fuller statement was needed.

Cardinal Ritter, Archbishop of St. Louis, expressed a desire to draw a distinction between what is laid down by Christ and what is not. There was a necessity for reformation in the second century. There was a particular need to distinguish between modern man and 16th century man. The pastoral needs were paramount. A union between faith and liturgy must always be kept.

Bishop Hermann Volk of Mainz, urged a spirit of simplification. He wanted to cut out all features which come from human vanities, such as pomp and circumstances. Especially in pontificabibus.[10] Exaggerations there are intolerable. This should be made to appeal to the separate brethren, and apply to vestments, music, art, everything. The liturgy

---

[10]Matters relating to the pontificate of the Pope.

is often the only opportunity the faithful have of coming into contact with the Divine. Mass must try to avoid legalism.

A missionary bishop said that the tension between tradition and revision should be solved by adopting a via media!"
[...]
Cardinal Ruffini, Archbishop of Palermo, spoke against the points made by Cardinal Ottaviani and said that this was not a theological dissertation, but a liturgical textbook. It was evident to many who had pastoral instinct that Latin was not enough. The vernacular was essential for the participation of the faithful; also the proclamation of the word with dialogue among the people. Exceptions should be made for solemn occasions, priests' conventions etc., when Latin only could be used. Translations should, of course, be approved. In his opinion people could not attend, let alone take part in, the Divine Office, because of Latin.

Cardinal McIntyre, Archbishop of Los Angeles, spoke in defence of the use of Latin whose retention in these days was especially urgent.

Cardinal Léger, Archbishop of Montreal, strongly approved of the Schemata. He wished to press for an immediate sub-Concilium to revise the liturgical books, not to wait for the end of the Council, and stressed some paragraphs as being of primary importance, as most countries are missionary countries.

Cardinal Godfrey, gave general approval to the Schemata. He could see the usefulness of the vernacular in the mission field etc., but Latin in the Mass should not be touched. There was a danger of confusion in neighbouring districts. And he would rather have tranquillity after the Council than confusion. The fact that a ceremony was introduced in the twelfth century was no argument against it. All ceremonies should be scrutinised according to their present usefulness, not as if they were archaeological pieces in a museum, in which only the antique had value.
[...]
Patriarch Maximos IV, Saigh of Antioch for the Melchites, said that the Roman Church used Greek until the 4th century, and Latin was introduced because it was the vernacular language of the people of Rome. It was not until the middle ages that the Latin language became the universal language of the Church. In the East all languages were

"The basis, in Pawley's understanding, of the Church of England as a church both catholic and reformed.

potentially liturgical languages. He favoured regional conferences of bishops [. . .]

6TH GENERAL ASSEMBLY 24TH OCTOBER

The discussion again centred round the Prooemium[12] and the first chapter of the Schemata on the Liturgy.

Cardinal Gracias, Archbishop of Bombay, urged a very great increase of discretion for Episcopal Conferences in missionary countries. Some of the minor sacraments must be entirely in the vernacular. The liturgy was in part instruction. It was the Verbum Dei in action and therefore must at all costs be made clear. The greater part of his faithful were illiterate. They heard, but did not read. There is no longer East or West as these terms used to be thought of, but a new church of the Gentiles. The vernacular is also necessary to put an end to 'all this bickering about the meaning of documents.'

It would be wiser to make Russian the language of the Church than Latin! He asked for simplification of episcopal vestments. At Vatican I Manning[13] joked that the bishops coming out among the crowds looked like a dramatization of the parable of Dives and Lazarus.

Cardinal Bea said that the Council should leave open the possibility of entirely new rites. The Ecumenical Movement had opened great new possibilities in this field and no door should be shut to developments.

Cardinal Bacci, (the Latin expert)[14] maintained that the participation of the people should be brought about by other means than the introduction of national languages. Epistles, Gospels etc. in vernacular tongues were no better understood by the people. It was possible for them to be embarrassed as e.g. by the story of Susannah. (general expressions of derision in S. Peter's). He even spoke against the indiscriminate use of vernacular testaments. Episcopal conferences would lead, he thought, to diversities hurtful to the Church. This whole speech was very badly received.
[. . .]

[12] Preface or introduction.

[13] Henry Edward Manning (1808–1902), Archbishop of Westminster, 1865–1892; created Cardinal 1875.

[14] Antonio Bacci (1885–1971), Cardinal-Deacon of Sant'Eugenio, 1960–1971; Titular Archbishop of Colonia in Cappadocia, 1962. He was strongly opposed to the use of the vernacular in the Mass. In what was known as the 'Ottaviani Intervention', he and Ottaviani sent to Pope Paul VI, with a short covering letter from themselves, a study by a group of theologians under the direction of Archbishop Lefebvre criticizing the draft Order of Mass of the revision of the Roman Missal.

Bishop Van Lierde, Vicar General for the Pope of the Vatican City, urged for greater clarity in the relations between the Liturgy and the spiritual life. The suggestion in the text that the Liturgy was the *only* means of redemption was dangerous. Doubtful relics should be scrutinised by a special commission. He also wanted a common attempt to introduce the greater Christian feasts into public life: Advent, Christmas, Ascension, even Corpus Christi.

[. . .]

Archbishop Šeper of Zagreb asked for a modification and clarification of a section which was better expressed in Mediator Dei,[15] concerning the relation of the sacrifice of the altar to the salvation achieved upon the Cross. Account should be taken of Protestant insights in this matter.

Report No 52.   9 November 1962

7TH GENERAL ASSEMBLY, OCT. 26TH

Discussion continued on the Liturgy [. . .]

Cardinal Siri, Archbishop of Genoa, said that they should have in mind the receptivity of the minds of the laity. Exaggerations would only confuse them. He advocated a mixed communion on the liturgy and the Discipline of the Sacraments to deal with details.

Bishop Bekkers of the Hertogenbosch, Holland, spoke on behalf of the Dutch episcopate and said that all agreed with the Prooemium and Chapter I. Their theological objections were small; in all things pastoral considerations were to prevail. Someone must consider, he went on, whether the Holy See ought to be leaded [*sic*] with the responsibility of deciding all the questions which might be referred to it. Unless regional conferences of bishops were give a wide margin this was what would be likely to happen.

[. . .]

Bishop Luigi Carli of Segni, Italy, was of the opinion that the place of the Liturgy in the life of the Seminarist was exaggerated. Good Liturgy grew naturally out of holy lives. There should be a central expert international commission of appeal in liturgical matters. He also made

---

[15] Encyclical issued by Pope Pius XII in 1947 regarding the participation of the faithful in the liturgy.

a very strong attack on the dangers of regional episcopal conferences, as lending to excessive variety.

Abbot Christopher Butler of Downside, who subjected us to a great flow of Oxford Latin, said that any doctrinal consequences of changes opposed in the constitution should be made clear. You could go a long way in custom without affecting doctrine at all. Where there was no such change proposed, this should be made clear.

Bishop Demetric Mansilla Reoyo, Auxiliary of Burgos, Spain, asked that a list be made of these extra-liturgical devotions which were (a) permitted and (b) commended. There was much regional variety before Trent, which Trent usified to the good of the Church. (Our minds thought of Cranmer, and the rites of Sarum, York and Hereford).[16]
[. . .]

Abbot Benedict Reetz, Abbot General of the Benedictine Congregation of Beuren, Germany, complained about an opening sentence which was too bald. 'Latina lingua in Liturgia servetur'.[17] What was to happen to Gregorian chant, however, he asked, if the vernacular be used. (Let the Church of England answer that one).[18] He wanted the vernacular to be used up to the Offertory, then Latin for the canon. On the whole a surprising and unconvincing defence of Latin coming from one of the Benedictine abbeys which has been a spearhead of liturgical reform.
[. . .]

Bishop Le Cordier, Auxiliary of Paris, said that he worked in an 'urban agglomeration' with youth etc. who were 'post-Christians', but he had good lay witnesses at work in factories, prepared to suffer for their faith. A Church which was truly a Mater et Magister[19] would talk to her children in their own language.

Bishop Rau of Mar del Plata, Argentina, spoke for Latin America, asked for not only a wider use of the vernacular, but for a reconsideration of any and every gesture and notion. The Liturgical Movement had already shown itself to be a direct inspiration of the Holy Spirit. Latin was not understood, especially in 'Latin' countries! Liturgical participation of the people was only possible if they were fully understanding what was

---

[16]In the Book of Common Prayer, of which Cranmer was the substantial author, these early rites were drawn together and given a new and distinctive form as the voice of a Reformed church.

[17]'Latin [should be] preserved in the liturgy'.

[18]In the Church of England, while the Psalms are often sung to Anglican psalm chants, both Psalms and canticles may still be sung to Gregorian chants, for example at Compline.

[19]*Mater et Magister* (Mother and Teacher), 1961 encyclical issued by Pope John XXIII.

going on. No commentary could take the place of understanding the text. No valid historical case existed against the use of the vernacular. [. . .]

Bishop Stanislaus Lokuang of Tainan, China, said that regional conferences should not make the changes, but should make suggestions to a central international committee. It was wrong to say that Liturgy, as such, was the gift of God, but the gift was grace, of which the Liturgy is a fruit.

Bishop Clemente Isnard of Nova Friburgo, Brazil, speaking on behalf of all the hierarchy of Brazil, argued that it was no good quoting Canon Law to the Council as something binding. The Council was above Canon Law and should change it where necessary. What was the point of granting 'permission to suggest' to bishops – even laity could do that!

One of the most amusing features of these discussions is to note the difference between the actual substance of the speeches, and the report on the day's deliberations as published in the following *Osservatore Romane.* On the above discussion the report read: 'The Council Fathers' discussion on these points was done with mutual exchange of each one's learning and experience. It is not a matter of opposing positions, but of a common and fraternal research through the free expression of different points of view, of liturgical practice always more suited for the realisation, on the catechetical and pastoral planes, of the very end which the Church sets for itself in carrying out its divine mission: the salvation of souls.'

9TH GENERAL ASSEMBLY OCTOBER 29TH

Discussion on the Liturgy was resumed, still on the Prooemium and Cap. I.

Bishop Santin of Trieste said that 'adaption' was not necessary for old churches, but rather a deeper piety and more active participation, much of which could be achieved without a single change in the liturgy. Adaption in ritual, however, was possible and necessary. Bishops should go away from the Council and think this out, then report findings to regional conferences.

Bishop Battaglia of Faenza, Italy, reported that there was no mention of the Blessed Virgin Mary in the whole schema. He appealed for some insertion with the phrase 'in opera nostrae salvationis'.[20] He also made a frantic appeal for the retention of the Latin language.

[20] 'In works of our salvation'.

Archbishop Melendro of Anking, China, (in exile), was anxious that the pendulum be not allowed to swing too far.

Report No 53.   7 November 1962

10TH GENERAL ASSEMBLY OCTOBER 30TH

Discussion was resumed on the 2nd Chapter on the Liturgy.

Cardinal Godfrey spoke first on certain difficulties which arose in his parishes: (i) masses tended to succeed one another every half an hour and therefore a homilia in every mass was not practicable, nor public prayers. (ii) the place for the vernacular was in the private prayers of the faithful, not in the public prayers of the priest. (iii) Communion in both kinds. Doctrinal difficulties had been raised by Protestants against the practices of one kind as used in the Roman Church; the general adaption of two kinds would therefore be constructed as an admission of doctrinal error. There were hygienic reasons against it: lipstick on the chalice (would the women use liturgical colours?) (a heavy-handed effort at a joke). There was also the case of alcoholics. (iv) Concelebration was all right, e.g. on Holy Thursday when all the priests stood around the bishop. Conditions otherwise should be very carefully stated in the schema.

Cardinal Gracias, Archbishop of Bombay, urged that unless the great questions (the use of the vernacular, adaptions of rite, and episcopal conferences), were clearly settled in the first chapter, it was going to be very difficult to consider the subsequent chapters. He stood against communion in both kinds in India for special reasons. He made an impassioned appeal for prayers for India and said that the 72 Indian bishops were having to consider whether to return to their country because of the grave military situation.[21]

[. . .]

Cardinal Alfrink, Archbishop of Utrecht, said that nothing was clearer in sacred scripture than that Christ instituted the sacrifices of the Mass under two kinds. It was agreed that it was difficult to carry this out at every Mass, but opportunities ought to be more frequent than the occasions mentioned in the chapter. Every congregation ought to be familiar with the practice, which must be worked out by the episcopal conferences.

---

[21] On 20 October 1962, Chinese forces had attacked India in the Himalayan border regions. After an intensive conflict a cease-fire was agreed on 20 November.

Cardinal Ottaviani [. . .] The reform of the Mass was a very awesome thing [. . .] Communion in both kinds was quite impracticable. The Scriptural arguments were not conclusive in this matter of detail. Christ was not trying to write rubrics. (He was 'gonged' into silence after 15 minutes!)

Cardinal Bea said that the word 'convivium' in the Preface should be substituted by 'sacrificium'. To 'sacrificium laudis' add 'et propitiationis'.[22] These two emendations come from Trent. The Homilia was already prescribed by canon law at which the faithful were present on Sundays and feast days. The question of communion in both kinds was disciplinary, not dogmatic. Pius IV allowed the chalice to certain areas of Germany two years after Trent. The Cardinal quoted several other instances of papal permissions for this privilege.
[. . .]
Archbishop Ermenegildo Florit of Florence [. . .] wanted homilia only at the more solemn masses. This should be strongly encouraged. (None of the speakers so far seemed conscious of the desire of the Liturgical Reformers that the Sacrament and the Word should almost never be separated, and that if necessary the number of masses on a given Sunday should be reduced. c.f the Book of Common Prayer – where there is a sermon the faithful should not communicate without having heard it.[)]
[. . .]
Bishop Bernhard Stein, Auxiliary of Trier, said that there must be a determined effort to make the word of God really understood in the celebration of the Mass. The whole conception of the Verbum Dei must be restored to its proper place.
[. . .]

11TH GENERAL ASSEMBLY OCTOBER 31ST.

Discussion centred on [. . .] the Schemata on the Liturgy.

A notice was given out forbidding the fathers to 'circulate' one another without the permission of the presidents.
[. . .]
Cardinal Caggiano of Buenos Aires approved of concelebration especially at ordinations and Maundy Thursday. It could be extended to sick priests.
[. . .]

[22] 'The sacrifice of praise' 'and atonement'.

Bishop Iglesias Navarri of Urgel, Spain, was against communion in both kinds. This was rendered quite unnecessary by decisions of private councils. Concelebration, he thought, only for the ordination of priests.

Bishop Nueir, Auxiliary of Tebe-Luxor for the Copts, pleaded for liberty to use leavened or unleavened bread because of difficulty of getting the necessary type in certain circumstances.
[...]
Bishop Devoto of Goya, Argentina, thought that there had been too much detail so far in the Council. He asked that the priest be allowed to face the people, and that considerable streamlining of ceremonial in the Mass should take place. A priest's intentions must not be able to be bought, or, if they were for individuals, to be for others than those present in public masses.

Bishop Nagae of Urawa, Japan, felt that lections and hymns at least should be in the vernacular. Perhaps in countries of the Latin language, they might wish to retain this language, but there was no question that it was possible in missionary lands. The people of Japan would never be able to say even the Lord's Prayer in Latin.
[...]
Bishop Da Cunha Marelim of Caxias do Maranhão, Brazil, was against communion in both kinds because of infectious diseases. The westward position for the mass should be reserved for special cases under permission of the ordinary. Otherwise the faithful would be more inclined to watch the face of the celebrant than to contemplate the face of Christ.

Archbishop Weber of Strasbourg, said that a large number of French bishops were in favour of communion in both kinds. The schema left discretion to bishops, which was as it should be.

Bishop Elchinger, Assistant Bishop of Strasbourg, wished for a more clear exposition of one section, that any changes were by way of evolution of a new liturgical understanding. Conservatism must be resisted for the sake of youth, who could not 'take' formalism and pomposity. They must have a rite that conveyed the mystery of the Incarnation without the unnecessary mystification of unknown ceremonies. If young people did not find communion with the divine within the Church they would go and find it elsewhere.
[...]
Archbishop Neofito Edelby, Titular of Edessa of Osroene. After a very clear advocacy of communion in both kinds, he accused the Council of being under a psychological prohibition lest it should seem to be

under pressure from the 'separated brethren', and less there should be any 'loss of face'. In any case intinction should solve the problem if there was any practical difficulty. The eastern churches, he said, had kept to the 'catholic order' through the centuries. Nevertheless there should not be sudden abandon, but gradual experiment, in the west.

Bishop Peter Pao-Zin-Tou of Hsinchu, Formosa, said there should be clear division between the three parts of the Mass. The use of the vernacular in the Mass of the catechumens would be immediately welcome in China. He thought that the post communion part of the mass was too short and the faithful had scarcely time enough to return adequate thanks before leaving the church. Why not therefore transfer the Gloria to the end of the service? Anglicans exchanged grins.[23]

[. . .]

Bishop Jan van Cauwelaert of Inongo, Congo, said that the bishops of Africa, Madagascar 'and the other islands' were very much in favour of the extension of concelebration. In fact 260 bishops supported the proposals of Cardinal Léger that the matter be left in the hands of individual diocesan bishops. This bishop made a very moving appeal for a new spirit in legislation which was loudly applauded. (Applause is officially not permitted in the Council).

Bishop Boillon, Coadjutor of Verdun, France, made the point that the sick can often only receive liquid. In that case communion must be administered in the second kind.

[. . .]

Report No 54.   12 November 1962

12TH GENERAL ASSEMBLY NOVEMBER 5TH

There were no meetings of the General Assembly on November 1st, 2nd and 3rd, as S. Peter's was being prepared for the celebrations of the 4th anniversary of the Pope's coronation on Sunday November 4th. Discussions on Cap I of the Schemata on the Liturgy were resumed on Monday Nov, 5th.

Cardinal Confalonieri of the Curia made an attempt to suggest that discussion be limited as far as possible to the actual text of the Schemata. This suggestion was not well received.

---

[23]This is the format as set down in the Book of Common Prayer.

Cardinal McIntyre of Los Angeles said that the mass was intelligibly and reasonably performed in the U.S.A. The Epistle and Gospel were read in English and then explained. This was quite enough. There was no need to interrupt the Latin. Sufficient manoeuvre was already allowed by existing formularies.

Bishop Duschak, Vicar Apostolic of Calapan, Philippines, said that there had already been dozens of changes in the ordo missae.[24] All changes should be as far as possible returns to the original forms and simplicities of the Liturgy as far as they were made clearer by advancing liturgical studies. We should not, he said, be hesitant to adopt radical changes provided they help to restore the original commemoration, in its simplest form, to the affection of the people. Christ sat in the middle of the people using the language of the times [. . .]. Then let a totally reconstituted and renovated Liturgy draw all together again, separated brethren and all. This would then indeed be a Concilium Unionis.

The substance of this speech was relayed to my wife on the telephone by the B.B.C. correspondent in Rome, before it was delivered in S. Peter's. Later the bishop concerned held a press conference at which he expounded his points once more. So much for the 'secrecy' of the Council's deliberations!
[. . .]
Bishop Bandira de Mello of Palma, Brazil, said that the Roman rite had evolved spontaneously from the first century and no doubt S. Peter himself had a hand in it. It was therefore a sacred trust which would be tampered with only at peril.

Bishop Cousineau of Cap Haitien, Haiti, hoped that the Council would not hesitate to institute and introduce new prayers into the canon itself if it felt that God's truth was more clearly expressed by so doing. There must be no unchangeable sanctity about the forms of words [. . .]
[. . .]
Bishop Seitz of Kontum, Viet Nam, asked for the significance of the offertory to be more clearly expressed in words and ceremony. Let the people both eat and drink the Body of Christ without limitation. The use of Latin at any point was nothing but a hindrance in the Far East.
[. . .]

---

[24] Ordo Missae (Order of Mass) is the set text of the Roman Rite Mass. In 1969 Paul VI promulgated the *Novus Ordo Missae* (New Order of the Mass or the New Ordinary of the Mass, not the official name). The *Novus Ordo Missae* is the ordinary form of the Roman Rite; the Traditional Latin Mass is the extraordinary form. Both are equally valid, and any qualified priest can celebrate either.

13TH GENERAL ASSEMBLY NOVEMBER 6TH

Discussion continued on Cap II

Bishop Pildáin y Zapiáin of the Canary Islands, Spain, said that a more fluid form of prayers in the Mass should exist for topical needs, particular biddings, etc. The homeless, the unemployed etc. should find that their needs had a recognisable place in the Liturgy itself.

MOTIONS FOR CLOSURE

After a few speeches it was announced that 'the Sovereign Pontiff had given to the Committee of Presidents the right to call for a vote for the closure of a debate when, in their judgement, the subject had been sufficiently treated and there were still Fathers down to speak'. This kind of notice is always repeated in the five languages French, Spanish, English, German and Arabic, which is no doubt evidence that not all the bishops can be assumed to understand Latin.

A vote for closure was taken, which was almost unanimous:

'Surgant qui consentitunt cession sessionis'

'Surgat qui nelant'[25]

Laughter and clapping when no one stood for the 'Noes'.

Discussion then turned to Cap III which deals with the Sacraments and Sacramentals.

Cardinal Ruffini, Archbishop of Palermo, asked that there should be a clearer distinction between the two. The former were instituted by Christ and were effective ex opera operato, the latter were instituted by the Church and were effective ex opere operantis.[26] Therefore let there be no change in the former, but perhaps in the latter.
[. . .]
Bishop Franz Hengsbach of Essen, said that:

1. The Sacraments in general are also discussed under other headings as well (Commission on Sacraments for example). He therefore called for a rearrangement of the material by a commission.

---

[25] Would those who consent to this session's closure stand'; 'Would those who don't, stand'.
[26] 'Ex opere operato' – 'by the work done', i.e. sacraments confer grace when the sign is validly effected. 'Ex opera operantis' – 'from the work of the worker', i.e. a term mainly applied to the good dispositions with which a sacrament is received, to distinguish them from the 'ex opere operato'.

2. Confirmation concerns the Laity. This should be discussed also with them.
3. The sections on Baptism of Adults and Confirmation should be run together. No one should be baptised as an adult without proceeding at once to Confirmation. A unified rite of Christian Initiation should therefore be worked out. This all sounded very Anglican.

[. . .]

Archbishop Capozi of Taiyuan, China, made a very strong appeal for a lively interpretation of all Sacraments and sacramentals by the celebrating priests, and the avoidance at all costs of formalism. The privilege of the cardinals of hearing confessions everywhere should be extended to every bishop.

Archbishop Kozlowiecki of Lusaka, Northern Rhodesia, drew attention to the shortage of priests and suggested that very much more use should be made of the laity e.g. for catechism. Priests in the mission field must be liberated as much as possible from administrative matters, and even from spiritual ones which could be accomplished by the laity.

[. . .]

Bishop Lebrún of Valencia, Venezuela, suggested that the privilege of baptism by laity should be extended because of the shortage of priests and difficulties of travelling.

Archbishop Salazar of Medellín, Colombia, speaking on behalf of all the bishops of Colombia, said that there should be two separate orders of confirmation, one for infants, one for adults. The regulations and canons about penances were too complicated. A form of interrogatory confession for those who were in articulo mortis[27] should be compiled. There should also be more liberty for provincial bishops. A uniform burial rite should exist for all classes, rich and poor! [. . .]

Bishop Cabrera Cruz of San Luis Potosí, Mexico, said that the shortage of priests made the practice of nuptial masses almost impossible in busy parishes. The married should therefore be encouraged to go to communion as soon afterwards as possible (c.f. Book of Common Prayer). Mexican accent very difficult to hear.

[. . .]

---

[27] 'At the moment of death, or a moment before death'. The phrase applies especially to any significant statement that a person consciously makes, such as an admission of guilt or a sudden act of contrition, just as he or she is about to enter eternity.

Report No 55.   12 November 1962

14TH GENERAL ASSEMBLY NOVEMBER 7TH

Discussion was resumed on the Liturgy [. . .]

Bishop Pierre Rougé, Coadjutor of Nîmes, said that the proposals concerning the rite of Unction had perhaps been thought to be contrary to the findings of the Council of Trent. This was not so if reference were made to the theological sections of a sacrament previously ordained by Christ. The prayers in the ritual had always asked for the recovery and good health of the recipient. How could that be if the sacrament were always only intended for those in articulo mortis.[28]

Bishop Angelini, titular of Messene, said that one of the results of the practice of waiting for a person to be in articulo mortis was that the ministration was lost altogether. Much better, therefore, for it to be used in general sickness. In primitive peoples, under the present conditions, far from healing, it kills from fright. The rite needs to be very much simplified, e.g. by the provision that it could be performed on the forehead only.

Bishop Kempf of Limbourg was of the opinion that even if the scope of this sacrament were broadened, they should not lose sight of the fact that it was *also* a sacrament of death, the anointing of the body for the passage out of this life into the life of resurrection.

Bishop Isnard of Nova Friburgo, Brazil, made a plea for the use of confirmation after the age of full reason. The change of the times, universal education etc. demands this.

Bishop Sansierra of San Juan de Cuyo, Argentina, said that the promises of baptism were such as were administered to a child per sponsores. By the time a child was ready for confirmation he should be adult and the promises should be more extensive, containing promises to Christ and the Church. The ritual and the rite of marriage should be amplified to give the pair much more to say and to do. Let the blackness of funerals gradually be exchanged for something better corresponding to the real theology of the matter.
[. . .]
Bishop Sibomana of Ruhengeri, Ruanda, said that on behalf of some of his own neighbours, they welcomed the provision in par. 49 that there might be incorporated into the rite of Baptism such local customs as might be edifying. There were in some parts of Africa certain initiatory

---

[28]See p. 155, n. 27.

rites which could easily be so incorporated. Many people in his part of the world took baptism very seriously and found the present ceremony rather short and unimpressive.

[...]

Bishop Wojtyła, Vicar Capitular of Cracow,[29] said that the pastoral aspect of the sacraments should certainly be kept on top. Christian initiation should not be thought of just as consisting of Baptism, but also of all Christian instruction and catechetical preparation for confirmation, leading up to first communion and this ought to be the order of the rites. (How Anglican can you get?) I made a mental note that we might send in a memorandum to the effect that this was very much the mind also of the Anglican Communion, and that the following out of the ideas had been found to be pastorally very profitable.

[...]

Bishop Malula of Leopoldville, Congo, asked that the bishops of the Catholic Church should unite in approving once more the ancient principle of diversitas in unitas; but then, like the Magi, offer each one what was their own, in union with their fellows. Let there be in effect national churches united by a common allegiance.

[...]

Cardinal Frings, Archbishop of Cologne, spoke of proposals for a further reform of the psalter, not in accordance with classical Latin, but of patristic. Let the Vulgate stay where it can; if not let it be compared with the Hebrew version of Jerome. There should be liberty left to episcopal conferences to allow certain people to be dispensed from the breviary in Latin. Many ordinands came these days from schools where there was no Latin. They were therefore a special case.

Cardinal Ruffini, Archbishop of Palermo, asked that the imprecatory psalms from the Breviary be left out; likewise psalms which used a non-Christian view of the after-life.

[...]

Cardinal Léger, of Montreal, made some totally radical suggestions for the clergy in parishes, as to the recitation of lauds, vespers and 'lectio divina'. The busy parish priest was sanctifying all the hours of the day by his work. The universal imposition of the same rule of prayer on religious and on parish priests was useless [...]. The bishops had a solemn obligation for the clergy in this matter. The disobedience which the present rule forced upon the parish clergy was most destructive of a good spirit. He, further, made an appeal for the vernacular in the Divine office in certain regions, and under

---

[29] Karol Józef Wojtyła (1920–2005), Pope John Paul II, 1978–2005.

necessary circumstances. Great dangers of formalism existed if these suggestions were not implemented.

15TH GENERAL ASSEMBLY NOVEMBER 9TH

Discussion continued on Cap IV concerning the Divine Office.

Cardinal Cerejeira, Patriarch of Lisbon, spoke first and said that care must be taken to avoid the dangers of 'activism' and 'Americanism' and not to let the spiritual office of the Church be swamped by daily necessities. The life of prayer must be preserved. Nevertheless the 7 hour offices, as at present constituted, were not convincingly arranged, and should be reconsidered.

Cardinal Spellman, Archbishop of New York, said that when innovations were made they must not be allowed to be just antiquarian and academic. The vernacular would be quite permissible for private recitation, though it should be borne in mind that the priest even in private recitation was offering the public prayer of the Church.
[. . .]
Cardinal Godfrey, Archbishop of Westminster, said that exaggeration had been made of the need for removing the 'burden' from the shoulders of the clergy. He had never heard a priest complain of the difficulties. There was always a danger of 'activism'. He appealed for the keeping of the old traditions, and insisted that the Breviary must continue in Latin; otherwise they would seriously undermine the possibility of Latin. There should be no further abbreviations. [. . .]

Cardinal Bacci of the Roman Curia, said that $4/5$ of the Breviary was from the Old Testament. This should certainly be revived. At least $1/3$ of the Psalms were unsuitable for recitation in the Christian Breviary. Historical lections should be improved and brought up to date, particularly the history of the Saints. A Commission to carry on this work after the Council would be desirable.

Cardinal Bea said it was not necessary for the Council to decree that a revision should take place. It had begun and was already going on and would continue under the papal decrees. What the Council should do is to lay down clearly the general rules which should govern the revisions; concerning the respective obligations of the religious and the secular; concerning the relation of choir offices to private recitation, and particularly concerning the participation of the laity in the Office from time to time. He made an appeal that the above measures would save a lot of time.
[. . .]

Bishop Weber of Strasbourg on behalf of most of the bishops of France, said that priests who were actively engaged in the apostolate could not possible fulfil all the obligations of the canon law. The Council should lay down the obligation of reciting the office as far as possible. There should then be a thorough revision with the needs of the parish priest in mind, if he was to fulfil his duties.

Bishop Franić of Split, speaking with the consent of all the Yugoslav bishops, said that in their circumstances, with few priests, they were overwhelmed with the obligations. A certain telescoping of the obligations (e.g. meditation into the office etc.) should be undertaken. [. . .]

Bishop Reh of Charleston, South Carolina, said that the whole breviary was designed for choral recitation. How could it therefore be well conceived for the harassed parish priest. The prayers, for one thing, were often responsory. There should therefore be a totally different type of private prayer evolved for the use of the individual priest saying the Breviary alone. [. . .]

Report No 56.   14 November 1962

16TH GENERAL ASSEMBLY NOVEMBER 10TH

Cardinal Ruffini, the reactionary Archbishop of Palermo, was in the chair for this Session and he announced at the beginning that there was to be no more applause. Discussion [. . .] on the Divine Office continued.

Bishop García, titular of Sululos (Spanish), said that there was too much of the Old Testament in the Breviary. This should be rectified with the greatest care by the substitution of the New Testament and patristic passages. [. . .]

Bishop Levan, Auxiliary of San Antonio, Texas, was of the opinion that the more extensive use of the vernacular in the offices, especially in public recitation, would be a help not only to the faithful of the Roman Catholic Church but also to the separated brethren. [. . .]

Archbishop Plaza of La Plata, Argentina, made a speech against those who too easily threw down the cult of images. He wanted to restore Our Lady of Ransom and Our Lady of Mount Carmel to the calendar. (They were expunged at the last revision).

Bishop Čule of Mostar, Yugoslavia, asked that there should be a distinction between the saints of the 1st class, whose lives were of universal importance and those who were of only local concern. A strong plea for greater recognition of S. Joseph was then made. There were too many members of small religious orders being canonised. This man was stopped by the President.

Archbishop Melendro of Anking, China, (in exile), made a plea for the cultus of Mary who was the best of all introductions to the person of Christ. This speech got so sermonical that the President eventually said:

> Omnes episcopi praedicatores sunt; praedicatoribus non praedicatur.[30]

17TH GENERAL ASSEMBLY NOVEMBER 12TH

[. . .] Discussion was then resumed on the 5th, 6th, 7th and 8th Chapters of the Schemata on the liturgy. The fifth chapter dealt with the liturgical year, the sixth was on the liturgical vestments and instruments, the seventh chapter concerned sacred music and the eight and last on the sacred art.

Cardinal Camara, Archbishop of Rio de Janeiro, urged the greater competence of clergy in sacred music, starting at the Seminaries; particularly in the matter of Gregorian chant.

Cardinal Feltin, Archbishop of Paris, wanted a fixed Easter on the first Sunday of April.

Cardinal Rugambwa, Bishop of Bukoba, Tanganyika, wanted a permanent Commission of music experts to be able to encourage the development of native music especially in the new countries.
[. . .]
Archbishop Melendro of Anking, China, (in exile [. . .]) thought that modern art had gone too far in banishing pictures. The Council should lay down that in all churches there should be at least a picture of Our Lord and Our Lady, preferably on the altar.
[. . .]
Archbishop Khoury of Tyr, Lebanon, wanted a redefinition of a liturgical day. There was a general practice for a liturgical day to run from vespers to vespers. He would prefer midnight to midnight. He spoke

---

[30] '[While] all bishops are preachers preaching should not be undertaken for the sake of preachers.'

for greater caution in the mitigation of fasts. There was a tendency to give in too easily to the laity of the modern world.
[. . .]

19TH GENERAL ASSEMBLY 13TH NOVEMBER

Cardinal Ottaviani returned to the Assembly today. His absence had been much commented upon in the Press and elsewhere and the fact that he had not been present since having been 'gonged' by the chairman (followed by applause) was in some quarters interpreted as pique. He chose, however, to return when the same chairman (Cardinal Alfrink) was presiding.

A ruling was made that amendments could be read out but not discussed at length.

Discussion continued on the [. . .] Liturgy.

Bishop D'Amato, Abbot of S. Paul Outside the Walls, made a plea for the universality of plainchant. Students from all nations in Rome, especially Africans and Asians said how easily they picked it up, starting from their own musical traditions. Gregorian chant did not, he said, go easily into any other language than Latin.

Bishop Almarcha Hernandez of León, Spain, asked that use be made of the treasures of music which existed already. Why hanker after more where there was this inexhaustible feast! A forlorn cry for traditionalism. Much Gothic architecture was destroyed at the Reformation, and there was now much danger that modern styles would obscure the value of what had gone before.
[. . .]

CULT OF S. JOSEPH

Cardinal Cicognani intervened at this juncture with a message from the Pope. He announced that the Holy Father had decreed that the name of S. Joseph should be inserted in the Canon.

This announcement was regarded by our friends in the Council at first sight with unconcealed dismay, lest its publication should seem to be the puny first-fruits of the great deliberations:

> Parturiunt montes,
> Nascetur ridiculus mus.[31]

---

[31] 'Mountains will go into labour, and a silly little mouse will be born.' Horace, *Ars Poetica*, line 139.

Some said that perhaps the Pope by deciding to take it on his own shoulders as a Motu Proprio[32] had avoided this very possibility. Others said that we must bear in mind that the Pope was under continual pressure from the 'Integrists'. In making them this petty concession perhaps he was hoping to put himself in a position in which he would later be able to say to them 'You've had what you asked for – now be reasonable and let the others have a turn.'

The discussions continued on the subject of the Liturgy.
[. . .]
Bishop Kowalski of Culma, Poland, wanted all jus liturgicum[33] kept in Rome. It had been one of the surprises (to me at any rate) to find how the Poles seemed to be conservative to a man. One supposed that sovietisation might have chastened them. But they were previously very reactionary. The Polish National Catholic Church in America, I imagine, represents the skimming off most of the reforming cream.

Bishop Taguchi of Osaka, Japan, appealed for simplification of the appearance of churches and of bishops! The Cappa Magna was not a thing which appealed to the Japanese, nor was the taking on and off of mitres during Mass.

Bishop Volk of Mainz, said he was authorised by the Secretariat for Unity to move an amendment to the effect that all parts of the Mass which could be sung by choir or people should be able to be sung in the vernacular, whether to Gregorian chants or not.

This completed the discussion on that part of the Schemata which concerns the Liturgy.

Report No 57.   16 November 1962

19TH GENERAL ASSEMBLY 14TH NOVEMBER VOTE ON THE LITURGY

Before proceeding to the new project on the Sources of Revelation, the Secretary General read (followed by translations in five languages) a communication in the name of the President, Cardinal Tisserant:

['·']With the completion of the discussion of the project "De Sacra Liturgia" it is proposed to proceed to a vote on the following Order of the day:

[32]A document issued by the Pope on his own initiative and under his own name.
[33]Liturgical jurisdiction.

1. The II Vatican Ecumenical Council, having seen the project "De Sacra Liturgia", approves its directive criteria which are intended to render, with prudence and comprehension, the various parts of the liturgy itself more vital and formative of the faithful, in accordance with present pastoral requirements.

2. The amendments proposed in the conciliar discussion as soon as they are examined and compiled in due form by the Council Commission on Liturgical Matters, should be submitted without delay to the vote of the General Congregation, so that its votes may serve for a final rendition of the text.'

This was eventually voted on and carried with only about 50 votes against, some 2,200 voting. The general principles of the Schema had thus been approved. This was regarded by one and all as a great gain.

Cardinal Ottaviani opened the discussion on the Sources of Revelation [. . .]

He then made a general declaration on the functions of a Council in relation to doctrine, which was to bring about *incrementum*, not *renovationem*, of the faith.[34]

Cardinal Liénart, Bishop of Lille, said that the Schema was a completely inadequate presentation of the situation. There was but one source of revelation, from which the two here mentioned flowed. Even Trent said that. The word of God incarnate was the original fount, which he allowed to flow on through the Apostles. The Holy Ghost was speaking through the Apostles before the New Testament was written. The style of the Schema was cold and scholastic. One could not speak so of God's previous gifts.

The Cardinal went on to say that they should have the sense to begin this Schema (in the presence of the observers!) with a clear declaration of their trust in the Word of God. This would have been a better thing to do than to correct errors. Their faith, he said, must not be founded on scholastic disputations, but on the whole word of God. The whole Schema should be rewritten.

Cardinal Frings, Archbishop of Cologne, referred to the speech of Cardinal Ottaviani, and that the Cardinal had said that the first duty of the pastor was to preach the truth. But there were two ways of preaching the truth: one which pleased and one which repelled. In this Schema

---

[34] 'Growth', not 'renewal'.

they did not have the Church speaking as Mater et Magistra,[35] but like a strict schoolmarm! He backed up Liénart in saying that this habit of speaking of the two founts was not really patristic, but dated from the 19th century historicism.

[. . .]

Cardinal Ruffini, Archbishop of Palermo, then came to the rescue. This had all been prepared with great care etc. Why throw it out without giving it a hearing? If they were to have another Schema, they should have to consult all the fathers again and so on ad infinitum.

Cardinal Siri, Archbishop of Genoa, agreed that the Schema was not perfect, but should be used as far as possible. 'Modernism' was still alive and had in fact grown since Vatican I and constituted a real danger. The Bishops of Italy yesterday had decided:

a. There was not an equal proportion between Scripture and Tradition,
b. it should be made clearer that Tradition needed to be interpreted almost entirely by Scripture.

Cardinal Quiroga y Palacios, Archbishop of Santiago de Compostela, maintained that it would not be right to reject any schema at this stage. If necessary it could be amended. The Church must obviously take into account the result of modern scholarship. Expressions and terminology should be as intelligible as possible.

Cardinal Léger, Archbishop of Montreal, wanted a revision of the whole thing in such a way as to show recognition of the great fruits of modern biblical scholarship. The present scheme:

1. had too much dogmatic certitude about things which were not yet decided,
2. the whole tone of the Schema should be made positive,
3. the mentality of the Schema should show confidence in the Holy Spirit without fears of errors; let then the doors be open to all the fruits of modern biblical scholarship.

[. . .]

Cardinal Alfrink, Archbishop of Utrecht, thought that there had been no real attempt to improve upon the doctrine of Trent, even though so much in the biblical field has happened in the meanwhile. The Schema missed great opportunities of removing misunderstandings which offended the separated brethren.

[35] Mother and Teacher.

[. . .]

Cardinal Ritter, Archbishop of St. Louis, suggested that the whole Schema be thrown out and that a new start be made. It was in no sense adapted to the needs of the present day, less clear even than Trent [. . .]

Cardinal Bea did not think that the Schema corresponded with the Holy Father's intentions for the Council which was that doctrines should be brought up to date. The Schema was completely lacking in pastoral sagacity. The whole affair lacked also any idea of the ecumenical problems. All this with an overtone which was most moving.

Patriarch Maximos IV Saigh of Antioch of the Melchites, spoke again in French without apology. This was no time for definitions about the relation of Tradition and Scripture, but about the relation of both to the needs of the modern world. This Schema just represented the formulars of previous years. He renewed his appeal to get down as soon as possible to the Schema De Ecclesia, which was at the back of it all, without which all must remain confused.

Archbishop Soegijapranata of Semarang, Indonesia, spoke in the name of all his bishops. This Schema would be a hindrance to unity because it did not face up to any of the problems. It would make the whole world think that the Church was not abreast of the problems of the present day. Attention should be paid to the relation of revelation to the magisterium of the Church.

Report No 58.   20 November 1962

20TH GENERAL ASSEMBLY NOVEMBER 16TH

[. . .]

Cardinal Tisserant spoke first and said that the Pope was well aware of the difficulties of modern biblical scholars. He was carrying on the work of Pius XII, who always tried to help them.

Patriarch Cerejeira of Lisbon thought that it would not be fair to the observers to let them suppose they could compromise with the truth in order to oblige. The situation of the world demanded that they should say what they had to say, without respect of person.

[. . .]

Cardinal McIntyre, Archbishop of Los Angeles, gave general approval to the Schema. There was in fact much freedom in the seminaries. Any other line of teaching than that of the Schemata would confuse the laity. It would be wrong to set aside what so many experts, teachers, and even Popes, had handed down to them as a sacred treasure.

Cardinal Caggiano, Archbishop of Buenos Aires, said that they had all had a hand in the preparations of the Council. The Schema was drawn up by a most carefully organised network of experts, leading up the Pope himself. [. . .] It was their main duty to carry on the main lines of tradition. What could be done to take into account modern knowledge should be gladly accepted. It would not help the separated brethren to pretend that Catholic doctrine was other than it was. The Pope's intentions were that they should express things in a pastoral way, not that they should minimise doctrine. This, in his judgement, had been done.
[. . .]
Cardinal Urbani, Patriarch of Venice, liked the Schema. Recent biblical developments had done harm in seminaries. Admittedly the expression was in some places too scholastic. Exegetes must be allowed to do their work, but they must be warned that their studies could easily bring about much damage. But on the whole they should be encouraged [. . .]
[. . .]
Archbishop Bengsch of Berlin, did not think that the Schema tallied with the minds of the fathers, especially in the spirit which dealt with the hard labours of those who were trying to explain the Bible to people. It shut doors which not even Trent or Vatican I had shut. Everybody was under the threat of modernism, whether in East Germany or elsewhere. What was needed were clear words concerning the content of the Scriptures. The Schema went out of its way to make difficulties for the separated brethren, especially the heading of magisterium ecclesiae. He could not, he said, go back and give his young confessors a stone instead of bread.
[. . .]
Archbishop Florit of Florence, said that the scholastic method of presenting doctrine was not well adapted to the modern mind. Biblical studies in particular needed a different approach and every effort should be made to make an opening for the new techniques.

Dom Christopher Butler, Abbot of Downside, was against the Schema. It did not fulfil the intentions of the Holy Father. There was no reason why the domestic quarrels of the Catholic Church should be broadcast to the world. Many questions were spoken about dogmatically which were not settled even by the scholars who were investigating them. Some had said that this Schema would do as a basis for discussion. It had already shown itself to be a source of real divisions. It was therefore unsuitable. There should therefore be a meeting between the champions of both sides to see if there could be a basis for a new constitution.

21ST GENERAL ASSSEMBLY NOVEMBER 17TH

[...]
Discussion on the Sources of Revelation then continued.

Cardinal Döpfner, Archbishop of Munich, spoke for an immediate vote and for the writing of a new Schema. He said that the Schema had had a very sticky passage through the various committees. Much of what had been said in the session had already been said in the Central Commission and had been ignored.

Cardinal Ottaviani, President of the Theological Commission, denied that the Schema had been arrived at by anything but the most democratic methods.

Bishop Parente, Assessor at the Holy Office, said he spoke not as an assessor of the Holy Office, but as a pastoral bishop. (He has no effective diocese at all). This was greeted with derision.

Archbishop Zoa of Yaoundé, Cameroons, said that the thing should be entirely rejected. He spoke on behalf of a very large group of African bishops. They approved of what Abbot Butler had said.

Bishop Pourchet of St. Flour, rose to support Abbot Butler's proposition.

Bishop Hakim, of Akka of the Melchites, Israel, also wanted the Schema rejected. He spoke in French, without apology. Ignoring the whole witness of the Eastern Church, and the entire tradition of the Eastern fathers, the theologians of the Roman Curia had succeeded in putting forward a theology of the word of God which was narrow and local instead of catholic.

Report No 59.   24 November 1962

22ND GENERAL ASSEMBLY 19TH NOVEMBER, 1962

Discussion was resumed on the Schema on the Sources of Revelation.
[...]
Cardinal Gracias, Archbishop of Bombay, said that the Schema had had so much opposition that in amending it, it would become unrecognisable. There were not enough representatives of the mission countries on the committee. Let there be another and new Schema.

Cardinal Meyer, Archbishop of Chicago, spoke for the rejection of the Schema because it could not possibly be a basis for unanimity.
[...]
Bishop Martin, Vicar Apostolic of New Caledonia, said that there should be nothing in the Schema which would even suggest the possibility that tradition is ever anything but interpretation of Scripture.

Bishop Henríquez, Auxiliary of Caracas, Venezuela, spoke for all the bishops of Venezuela. He asked for the whole Schema to be rejected and for another to be written in close contact with the Biblical Institute.

Bishop Griffiths, Auxiliary of New York, quoted 'Lord, we have toiled all the night and taken nothing. Nevertheless at thy word we will let down the net.' He suggested making the best of the Schema and asked to hear the experts on both sides.

Bishop De Smedt, Bishop of Bruges, spoke for the Secretariat for Promoting Christian Unity. He said that the Schema failed in this matter of unity. Hitherto one of the hindrances to unity had been the fact that each side had expressed its interpretation of the depositum fidei[36] in language and terminology which was unfamiliar to the other. Care should be taken to see that this was brought to an end by this Council. There must be an entirely new method, free from any suggestion of opposition or urge for conversions. To restate the Schema in these terms would not be easy. There was no need to minimise Catholic truth for the sake of friendliness. Yet they must at least know what the Orthodox and Protestants said about these things.

The Secretariat for Unity was set up by the Pope to help other commissions. It offered to help the theological commission in this matter. They declined. He went on to say that there was a noticeable difference between the 'Ecumenicity' of those who lived side by side with the separated brethren.

He finished with a most moving peroration (which I had to admit moved me nearly to tears) saying that the whole Schema was actually a retrograde step at the very point where progress really could be made – not in union but in the possibility of dialogue – now and in the future. This Schema as it stood would close the doors for a long time and the 2nd Vatican Council would be responsible for a very great mistake.

---

[36] 'Deposit of faith'. The apostles entrusted the 'sacred deposit' of the faith, contained in sacred scripture and tradition, to the whole of the Church.

This was received with applause, in spite of previous prohibition. Ottaviani left the Aula during the speech! (The speech was afterwards seen to be of the greatest importance in the Council and undoubtedly influenced the voting).

24TH GENERAL ASSEMBLY NOVEMBER 20TH

Discussion on the Sources of Revelation continued.

After about half an hour of speeches, it was announced that a vote would be taken on the proposal of the Council President on the question *whether* the discussion should be stopped on the whole Schema and a new one prepared *or* whether the Council should proceed to a discussion of the detailed chapters. This was intended, and treated, as a trial of strength. The result of the voting was:

| For abandoning the Schema | about 1300 |
| " continuing " | about 800 |

which was received with a gasp of surprise by all; nobody, not even the most sanguine, having expected the 'liberals' to be so strong. All our friends, from Cardinal Bea downwards, were very pleasantly surprised. Incidentally although a record of a vote having been taken was published in the *Osservatore Romano* the next day, no figures appeared. They were, however, published in the big national daily the *Messagero*.[37]

It was, however, immediately announced that for a resolution on a doctrinal matter of this character to be effective, a majority of 2/3 was necessary, which this was not. The decision was therefore set aside and the Schema was proceeded with. This seemed at first sight to be a clever manoeuvre by the integrists of the form in which the question was put i.e. if it had been put the other way round the 2/3 majority would not have been necessary. It was later agreed that this was not the case and that the procedure, though unfortunate, was regular. The majority were encouraged by their win, but said that it just fell short of the necessary 2/3.

24TH GENERAL ASSEMBLY NOVEMBER 21ST

The following morning, however, it was announced that the Pope had decided that it would not be practicable to discuss a Schema against which more than half the Council had voted. He therefore

---

[37] Italian daily newspaper published since the late 1870s.

ordered that discussion on it should cease and that a new Commission, representing both the Theological Commission and the Unity Secretariat, should sit and draw up a new one.

This was greeted with applause. The privileges of the autocratic papacy were thus invoked to save the democratic council from the consequences of its own rules. Almost everybody regarded this as a very wise move. It should perhaps be interpreted as the Pope acting as a good pastor rather than as a theological liberal. The communication from the Pope ended with the statement that the fundamental doctrines of the Church on these matters had already been laid down at Trent and Vatican I.

There were desultory speeches on the same theme during the morning of which the only notable one was that of:

Dom Christopher Butler, O. S. B., Abbot of Downside who hoped they would exclude from the Schema everything which hampered the liberty of scholars on things which were not as yet defined. Nothing should be put in which favoured one school of thought at the expense of another. There had been unworthy things said in the assembly the day before which really impugned the honesty at the Pontifical Biblical School and such scholars. This should not be done.

OBSERVERS' MEETING

The usual Tuesday evening meeting for the Observers was called by the Secretariat for Unity on November 20th, and the subject was that of the Sources of Revelation, the current one on in the Council. We were addressed first by Fr. Yves Congar, O. P. Members of the Secretariat for Unity were also present.

He began by commenting on the remark of Bishop Guerry (of Cambrai) in the Assembly where he said that there was no necessary opposition between doctrine and pastoral needs. Those in favour of the Schema, in the opinion of Fr. Congar, were too intellectualist. There were, he thought, two concepts of ecumenism:

Doctrinal. The partisans of the Schema saw tradition only in doctrinal form. For them ecumenism consisted merely in being polite to one another.

Realistic. The belief that there was a real dialogue which was able actually to mould the tradition in such a way as to make it more potent as a vehicle of ecumenism:

Fr. Congar went on to say there were two streams of tradition:

a. The written word,
b. The oral tradition which consisted not only of the spoken word, but also of a whole instinctive spirit in the Church.

The texts in Holy Scripture about the Eucharist were few and not very informative from the point of view of one wishing to celebrate the Eucharist. The real spirit was handed on by the instinctive tradition, c.f. the difference between instruction and education.

A second example was the ordination of priests. The actual tradition sacerdotii was accomplished by the laying of hands by the presbytery without a word spoken.

There were *three tensions in the Council.*

1. *Sociological.* The opponents of the Schema were German, Dutch, French, French African, Indonesian etc. Then there was the Irish group, (especially N. America); then the Italo-Spanish. One could not push differences so far as to cause rupture between the groups. Catholic unity was too valuable to sacrifice.

2. *Academic.* The difference between l'église 're-sourcée' and l'eglise non-re-sourcée'* The return to sources, biblical or patristic had already made a great division. The other side had learnt all their theology from manuals. The 're-sourcées' went back to the Greek fathers as well as the others.

   *He meant a church which has or has not had in effect a biblical and patristic reformation.

3. *Between the Holy Office and the rest of the Church.* The various commissions were chosen widely, except for the Theological Commission.
   In the latter the consultors were not able to speak, as in the other Commissions. The Theological Commission was very conservative: it would have no relations with any other commissions, let alone the Secretariat for Unity.

Professor Cullmann said that the problem brings up the question of the norm. For Protestants the norm was Scripture, for Catholics otherwise. Is that so? If so what was the Catholic norm?

Congar said that tradition must itself find its norm in the magisterium because it had had to decide what Scripture was. A norm must be *living*. The Scripture was fixed. He added that he would like to introduce into

Catholic theology the word 'indefectible' as well as infallible. The latter was applied only to acts; the former to a whole activity. Indefectible admits the possibility of occasional error while guaranteeing the whole process.

Archbishop Heenan, who was present at all this session, then said that as there were bishops present he felt it his duty to say that he, probably they, disagreed very strongly with what had been said, especially the last section. He did not want the observers to get a false impression.

The meeting was then electrified by the principal Russian observer *Borovoj*, who, with many dramatic gestures, then got up and said that for the Orthodox the relations between Scripture and Tradition presented no problem. They had always had an 'orthodox' doctrine.

Then, with accelerating gestures and with great force of declamation, he turned towards where Cullmann and Schlink were sitting and said: 'I wish you Protestant theologians would realise the harm you are doing in picking the Bible to pieces, with your Formgeschichte,[38] without giving people positive doctrines to put in its place. You make mistakes in publishing your immature conclusions. The atheists among whom we have to live use your confusions to demonstrate that all Bible teaching is discredited. You manufacture a weapon with which they can beat our backs. Have you no more sense?'

At this point the meeting broke up.

Report No. 60   25th November, 1962

25TH GENERAL ASSEMBLY NOVEMBER 23RD

Discussion began on the Schema on Communications Media, press, radio, cinema, and television. The Secretary General announced that following this, the Council will discuss the decree on the Unity of the Church, which is called *Ut unum sint*, which will be followed by a project for a constitution concerning the Blessed Virgin Mary, called 'De Beata Maria Virgine'. This project was distributed to the fathers on this date, together with a project on the Church, 'De Ecclesia', which are in a single volume.

[. . .]

---

[38] *Formgeschichte* (form criticism – classification of Biblical texts according to literary form) was introduced by the German Old Testament scholar H. Gunkel (1862–1932), and applied to New Testament studies.

26TH GENERAL ASSEMBLY

Discussion on the Communications Media continued. It was announced that the special commission for the revision of the project on the Sources of Revelation had been constituted. Cardinal Ottaviani and Cardinal Bea are to be joint presidents(!) Other members are: Cardinale Liénart, Frings, Ruffini, Meyer, Lefèbvre, and Michael Browne. Members of the Theological Commission and the Secretariat for Unity are also said to be taking part. These discussions should be interesting!

[. . .]

Report No. 61   1st December, 1962

27TH GENERAL ASSEMBLY NOVEMBER 26TH

It was announced that as soon as the discussion on the project concerning *Communications Media* was finished, the Council would move to examine the Schema on the *Unity of the Church* prepared by the Commission for the Oriental Churches. There would also be separate treatment on the same subject based on the project prepared by the Theological Commission and the Secretariat for Promoting Christian Unity. Reservations for speaking time on the discussion of the Schema on the *Church* were also now being accepted. This would immediately follow up *Ut unum sint*. The Project *De Beata Virginis* would be considered with 'De Ecclesia' of which it formed a part.

After an hour's further debate on the *Communications Media*, it was decided to cease the discussion, and a start was made on the Schema *Ut unum sint* which was introduced by:

Cardinal Amleto Cicognani as President of the Preparatory Commission for the Oriental Churches. He said that this Schema was mainly concerned with the churches of the ancient East. There were difficulties in the way of union. This document was intended to explain the doctrine of the Church in such a way as to make the path of union easier [. . .]

Father Athanasius Welykyi of the Order of St. Basil the Great, who was the Secretary of the Commission for the Oriental Churches, to read the report on the project. Although, he said, this was only concerned with the Eastern churches, the principles were of course universal. They were not concerned primarily with theological unity. That was not in question. An attempt had been made to use terms familiar to Oriental ears, rather than scholastic language.

The situation of the East, he continued, was not just a schism, but a separation. Fratres separati was therefore a term of endearment, not of hostility. The first step towards unity must be psychological. It must be the declaration by a council that all easterns who come to find unity with the One Church would be able to preserve their own rites.

Cardinal Liénart, Bishop of Lille, said that the tone of the Schema was all wrong. It spoke in a too authoritative way of the duty of others to return to unity with them. It was too pleased with itself. It was clearly not able to be of much pastoral use.

It was no use talking about the East alone, as if the East were one Church – this was a great psychological mistake. And one could not treat the East apart from the West. They should be speaking at the same time of the Protestants and Anglicans who were baptised Christians. This should be referred to the Secretariat for Unity.

Cardinal Ruffini, Archbishop of Palermo, thought that this Schema should be put together with the one 'De Ecclesia.' It was dangerous, when talking of unity, to use language which gave the impression that the Church was nothing else than a vehicle for bringing about the union of Christians.
[...]

28TH GENERAL ASSEMBLY NOVEMBER 27TH

[...]
Discussion on the Schema on the Unity of the Church was then resumed.

Report No. 62   4th December, 1962

30TH GENERAL ASSEMBLY – 30TH NOVEMBER

[...]
Discussion on the Schema on the *Unity of the Church* then continued.

Cardinal Wyszynski, Archbishop of Warsaw, said that the urgency of these days, especially as seen by those who were suffering oppression, was compelling to unity. The doctrine of the Eastern fathers led all towards the same goal.

Cardinal Bea. This Schema was not compiled as an isolated doctrinal exercise but as an opportunity of expressing the Latin churches' admiration and friendliness towards the Oriental Church.

Many things overlapped with those prepared by the Secretariat for Union. They should therefore be run together if possible, after they had done Chapter II (de ecumenismo) in the Schema De Ecclesiae.

Provision should be made for combined liturgical prayer. There must be a distinction between doctrine itself and the way in which it was expressed. It was in this latter that much improvement was possible.

Unidentified – probably Archbishop Harmaniuk of Winnipeg, for the Ukrainians, wanted a mixed theological commission consisting of Catholics, Orthodox, Anglicans and Protestants to work out a unified basis of total reunion. It was no good attacking the problem piecemeal. [. . .]

Bishop Franić of Spalato, Yugoslavia, said that this must be considered not 'ex libris' but 'ex vitae'. Before the war thousands of their people went over to the Orthodox for 'opportunist' reasons. They would not now be won back by aggressive ecumenism. It should be more clearly stated that this was a schism between two churches through the faults of both and as two churches they should make entirely mutual approaches again. He proposed certain 'penetential' [*sic*] emendations expressing the acknowledgement by Catholics of their faults.

Archbishop Hayek of Aleppo of the Syrians, thought that the Eastern question must at all costs be kept separate. There must be talk of Oriental churches, for there were so many. There was also need to speak of the Latin and Eastern churches as parallel, and never of return of the latter to the former.

Archbishop Heenan, of Liverpool, thought that it had been a pity to start this with the Eastern churches. The nearer they were the harder it was to find unity. To Protestants they could easily say that they could not love Christ unless they also loved the Blessed Virgin Mary. In the case of the East the greatest reasons of schism were envy and jealousy. He regretted the absence of observers from Constantinople and Athens, and from the total Orthodox world with the notable exception of the Russians. He was thankful that the Archbishop of Canterbury had so readily responded to the Pope's invitation. There was among Anglicans and Protestants a much more ready understanding of the problems at issue, and a greater willingness to try and solve them.

I saw Archbishop Heenan after the Council and thanked him for his kind references to the Archbishop of Canterbury and the Anglicans in general. Heenan purred with pleasure and said he hoped that I would pass the news on to Canterbury, which I hereby do. I refrained from observing that our keenness to be represented in Rome was partly inspired by the prospect of discussing the issues in a climate more favourable that that provided by the R.C. hierarchy in England.

I ventured to question his assessment of the Eastern affairs. My information was that the Orthodox as a whole had been double-crossed by the Russians, who were themselves probably acting in answer to political dictates in order to embarrass the Romans. [. . .] Heenan said he was not sure if my intelligence was right. I said that Athenagoras was certainly disposed to cooperate personally though, like the Pope, he was surrounded by some backward-looking reactionaries. We both laughed ecumenically and went our ways.

It was announced that on the following day discussion would open on the Schema *'De Ecclesia'*. This represented the failure of Ottaviani to postpone this debate until the following session.

31ST GENERAL ASSEMBLY 1ST DECEMBER

[. . .]
Cardinal Ottaviani in typical vein (he is very humorous, and a consummate spontaneous orator in Latin) said that no doubt the 'opposition' had already prepared another Schema, so he would confine himself to saying that the Schema was neither unecumenical, scholasticus, non-pastoralis, or any of the other usual things. 'Tolle, lege; non substituatur'.[39]

Bishop Franić, of Spalato, Yugoslavia of the Holy Office, was put up as official 'relator'. The Schema was the result of much labour. It represented the simple doctrine of the Church received from the past, unalterable etc. as one, indefectible, infallible etc. It should also be noted that a great effort had also been made to make it agreeable to modern biblical scholarship.
[. . .]
Cardinal Alfrink, Archbishop of Utrecht [. . .] There was, he thought, too much insistence on the rights of the Church. There should be much more talk about the liberties of other people which is [*sic*] to be preserved by the Church. The Schema about the Blessed Virgin Mary should be joined on this.

---

[39]'Take up and read; there is no "alternative"'. The first part of the quotation stems from St Augustine's *Confessions*, book VIII, chapter 12.

Cardinal Ritter, Archbishop of St. Louis, said that the bishops were not the whole of the Church, and more should be said about the other orders. There should also be more about the liberty of Christians in general rather than about the rights of the Church.

Bishop Bernacki, Auxiliary of Gniezno, Poland, remarked that there was no chapter about the Pope. They owed this also to the separated brethren.

Bishop De Smedt of Bruges said that the Schema took some account of modern theology, but has many defects.

1. Too much 'triumphalismus', pompous, romantic, as in *Osservatore Romano*. This was far from the humble language of Scripture; from the solid style of the Eastern Church.

2. Clericalism. The whole was like a pyramid, with the Pope at the top and the people at the bottom, ecclesia doces et discerns.[40] Much use should be made of the place of the laity, especially of their part in the life of the Church. There was also too much episcopolatris.

3. Iuridicism, legalism. All validly baptised Christians were members of the Church. The language concerning the separated brethren was arrogant.

Bishop van Cauwelaert, of Inongo, Congo, thought that there was too much legalism about the whole Schema, and not enough of the joyful news of the new redeemed community in which all men can find the home they need, and all the graces. The social work of the first apostolic community was itself an impulse for the growth of the Church. It would help if the Church were more liable to learn from the world around it what it has to teach. Let us talk, he said, less about asking the Protestants having to submit [*sic*] to an authoritative power they don't understand, but rather let us invite them to cooperate in the work of Christ. The whole thing should be radically revised.

The general feeling among the observers was that this had been a disappointing start to the discussion, being too 'conformist'.

Our friends among the Romans said that they were being very careful not to allow a climate of sympathy to build up around Ottaviani. The debate would probably 'hot-up' later.

---

[40] 'The teaching and learning Church'.

Report No. 63   5th December, 1962

32ND GENERAL ASSEMBLY 3RD DECEMBER.

Discussion of the Schema on the Church continued.

Cardinal Spellman, Archbishop of New York, gave a warning against too high ideas about the place of the laity in the Church. There were great opportunities of services already open to them which had not been taken up, without opening up new ones.
[...]
Cardinal Gracias, Archbishop of Bombay, thought that the Schema had great faults but could be adopted by a special commission [...]. The attitude of the Catholic missions to non-Christian races and nations must be more modest, or they would invite persecutions. They should show knowledge of all different modes of thought of Asian philosophers concerning the Christian community.

Cardinal Léger, Archbishop of Montreal, wanted a permanent sub-council to be set up for carrying out in detail the will for renewal so clearly shown already. There should be clear voting and decisions now about the Liturgical Schema so that they could go home with clear ideas and begin work at least in that department.
[...]
Archbishop Kominek, titular of Eucaita (Polish), preached a short homily on the birth of the Church at the foot of the Cross (Our Lady being the first member), which started a notable movement towards the coffee bars.

Archbishop Marty of Rheims said that the Church was essentially a mystery. The Schema made too much of it as an institution. Some people could even make a juridical institution of the Holy Trinity! The same was true of the treatment of the hierarchy. The relation of the laity to the hierarchy was too much like that of troops to a commanding officer. The Mission of the Church was inadequately expressed. It was not to bring salvation to men – this was done by Christ alone. The office of the Church was to announce the grace of Christ available.

Bishop Huyghe of Arras thought that the Schema [was] too inward-looking. It lacked evangelical spirit. It was subject to all the objections brought against the 'two fontibus';[41] too pompous, too scholastic,

---

[41] Two sources.

out-of-date, too juridical. It should be totally re-written by people who came straight from a reading of the gospels.

Bishop Hurley of Durban spoke for the total re-writing of the Schema according to the new principles of unity. Much has been written, he said, of a new conception of the Church, which had been entirely ignored.

Bishop Rupp of Monaco made a very strong appeal for the decentralisation of the Church and the ending of the 'baroque' age of church government.

33RD GENERAL ASSEMBLY DECEMBER 4TH

The discussion on the Schema on the Church was resumed.

Cardinal Frings, Archbishop of Cologne, said there was nothing in the Schema of the Greek tradition about the Church. [. . .] He asked for the doctrine of the Church to be rather scientific, catholic, ecumenical, than juridical. The whole thing, he thought, was unworthy of an ecumenical council. It should be sent back for thorough revision.

Cardinal Godfrey, Archbishop of Westminster, was generally in favour of the Schema. He found it difficult to know in his nation what people actually believed. Now the 'state Church' since the Reformation, called itself the 'catholic' Church. They were called the 'Romans' while there were others who called themselves 'Anglo-catholics'. Let no one think that the non-Catholics were close to them in the faith, and no one should come to England thinking that the problem was easy. They must be charitable, but that does not involve them in making concessions in doctrine or morals; that would be very stupid. It would be no help to the separated brothers, but an obstacle. He spoke frankly lest after the Council it should be thought that they should in any way have changed everything. Caritas sine scientia errat.[42]

Cardinal Suenens, Archbishop of Brussels-Malines, asked what was the main thought of the Council? There should be a coordinating theme. Vatican I was a council de primatu pontificis. Vatican II should have ecclesia Christi gentium.[43] If this theme, which came from the Pope, were acceptable, then they should reconsider the Schema.

The general subject was the Church; what it was, what its job was. He proposed a whole re-arrangement of the Schema in detail. There was

---

[42] 'Love without knowledge is mistaken'.
[43] Vatican I was about the primacy of the Pope. Vatican II should be about the Church of Christ for the nations.

not time or space to talk about the rights and privileges of the Church, but rather of its world. The doctrine of the Church would be clarified in the vigorous prosecution of this programme. As the successor of Cardinal Mercier, he prayed that the work of the Secretariat for Unity would be a pattern for all.

Cardinal Bea said that the present doctrines of the Church began to take their shape at Trent, when the world was so troubled that no one could think clearly. Vatican I was interrupted by wars. Now all separated brethren and they had been thinking about the Church afresh. It was, therefore, up to them to make a real contribution to its clarification.

There were, he felt, certain things to the Schema which were missing. The evangelical commission of the Church must come earlier and be more prominent. And what about the question of who were members of the Church. This was not the time to put out a definition of this, for it was under discussion by scholars.

There should be much more reference to the Scriptural origins of the collegium episcoporum. Then let the office of the papacy be fitted naturally into this. Let all the questions come from the most reputable and ancient sources. A lot of the doctrine under this head is obscure, and should be clarified [. . .]

The root trouble was that the Schema did not correspond to the intentions of the Holy Father, which were that the doctrine of the Church should speak clearly out of its pages and not only to theologians and priests and Catholic faithful but to all Christians, and even to the world.

Cardinal Bacci thought that they should speak of fratres seiuncti,[44] not separate. The former was less offensive, as not involving them in the guilt of a deliberate act of separation. They must be careful to give the separated no suggestion that there were divisions as to doctrine. [. . .]

Archbishop Guerry of Cambrai objected to the suggestion in one of the chapters that the authority of the bishops derived from the Pope. Also the totally juridical treatment of the relation of the Pope to the bishops. This relationship was never mentioned except as juridical. The main idea should be that of a father of a family. [. . .]

[44] 'Separated brethren'.

Report No. 64   7th December, 1962

34TH GENERAL ASSEMBLY 5TH DECEMBER

[. . .]

Cardinal Ruffini spoke first and said he was generally in favour of the Schema.

Cardinal Montini, Archbishop of Milan [. . .] They had heard many theories of the episcopate put before them in the past. But there was no coherent theory of the episcopate here. What was its real job in the Church? What was the place of the Papacy in the Church? What was the real function of the college of the bishops?

[. . .]

Patriarch Maximos IV, Saigh, of Antioch of the Melchites, said that the Schema did not correspond to the Pope's ecumenical intentions.

1. The use of the metaphor of an army ready for battle was not good for these days. There was a spirit of triumphalism which was to be deplored.
2. Ecumenism was conceived too much in the way of submission.
3. Titular bishops were not given full treatment. Were they real bishops or not?
4. The language concerning the Pope was terribly exaggerated. Was the Pope the only successor of Christ?

A certain theological school[45] was continually forcing its theories on the notice of the Council. Let the Council have a mind of its own.

The Primacy of the Pope was not in the succession of the Caesars, but of Christ. Christ always associated authority and love. There were those who exalted the Papacy to divinity. He read some terrible extravagances from an Italian church magazine. Let the world see that this was a primary of service, not of power.

[. . .]

35TH GENERAL ASSEMBLY 6TH DECEMBER

Discussion on the Schema on the Church continued.

[. . .]

This was a singularly uninteresting morning's debate [. . .]

[45]Presumably meaning Thomism, but possibly Scholasticism.

36TH AND LAST ASSEMBLY 7TH DECEMBER

[. . .]
Discussion on the Schema on the Church was resumed.

Cardinal König, Archbishop of Vienna, said that there should be certain improvements. In particular the missionary function of the Church should be clearer.

Cardinal Lefebvre, Archbishop of Bourges commented on the total lack of mention of the Caritas Christi,[46] which should be the chief motive of the mission of the Church. Under this inspiration the whole nature of the various orders of the Church, bishops, priests, deacons and laity would take on a different character, the clergy more humble, the laity more active.

Bishop Ghattas, of Thebes, Egypt, said that the tradition of the East always spoke of 'the churches', taking account of the collegiality of the episcopate. It was therefore arrogant to speak dogmatically of the necessity of union with the see of Peter. It should be held up as a rallying point that Rome should be a centre, Baptism should be the unifying factor among all the Christians.

Bishop Ancel, Auxiliary of Lyons, said that the juridical organisation of the hierarchy should not conflict with the evangelical aims of the Church, and in so far as it does it should be radically reformed.
[. . .]
Bishop Volk of Mainz thought that the Church should be conceived of not so much as the means of grace, but as the fruit of grace. The Schema should be more clearly seen to come out of Scripture. [. . .]

Dom Christopher Butler, Abbot of Downside, hoped that they would not define any new doctrine. There had been many objections to the Schema, and there should certainly be a very radical rewriting.

There had been very much new thought about the nature of the Church since they had thought of it as exclusively the company of those in communion with Rome only. They should define the limits of speculation and then encourage the theologians to go ahead within those limits.

The 'doctrinal mission' of the Church must be to open up the word of God for people's edification.

---

[46] God's love.

Report No. 65   2nd March, 1963.

THE INTERIM

There were of course many reviews in a variety of newspapers about the first session of the Council and speculations about the second. All the papers which I have read agree in thinking that the first session has been successful; that the party of reform showed itself to be much stronger than it was expected to be; that much acceleration of business will be necessary in the next session and that nobody should be too sure in their prophecies about the second session.

Our friends in Rome were pleased with the progress, some of which astonished even them. In particular they rejoiced at the recognition accorded to Cardinal Bea and his Secretariat.

There were some who advised caution. They said that Ottaviani is a very powerful man and that of course machination will be going on in the interim to ensure that not too much ground is gained by the liberals in the next session.

THE BUSINESS COMMISSION

Soon after the last sessions the Pope appointed a septemvirate to review all the Schemata which had not yet been dealt with, to streamline them and where necessary to revise them 'in the light of experience gained in the first sessions', i. e. to see that the Holy Office do not have it all their own way and that the point of view of the liberals finds free expression; also to remove language and expressions which might be offensive to non-Catholics. The seven were Cardinals

Cicognani	Döpfner
Confalonieri	Suenens
Spellman	Alfrink
Urbani	

The three on the left are conservatives, those on the right liberals, and the seventh I do not know about. He is the Pope's successor at Venice. [. . .]

Report No. 68   11 May, 1963

ARRIVAL. I returned here on May 3rd, and propose to stay until June 19th [. . .]

THE AMERICANS I came out here via Berchtesgaden, where I had been asked to address an assembly of the American chaplains in Europe, the American Forces chaplains in Europe, and a holiday conference of their lay people, about 250 people in all. They were very interested in the theme (Unity and the Vatican Council), very enthusiastic about the improvement in relationships and seemed aware that there is a struggle going on in the R.C. Church in the States to minimise the hardness of the (mainly Irish) diehards.
[...]

ARCHBISHOP HEENAN

You will know that the Archbishop has had a motor accident, which has prevented him coming to Rome for the present sessions of the Union Secretariat. Willebrands thinks that Mgr. Heenan must be out of the running from Westminster, or else the announcement would have been made by now [...]

THE COORDINATING COMMISSIONS

These are said to have done their work pretty drastically, both in spirit and in letter, i.e. they have rewritten and shortened schemata 'in the spirit of the debate of the first part of the Council'.
[...]

Report No. 69.   22nd May, 1963

THE POPE'S HEALTH

I have been trying to refrain from unnecessary alarmist reports about the above, partly because even the reliable sources of information seemed uncertain about it. But I have just been with Cardinal Tisserant, the Dean of the Sacred College, who puts the matter beyond doubt. The Pope, according to him, is gravely ill and 'can not last long'. In answer to my question whether he will live to the next session of the Council he said 'most probably not'. On return from the visit I hear that the Pope has missed his usual Wednesday audience, for the first time. We must therefore presumably expect his end during the next months.

PROTOCOL

I wonder if you have any official information as to what would be the correct procedure in the event of the Archbishop needing to send a message of condolence in the event of the public announcement of his sickness or in the case of his death. There is obviously here a slight urge on the part of the unity Secretariat to get everything concerning the 'separated brethren' to reach the Vatican via them. The Secretariat of State, on the other hand, do not want to renounce any privileges. My feeling is that we should be careful to reserve our rights as a Church to continue direct access to the Pope by whatever means have hitherto been used [. . .]. I am told that in the event of the death of a Pope the Secretary of State goes out of office immediately and that correspondence for the Sacred College is addressed to His Eminence the Cardinal Camerlengo, who is the temporary post-box for the College.
[. . .]

Report No. 70   27th May 1963.

THE POPE'S HEALTH

This now seems to be expiring and his death may have occurred before you get this. In any case it is time to consider what you would do in the way of sending a delegation to the funeral. I am proposing to be here until June 19th, though if the Pope were to live that long I could stay longer [. . .]

A NEW ELECTION

To judge by precedents a Conclave would be held about a fortnight after the decease [. . .] At least that is what the Secretariat told me this morning. My memory was that the election took much longer.

I must now attempt to prophesy as follows. The continuation of the Council is obviously the major feature in the election of the new Pope. You will no doubt know that the decision to continue or not to continue rests entirely with the new Pope, who can either erase the Council as though it had never been, or can in five minutes validate all its previous proceedings.

All my sources of information without exception say that it is unthinkable that the cardinals should elect a man who would not carry on the Council, and I think the same. The dominant influence being Italian there are three currents which determine this, one that the bishops would so obviously want it to continue and the Cardinals would wish to satisfy them. Second that a decision to discontinue would clearly be interpreted by the whole world as an act of great impiety against the memory of such a beloved figure as the present Pope, and the concepts of 'bella figura' and 'bruta figura' loom large in these quarters.[47] Thirdly, I imagine that even die-hards want to continue the Council in order to clean up the 'heresies' that are abroad.

It is therefore possible that they may elect a Pope just for the purpose of bringing the Council to a safe conclusion. In that case it might be an old man, such as Cardinal CICOGNANI, the Secretary of State. There are more people who seem to favour this than I should like to think. He would be a colourless chairman, and it is said of him that he has been scrupulously fair in chairing the Oriental Commission even when it went against his own ideas. But he was responsible for the bad text of the Schema on the Oriental churches and reunion which has had a severe mauling at the Council. He is at heart a reactionary, though mild. And he is 81! I think there is no possibility of the election of Cardinal BEA, though some speak of it.

The favourite is undoubtedly MONTINI of Milan. By that I mean that the bishops would elect him in, and the Italian population. Though with the Conclave you can never be sure. It is a proverb that he who goes into the Conclave Pope comes out a Cardinal. Pius XII was an exception to this. Montini's left-wing sympathies are said by some to tell against him. Assuming that it has to be an Italian, he would suit us best. I was among the group who stayed with him in 1956.

Among younger Italian cardinals there is CONFALONIERI, who is a canonist and administrator, colourless and safe. The extreme right, from whom God preserve us, is SIRI of Genoa.

If the Pope dies in the course of the Council that will make the ensuing Conclave different from most in that the College of Cardinals will know one another fairly intimately. I think this would tell in favour of Montini. On the other hand it could make the possibility of a non-Italian Pope much greater than it otherwise would be. There are too many unknown factors for it to be possible to prophesy on that issue. If it were a non-Italian the most likely name among those I have heard is that of Suenens of Malines-Brussels. He has expounded some revolutionary new ideas at the Council, and been loudly applauded,

[47] The 'beautiful figure' and the 'ugly figure' (i.e. making a bad figure, or presenting a bad image).

(on the Laity, on the reform of the religious orders, on the Liturgy and Ecumenism). But he has a very conservative side as well, as you might expect from Belgium, and he is a great devotee of the cults of the B.V.M. A strange mixture.

In the event of the Pope dying within a week or so, would you wish me to extend my stay here to cover the period of the Conclave, Declaration, Coronation etc? I am inclined to believe the Romans would think it odd if I went home in the middle of it all.

In the event of the death, election etc. being before the end of July it is thought here that that would not affect the date of the reopening of the Council.

Report No. 71   31st May 1963

[. . .]

THE POPE'S LIFE

I think that by this time you receive this the Pope will have died, in spite of totally unfounded rumours and even reports (e.g. in the *Times*) that he has revived. The strange drama has been enacted here of the *Osservatore Romano* continuing to put out entirely falsely optimistic reports while the secular papers are speaking of 'the transparent lies' of the Vatican press. The power of rumour in this town is quite terrifying. I was told at 5 p.m. today by Fr. Boyer in the Biblical Institute that the Pope was dead. Even I was disposed to believe that he was right. But it was an unfounded rumour. It is said in the secular press with an obvious double-entendre that 'they will believe anything in this city'.

The Pope has had cancer of the stomach and of the prostate gland. The Vatican papers have persisted in calling it a 'tumorous Growth'. One can not help thinking that this strange behaviour dates from the days when every effort was made to hide the death of the Pope because of the possibility of violent attempts to impose a new Pope on the Conclave.

THE FUNERAL

I am informed by the Minister to the Holy See that in past cases the 'entombment' has happened on the fourth day after the death. This has been semi-private, i.e. nobody more remote than diplomatic representatives has been present. The Requiem is on the ninth day, unless that is a Sunday. It is to that that presumably representatives of other churches will be invited. Incidentally, will our representative represent the C. of E. or the Anglican Communion? Or the Archbishop of Canterbury?

[. . .]

THE CONCLAVE

I think I ought to say that the best informed people here do not attempt to prophesy, and I am sure you will not expect me to do so. Nobody does any more than make a list of the possibilities, and this I have already done. To my previous list I think I would now add that of Cardinal de Joiro, a moderate conservative. But we must bear in mind that John XXIII wasn't on anybody's long list

[. . .]

I hear from reliable sources that the Pope held a Consistory on his death-bed and made some new cardinals. The Pope has delivered a testament to the Cardinal Secretary of State asking that the Council should continue. This confirms my previous belief that the Conclave will elect a man who will fulfil this pious wish.

[. . .]

'THE WOOLWICH SCANDAL' (I use the Archbishop's own description)[48]

I am afraid that this has now reached the English theological colleges here, the Gregorian University, Cardinal Bea and members of the English and American congregations and has done us much harm. I have asked the English book-shop to stock the Archbishop's pamphlet. I am presenting Cardinal Bea with a copy of the Archbishop's pamphlet and of the speech at Louvain which I hope will act as an antidote. The book has also caused wide distress in America. When Professor Schlink was here a week or two ago he commented upon it unfavourably. I have done my best to explain the motives of the book, though not to hide the fact that it is a tactical mistake. Incidentally, I gather from both R.C. and Episcopal Americans

---

[48]The rumpus caused by the publication earlier that year of the polemic *Honest to God* by the Bishop of Woolwich, John Robinson. The book, which appeared to challenge a variety of conventional doctrines, not least about the nature of God, appropriated and popularized certain phrases adopted by Dietrich Bonhoeffer, but very much on its own terms. It was an almost immediate bestseller, and very much a phenomenon of the day. Archbishop Ramsey wrote a riposte which was not widely regarded as his most successful work.

here that Tillich's[49] stock is pretty low in America. He is called the cocktail party theologian and judged to be incomprehensible. Someone said 'the best known and least read theologian in the States.'

CARDINAL BEA

I had a long session with the Cardinal last week. He had enjoyed his time in America and seemed to think that there was a better spirit there now. He said that Küng had overstepped the mark there a bit, and this seems now to be a fairly common verdict. He was apparently misunderstood in Britain in one or two instances. I think he would now do well to lie low. The Cardinal had attended a meeting in Geneva with the W.C.C. on mixed marriages. He said it was difficult to deal with the Protestants because they differed among themselves as to the theological nature of marriage. I said that this did not apply to the Anglicans, and he agreed. He asked me to send his greetings to the Archbishop of Canterbury, which I hereby do.

[. . .]

Report No. 72   6 June, 1963

THE OBSEQUIES OF POPE JOHN XXIII

The date of the official public Requiem has been changed from Saturday June 15th to Monday June 17th. I have heard from the Bishop of Ripon that he is expecting to come, and I think I look forward to seeing him again.

THE CONCLAVE AND CORONATION

The Italian newspapers carry the suggestion that the cardinals will want to have the election over in time to crown the new Pope on the feast of S. Peter and S. Paul, June 29th. I should have thought that this was for them an irresistible temptation to make the best propagandist use of the moment.

---

[49] Paul Tillich (1886–1965), German theologian by then living in the United States; in the eyes of the broad reading public perhaps most notably author of *The Shaking of the Foundations* (London, 1949).

ITALIAN PRESS COMMENTS

The late Pope has had an exceedingly good writing-up, as might have been expected, even when making allowance for habitual Italian exaggerations. The main achievement with which he is credited is that of having flouted the wishes of his Curia and given free rein to the liberal aspirations of the Church in other parts of the world than Italy. The only word of criticism (and this is always very gently put) is that he did not realise what would be the effect in Italy of his 'leftist' political utterances. It seems to be universally assumed that these were the cause of the swing in the Italian elections. It is said even in moderate circles that this might give the Italian cardinals an excuse for 'ganging-up' against the progressiveness in the forthcoming election which they would not otherwise have. It would be sad if that proved to be true.

[. . .]

FURTHER INFORMATION ABOUT THE CONCLAVE ETC.

The Requiem on the 17th will be in fact a novemdiale, counting from and including the day of the entombment and then excluding the two Sundays and Corpus Christ, which are not counted.

The Conclave will begin at 6. p.m. on the 19th, though the elections will not start until the following day. President Kennedy, who had planned to arrive in Rome on the 20th at the end of a tour in Europe has decided not to cancel his appointment.

The reviews in the newspapers about the election of the Pope are very confusing. I suppose they have to prophesy to please their public but their assessments are often based on misinformation and are contradictory.

Two matters seem to be fairly well agreed upon, and both are disappointing. One is that the election must take into account the political situation in Italy. The Christian Democrats were returned at the recent election with a very much reduced majority and rely on cooperation from the Socialists. Their government is thus very tenuous. The last Pope having caused a swing to the left, the reviews say, the new one must surely correct the tendency.

The other thing on which the reviews seem agreed is that Montini's chances have grown much less in the past two years. He has become cautious and diplomatic and has even involved himself in palpable contradictions. But they may be wrong about this too, though I have heard it in other circles.

The reviews give a larger chance than I should have thought to Lercaro of Bologna. Taking advantage of those I have read the colourless Confalonieri is the favourite.

Report No. 73	17th June 1963

[. . .]

THE ELECTION

The press notices here grow more and more like those for the last week before the 'Grand National' in England.[50] You could almost have a daily call-over and shorten or lengthen odds accordingly. At the time of writing the candidature of Cardinal Montini continues to be played down and that of Cardinal Lercaro of Bologna played up in his place. There is no doubt in my mind that in the general public opinion Confalonieri is the favourite. Urbani of Venice and Costaldo of Naples have been increasingly canvassed and there is no doubt that they must be put on the 'long list'. I imagine that the former is the more progressive of those two, and that we might do much worse than to have him. He has at least a lot of experience behind him, and was chosen by the last Pope to be his successor of Venice. It becomes evident that in this method of election and under this present state of tension (there is not usually a dominating issue in an election) almost nobody will get the candidate they really want and they will have to agree on a 'third man'.

I am sorry to see that the newspapers include among the papabili the name of Antoniutti, one of the more recent creations. I had understood that he was 'kicked upstairs' for having made a really bad job of being Nuncio in Spain. He is of the extreme right wing and is a personal friend, it is said, of Franco.

THE U.S.S.R. AND THE REQUIEM

A shudder has been caused in Rome by the announcement that the Soviet Union are sending as their representatives two excommunicated Lithuanian R.C. priests. These men are excommunicated latae sententiae[51] for being 'Quisling' administrators

---

[50] A famous horse race and something of a national event which attracts a great deal of betting on favourites of one kind or another.
[51] 'Sentence already passed'.

under the regime of 2 dioceses whose bishops are in prison. The photograph in the press shows them arriving in Fiumicino airport in lay dress accompanied by a member of the Soviet police. The last I heard of it was that the cardinals were to meet to decide whether or not to receive the delegation.

It seems to me, and to everybody, that this is both a calculated insult and a deliberate embarrassment. It will enable the conservatives in the Curia to say to the rest 'You see what Pope John's overtures to the left have led to', and so favour the election of a right-wing pope.

[*Added by hand*] *P. S. This is misinformation. See next report*

THE NEXT SESSION OF THE COUNCIL

Cardinal Léger of Montreal recently said that shortly before he died the Pope sent and offered to the Oecumenical Patriarch of Constantinople that if he wished to attend the next session he could have the use of Castel Gandolfo. It is not known if it was accepted.

It occurs to me that there is every possibility that a reforming pope, if he were to be elected, might want to postpone the next session of the Council, so that we must not necessarily be disappointed if that happens. The revised abbreviated agendas were to have been sent out at the beginning of June to the bishops. Any Cardinal elected pope would not necessarily have studied them in detail, unless it was Tisserant or Confalonieri. A reforming Pope might therefore feel that he should study at length after he has got his breath and then sent them off at leisure.
[...]

THE POPE'S SARCOPHAGUS

I am sorry to see that part of the inscription on the above, recording the achievements of the late Pontiff, includes the (to us) unacceptable claim that he worked hard.
> 'UT OMNES FRATRES CHRISTIANOS SEPARATOS
> IN UNUM OVILE REDUCERET'
'Ecclesiam' might have done, but not 'ovile'.[52]

---

[52] The Pope worked hard 'to bring back all separated Christian brothers into one sheep fold'; 'church' might have done, but not 'sheep fold'.

Report No. 74   19th June, 1963

THE ELECTION

The cardinals are being walled up this afternoon and it is expected that the election will be completed on Friday or Saturday. I hope to be spared the humiliation of hearing that the Pope is somebody whose name I have not even mentioned in these reports, but I give due notice that that is not impossible. The latest developments here are that we hear much more of the candidature of Antoniutti from civilian sources than we should like to hear. I have already made reference to him and he is very right wing. The Legation here fancy Marella, with Confalonieri as second. The Unity Secretariat, on the other hand, think Antoniutti quite impossible and still have Montini or Lercaro at the top of their lists. I hope it isn't wishful thinking on their part. Some sides, and indeed all sources that I have seen or heard, think it impossible that the new Pope should not want to continue the Council.

I have tried out my idea that even a 'liberal' pope might want a postponement of the Council and this seems to be generally admitted. So we must not be disappointed if that is what happens – it could be a good thing in the long run.

THE REQUIEM

The Bishop of Gibraltar and I attended this on Monday the 17th. Although it was celebrated by the French Cardinal Tisserant there was no trace of liturgical reform. The Earl of Perth,[53] as you know, represented Her Majesty, and we had the honour of dining with him on the evening of the previous night.

We were surprised that there were not more representatives of churches. The Russian Observers were there as usual, pushing themselves to the fore and making sure that they were photographed every few yards. There was also a delegation from the Russian émigré Church in Europe, Schlink from Heidelberg, Vischer from Geneva and a representative from the Methodists.

THE ENTHRONEMENT AND CORONATION

There is a very strong current of opinion that in spite of the short interval involved June 29th (the feast of SS Peter and Paul) will be

---

[53] John David Drummond, eighth/seventeenth Earl of Perth (1907–2002), minister of state for colonial affairs in Harold Macmillan's Conservative government, 1957–1962.

the date. In fact a very reliable source, coming straight from Cardinal Tisserant, said that arrangements were being made prior for that day, and that it would be up to the new Pope to cancel them if he wishes. Invitations will not be sent out to other churches though, if they send them, their delegations will be welcome.

I was surprised and disappointed to find that both Schlink and Vischer think it would be wrong for them to be represented at a coronation, because there is a complex of dogmas concentrated upon this occasion to which they have objection. I argued that the position did not seem to me to be materially different from that of the Observers at a Vatican Council. I added that in my view it was most important that as many as possible of the Observers should be sent as delegates to the enthronement and coronation. If it were an acceptable Pope it would signify our encouragement; if it were an unacceptable one it would be a demonstration in support of our friends to show that our desire for better relations did not change with the change of the papacy.

It is important in this connection to remember that the main ceremony involved is that of the Enthronement of the Bishop of the diocese of Rome. All that takes place inside the Basilica is the enthronement. The Pope is enthroned by the Dean of the Sacred College. It is at this that delegates would occupy seats of honour and I do not see that any delegation would be in any way compromised by being present at it. The assembly inside the Basilica then moves out in casual disorder to S. Peter's Square, where the Pope appears on the balcony and is crowned with the tiara. Nobody is officially present at this ceremony except the small party on the balcony. The origin of the ceremony is that of investiture with the sovereignty of the Vatican kingdom. The Pope is only crowned by the senior cardinal deacon. Our friends in the Vatican will get additional delight if they have to see Montini crowned by his enemy Ottaviani. In the processions the mitre is always carried before a tiara. Both ceremonies are formal public recognitions, comparable to the enthronement of a bishop in an English diocese. They have no legal or sacramental significance. Cases have occurred in which cardinals who were only in priest[']s orders have been elected Pope. The last case was that of Gregory XVI in the middle of the last century. Such a man became Pope immediately on acceptance of election. Cardinal Tisserant will enthrone the new Pope as Bishop of Rome. I am inclined to think that you would be wise to refer to the whole ceremony in any public statement as the 'Enthronement and Coronation of XXXX as Bishop of Rome and Pope'.

[. . .]

THE U.S.S.R. DELEGATION TO THE REQUIEM

My item on the above was based on misinformation contained in the newspapers. The men who represented the U.S.S.R. were not excommunicate; they were in fact vicars capitular duly elected by the Chapters of the dioceses whose bishops were in prison, to act as Ordinaries during the bishops' inhibition. This is in full accord with canon law. It is interesting to note how the Vatican are dealing with the situation in the countries east of the iron curtain, where bishops are under civil censure. A member of the cathedral chapter is elected to be the legal Ordinary of the diocese and a priest in the diocese is then consecrated bishop to a titular see to perform the episcopal functions. He does not have full canonical jurisdiction, which resides legally in the Ordinary.

THE SECRETARIAT AND THE FUTURE

All the staff seem to be optimistic. Willebrands today said that an unprogressive Pope might hold up the work of the Secretariat in certain respects only for a period, but there was no possibility of its being closed down. He said that there had been critics of the late Pope's attitude to politics, to ecclesiastical administration, and his attempts at theology, but nobody had dared gainsay his attitude to ecumenism. The Unity Secretariat regarded as symptomatic that although most of the caretaker cardinals are reactionaries nobody has dismissed Capovilla the late Pope's chief chaplain, who is being allowed to stay on to see if the next Pope wishes to continue him in the service. In the last interregnum there was a thorough and immediate clear-out of all Pius XII's staff.

Report No. 75   21st June, 1963

A CORRECTION

In a previous report (No. 72) I referred to Cardinal ROBERTI as a liberal. This was mistaken. He is a Curia Cardinal and a canonist. He is spoken of by some as being, because of his neutrality and legislative experience, a good man to bring the Council to a conclusion and to implement its deliberations. He is most unimpressive to look at.
[. . .]

THE CONCLAVE

The cardinals were walled up on the 19th and there were four votings yesterday the 20th. The smoke is put up the chimney after every second vote if they are negative. All four votes yesterday have been negative. Apparently the method of voting is straight, with no proposition of candidates. The cardinals adjust their votes each time according to the 'form' of the previous voting. The first vote of all is a 'homage' vote from which an election is not usually made.

The appearance on the balcony is said to be generally about half an hour after the acceptance of the Papacy.

THE CONCLAVE ORATION

This was preached before the cardinals on the evening of the 19th before they were enclosed. It was preached by Mgr. Amleto Tondini, the Latin expert of the department of 'letters to heads of state.' It was heavily dosed with the 'rightest' sentiments, and was obviously 'inspired' by some of the influences in the Vatican unfavourable to us.

The oration was as nearly critical of Pope John as it dared to be. After lengthy eulogies of him it said that he had left a difficult task for his successor. The people recognised in him goodness and a desire for peace, but were those yearnings the only needs of mankind which it was the Church's duty to satisfy! A more important task of the new Pope would be to safeguard the Catholic faith against the dangers of modernism and relativism. The Pope's aim in calling the Council had been to safeguard the Catholic faith by demonstrating its adaptability to the needs of the present day. He also had invited the separated brethren 'being desirous to provide more securely for their eternal salvation, to return to the Church of Christ'!!! (One is conscious here of a deliberate, arrogant return to the offensive type of pre-Roncalli).

As if the foregoing weren't enough the orator went on to say that the new Pope would certainly have to bring the Council to a conclusion at some time or other, but he would have to consider very carefully whether the present was the best time to do so. He said that the Catholic Church must beware of toying with communism or with any other set of erroneous ideas which were deceiving mankind at the present moment. The proper course for the new Pontiff to adopt was to show the world that the Catholic Church was not to be blown away by every blast of strange doctrine, but that its dogmas were unchangeable. He should steer the ship of Peter for the advantage of all, but particularly of the Catholics.

This oration, which was obviously inspired by the extreme right of the Curia, caused a wave of irritation to sweep over the city of Rome. There was however a credible source of information, stemming from members of the Sacred College itself (who were not as yet enclosed) that such a speech would probably have the effect, if it had any effect at all, of encouraging the 'left' and perhaps even of moving to the left some of the waverers in the centre, who would thus have had a gratuitous demonstration of what they might be in for if they had a Pope of the right. The Secretariat for Unity say we are to disregard it.

| Report No. 76 | 21st June, 1963 |

POPE PAUL VI

Cardinal Montini was elected this morning after the first count of the day and in a comparatively short conclave. I was present in S. Peter's Square, having hurried down there after seeing the white smoke on the television. The timing made Montini's chances very high and there was general expectation in the square that it would be him. I met the Unity Secretariat men there and enjoyed their company throughout. The Cardinal Deacon (Ottaviani) had to announce the election and he did it with gusto considering how unacceptable it must have been to him. He will also have to perform the coronation.

All the Secretariat staff and several other people I met think it quite possible that the reactionary oration (which was summarised in the last report) at the Conclave might have had an effect contrary to what was intended.

There is considerable pleasure that the new Pope has taken the title of the Apostle of the Gentiles and it is hoped that this is significant. The idea of Paul at the helm of the ship of Peter is a suggestive one.

The Pope eventually appeared on the balcony and gave a blessing. The applause in the Square was most moving. I must admit that I was very moved at the announcement. I was naturally thinking of the thrilling time we had at Milan in 1955 [*sic*] with Montini and of how he had said that we should live to see considerable change in Christian relations in our lifetime.

I went back to the Secretariat afterwards and asked if I could procure a bottle of champagne and bring it in, which I did. We then all toasted the new Pope and the cause of Christian union. Willebrands made a neat little speech in which he said that this was certainly a great day for them, and he was sure it would be also for the Church of England. He said that the spontaneous response of the Church of England to the policy of John XXIII had certainly been appreciated in Roman circles, and who was to say that it was not without influence in the course of events which had led to this happy moment.

This has been an exciting day and I will refrain from attempting any further evaluation of the new Pope except to say that in my opinion Pope John's surprising overture, which was endorsed by the bishops in Council more strongly than we could have hoped, has now penetrated right into the Vatican itself to be a certain sign that God's hand is guiding our brethren of the Roman Church to better things. Nobody should suppose that Paul VI, or any other Pope, can undo the tangled skein of 400 years separation in a generation. But his election is certainly further confirmation that it is worth our while pursuing the path we have begun and that there is real ground to hope and pray for the eventual reunion of Christendom.

Report No. 77	26th June, 1963

POPE PAOLO VI

It still seems too good to be true that Cardinal Montini was elected Pope, and everybody here is very happy about it. There can now be no doubt that the papers were deliberately trying to play down Montini's candidature for political reasons. I hope it is realised what 'being Political' amounts to in Italy. Any Pope or Bishop who dares to say (what is evident to the eyes) that there is a gross maldistribution of wealth in Italy, is being 'political' and is guilty of 'leftist' tendencies. Anyone who says that atheistic communism is a danger to the liberties of man tends to be called a 'rightist' or 'neo-fascist'. Very often what is called 'political interferences' is a necessary and reasonable application of the second Commandment in cases where to be silent would be to betray the gospel and the priestly office. Similarly, to be known to have views about the reform of the Curia is to be 'political'. In all these senses Montini is a 'political' Pope, and long may he continue to be so.

There have of course been many speculations as to how the election came about. It was accomplished quickly, and with no bones broken. It is said that he was elected on the first day and asked the cardinals to 'sleep on it'. Two of his protagonists are said in all the papers to have been decisive. The flamboyant Cushing of Boston is said to have swayed all the South American cardinals and even to have stampeded Spellman of New York. But it was apparently Micara, one of the old curia cardinals, who persuaded his curia brethren that they stood no chance, and also that there must be no bargaining. In some previous appointments there have been instances of mild simony when a Pope has been elected after promising to have someone of the opposite faction as Secretary of State. Montini evidently did not do this, as he immediately confirmed Cicognani, John XXIII's nominee, in his office. Incidentally, the newspapers have taken to referring to the 'rightest' or 'integrist' cardinals also as the 'dogmatists'.

THE ESTABLISHMENT AND THE ITALIAN PRESS

I have recently written five letters to editors of Italian magazines and newspapers correcting the continual suggestion that the Queen is hierarchical head of the Anglican Church and that the establishment is more onerous than it is in fact. It may interest you to hear that the article by Alberto Spada of the Europeo was headed 'Pope and Queen'. It carries a photograph of the Queen 'as Head of the Anglican Church consecrating Guildford Cathedral'. This is really intolerable, and I am taking some cuttings to Cardinal Bea. In my mind one of the strongest arguments for disestablishment (for which I am not a fanatical enthusiast) is the false impression it gives of the whole Anglican Communion. I had to explain to the Abbot General of the Benedictines that the Queen had no relationship to PECUSA – it is a bad as that. Fortunately the articles always all call her the 'Head of the Anglican Church' which one can deny outright. It is surprising how few people realise that such connections as there are obtain only in the two English provinces, not even in Wales or Scotland.
[. . .]

THE SECOND SESSION OF THE COUNCIL

I have just been told by the British Minister that the Council will re-assemble on September 29th. It is interesting to note, that for the first time, the Council is to have as its opening (or closing) date, a day which is not a feast of the Blessed Virgin Mary.

COMMUNICATION WITH THE POPE.

I have written a personal letter to the Pope on the strength of my personal association and hope this will reach him. I wish it had been possible to have an audience before we come away next Monday, but it would not be reasonable to ask, though I have given him notice that I intend to ask for one next time. It might be possible to exploit this situation so that we have a really trustworthy straight 'private line' to His Holiness. I have just been with Cardinal Tisserant who, without my mentioning the matter said 'You should use your previous acquaintance with the Pope to see that he has *direct* information about what is in your minds.'

CONTINUATION OF THE COUNCIL

Cardinal Tisserant told me today that he thought the Council must almost certainly have a third session, in the Spring or Summer of 1964.

Report No. 78   1st July, 1963

CARDINAL BEA

I had a farewell interview with the Cardinal last Friday 28th June. He asked me to convey his greetings to the Archbishop of Canterbury. He is hoping to have at least a month's rest during the summer.

Concerning the conclave he confirmed what had been rumoured in the papers, that the 'right' hadn't really a candidate who stood a chance. Cardinal Micara, one of the Curia cardinals, therefore suggested that the 'right' should own themselves defeated and support the 'left' which they meekly did. He was supported by Cardinals Testa, Cento and Confalonieri.

THE COUNCIL

Everybody now seems to think it is likely that there will be a third session of the Council, perhaps after Easter 1964.
[. . .]

R.C. ARCHBISHOP OF WESTMINSTER

The Apostolic Delegate[54] was in Rome on Friday last and had an audience with the Pope, presumably for this purpose. Cardinal Bea is against Heenan's nomination and in favour of Holland of Portsmouth, though he would welcome Abbot Butler providing he has the necessary administrative capacity about which he is not certain.

---

[54] Gerald O'Hara (1895–1963) was the Apostolic Delegate to Great Britain from 1954 until his sudden death on 16 July 1963.

THE POPE

I had intended to return, as you know, on Monday July 1st. According to the usual pattern of events out here I learnt at 10.30 p.m. the previous evening that the new Pope wished to see us the following day at noon. Accordingly I rearranged my passage and was able to be at the audience, at which His Holiness received the two Russian observers, Bishop Kotliarov and Archpriest Borovoj, the Bishop of Ripon and myself, Brother André of Taizé and the Rector of the American Episcopal Church in Rome.

This was the first private audience of the new Pope's reign other than those normally given to Heads of State and their representatives and to Roman Catholic prelates.

His Holiness received us in the Library most cordially. He spoke specially warmly to the Bishop of Ripon and to me as 'old friends'. He spoke of our meetings at Milan and of his being our guest at the American Church House. We were all very moved by the occasion not least the Pope himself. He said he had pledged himself to work for Christian unity, and we should find him true to his word.

As the Russian observers were present, we made no speech in return (I will explain this in private), but made it abundantly evident that we were very pleased at his election and that we would pray and work for the unity we all desired.

I was able to renew my contact with Don Pasquale Macchi,[55] who was the Pope's chaplain at Milan in 1955 [sic], who has come with him to the Vatican, and who is to remain in the same post. I asked him whether we could use him as a channel of direct communication with the H.H.[56] and he said we could. If therefore there is ever anything of a very confidential kind which we wish to communicate, this would be a reliable channel.

THE CORONATION

This happened outside S. Peter's on Sunday evening June 30th. You will have seen accounts and pictures of the ceremonial. We had exceedingly prominent places behind the cardinals. The whole scene was splendid in the extreme. It cried out loud for large doses of

---

[55] Dom Pasquale Maachi (1923–2006), private secretary to Paul VI; made a bishop by John Paul II in 1989.

[56] Presumably His Holiness, i.e. the Pope.

liturgical reform, though the main principle was good, and the Pope's mass was a dialogue, with hearty participation by French, Belgian, German (and Anglican contingents). The Pope in his address said how wonderful it was that the epistle and gospel were repeated in Greek. He should have said that it would have been better if only they had been repeated in Italian for the benefit of the 150,000 on foot for the service.

The papal allocution was very good. It was delivered in Latin, Italian, French, German, Spanish, Portuguese, Polish and Russian (i.e. sections of the oration in each). It was again Christocentric, and the only time Our lady was mentioned it was in the words of the Magnificat. There was a considerable exhortation to the Uniate churches to respect the authority of the Holy See!

THE RUSSIAN OBSERVERS

These two, Bishop Kotliarov and Archpriest Borovoj continue to be an embarrassment (perhaps deliberately?) to the Secretariat and to us. They informed the World Council of Churches that they had no intention of coming to the Coronation, and then came. Kotliarov has continuously said he did not speak English. Today I started to speak to him in French, and he asked me to speak in English because he did not understand French. I was able to reply that in December he asked me to speak to him in French because he did not understand English etc. There are those who suggest that his elevation to episcopal rank since the last session of the Council is a subtle political move.

The Americans frequently 'get at' me about Kotliarov, saying that they have him on every black list in the White House. I have answered that as Anglican observers we could do nothing about this, but suggested that if it were true the American Embassy could reasonably protest to the Vatican.

The two of them embarrass us all by continually forcing themselves into the front row of everything which happens. I managed to engineer today that the two bishops, i.e. Kotliarov and Ripon were presented to the Pope first. There is evidence that Borovoj is straightforward and is being watched by Kotliarov. The former warned Willebrands secretly not to communicate with anyone on his journey back from Moscow by train, and Willebrands is aware of having been followed several days after his return via Vienna.

This is one of the many reasons why it is so desirable that the Oecumenical Patriarch of Constantinople should send a representative, who should be a bishop, who could then be accepted

by all observers as their leader. Can Lambeth suggest this to Constantinople?
[. . .]

THE CORONATION (FURTHER)

I omitted to mention above the matter of the tiara. This was put upon the head of the Pope (to the amusement of many) by Cardinal Ottaviani; with a formula which ought soon to be forgotten. Phrases like 'princeps principum'[57] etc. came over the air.

The interesting and (we hope) significant thing was the shape of the new tiara. Instead of the old baroque shape (like that of a guardsman's bearskin) the artificers of Milan had made him a new tiara in bright metal (burnished steel? aluminium?) of the same shape as the old Byzantine mitre, rather like a beehive. Was this a deliberate reversion to the forms of the Popes of the undivided Church?

Montini behaved very humbly through it all. He is a man who could not 'put on airs', no matter how high one exalted him. His chaplain told me he spent the whole night awake in prayer between the first vote which elected him and the second which he accepted immediately.
[. . .]

Report No. 79   20th September, 1963

ARRIVAL

I arrived here on Sept. 18th. and hope to stay to the end of the next session of the Council, until about Dec. 10th. The Council ends on the 4th December.
[. . .]

THE COUNCIL – THIRD SESSION

It now seems to be taken for granted that there will be a third session of the Council, probably May – July next year.
[. . .]

THE INTERIM.

The coordinating commissions of the Council have been hard at work and have been trying to carry out the late Pope's directive to shorten,

---

[57] 'The first of the firsts'.

conflate, and where necessary rewrite, the Schemata of the last session. I am informed that 20 Schemata have been reduced to 17, and that the present Pope thinks even they are too long. The new Schemata (four of them at least) are in our hands: they are much shorter than their predecessors. These schemata have been out to the bishops and have been digested by them. The new Pope has not altered any of them so far, and they have come out over the seal of John XXIII.

THE NEW POPE, PAUL VI

The Pope continues to run true to form. Mgr. Willebrands told me today that the Pope sent for him last week and asked about the work of the Secretariat at length. This is more than his predecessor did. He told W. that he had said unity would be a preoccupation of his pontificate and that he meant what he said.

The *Osservatore Romano* has twice shown pictures of the Pope saying Mass in a plain long 'gothic' chasuble. I append one of them. This must be the first time a Pope has been seen in this garb since the Reformation. He is obviously establishing himself in the affections of all his staff here as a most devout industrious and learned Pope with a very wide view. It is fair to say that whereas they loved Pope John they admire Paul VI. That does not mean to imply that Paul is cold. He takes longer to know and is less spontaneous; he will certainly be a great Pope. Everyone is agreed in saying that the two men are providential. Paul could not have made the 'breakthrough' which John has accomplished, and John could not have steered the outcome as judiciously as Paul will do.

ARCHBISHOP OF WESTMINSTER

There is no doubt that the nomination of Mgr. Heenan was a surprise out here, as well as at home. The long delay had been interpreted as meaning they were trying to find someone else at all costs. I find that my guesses from England correspond to what is supposed out here, viz. Heenan was appointed because of the unity angle. It is recognised that the English episcopate didn't want him for reasons that are not difficult to guess. But he has talked so much about unity that he will have to attempt to implement the decisions of the Council.

This is a confidential report. I don't think readers will need informing that Archbishop Heenan will want careful watching. He is concerned with unity but is at the same time a very zealous Roman Catholic and a very forceful and persuasive prelate. Perhaps he has been raised up to encourage zeal in the Church of England. I think our friends in the religious orders will have been disappointed, though the hierarchy will rather have had Heenan than any religious at all. It was amusing to notice that Dom Christopher Butler's assessment of Heenan in the *Sunday Times* said that 'Dr Heenan has had a very thorough theological formation'; and formation is of course to be distinguished from, in fact contrasted with, education, in Roman parlance.

My own view is that Heenan is the best we could have expected unless we could have had Holland of Portsmouth (assuming of course it could not be a religious). But he is not a man of wide vision and I'm afraid he is not a man whom people really trust. Even ordinary people sense this very much.

UNITY IN ENGLAND

Having been bold in the last paragraph may I stick my neck out further and express the hope that the C. of E. will quickly evolve machinery to deal with the new situation which I should say is already created by Heenan's appointment, and which will in any wise come about after the Council – i.e. the situation whereby the Roman Church in England will start using the new 'unity' situation as a means of further propagation of the faith? And they of course will be highly organised and will have a programme controlled by the hierarchy. Has the C.F.R. given thought to this, or does it reckon to deal with this situation? [. . .] We need to have a centre to which all Anglicans (and others?) can address questions about Roman relations, which shall ensure that trained speakers are available in all areas, shall weigh reports of Roman misbehaviour and (where advisable) pass them on to Heenan's committee, and a thousand other things. Is John Kelly's committee able to do this?
[. . .]

REPRESENTATION IN ROME

I wonder if any thought is being given to the future of this assignment? It is evident to me that when the Council is over there will be scope and opportunity, if not an actual request, for an Anglican officer in Rome, and an Anglican centre. I would gladly write at length on suggestions about this if asked to do so. If this is to come into being in a year or eighteenth months' time surely now is the time to be planning the finances. As we have our men at Geneva and back that whole enterprise to some thousands per annum I hope there would be a case for this too. No doubt in the future it will have to have an Anglican Communion angle and sustentation?) etc. That will not be for me to decide, but I do recommend strongly that it be kept in mind. The chief reason for it is that the Romans would welcome it: they are very flatterous about us sometimes and speak very generously of what we have to contribute.

Report No. 80   24th September, 1963

THE POPE'S VISIT TO THE ENGLISH COLLEGE

On the 22nd of August the Pope went to the summer residence of the College during his stay at Castel Gandolfo. In the course of this visit the Rector said:-

> the 'vocation' of the students of the English College will be to work in England for the salvation of the souls and for the conversion of many brethren separated from the Holy See. The alienation of our country from the Catholic faith was a most sad event, but now the darkness seems slowly to be dispersing, and we continually pray that the Lord may hasten the great day when finally England may again be called The Dowry of Mary.

Responding to the Rector, the Pope expressed:

> 'sympathy, affection, admiration for what English Catholics are doing and for what they represent in the Church of God', adding that 'they constitute one of the strategic points, it may be said, in the life of the Church'. The Pope then hoped that the action of English Catholics might attain 'the most joyous and', that is that it might be possible 'in very truth to greet England once more as the Dowry of Madonna, and that its inhabitants, with all others who share their nationality, may all become sons of the same Church, of the same faith, with the confidence in their hearts of Christian salvation.'

It seems only fair to quote this kind of lapse on the part of the Pope. But what else could he say to the English College? The Rector of the College is a rather unprepossessing Irishman of the hard school called Mgr. Tickle (!); friendly to speak to, but with no vision.
[...]

THE POPE AND THE CURIA

The Pope has announced the general terms of his intentions of reform for the Roman Curia. This is no surprise, for he himself has often adumbrated it, notably in what was regarded as his 'pre-election' speech in Milan. The reform is of course long overdue and is strongly desired by everybody except the Curia itself. The main intention is to internationalise it, to streamline it and to think out its fundamental significance in relation to the Papacy and the episcopate. The general complaint has been that the Curia has been able actually to interfere with the running of dioceses. I imagine that this is a long-term project, though the Pope made it clear that he is going to do it largely on his own.

[. . .]

WILLEBRANDS AND THE SCHEMATA

I had a long talk on arrival with Willebrands and expressed my view that the Schemata represent an immense advance on their predecessors, on which we congratulated the Secretariat. We hoped of course that more ground would be won in the second session. Willebrands said we must be prepared for the integristi to fight back hard and there was always the possibility of their regaining some ground, though he hoped not. The part of the Schemata de Ecclesia of the papacy was very disappointing and in my view represented a worsening of the position at Vatican I. Willebrands said that they were not satisfied with it but I could not pin him down to saying how it could now be improved upon. The 'Explanations' are very bad and merely demolish 'straw arguments'. Whoever thought that infallibility meant that the Pope could predict next week's weather?

In my view the two main points won were the recognition that all the baptised were members of the Church (on whatever footing) and the implied admission (in de Ecumenismo) that there was schism within the Church (i.e. in recognising the Orthodox as Ecclesiae Orientales). I asked whether that did mean giving up some of the position of Trent and Vatican I by which actual communion with the successor of Peter was an essential condition of membership of the Church. He said that he hoped we shouldn't call it that but a 'clarification of an idea'. That seemed to me to be a pregnant remark and perhaps a momentous discussion. In countless conversations I have never yet heard anybody of Willebrands' authority say so plainly how they intended to get round this kind of difficulty.

I asked him how the R.C. envisaged the development of their present approaches to the Orthodox. The Pope had said that he wasn't thinking in terms of 'submission': but what I said [was] that it was surely already obvious that neither the Orthodox nor we could make unity in any form on the basis of the infallibility per se of the Pope.

[. . .]

I asked if the differences between the Roman and Anglican doctrines about the Eucharist could be regarded as a diversitas espressionis,[58]

---

[58] 'Difference of expression'.

and he said he thought not. But I am not sure how really conversant Willebrands is with our theology.

[. . .]

Report No. 81   30th September, 1963

CARDINAL BEA

I had an introductory interview with the Cardinal who seemed to be in very good health. He agreed that the new Schemata were a great advance on the old ones. I said that the 'Explanations' offered in de Ecclesia about the nature of the infallibility of the Pope were disappointing and were not in fact explanations of our difficulties at all. He said we should wait and see what came out of the Council. I asked if he thought that the 'Liberals' should gain further ground at this session, and he said he thought it was possible.

He repeated that it was now quite certain that the Secretariat would continue after the Council. There would be a third session of the Council, and the Cardinal thought this more likely to begin soon after Easter than in the autumn.

[. . .]

ARCHBISHOP HEENAN'S ENTHRONEMENT

The press men who are here for the opening of the Council have obviously been given a good impression of Heenan and seem to think that he is bound to live up to his professions of friendliness. I am amused by his conception of 'building a bridge to Lambeth', and hope it will be made wide enough for two-way traffic.

[. . .]

LIGHT RELIEF

The reassembly of all the personalities of the Council has brought its crop of stories. One of the most attractive is that the conservatories [*sic*] in their confessions now habitually say 'Bea culpa, Bea culpa, Bea maxima culpa'.

THE SECOND SESSION AND AFTER, SEPTEMBER 1963–SEPTEMBER 1964

Commentary: September–December 1963 – the second period of the Council

When the second period of the Council opened in September 1963 Paul VI had replaced the deceased John XXIII as the Roman pontiff. During this period the discussion on *Lumen Gentium* continued and the Council Fathers also began discussing *Unitatis Redintegratio* (Document on Ecumenism).

Lumen Gentium had been revised in the interim and when the Council Fathers assembled anew they turned their attention to the question of co-operation (*cooperentur*) which emerged as one of the key words in the vocabulary of Vatican II in the sense of collegiality. The question of whether Mary's role in the Church should be treated in a separate document or not was also debated; eventually the Council voted for implementing it within the larger Constitution on the Church which was finally ratified by the Pope in November 1964.

On 18 November 1963 the Council Fathers were finally ready to debate the long-awaited schema *De Ecumenisme* (On Ecumenism). The document had been prepared by the Secretariat on Christian Unity and consisted of five chapters that addressed the principles and practice of Ecumenism, Christians who were separated from the Catholic Church, the Christian attitude to non-Christians (especially Jews), and the question of religious liberty. Rather than referring to Protestants as 'heretics' and to Orientals as 'schismatics', the schema spoke of these as 'separated brethren'.

It was, however, the question of the relationship to the Jews which proved contentious. It was the German Cardinal Bea who presented chapter 4 on the Catholic relationship to the Jews. He said that this relationship was an important issue because of the violent outburst of anti-Semitism that had culminated in National Socialism. After the Holocaust the Church could no longer project any form of anti-Semitism.

The question of religious freedom was presented by Bishop De Smedt, who asserted that religious liberty was part of the Catholic tradition and not a break with the past. Although many applauded

De Smedt's speech, some feared that religious liberty did not so much represent the Catholic past as deviate from it. The discussion on the Jews and the question of religious freedom was deferred to the Third Period.

At the end of the Second Period the Decree on Liturgy and that on *Inter Mirifica* (Decree on the Media of Social Communications) were solemnly ratified.

Report No. 82   1st October, 1963

THE SECOND SESSION

This opened on Michaelmas Day, Sunday 29th September in S. Peter's Basilica with the usual ceremonies. The Mass was celebrated by Cardinal Tisserant, the Cardinal Dean. This was followed by the profession of faith of the Pope and the Secretary General of the Council and the Pope's absolution.

THE OBSERVERS

Their number has increased slightly since the last time. There are two Russians there this time, Borovoj and a new one called Ilic, who is said to be a Canon of Leningrad Cathedral.

[. . .]

You will perhaps realise that in addition to our delegation we have the Bishop of Nagpur (Sadiq), who comes in the name of the W.C.C., the Bishop of South Kerala (Leggs), who is Moderator of the Church of South India, and a man called Norgren of P.E.C.U.S.A., who is also under the umbrella of W.C.C.

The Observers came here for a discussion and lunch on Saturday and we planned our campaign. It is intended to send general Observers' reports as well as mine. Miss Johnstone is installed as secretary, and is very satisfactory.

[. . .]

It is intended that Observers' reports will be sent when Schemata are completed. General progress of the debates will be shown in my series.

THE POPE'S SPEECH

This was very satisfactory. It continued the Roncalli tune and went to the length of admitting Roman Catholic responsibility for the divisions in the past. We now look out for the next stage, which is the admission that the Roman Church is also partly responsible for the continuation of divisions in the present. [. . .]

Report No. 83.   2nd October, 1963

SECOND SESSION OF THE VATICAN COUNCIL

37TH GENERAL SESSION, MONDAY 30TH SEPTEMBER, 1963

The session began with a Mass in the Ambrosian rite said by the new Archbishop of Milan.

PRELIMINARIES:

It was proposed to admit laity who are to be 'auditors'. They can be called upon by the same rules as the Periti.

> A rule as propounded whereby speakers must give three days' notice before speaking and should, if possible, submit the whole text of their speech. This was received with a smile.

SCHEMA 'DE ECCLESIA'

[. . .]

Cardinal Ottaviani and Cardinal Browne read formal introductions to the lay out [*sic*] of the Schema. The text of these introductions had already been distributed.

[. . .]

Cardinal Frings of Cologne spoke for the bishops of Germany and Scandinavia. He said that the Schema was on the whole placet[1] because it is clear and pastoral. It is a great improvement on its predecessor. It avoids the bombast and pride of the former and is more firmly rooted in the Scripture.

[. . .]

---

[1] 'It pleases', i.e. 'pleasing'.

Patriarch Cilicia of the Lebanon made a reactionary speech saying that the essential difference between laity and hierarchy should be emphasised, and also that the non-Catholics should have made it clear to them that defective faith is an impassable barrier to union.

[. . .]

Archbishop Ngô-Din-Thuc of Huê, Vietnam wondered why there were not Buddhist, etc. Observers. Similarly, among the Christian Observers, he thought there were not sufficient Asiatics.

Bishop Gargitter of Bressanone wanted further clarification of the relations between the Pope and the college of bishops. He thought the Schema did not give sufficient teaching on the place of the laity.

38TH GENERAL SESSION, TUESDAY 1ST OCTOBER.

Cardinal Rugambwa of Bukoba, Tanganyika, made an impassioned appeal for the overriding importance of the missionary function of the Church.

Bishop Hermaniuk of Winnipeg, of the Ukrainians in Canada, commended the scriptural basis of the Schema and its foundation in the fathers, especially of the Greeks. He thinks the ecumenical spirit is also commendable.

[. . .]

Bishop Gasbarri of Velletri, Italy regretted the omission of any reference to the problems of the relations between Church and State.

[. . .]

Bishop Arceo of Cuernavaca in Mexico said the separated brethren are often able to speak with reason against exaggerations in the devotion to the Saints. The chapter de Sanctitate Ecclesia should take account of this fact for the avoidance of misunderstanding.

Cardinal Browne summed up.

[. . .]

Report No. 84   4th October, 1963

39TH GENERAL SESSION, WEDNESDAY 2ND OCTOBER.
INTRODUCTION TO DE ECCLESIA.

Cardinal Gracias of Bombay thought the introduction should contain something about the history of salvation and the place of the Church in it. 'Too many cooks spoil the broth', there are too many signs of unresolved differences.

In 'missionary countries' the Church must learn to shed all ideas of ruling of kingdoms and of authority, except in the scriptural sense. They were a negligible community, and should behave accordingly. Some Christians can be more papal than the Pope. He quoted Newman,[2] who said that growth without improvement is no use: quantity without quality is often the aim of missionaries. The Church must be aware of this. The language of services should be more prominent in the Schema.

[. . .]

Archbishop de Provenchères of Aix, France said it was important to decide whether the Church was a sign of the union of men with God, or whether it was the actual means of a union.

[. . .]

Dom Christopher Butler referring to the paragraph about the non-Catholics, said, these separated communities were not simply natural communities, but supernatural. They are therefore in a real sense related to the Church.

There is a distinction between the regnum Dei and the regnum Christi.[3] You cannot equate the Church with the regnum Dei, it is subject to it, receives it, appropriates it. You can only make this equation in the case of the regnum Christi.

40TH GENERAL SESSION, THURSDAY, 3RD OCTOBER.

Further speeches on details of the schema de Ecclesia, and further repetitions of points already raised. But three contributions were of importance or interest or both.

Card. Bea reminded the Council that it was the Pope's desire that the statements of the Council should manifestly spring from scripture. It is also very important that separated Christians be shown the scriptural foundations of the Council's formularies. In this light, the Schema has serious defects. For example, it is often said in the Schema that the Church must be a unity etc., but no scriptural proofs for this are given. Ever since the Reformation the understanding of this idea has

---

[2] John Henry Newman (1801–1890), pioneer of the Oxford Movement who left the Church of England in 1845 and converted to Rome; created Cardinal in 1879. Not a few regarded Vatican II as 'Newman's Council'. He is claimed by both the Anglican and Roman Catholic churches as one of their own.

[3] 'God's kingdom' and the 'kingdom of Christ'.

been a cause of division and the Schema does not help. Often in the text scripture is used wrongly. [. . .] When it comes to arguments from tradition, it is no good trying to convince non-Catholics of the truth of Catholic positions simply by quoting recent Pontifical statements, and this is particularly so in the case of references to the B.V.M. The Council should find and use the *common* faith ante-dating the 11th century schism. This is the only possible foundation. When, e.g. the Schema asserts that episcopacy belongs to the sacrament of order, it is only asserted. There should be argument documentation from antiquity. Similarly, in the Schema, when the Papal prerogatives are referred to, only recent statements from canon law are cited. This will not do – and it is especially irrelevant and harmful in relation to Eastern Christians who do not accept the authority of such canon law. The whole thing should be revised in this light. [. . .] And the only scriptural arguments used should be based upon exegesis acceptable to modern scholars. Other sorts of arguments are of no help in creating unity with the separated brethren, and the Council should remember that this cause of unity is one of the primary purposes of the Council.

Archbishop Heenan, speaking in the name of the hierarchy, spoke characteristically! He found the section (paragraph 9) on non-Catholic Christians defective because it did not sufficiently emphasise the duty of preaching to non-Catholics and bringing them into the Catholic fold. All Catholics had the duty of the apostle, and non-Catholics ought to know that the Church would never be satisfied until they were converted to her [. . .]

Bishop van Velsen of South Africa spoke of paragraph 9 in another voice. (Curiously, his points are omitted from the official press release summarising the day's proceedings. Accidentally? Deliberately?) Nothing was made of the (common) faith in Scripture as the Word of God. It is said that they have baptism, yet nothing is said about what 'body' they are incorporated into by baptism. Nothing is said about their order: priesthood, episcopacy – nor about their eucharist. And financially, nothing is said about the question of the papacy in relation to these non-Catholics. The Bishop did not go on to say what he wanted said about these matters in the Schema, but it may be significant that one voice has raised the question.

HEENAN'S SPEECH.

My comments are these:-

This only confirms what I have never ceased to say, that Heenan is a dyed-in-the-wool reactionary.

Does this mean that the proposed Lambeth bridge is to be built for one-way traffic only?

Heenan is chairman of the committee of the Roman Catholic hierarchy in Britain for 'ecumenism'. He said he was speaking in the name of all the episcopate. Is this then their combined conception of ecumenism? What then does it mean to them but a convert-drive, disguise it how you will?

Does Heenan not realise that though this speech and the enthronement speech do not seem inconsistent to him, to the ordinary Christian they indicate a quite transparent duplicity?

This gives encouragement to anyone in the Church of England who feels inclined to continue anti-Roman propaganda.

This confirms our belief that we can as yet expect little ecumenical advance in England. If we wish to follow up the intentions of the past Pope and the present one we must do so outside England.

The comment of a prominent American bishop was that there are more than enough non-Christians in England and U.S.A. or elsewhere for it to be right for us to have time for convert-catching.

This was not the voice of Pope John, nor is it that of Pope Paul.

Report No. 85   8th October, 1963

41ST GENERAL SESSION, FRIDAY 4TH OCTOBER.

The discussion of Chapter 1 of de Ecclesia was continued and concluded, and discussion of Chapter 2 begun. Once again (in regard to Chapter 1) little that was new was said. [. . .]

Archbishop Baudox of St. Boniface, Canada, dealt with paragraph 9 and repeated the Abbot of Downside's criticism, viz. that it treated non-Catholic Christians only as individuals. He even elaborated the Abbot's point by saying that these separated communities possess (as it were) the marks of the Church, sacraments, preaching of the word of God, and that they doubtlessly bring men to God. This should be recognised in paragraph 9.
[. . .]

Chapter 2

Cardinal Spellman roundly condemned the proposal for a permanent diaconate, on the ground that it would lead to a diversion of what would otherwise be vocations to the priesthood.

Cardinal Ruffini did the same [. . .]. The Bishops may have the Pope's 'permission' (from time to time!) to meet and teach, but there are no grounds for the notion of 'collegiate' episcopacy as defined in the Schema. The Pope has no need of such a College to confirm his teaching.

Cardinal Bacci, to complete a trio of the Sacred College, took the same line on proposals for the diaconate.

The other speakers were generally of a very conservative kind and in particular *Bishop Pocci* (speaking on behalf of *Cardinal Micara*) took the fully 'integrist' line, and said that the Council ought to concern itself with the condemnation of errors – of which there were many, often supported by dignitaries (!). Earlier councils had pronounced Anathemas – and so should this one.

In relation to Chapter 2, it was the conservatives' day, and no one spoke with any force against them

42ND GENERAL SESSION, MONDAY 7TH OCTOBER.

[. . .]

Cardinal König emphasised the power of a Council as expression of collegial power. But there should be more said about the formation of the bishops outside the Pope. This makes little advance on Vatican I. He defended the text against Ruffini's attacks concerning the uniqueness of Peter as the foundation-stone. There should be more development.

[. . .]

Cardinal Alfrink – Whenever the Schema speaks of 'Peter with the Apostles' etc it should read 'Peter and the *other* Apostles.'

Patriarch Maximos IV – Vatican I defined the Primacy. The real obstacle to unity was not the Primacy itself but the excessive doctrines concerning it and its juridical expression. Paul VI told the Council not just to repeat Vatican I but to suggest new interpretations.

This Schema should therefore express with a sane balance the relations between the Pope and the bishops [. . .]

Bishop Zazinović of Jugoslavia – The bishops as a body are unusual to the task of governing the Church. Insistence on collegiality could weaken the Primacy. It would be better to make no change in the traditional practice. Still, it would be advisable to set up a permanent episcopal commission with representatives of all nations, with regular meetings, and with authority to decree changes even in the prevailing practice of the Roman Curia.

Bishop Beck of Salford spoke on behalf of the English bishops for a closer definition of the office of the priesthood, particularly of the sacrificial priesthood. The importance of emphasising this in ecumenical work (!).

(continued in report No. 86)

Report No. 86   10th October, 1963

42ND GENERAL SESSION, MONDAY 7TH OCTOBER (CONTINUED)

Bishop Beck of Salford (continued) [. . .]

(it is amazing how English Roman Catholic bishops seem to interpret their ecumenical role as being the reiteration at every possible opportunity [of] those particular doctrines which provoke separation).

43RD GENERAL SESSION, TUESDAY 8TH OCTOBER.

Before the speakers began to address the Council, the General Secretary announced the procedure to be followed in voting on the individual amendments proposed for Chapter II of the schema on Sacred Liturgy.
[. . .]

Continuation of debate on Chapter II of the Schema on the Church

Cardinal de Arriba y Castro, Archbishop of Tarragona, Spain said the insistence on the concern of the Church for the poor should not be interpreted as though the Church intends to do nothing to improve the living conditions of those in want. No true member of the family of God will ever allow anyone to suffer much less die of hunger. But mere help is not sufficient. There is a serious obligation to help better the over-all social situation. We should not leave to the Marxists the task of improving the social conditions of the vast masses of the poor. Christ's commandment of love demands that we be interested in the poor and this is not a mere counsel, but a precept. The improvement of the poorer classes is a most urgent duty. Fulfilment of this duty would be greatly helped by organizing in Rome a central office, or Sacred Congregation, to coordinate study on social problems and assist in promoting social justice everywhere in the world.

Cardinal Gracias, Archbishop of Bombay considered the use of scripture in arguments proposed in the schema should conform in all respects to the principle of sound scholarship and exegesis. This document should reflect the Church's veneration for sacred scripture. As for the arguments from tradition, it would be advisable to use only the earlier sources for arguments on points of disagreement with our separated brethren. But this schema is not intended only for them; it is designed as a foundation for the renovation of the Church. Consequently we should use all the riches of tradition, of whatever period, in order to present an integral image of the Church [. . .]

Cardinal Landázuri Ricketts, Archbishop of Lima, Peru – In the discussion on the advisability of a permanent diaconate, it should be borne in mind that there is no question of laying down universal legislation. As for the objection that the presence and activity of married deacons in the Church might have unfavourable repercussions on the tradition of clerical celibacy, it should not be forgotten that all necessary precautions are to be taken by the Church. If it is objected that this provision might eventually diminish the number of vocations to the priesthood, there is the possibility that any such eventual diminution might be overbalanced by an increase in the greater overall number of workers for souls. Besides, the work of these deacons is intended to deepen the spiritual life of many of the faithful and this in itself would be a stimulus to more vocations.

Cardinal Suenens, Archbishop of Malines-Bruxelles, Belgium continued the discussion of the oportuneness of restoring the permanent diaconate, and said it should be borne in mind that this was a question pertaining to the very constitution of the Church. It has not arisen merely from the necessity of meeting local needs in various parts of the Church; it proceeds not from natural but from supernatural realism. The argument in favour of this diaconate is based on the fact that the work to be entrusted to such deacons would proceed from the order they have received; there is no question of work which could just as easily be done by dedicated laymen. Simple natural gifts would not be sufficient, even with the special grace of Baptism and Confirmation. The purpose of this restoration would be to attribute greater prominence to the diaconate in the Hierarchy of the Church

[. . .]. The task of the Church is not to issue a universal decree but only to make it possible for the Church not to fall short of its duty where this is necessary. There can be different solutions of the problem for different places, but the supreme law must always be the salvation of souls.

[. . .]

Archbishop Staffa, Secretary of the Sacred Congregation of Seminaries and Universities considered the use of the phrase 'undivided subject of full and supreme jurisdiction in reference to the Roman Pontiff and the bishops of the Church' gave rise to certain doubts and uncertainty. It would be much better to retain the doctrine set forth by many theologians at the time of the first Vatican Council and to maintain that supreme power over the entire flock of the faithful was entrusted to Peter and to Peter alone. Since everyone agreed that the Pope always had ultimate power over all the bishops, it would be advisable to retain the doctrine that full and supreme power is vested solely in the Pope, independently of consultation with others. The bishops of the world must cooperate with the Roman Pontiff but it belonged to him to exercise eventually the supreme power of decision. (There you have the supreme doctrinal clerical view in all its nakedness).

[. . .]

Report No. 87   10th October, 1963

OBSERVERS' MEETING, TUESDAY 8TH OCTOBER.

De Ecclesia. Chapter II

[. . .]

Dr. Lukas Vischer said he felt the priest was much more the successor of the Apostles in the sense of being the celebrant of the Eucharist (para. 14). He wanted much more reference to the Holy Spirit.

Prof. Schmemann thought the whole document too Latin. Not enough appeal to later Ecumenical Councils. Even chapter 16 de Collegio Episcoplai ejusque Capite[4] tells us more about the Pope than about the bishops. This appears to an Orthodox quite bizarre. It is an address

---

[4]The College of Bishops has no authority unless united with the Roman pontiff, Peter's successor, as its head.

to the Pope, with an apology for the existence of bishops. There is a fear of approaching the doctrine concerning the Pope.

Prof. Cullmann

1) Of what sort is the primacy of Peter among the twelve before the Resurrection?
2) What is the character of the primacy of Peter after the Resurrection before he leaves Jerusalem, among the Church of Jerusalem?
3) What is the nature of the primacy after Peter's departure? His church tradition and his life study leads him to agree with Ruffini (!) that the bishops are not the successors of the apostles, who were eye-witnesses of the Resurrection.

The lecturer (Mgr. Philipps of Louvain) said it was not for us to justify the position of the papacy – that was done once for all at Vatican I. He answered Cullmann's last point (or tried to) by quoting the incorporation of Matthias into the college.

[. . .]

Canon B. C. Pawley (C of E) said that speaking as a member of an episcopal church he found the Roman Catholic use of the office of a bishop uncertain not only because of the intrusion of the Papacy but also because of:

1) the cardinals,
2) Titular bishops with no jurisdiction,
3) Missionary bishops with no de jure seat in council
4) Praelatura nullius,[5]
5) Those very independent and Presbyterian phenomena, the Religious Orders, exempt from Episcopal jurisdiction.

New forms of episcopate (as in South India) had soon been able to teach us lessons.

44TH GENERAL SESSION, WEDNESDAY 9TH OCTOBER

Moderator: Cardinal Suenens

Chapter II of de Ecclesia

Cardinal Liénart of Lille said we must never speak of Peter and the Apostles as if they were separate. The whole Scriptures must be read

---

[5]'Prelature of none', usually reffering to a titular bishopric with jurisdiction over a territory not in a diocese but subject to the Holy See.

together [. . .]. So he made the college. The college therefore came before Peter, who had the special job of confirming his brethren (not his slaves) in the faith. There was to be a link of charity between them. Their first preoccupation after the Resurrection was to fill up the number of the college. Then they began the preaching. The exercise of authority came spontaneously. The gospel never interprets authority in terms of power but of service.

Cardinal Richaud, Archbishop of Bordeaux – The permanent diaconate will do no harm to the presbyterate. He remarked on the institution of the diaconate in the New Testament which was for practical administration and needed so far no seminary training. The present pastoral needs suggest that there should be a greater concentration of priests in towns, which would make the provision of this kind of ministration more necessary.

[. . .]

Bishop Ataún, coadjutor of Cadiz, Spain said that the section on the priesthood did not sufficiently refer either to the biblical foundation on which it should rest, nor did it properly relate to the High Priesthood of Christ.

[. . .]

Archbishop Conway of Armagh, Ireland criticised several omissions and deficiencies, especially in treatment of the priesthood. It deals with bishops in nine pages, but gives only half a page to priests. Even this is not about priesthood itself, but only in its relation to bishops [. . .]. Priests are mediators between God and man! They handle the precious Body and Blood, they absolve in the name of Christ. There being such a critical shortage of priests throughout the world, the function of the priesthood should be exalted. It should have a separate chapter.

Several speakers in the course of the morning expressed anxiety lest whereas Vatican I offended by not giving sufficient attention to the episcopate, Vatican II might make the same mistake with regard to the priesthood.

Bishop Franić of Spalato, Jugoslavia, on behalf of all the bishops of Jugoslavia, was strongly against the introduction of the married diaconate, whose wives (and children!) might be the ridicule and the scandal of the Church. In the Orthodox Church there was obviously a greater esteem for the unmarried, from whom alone bishops were appointed!
[. . .]

Report No. 88   11th October, 1963

45TH GENERAL SESSION, THURSDAY 10TH OCTOBER.

Still on Chapter II of de Ecclesia.

Bishop Schick, auxiliary of Fulda, Germany, in the name of the bishops of Germany, called for a more thorough treatment of the theological functions of the priesthood, especially 1. Cor. 12, the Eucharistic foundation and the general New Testament background. The implications for the local church of the theology of the universal Church should be more closely defined.

[...]

Archbishop Descuffi of Smyrna, Turkey made a very reactionary speech. For the sake of the observers etc. it should be very clearly stated that the Pope has absolute and sole authority of declaring infallibility without the consent of the Church.

[...]

Archbishop Yago of Abidjan, West Africa said that against the restoration of the diaconate it had been objected that we should not return to the conditions of the first century in the Church. But it is evident that in many areas the Church is actually living for all practical purposes in the first century [...]

[...]

Archbishop Vande Hurk of Medan, Indonesia, in the name of the Indonesian bishops, said it cannot be demonstrated with certainty that the apostles set up individual bishops as heirs of their authority and as real successors. This is a historical question which the Council should not undertake to settle. The text should not refer to a bishop and his diocese, but rather to the bishop and the Church entrusted to him. The bishop exists for the Church, not the Church for the bishops.

[...]

46TH GENERAL SESSION, FRIDAY 11TH OCTOBER.

Chapter II of de Ecclesia continued.

Cardinal Quiroga y Palacios of Santiago de Compostela, Spain, spoke against the conception of the collegiality of the bishops, considering it neither founded in scripture nor to have other significance. The single bishop working in union with the intention of the Holy Fathers was the characteristic form of the Church.

Archbishop Slipiy of Lvov, Ukraine, recently liberated from long incarceration, gave a long history of the Church in the Ukraine. The bishops do not form a college – this is a quasi-political conception. The bishop is given full powers which are not modified by his membership of the college. The Pope is 'bishop of the Church' and receives his authority directly from Christ.

Bishop Costantini of Sessa Aurunca, Italy, said the Schema put too much stress on priests and deacons. There is no cogent reason for restoring the diaconate as a permanent rank. In case circumstances in a particular locality should demand services which can be rendered only by a deacon, the problem can be solved by ordaining qualified lay-brothers in religious communities [. . .]

Bishop Casamandari of Ciudad Juarez, Mexico said that in many parts of Central America many marriages were not able to be celebrated in church for lack of priests. It should therefore be possible for the new deacons to be able to do this. There should at least be a period of experiment.

[. . .]

Archbishop Gouyon, coadjutor of Rennes, France, considered the primacy of Peter and the collegiality of the bishops was inseparable.

This bishop pointed out that when the Pope consecrated bishops he did so alone, because he was 'all the bishops'. Where does this get us? Is this another sign of insecurities of the Roman Church in exercise and conception of the episcopate?

[. . .]

Bishop Bettazzi, Auxiliary Bishop of Bologna said the concept of episcopal collegiality constituted no danger to the Primacy [. . .]. This doctrine was not a theological or canonical novelty. When a bishop was consecrated he contracted a close bond of union with the particular church to which he was appointed. The will of the Holy Father could break this bond by transfer to another diocese, but could never sever the bond linking the bishop with the Universal Church.

[. . .]

47TH GENERAL CONGREGATION, MONDAY 14TH OCTOBER.

Cardinal Frings of Cologne said the concept of collegiality in its juridical sense was not found in the earliest fathers, but neither was the primacy of the Pope. But they both come unmistakeably out of the later tradition as history evolved. The primitive Church was made up of many elements. The two were clearly present by the time of Cyprian. S. Augustine, speaking of the Donatists, said that they did want to form part of the college.

The collegiality of the episcopate was therefore quite as clear and authoritative as the Primacy in Vatican I and the Assumption of the B. V. M.

[. . .]

There were three speakers at this period who vainly repeated the text book doctrine of Vatican I, who were obviously creating impatience among the fathers.

[. . .]

Bishop Vion of Poitiers said the schema was still too much concerned with the bishop[']s duty of ruling rather than with the apostolic duty of serving.

[. . .]

Bishop Kémérer of Posadas, Argentina, in the name of bishops of Latin America, made a very impassionate appeal for the diaconate without which the Church in many parts of Latin America could scarcely survive. This was applauded.

Archbishop Zoungrana of Quagadougu, Upper Volta, Africa, was against the permanent married diaconate because of the fatal consequences in Africa to the future vocations of the priesthood [. . .]. At the end of the speech he said that if in any province it should be necessary to have permanent married diaconate, they should be able to apply to the Pope. It was not for a council to make this immense change general.

Bishop Carli of Segni, Italy, who is apparently very much in the pocket of Ottaviani, Ruffini, etc., wanted corpus, or even familia, episcoporum, rather than collegium.[6] The bishops have no corporate existence apart from the Pope.

The introduction of the idea of the collegiality seems to compromise the absolute privilege of the Pope. (Note: the vote on this will be the clearest indication of progress or reaction on the part of the bishops).

The expression of infallibility was not as clear as in Vatican I and there was a danger of the charisma being lost in the collegiality. Whenever the Pope spoke infallibly he involved the college!

48TH GENERAL CONGREGATION, TUESDAY, 15TH OCTOBER.

[. . .]

ENGLISH COLLEGE

With the whole hierarchy, I got an opportunity to say to the Rector how disappointed we had all been at his utterance on the occasion of the Pope's visit. That had evidently been brought home to him by others.

I sat next to Archbishop Heenan and was able to refer to his speech about conversions, showing him that we wanted to know was what was left of Ecumenism after that. He said it would be made clear when we got to de Ecumenisma.

ARCHBISHOP HEENAN

I sat next to Archbishop Heenan at a party the very next day and was able to let him know that I had not had a lot of correspondence about his speech. He has since been reported as saying at a press conference that one can not distinguish in the Council at this session 'progressives' and 'reactionaries'. That is absurdly untrue. Admittedly the issues aren't so sharp because the progressives have had so many of their points now incorporated in the Schema but reactionaries are still very distinguishable, Heenan himself in the front ranks of them.

[. . .]

---

[6]'Body, or even family, of bishops, rather than college'.

Report No. 90   16th October, 1963

OBSERVERS' MEETING, TUESDAY, 15TH OCTOBER.

Bishop Cassien, Director of the Orthodox Theological Institute St. Serge, Paris, made a general plea for some strictness in the use of theological terms. Our use of them has often been more poetical than scientific. The flame is often used as a metaphor, as expressing the Holy Ghost in relation to the Church. But it is not scientific.

It is said that the Holy Ghost reveals Christ to the Church. But how? In the Conception? In the Parousia?

Mgr. Willebrands said that Cardinal Bea had complained in the Council about the inexact use of Scriptural notions in the Schema and had sent a detailed list of passages.

Prof. Caird, Congregational, said that what is said of the Apostles is often transferred to the bishops without care. Some of the characteristics of the Apostles (e.g. eyewitnesses) were not able to be handed on. In Matt. 18,18 the Apostles are representatives of the whole people of God, not predecessors of bishops. Note the immediate previous context, and that which follows. It is therefore dangerous to apply binding and loosing to the episcopal office on the strength of these verses.

Fr. O'Hearne,[7] Passionist, U. S. A., agreed with Prof. Caird as exegete. The whole passage was addressed to the disciples. But this did not render less strong the other texts in which all seemed entrusted to the Apostles.

The mystery of the Council of Jerusalem in which James, not one of the twelve, was in a prominent position. But now the power to bind and loose was also passed on to priests by the college of bishops.

Rev. El-Moharaky, Copt from Cairo, said that a tradition to be catholic must be in accord with the Scriptures. A council to be ecumenical must be in accord with the three sources of truth; Scriptures, Tradition, and Councils. The action of the Pope in Vatican I in declaring himself infallible is not in accord with these criteria.

If Christ were the corner stone of the Church, Peter could not be the rock. But the rock was the teaching revealed by Christ, later defined by really ecumenical councils. In this sense every bishop was infallible in a

---

[7]This is an error. The person referred to is Fr Barnabas Ahern, as correctly spelled in Report 97.

way whenever he taught in the name of the Church. Paul's conversion of Peter.

Prof. Oberman, Congregational, U. S. A., was surprised that there was no discussion whatever of the position of S. Paul, with its suggestion of the charismatic character of the office of the Apostolate [. . .]

Prof. Skydsgaard, Lutheran, University of Copenhagen, said that the Pope in his inaugural address said the Church was a mystery which should be continually explained. There was something completely lacking in the nature of the Church. It was an essential characteristic. The Schema spoke of the mystery in a one-dimensional way. The mystery of the people in its pilgrimage, in his relations with his people. As with Israel so with the Church. The history of the new Israel was also a mystery, in darkness. The sin of the people of God made it so. God was in the midst of his people as the one who was continuously redeeming them. This belonged to the core of ecclesiology. The paradox was to be kept before the people. The prophetic word of God's wrath and mercy must never be absent from the conception of the Church.

The restoration of this dimension was also the key to the possibility of ecumenical progress.

Prof. Cullmann, of the Universities of Basle and Paris, put hope in the new chapter de populo Dei.[8] It was necessary to recite the 'histoire du salut'[9] at every turn. We are the point in the 'histoire du salut' in between the Pentecost and the Parousia. This was the hour of the Holy Spirit. He deplored the school of Bultmann which had done so much to destroy this classic sequence.

Cullmann asked if the 'propers' of the Roman Mass of the Holy Spirit were fixed for all time, for he thought they were drawn from too few sources. Should there not be citations from that classical chapter of the Holy Gospel, Romans 8? The Roman Mass only used the Johannine texts, good but incomplete.

Prof. McAfee Brown, Presbyterian, U. S. A., welcomed the rumour that the Schema might include the Schema of the B.V.M. What was said about her was best said in the context of the Church, rather than as a

[8]'Of the people of God'.

[9]Oscar Cullmann, 'L'evangile johannique et l'histoire du salut', *New Testament Studies*, 11, 1964, pp. 111–122, shows that the Gospel of John as narrative is full of salvation-history references, indicating that, in the author's opinion, the events outlined in the narrative happened in accordance with a salvation-historical timetable, as ordained by God (see John 1:17; 3:14; 7:6, 8; 8:56; 9:2–3; 18:32).

quasi-celestial personage. And the suggestion that anything that was said about her should have a strong biblical base was also welcome.

Bishop of Nagpur, India, spoke about the Church's function of mission. The Hierarchy should be shown primarily as missionaries. Unity was inseparable from mission. The urgency of the missionary situation was not sufficiently emphasised.

Canon Pawley, C of E., read the draft on one of the points which the Anglican observers will submit to the Secretariat on the Schemata; in which was emphasised the need, from the personal angle, to apologise first for the all too evident weakness of the Church in this world (where more evident than in Italy?) and only then to advance to the teaching that the Church is also equally certainly conscious of the mystery that, in spite of her weakness, she was the divinely instituted means of grace etc . . .

49TH GENERAL CONGREGATION, WEDNESDAY, 16TH OCTOBER.

The moderator informed the assembly that notwithstanding the vote the previous day to close the debate on Chapter II, several Fathers had availed themselves of the faculty granted in the rule of procedure to speak on this same chapter.

Bishop Ammann, titular Bishop of Petnelisso, in the name of five other bishops, said the concept of the collegiality of the bishops and of their dependence on the Holy See requires that efforts be made to maintain and to tighten the bonds uniting the hierarchy throughout the world with the Roman Pontiff. Nevertheless one might ask if this strengthening of union requires the presence of diplomatic representatives of the Holy See throughout the world. Many persons think that such officials as Apostolic Nuncios, Internuncios and Delegates are shadows hiding the genuine face of the Church. Their presence in a country seems to create the impression that the Church is imitating the secular powers, and the false impression is encouraged that, in one way or the other, the Church is mixing in international politics. It is time to put the representation of the Holy See in various countries in the hands of Patriarchs, Bishops designated by their respective national conferences, etc. These people know their own country better than outsiders, are thoroughly familiar with its language and traditions, and they are in a much better position to evaluate problems and decide on appropriate solutions. Why would it not be possible, if the diplomatic representatives are to be maintained, to appoint outstanding laymen instead of clerics? As witnesses to the faith they would be 'confessors' but not necessarily Pontiffs. The present system needs to be radically reorganised.

Bishop Carretto, Vicar Apostolic of Rajaburi, Thailand, in the name of the bishops of Thailand and Laos, said that in mission countries the scarcity of priests is such that they are not able even to preserve what the Church has already accomplished let alone engage in any activity of spreading the faith. This is the main reason why permanent deacons should be instituted in the Church. To forestall many of the objections which have been raised, the choice of deacons should fall on men who would be at least forty years old, men outstanding for the sincerity of their Christian life and their apostolic zeal. They should be financially independent and thus better able to act with upright intentions. If they are married, no permission should be forthcoming to pass to the priesthood, at least not as long as the marriage bond lasted. Such men would be able to act in several capacities to promote the welfare of souls and there is no reason why their labours should not be ennobled and sanctified by the special grace of the order of deacon.

Archbishop Zoghbi, Vicar of the Greek Melchite Patriarch for Egypt, considered the text of the schema was too unilateral in that it did not pay sufficient attention to the long-standing tradition of the Oriental churches regarding the collegiality of the bishops. The text placed so much emphasis on the authority of bishops and the Roman Pontiff that it failed to place in the proper light the figure of Christ, who is the source of all authority. Special care should be taken to eliminate the constantly recurring emphasis on the dependence of the bishops on the Pope. No one denies the authority of the Roman Pontiff over the entire Church, but this authority is not intended to destroy the power of individual bishops, rather to protect and safeguard it. An apparent obsession with the Primacy has beclouded the doctrine on Christ the High Priest. The greatest grace conferred on Peter was his membership of the apostolic college. The special mission to confirm his brethren was something added on to his basic apostolic vocation. The same is true of the place of the Roman Pontiff in the Church.

[. . .]

Bishop Drzazga of Siniando, Poland, in the name of the bishops of Poland, said the spiritual needs of the faithful were such that they could be met only through the priestly ministry strictly so-called. The restoration of the diaconate would really not make a substantial difference in the over-all picture. If such deacons were to be permitted in the Church, they should be held to celibacy. In cases where a married deacon might wish to advance to the priesthood, this would be impossible in the Latin Church. Consequently there would be the serious temptation to go over to one of the national churches where celibacy would not be required. The activities proposed for deacons could be taken care of by secular institutes.

The synod then passed on to consider Chapter III of the Schema, de populo Dei et de Laicis[10] [. . .]

Report No. 91   18th October, 1963

49TH GENERAL CONGREGATION, WEDNESDAY 16TH OCTOBER (CONTINUED).

Chapter III of the Schema, de populo Dei et de Laicis.

Cardinal Ruffini began the discussion on Chapter III by saying that no one denied the exalted function and duties of the laity in the Church. Today more than ever the hierarchy and the clergy were sorely in need of the assistance of the laity. Nevertheless this did not authorise us to speak of a 'mission' of the laity. They did not share in the mission conferred by Christ on the apostles, as though they were on the same level with the hierarchy in the task of evangelizing the world. Unless the unprecise terminology in the text was corrected there was a danger that pastors and bishops might encounter difficulties in cases where they must disagree with the laity. If the laity felt it had a juridical right to share in the ministry of the Church this could lead to a weakening of the position of the hierarchy. Pastors and people did not enjoy unconditional equality in carrying out the mission of the Church. In the schema certain passages from scripture and the fathers were quoted out of context or in a manner not really appropriate to the purpose in hand.

Cardinal Cento, Major Penitentary, said that the text of this chapter was of the utmost importance for the coming schema on the apostolate of the laity. Its provisions constituted the principle and foundation of this schema. What the present schema had to say on the quasi-episcopal aspect of father of families and on the priesthood of the laity constituted a valuable document for meditation of the clergy and laity alike.

Cardinal Bueno y Monreal, Archbishop of Seville, said for the first time a Council document made special mention of the laity and this

---

[10] 'Regarding the People of God and the Laity'.

represented an official appreciation by the Church of the importance of the laity. Perhaps in the past there had been too much insistence on the Oriental figure of 'the flock'. The concept of the people of God represented the external manifestation of the Mystical Body which really constituted the internal spiritual reality of the Church.

Cardinal Bacci of the Roman Curia thought great care should be exercised in speaking of the *universal* priesthood of the faithful. Their priesthood was not all-embracing. They had no power like ordained priests over the real body of Christ or over His Mystical Body [. . .]. The priesthood of the laity was of a generic, not proper nature and was intended to offer to God spiritual victims of praise.

[. . .]

50TH GENERAL CONGREGATION, THURSDAY, 17TH OCTOBER.

The discussion on Chapter III 'De populo Dei et Laicis'

Bishop Rastouil of Limoges said in the Old Testament the people of God was essentially priestly in character. The new people of God was the Church, which was priestly in the unique priesthood and in all its members through the effects of the Sacramental character conferred by confirmation. This character was a derivation of the priesthood of Christ. Thus the priesthood was the key to the explanation of the nature and activity of the Church, since the Church was a continuation of the active presentation of Christ in the world through and in the members of the Mystical Body. The chief priestly functions of the people of God were to praise God and bring in 'the other sheep'. The priesthood in Christ was the power of redemption; in the Church, the power to apply redemption. There should be a fuller treatment of the priesthood realized in Bishops, priests, and the laity.

[. . .]

Bishop Hengsbach of Essen considered the general language was not clear enough, it was more ideological than theological. The whole question of the apostolate should start from the theological conception and gradually move to practical implications. There was throughout a jealous tendency to guard the privilege of the hierarchy. It was now time to relax about this and to open the doors of opportunity to the laity. The laity must have a part in munere docendi.[11] In the New Testament the Holy Ghost is poured out indiscriminately.

---

[11] Canon law.

Bishop Wright of Pittsburgh, Pennsylvania, U. S. A., thought this was a great opportunity to give to the laity what they had been waiting for for several centuries, a coherent theology of the laity. It was time to make an end of the idea that the Roman Catholic Church was a sacerdotal church, whereas it was only the Reformation churches which had a place for the laity.

[...]

Bishop Dubois of Besançon, France, said that the conception of the populus Dei should be made broad enough to include all those who confess the name of God in any recognisable form; the Gentiles of the New Testament certainly, the Jews, possibly Muslims and Hindus. All in contrast with those who deny the existence and not the word of God.

Report No. 92   22nd October, 1963

51ST GENERAL CONGREGATION, FRIDAY, 18TH OCTOBER.

Cardinal Gracias, Archbishop of Bombay, said that paragraph 26 was too much weighted in favour of the hierarchy. The laity must not be thought of as sheep under a shepherd. This is now a bad metaphor – in the case of the Good Shepherd it is a different matter. They are condisciplati[12] with the hierarchy. Some members of the hierarchy neither seek nor want the collaboration of the laity and, when it is offered, give the impression that accepting it is something of a privilege for those who have offered to help. We must remember that the laity not only have a call and an invitation but also a right to share in the mission of the Church. This does not mean a share in the mission of the hierarchy, which must always be distinguished from the work of the laity.

[...]

Bishop Schröffer of Eichstätt, Germany, considered the people of God were not primarily a sacramental but a prophetic community. It was a mistake to speak of obedience in reference only to the laity. Were not the clergy also under obedience? It would be better to speak of the hierarchy 'and the rest of the people of God' rather than always opposing hierarchy and laity. The hierarchy was part of the people of God.

---

[12] Fellow disciples.

[. . .]

Bishop De Smedt of Bruges, said the doctrine of the universal priesthood was defective and should be amplified. Laity were called to lead a life of priesthood of Christ. They were under an obligation to lead a consecrated life . . . a living sacrifice. This sacrifice was at its height in the historic sacrifice of Christ.

[. . .]

52ND GENERAL CONGREGATION, MONDAY, 21ST OCTOBER.

[. . .]

Cardinal Meyer, Archbishop of Chicago, said, although baptism incorporated us into the Church, with all its privileges, we must not lose sight of the fact that the Church was a body of sinners. The mass was indeed offered, and pardon daily placed pro omnibus peccatis, erroribus et negligentiis nostris.[13]

He proposed an amendment corresponding almost exactly to one of the proposals in the comment of the Anglican Observers. (We later discovered he had been put up to it by the Secretariat, so that this represents a real immediate impact of the Observers on the Council).

Cardinal Ottaviani complained about certain periti who were distributing leaflets to the fathers trying to persuade them in favour of celibate deacons. They were acting ultra vires.

He proposed that the new situation for which the new type of deacon was proposed could be equally well filled by the office of acolyte.

ENTERTAINING CARDINAL DÖPFNER

We had this distinguished cardinal (the youngest of the lot, aged 48) together with Prof. Cullmann. In the course of dinner we asked him what he thought would be the distinctive results of the Council. He said we must prepare our people not to be disappointed with the absence of spectacular results, and on the other hand to appreciate the value of the 'new theological' outlook of the Schemata. It is not easy for those outside the Roman Catholic Church to appreciate at what cost this new outlook has been achieved. It dominates all the Schemata. To assess it we must compare the present Schemata with the originals. He also said that if, as he hoped, there are no further Marian definitions, this should be appreciated as a positive achievement. He also hoped

---

[13]'For all our sins, mistakes, and omissions'.

that the new permission to discuss and to pray together would make a tangible impression on the people. Even if they were unable to make changes in the mixed marriages legislation, he hoped there would be some organisation through which hard cases or mistakes could be rectified and regulated.

COST OF THE COUNCIL

Archbishop Heenan told us that the Council was costing £20,000 [*sic*] per hour, and that therefore a ten minute speech cost £300, £30 a minute. Even Toronto can't touch this.[14]

[. . .]

THE NEXT SESSION

Everyone is very anxious to know when the next session will begin, not least the Anglican Observers. There is now an impatience to get the Council over, and a general inclination to finish it in one more session which, it is hoped, will defer a lot of administrative decisions to post-conciliar commissions. I am not certain that these hopes will be realised. I think the most likely date for resumption will again be September.

53RD GENERAL CONGREGATION, TUESDAY, 22ND OCTOBER.

Cardinal Suenens, Archbishop of Mechelen-Brussels, said that we too easily lost sight of the fact that charisms still existed in the Church. Recognition of this fact was important for any well-balanced view of the Church. Such charisms were not mere peripheral phenomena nor accidental appendages to the Church but part of its nature. We must avoid giving the impression that the Church is no more than an administrative machine completely cut off from the influence of the spirit of God. This was the age of the Holy Spirit, who was given not only to pastors but to all members of the Church [. . .]. Any treatment of the Church which took up bishops and the hierarchy while saying nothing of the gifts of the Holy Spirit would be defective. It was a fact of history that some members of the laity had at times awakened a sleeping church lest the teachings of the Gospel were lost sight of. Charisms without a hierarchical direction would be a source of disorder, but a government of the Church which ignored charisms would be poor and sterile. The chapter should be revised with more

---

[14]This reference remains obscure but may refer to a meeting held under the auspices of the Canadian Council of Churches, founded in 1944.

emphasis on the freedom of the children of God in the Church. To show the world that we practised what we preached, we should provide for an increase in the number of lay-auditors with the representation on a broader international basis, the admission of women among the auditors, since women constituted one half of the population of the world, and representation likewise from the great congregations of brothers and sisters who contribute so signally to the apostolic work of the Church.

Bishop Ruotolo of Ugento, Italy, suggested there should be a separate Schema on the laity. More space should be given to the place of confirmation, which should be made more effectively the 'ordination of the laity'. The present emphasis on the laity should not be regarded as a novelty, but as an age-old tradition of the Church, starting from the Scriptures. The talents and experience of the laity should be used at every level of Church life, theological, administrative. There should be training colleges for laity.

[. . .]

Report No. 93   23rd October, 1963

OBSERVERS' MEETING, TUESDAY, 22ND OCTOBER.

Professor Müller of Louvain, gave an introduction to the part of the Schema which concerns the laity. The priesthood of the laity. Is it only metaphoric, by transfer of the language used of the real (!) priesthood, which is the ministerial or sacramental priesthood.

Note how the Sensus Fidei[15] is extended to the whole body, as is also infallibility. The charismata of the laity is therefore very much extended from what has been supposed in previous Roman Catholic pronouncements [. . .]. This, it is hoped, will have great ecumenical importance as offering a field for future dialogue. Many people think these notes should have been included in the text.

In this Schema the laity are not defined but described negatively, as being neither clergy nor laity. There are significant emendations proposed (page 10 and 11 of the second volume of emendations) which make an attempt at real theological definition.

---

[15] 'Sensus fidei' literally means 'sense of faith'; the theological meaning of both it and 'sensus fidelium' ('sense of the faithful') are set out in *Lumen Gentium.*

[. . .]

Dr. Steere (Quaker), said that the Schema should be careful of being guilty of 'abolishing the layman altogether' by merely extending to him metaphorically the language of the priesthood.

Note the habit of the Holy Spirit of speaking through the laity (Benedict, Francis, S. Catherine of Siena etc.)

Some references to what Tillich calls the 'latent church' of do-gooders who fear to be saved alone).

Professor Mathew (Mar Thoma Syrian Church of Malabar, India), said the hierarchy of the Roman Church seemed to be shy of using laypeople for the purpose of preaching.

Professor Berkouwer, of The Free Protestant University of Amsterdam, asked for further clarification of the concept of obedience, as distinct from submission on the part of the laity.

Dr. Horton (Congregationalist), considered the Schema ought to give guidance to the laity perplexed by the apparent impossibility of ministering truthfully to Christ in the Hall.

Pastor Roux (French Reformed Church) said a new conception of hierarchy could be a great help to large sections of Protestantism, especially where it suffers from a caricature of the conception of the universal priesthood of the laity.

Mgr. Willebrands said he would be glad if all could agree that the word 'hierarchy' could be taken to mean 'holy order in the whole Church of God'. Then there can be various degrees of office within the order.

Revd. El-Moharaky (Coptic Church of Egypt), reminded the meeting that when the Apostles wanted to replace Judas, the general laity chose two, from whom they appointed. Likewise at the appointment of the 70 it was the multitude who acted as C.A.C.T.M. before the Apostles laid hands on them. This principle is carefully preserved in the Coptic Church in the selection of bishops, priests and deacons.

Professor Schlink (Evangelical Church in Germany), referring to Cardinal Suenens['] speech in the Council, said that the Church is founded not only on the Apostles but on the prophets. They had the imposition of the hands, though they did not belong to the hierarchy. This charismatic function is essential to the Church. These two functions must be reconciled in all the churches.

[. . .]

THE PROGRESS OF THE COUNCIL

Bishops have been complaining (and so have the Observers) that progress is now very slow. Last Wednesday (23rd) the four moderators had a meeting (it is said) with the thirteen presidents to decide (a) who was really in charge, and (b) how to accelerate procedure. As a result of that the moderators have been throwing more weight about and things are moving more swiftly.

THE SCHEMA OF THE B.V.M.

The first thing the moderators (particularly Cardinal Döpfner) have done is to get the Council to make up their mind whether to have the constitution on the B.V.M. as a separate Schema or whether to include it in de Ecclesia.

The cardinal arranged for two speakers (one on each side) to address the assembly on Thursday. They were Cardinal Santos of Manila (conservative) and Cardinal König of Vienna (liberal). The speech of the former was very thoroughgoing. While admitting that the B.V.M. was of course a member of the Church Triumphant, he claimed that the nature of her membership was so different (because of her pristine sinlessness through the Immaculate Conception) that to include her doctrine in a Schema on the Church would be misleading. She related more naturally to Christology and to Soteriology than to Ecclesiology! In any case who knew whether new doctrines were going to be revealed through the Council about her.

Cardinal König started by saying that Mariology had had a big impetus in the past century and had been the occasion of much zeal in the Church. The Church was to be the main theme of this Council and it was not fitting that the B.V.M. should be absent from it if she was the 'crown and example of the Christian'. Mariology should not too readily be allowed to become a separate department of theology, lest it lead to exaggerations. The Council has already said clearly that it did not want new doctrines about the B.V.M., which would be the only excuse for a separate Schema. It was necessary for the clear conception of Christ as the only Mediator that the B.V.M. should be confined to de Ecclesia. There was a sense in which we were all 'mediators of grace' when we fulfilled our Christian membership. In that sense only the B.V.M. was Mediatrix gratiae.[16] The biblical references to the B.V.M. all related her to the Church, and in that context let her be proclaimed to the world.

---

[16]Mediatrix of grace (referring to the intercessory role of Mary).

There is no doubt that this vote, the result of which you may have read by the time you get this, will be one of the turning points of the Council. The 'conservatives' are working very hard to win it, and if they lose it will be a considerable defeat. It will demonstrate the power of the Council, it will represent a slight criticism in retrospect of the last two Mariological doctrines, it will show the kind of way in which we may hope for future developments. In fact, it will be the kind of fruit which we could hope for. If, on the other hand, the issue is lost to the reformers, there need be no great despondency. It will only show that the time is not yet, but that the number is growing of those who are working for better things.

[...]

RELIGIOUS LIBERTY

Two prelates from the other side of the Iron Curtain (Poland and Czechoslovakia) made impassioned speeches on Friday, 25th October[17] about the restrictions they are suffering. They were brought into the discussion on the nature of the Church in the hope that the language concerning the right and duty of the laity could be made more vivid.

That started me wondering about the question of religious liberty in general. While the Romans are thinking about it they might start at home and consider the cases of Italian Protestants who find it impossible to get permission to erect new buildings and of ex-priests in Italy who are victimised. The last Lateran treaty contains some very cruel clauses. And of course there is the whole question of Spain. We must try to let the Romans here see that we regard all these questions as related.

Report No. 94   25th October, 1963

54TH GENERAL CONGREGATION, WEDNESDAY, 23RD OCTOBER.

His Beatitude Paul II, Chaldaean Patriarch of Babylon, said the Council should avoid becoming involved in controversial questions such as the universal priesthood of the faithful. In any case, if it were not to be taken up, it should be very clearly explained lest it opened the door

---

[17] Either this is an error for Friday, 18th October, or the report was begun on 23rd October but not completed until after the speeches had taken place.

to interference by the laity in things which properly belonged to the Hierarchy. This question would be understood only with difficulty by the Oriental churches, for which there was only one priesthood, namely the one shared in by those who had received Holy Orders. The laity had the mission to preach the Gospel, not as sharers in the priesthood, but as witnesses to divine truth. The non-Catholic observers were present at the Council daily, assisted reverently at Mass each morning, and gave evidence of their good will and patience. It would be well to give them an opportunity to be heard at least once a week, either in the Council hall or elsewhere.

[. . .]

Bishop Przyklenk of Januaria, Brazil, wondered if a non-theological definition of the layman should be part of a dogmatic constitution. That the definition should be negative should not be surprising. There were only two classes among the members of the Church, and at times one could be described only in contrast with the other. In this dogmatic text doctrinal ideas were intermingled with disciplinary and pastoral considerations. Either the text should be purified of these non-dogmatic elements or the constitution could not be called 'dogmatic'. After the example of some other Councils the content of the constitution could be presented as 'the doctrine' on the Church.

Bishop D'Agostino of Vallo di Lucania, Italy, thought it would be more logical if the content of this chapter were presented as follows: Christ was the Head of the Mystical Body. All the baptised were incorporated into Him, therefore they all enjoyed equality, all shared in the priesthood of Christ and were all called to sanctity. The schema was inadequate on this last point. It should stress more insistently the holiness of priests, the obligation of all the faithful to pursue sanctity and the relationship of the evangelical councils to Christian life.

Bishop Moralejo, Auxiliary of Valencia, said that since most men, whether within or outside the Church, knew the Church only from its externals, our mode of presenting this schema should be in keeping with present day thinking. As it stood, it was not [. . .]

[. . .]

Bishop Arneric of Šibenik, Yugoslavia, considered the doctrine on the priesthood of the laity was of the utmost importance for areas where the Church could not function and where its Catholic action organizations were not permitted to carry on their work of deepening Christian life both within and outside the family circle. In many localities it was engaged in a struggle, not merely against atheism but actually against anti-theism, if the term could be used. In protecting the freedom of the Church's spiritual activity the laity would draw great inspiration and courage from realising their dignity in the Church and being conscious of what they could do to carry on the mission of Christ.

[. . .]

Bishop Primeau of Manchester, U. S. A., said the laity were not to be regarded as silent and passive sheep. They recognized in the Church not just a dry complex of laws, but a living body which was constantly growing and therefore subject to change. We needed a genuine dialogue between the Hierarchy and the laity, so that the latter might have a greater share in the life of the Church. It had been proven by experience that in many fields members of the laity were much more competent than the clergy or the Hierarchy. They had a genuine love for the Church and were animated with the spirit of reverence for their superiors in the Church. They wanted to do their part. Unless the Council determined the respective roles of liberty in the laity and authority in the Hierarchy there would be greater danger that dedicated laymen might lose interest in the mission of the Church, give in to discouragement and even eventually fall away. The obligations of the Hierarchy in this respect had particular importance when dealing with intellectuals in the Church, since it was necessary to acknowledge their right to freedom of interrogation and to intellectual initiative. Our text was too negative and too clerical. It might be said to sum up the duty of the laity as being: believe, pray, obey and pay. In their mission the laity should not be regarded as mere delegates of the Hierarchy, but as having their own proper part in the mission of the Church. We should put these principles into practice by giving our lay auditors an opportunity to be heard in the Council.

Bishop Scandar of Assiut, Egypt, asked that in any discussion of the mission of the Church special attention be paid to the importance of Catholic schools. Such schools were essential for the proper training of youth in the understanding and practice of their faith.

[. . .]

Report No. 95   25th October, 1963

55TH GENERAL CONGREGATION, THURSDAY, 24TH OCTOBER.

Continuing the discussion on De Ecclesia:

Cardinal Siri, Archbishop of Genoa, said that there was a danger about the text which concerned the subjection of the laity to the hierarchy. The separation of the chapter gave the impression that the laity were something apart from the Church. The analogical use of the idea of the universal priesthood of the laity was excessive.

The Church must always proceed with the greatest caution in the handling of the charismata, because of the danger of excesses, illusions and deception. But they must all be carefully kept under the authority of the Church.

Fr. Fernández, Minister General of Dominicans, spoke in favour of the unification and hierarchical control of the lay associates. They should be more adventurous, not sitting back and bemoaning what is going on in the world. What the world is misusing let Christians commend by its good use. There is too much canalisation of Catholic social work into 'charitable' work. The best 'social' work is for men to be exemplary citizens, industrialists, businessmen, politicians etc.

Bishop Cantero of Huelva, Spain, on the next sensus fidelium.[18] This was to be found in the whole Church and was an instinct both positive and negative. Sometimes the sensus fidei flourished in the people before it did in the hierarchy, and as such was in a certain way a fluid source of revelation. The history of the doctrine of the Immaculate Conception was a case in point.

Bishop Tracy, Baton Rouge, U. S. A., asked that the text which made race discrimination unthinkable for Christians should be even more clearly stated. He wanted a plain dogmatic definition (cheers).
[. . .]

Archbishop Hakin, Maronite of Nazareth said the Schema was made by bishops etc. who lived in places where the Church was still regnans. It should be acknowledged that the Catholic Church was really a very small minority. The whole Schema was still too pompous. How did the Fathers dare speak so disparagingly of women and the wives of the clergy? What about the east and the separated brethren? In many ways the woman was not sufficiently honoured, and in many ways parts of Christendom.

It was then decided by unanimous vote to discontinue discussion of Chapter III.

---

[18] See p. 235, n. 15.

It was decided to take a vote next week on the issue of whether the Schema de B.V.M. should be an independent schema or should be contained with de Ecclesia.

[...]

57TH GENERAL CONGREGATION, TUESDAY 29TH OCTOBER.

[...]

It was announced that a vote would then be taken on the question whether the Schema de B.V.M. should be included in the Schema de Ecclesia or stand by itself.

Notice was given that on the following day, by order of the Moderators, the five following general questions would be voted on, to accelerate the procedure. In each case the question was phrased, 'Should the Schema, in the opinion of the fathers, be arranged so as to teach that . . .'

1. The bishops embody the fullness of the priesthood.
2. The bishops are a college in communion with the Pope, their head.
3. The bishops acting in cooperation with the Pope, exercise full authority in the Church.
4. The bishops ought not to act apart from the Pope.
5. The institution of an order of permanent deacons is compatible with the teaching and order of the Church.

During the morning there was a general desultory discussion on Chapter IV, de Vocatione ad Sanctitatem in Ecclesia.[19]

We had already made representations concerning this section in our observations on the Schema. The congregation emptied itself into the bars for long periods of this discussion, and we had some profitable discussions. We were able to show our general attitude to the question, as follows:

a) We are also concerned in the religious life, which is highly prized in the Anglican Church.
b) We don't use the expression 'vocation to sanctity' solely concerning the religious life, because it is more aptly applied to the disciplining of every Christian.
c) We would hesitate to describe the religious life in terms of sacrifice. In comparison with the hardships of the secular

---

[19] 'On the call to holiness in the Church'.

priesthood in some areas it could be (and in the Roman Catholic Church is) a soft option.

Cardinal Döpfner, Archbishop of Munich, said the chapter should be rewritten along the lines of the following principles: a distinction would be made between the general means of sanctification and the special means provided by the Counsels, as also between the holiness conferred in baptism and the personal holiness which is a development of it. The description of holiness should pay more attention to the primacy of grace. There should also be a description of the theological concept and role of the Counsels and of the state in which they are professed, explaining these elements in a Christological, soteriological, eschatological and ecclesiological sense. Scripture texts should be used with greater caution and the chapter should be cleared of repetition and some superfluous elements.

[. . .]

Report No. 96   31st October, 1963

OBSERVERS' MEETING, TUESDAY 29TH OCTOBER.

[. . .]

The de Ecclesia still needed so much revision that it could not be adequately treated in this Council.

Canon Pawley, Church of England, said that in his opinion the Schema de Ecclesia and its discussion had shown how much the churches were in need of one another in the matter of church order, among other things. They were all to some extent caricaturing of what church order should be (and that is what hierarchy really meant). They had all been distorted to some extent, or were defective, because of accidents of history. The Roman Catholic distinction between ecclesia discens and ecclesia docens[20] was outrageous, and we therefore rejoiced to see the Roman brethren struggling free from that power and trying to find a place for the laity. The Church of England was trying to solve that problem as well, though of course for centuries the laity had had their place. The Church of England in England was perhaps too closely allied with the state, though not in other countries. In Protestant churches in practice the laity were often as tyrannical as the Roman hierarchy and the ministers were therefore 'stooges'. In other cases

[20] 'Learning church' and 'teaching church'.

churches were at the mercy of their theological faculties which was worse still (laughter), etc. etc. He hoped that all churches could feel their way back to a catholic church order together.

Archpriest Borovoj, Orthodox Church of Georgia, said that the question of the relation of hierarchy and lay people was well preserved among the Orthodox. [. . .]

The experience of Russian Christians underlined the importance of the laity in the life of the Church. When, for example, Roman Catholic Poland invaded the Ukraine and tried to convert the Orthodox population by force (said with a good gesture, and kindly accepted), some of the hierarchy defected, others converted in order to curry favour, but it was the lay people who put up the real resistance. Likewise, in the Russian revolution, many of the hierarchy were executed for civil crimes, some defected to the west, but it was in the laity that the whole body recovered the life which it now is able to live, under the most dangerous circumstances.
[. . .]

58TH GENERAL CONGREGATION, WEDNESDAY 30TH OCTOBER.

Discussion was continued on Chapter IV of the Schema de Ecclesia.

Cardinal Léger, Archbishop of Montreal, said:

1) Sanctity must not be represented in such a way as to appear unattainable by the laity.
2) We must therefore see that the 'evangelical counsels' are always carefully explained with that end in view.
3) Very great care must be taken to work out a theology of the sanctity of the laity *applicable to all.*
4) All sanctity must be carefully linked to the baptismal profession.

Cardinal Urbani, Patriarch of Venice, said that in commending the sanctity of the Church we must insist that the Church Militant was but a small part of the whole, and emphasise the intimate connection with the Triumphant and Expectant.

Cardinal Cento, Major Penitentiary, said the process of solemn canonisation resulted in the elevation of a large proportion of clergy and religious. This was liable to give a wrong impression. Efforts should be made to enrol a larger proportion of lay saints.

Cardinal Bea considered the Schema was not realistic enough. The Church was, and should be shown to be, a body of sinners. If it had not been the Reformation of the 16th century would not have been necessary! The whole Church, therefore, consisted of the perfected saints and those in the world who were being perfected. The scriptural quotations were not good enough. Very often mistakes were made in the applications of texts meant for the Apostles which were applied to all Christians. There were many texts in the New Testament, almost 20 in St. Paul alone, which were omitted but which could be used to present the entire doctrine of authority. Unfortunately no reference had been made to primitive tradition and this was a lacuna of great importance because any dialogue with our separated brethren on this question must be based on scripture and early tradition.

At the end of the session a motion for the closure of the debate was passed almost nem-con.
[...]

59TH GENERAL CONGREGATION, THURSDAY 31ST OCTOBER.

Still on Chapter IV of the Schema de Ecclesia.

Although at the end of the previous congregation a motion closing the debate had been passed, the ruling of procedure required that the list of speeches should be completed. The Council endured this with ill-disguised impatience, and the day's president, Cardinal Döpfner, ruled many fathers out of order for repetitio rerum quae iam longe tractate sunt.[21]
[...]

Report No. 97   7th November, 1963

60TH GENERAL CONGREGATION, TUESDAY, 5TH NOVEMBER.

The introduction to the Schema de Episcopis et Diocesis[22] was read by Cardinal Marella and the Bishop of Segni. These speeches seemed preoccupied with a desire to show how ready the Curia was to be reformed and not to stand in the way of the bishops. 'Qui s'excuse s'accuse?'[23]

---

[21] 'Repeating things that had already been drawn out [discussed]'.
[22] 'On bishops and bishoprics'.
[23] 'He who excuses himself, accuses himself.'

[. . .]

Bishop Rupp of Monaco said the very important question of an obligatory retirement age for members of the hierarchy was touched upon and then left hanging in the air [. . .]

[. . .]

OBSERVERS' MEETING, TUESDAY, 5TH NOVEMBER.

On the 4th Chapter of de Ecclesia, de vocatione ad sanctitatem in Ecclesia.

Introduction by Pere Lalande, Superior General of the Holy Cross Fathers.

This proved to be a most unprofitable beginning. To start with, the Observers were unprepared to discuss a Schema which they supposed had been 'shelved' for further editing. In any case, there had always seemed (to me at least) to be such a gap in thinking and even in terminology between ourselves (a fortiori the Protestants) and the Roman Catholic Church on this whole matter that it was difficult to know where to begin our work as pontifices. Presumably we should wish to demolish the whole scholastic moral theology and to start again in the general spirit of Anglican moralists (Kirk, Mortimer, etc.) to work out the proper relations between revelation and natural ethics. When the Roman Church said that of course all sanctity must be founded on the evangelical counsels they were in a world of discourse so different that it was difficult to comment.

The speakers eventually got down to saying that the foundations of the religious life as stated in the Schema should be more certainly illustrated by the Scriptures, as they easily could be.

Professor McAfee Brown, United Presbyterian Church, U. S. A., was grateful for the point that holiness was an aim for all, which ecumenically was most acceptable. Then a caveat about the absence of conception of justification, growth in sanctity by the redeemed sinner. Simul justus et peccator.[24] What Roman Catholic objection was there to this doctrine? If none, why should it not be better represented in the Schema? Emphasis should be laid on the fact that sanctity was first and last a gift.

Professor Skydsgaard, Lutheran, Denmark, said the chapter lacked Christological and biblical foundation. It lacked the 'radicalism' of the Kingdom of God. It was too moralistic and there were dangers of phariseeism, especially in the eyes of the world. [. . .]

---

[24] 'Simultaneously righteous and a sinner'.

Immense opportunities were given to the Roman Church to go out into the world with the message of the Kingdom of God. The very title of the chapter was wrong. It made of sanctity something to be achieved in the future. Sanctity was much more than that, it was something which we were now by a vocation.

He then went on to a rather narrow exposition of sola fide[25] which was slightly disappointing.

Mgr. Höfer intervened to say that the Roman Church had no general objection to Professor Skydsgaard's doctrine. They had the reality of which he spoke in their spirituality. But the foundation of it was proving difficult! They had been glad of Lutheran help. Much of their difficulty was a legacy of the middle ages. The lives of the saints as understood by the Roman Church surely put the matter of grace beyond doubt. Mgr. Höfer said that bad biographies of saints had led to much confusion.

Fr. Ahern, Passionist, asked that we should look at the rule of St. Benedict, of St. Bernard, the works of St. John of the cross and St. Theresa of Avila, which abound in the spirit of which complaint had been made. Historically it was Pietism, Quietism, Madame de Guyon, Fénelon, Bousset, etc. which started the rot. Since Abbot Marmion there had been a turn back to the right lines.

Mgr. Willebrands said that as long as the Roman Church persisted in speaking of a system of sanctity it was bound to fail in its task of explaining the true nature of redemption and sanctification.
[. . .]

Report No. 98   8th November, 1963

61ST GENERAL CONGREGATION, WEDNESDAY 6TH NOVEMBER.

Schema de Episcopis et Diocesis.

Cardinal Ruffini said some of the arguments of the day before would turn the Schema inside out. Most of them were invalid. The granting of juridical authority to episcopal conferences would lead to dangerous

---

[25] 'Only by faith'.

divergences and must certainly injure and diminish the authority of the Pope.

The solution was to divide episcopal faculties into two careful categories, one of which could easily and rightly be administered by single bishops (dispensation) and the other [of] which would contain those things which could only be handled by papal authority.

Cardinal König, Archbishop of Vienna, suggested that, because of the importance of keeping channels of communication open between the centre and the periphery (i.e. between the Pope and the bishops), it would be helpful to mention explicitly the annual, or at least semi-annual, convocation of the Chairmen of the National Episcopal Conferences, and other members of the hierarchy for meetings in Rome. This would be important also in maintaining relationships between missionary countries and the rest of the Church.

Cardinal Alfrink, Archbishop of Utrecht, considered there should be much more detailed treatment of the new theme of the collegiality of the bishops, and of the relation of the college with the Pope. It was frequently said that the organization of National Episcopal Conferences would be an expression of the collegiality of the episcopate, and that this would be even more true of the institution of one central organ in Rome to assist the Sovereign Pontiff on the government of the Church. But such an organ, whether composed of cardinals in charge of dioceses or otherwise, did not reflect the collegiality of the bishops nor would it be a parliamentary expression of their authority. The Council should also accept the Pope's invitation to offer suggestions about the new central body. The function of the Curia was not to stand between the Pope and the bishops. Whoever said the Curia Romana existed iure divina?[26] The Curia should be the administrative organisation of the corpus episcoporum!![27] Many more facultates could with safety be entrusted to episcopal conferences. (Sustained applause!)

Cardinal Bea said the principles of ecclesiastical organization should be drawn together from revelation, and this was much more important than just grouping together certain practical applications. According to St. Paul the Church was a spirit of each member, but always in close union with the others. Thus there was no danger of schism but everything contributed to mutual concern for one another. In the history of the Church, and as the result of particular circumstances, many institutions had grown up; the Patriarchates, the erection of

[26] 'By divine law'.
[27] 'The body of bishops'.

ecclesiastical provinces, the Roman Curia, among others. The role of authority was not to replace individual members in what they could do by themselves, but only to supply what they could not provide. This was true of any authority, but particularly of authority in the Church, and was particularly applicable to those special members of the Mystical Body who were the bishops, brought to Rome to work with the Pope in the way determined by him. This would have ecumenical importance because the traditional accusations of lust for power, ecclesiastical imperialism, curialism and centralization could not only be answered with words. The most effective reply was in a spirit of profound reverence for individual bishops.

[. . .]

Archbishop Gomes dos Santos of Goiania, Brazil, said the schema lacked general perspective, was out of harmony with the dogmatic teaching of the schema on the Church, favoured the position of those who regarded the hierarchy as strictly juridical, and pushed into appendices some matter of crucial importance. It needed to be completely redone and should be integrated with the schema on the cure of souls. More stress should be placed on the spiritual figure of the bishop and on the practical consequences of collegiality. The Roman Curia should have only consultative and executive powers. The National Conferences should have sufficiently wide authority to meet their needs without prejudice to the primatial rights of the Pope.

[. . .]

Report No. 99   11th November, 1963

62ND GENERAL CONGREGATION, THURSDAY 7TH NOVEMBER.

The debate was continued on Chapter I of the Schema on Bishops and the government of dioceses.

His Beatitude Ignace Pierre XVI Batanian, Armenian Patriarch of Cilicia, said that from the first Vatican Council it was known that the Pope had the fullness of jurisdiction, that his power came directly from God and was not subject to limitation by any human authority, and consequently he had the right to organize the Curia as he wished [. . .]. Every human institution had its weakness and we should try to correct them wisely and prudently. This did not mean publishing them and bringing them to the attention of everyone with the risk of scandalizing or shocking souls. It was not right to forget all the services rendered by the Curia and to concentrate only on its weak points.

Archbishop McCann of Cape Town considered that, in addition to the appointment of bishops from dioceses to the Roman Curia, it was essential that a consultative body be set up to represent the episcopate of the entire world. This organ would have periodic meetings in Rome with the Pope and the chief Curia officials for the discussion of all business concerning the universal Church. In order to prevent undue prolongation of the Council, this body of bishops could be empowered by the Council to decide certain detailed points. It would also have an important informative function for the Holy Father and his aides.

63RD GENERAL CONGREGATION, FRIDAY 8TH NOVEMBER.

It will be readily understood that with Maximos IV the 'temperature' of the Council was already beginning to rise.[28] Today it went up many degrees. The first inflammatory was provided by:

Cardinal Frings of Cologne, who is a man of great calm and dignity who commands the highest respect. Perhaps the cold Germanic manner, which was exceedingly courteous, added to the provocation. He said remarks recently made in the Council to the effect that the collegiality of the bishops had not been approved by the Council because the Fathers must wait for a definitive response from the Theological Commission were indeed amazing. They seemed to insinuate that this had at its disposal sources of truth unknown to other Council Fathers. Such observations also appear to lose sight of the fact that the Commissions were to function only as tools of the General Congregations and were to execute the will of the Council Fathers. The distinction between administrative and judicial procedures in the Roman Curia should be extended everywhere and include the supreme Sacred Congregation of the Holy Office. Its procedures were out of harmony with modern times, were a source of harm to the faithful and of scandal to those outside the Church. No Roman Congregation should have the authority to accuse, judge and condemn

---

[28] During the discussion of the schema on the bishops that took place on 6 November, Maximos IV had caused much excitement among the Council Fathers by calling for a structural change of the government of the Church. The present structure merely allowed the Curia to assist the Pope and did not, according to Maximos IV, answer the needs of the day nor reflect the collegial responsibilities of bishops. Further, he asserted, 'the present court reflected a certain particularism and was an obstacle to ecumenism' (Report 98, passage not included in the text). This was the first effort of the Council to implement a framework for collegiality into its structure.

an individual who had no opportunity to defend himself. With all due reverence and gratitude for the devoted individuals who spend their lives in the difficult work of the Holy Office he felt that its methods should be basically revised. It would be advisable to diminish substantially the number of bishops working in Curial Offices. No one should be consecrated bishop just in order to honour him or the office he held. If a man were consecrated bishop, then he should be bishop and nothing else. No one was ever ordained to the priesthood as a mark of honour or gratitude. Not a few of the tasks of the Roman Curia could be performed by laymen. Consequently, efforts should be made to use bishops, fewer priests and more laymen.

Cardinal Fring's speech had evidently proved to be too much for:

Cardinal Ottaviani, Secretary of the Holy Office who spoke with great vehemence in impromptu Latin, beginning 'altissime protestor',[29] so that the saying ran through the Council that Ottaviani had joined the Protestants. He said the opportunity must be taken to protest most vigorously against the condemnation of the Holy Office voiced in the Council hall. It should not be forgotten that the Prefect of the Holy Office was none other than the Sovereign Pontiff himself. The criticisms formulated proceeded from lack of knowledge, not to use a stronger term, of the procedures of this Sacred Congregation. No one was ever accused, judged, and condemned without a thorough previous investigation carried out with the help of competent consultors and experienced specialists. Besides, all decisions of the Holy Office were approved by the Pope personally, and such criticisms were a reflection on the Vicar of Christ. The five points recently submitted for the approval of the Council Fathers were drawn up by the Council Moderators. They should have been submitted to the Theological Commission for careful study, and the Commission would have been able to perfect certain expressions and eliminate certain obscurities. Those who proposed the collegiality of the bishops proceeded in a vicious circle, since they presumed that the Apostles existed and acted as a collegial body. From the collegial character of the Apostolic College they deduced the collegial character of the body of bishops. But even learned and experienced professors of Sacred Scripture would admit that these theses had no solid foundation in the Sacred Books. Defending collegiality entailed some limitation of at least the exercise of the Universal Primacy of the Roman pontiff. The fact was that Peter only had responsibility for the whole flock of

[29] 'I protest vehemently'.

Christ. It was not the sheep who led Peter, but Peter who guided the sheep.

This whole episode reflects the biggest clash of personalities and tendencies which we have seen in the Council. It was the bishops versus the Curia in a big way. We found ourselves, as always, metaphorically cheering the liberals. It seems to us most important that the Council should be made to prevail over (a) the Curia, (b) its own Commissions who, on the Council's own procedural rules, are there to do its will, not to be the big stick with which to beat it, and (c) the Code of Canon Law, which some people have the temerity to quote against the Council, forgetting that the Law exists for the Church, and not vice versa. For, unless the Council can swallow these three smaller fish, how can it hope to nibble at the Pope.

Cardinal Browne said no objection could be raised on theological grounds against the proposal to bring bishops to Rome to assist the Holy Father, but the Congregations constituted the Curia and the Curia belonged to the Pope [. . .]. If collegiality conferred on all bishops a right to co-government with the Pope, then he in turn had an obligation to recognize this right. This would inevitably lessen the power of the Pope, who would no longer have full jurisdiction. This would be against the constitution 'Pastor Aeternus'.[30] We should be on our guard.

[. . .]

THE JEWS

We have been circulated with copies of a new Chapter IV which it is proposed to add to De Ecumenismo. The covering notes say that it is non-political. Its main intentions are to make clear that the Jews are not to be blamed for the death of our Lord, to point out that we enjoy the same common heritage and that the Roman Church is against anti-Semitism in every form. We hide the fact, though the passage is in desuetude. But we do protest strongly against the inclusion of this Chapter in the Schema de Ecclesia [*sic*]. Our notes say, 'Although we entirely endorse both the spirit and the letter of the new Chapter IV concerning the Jews we most strongly urge that it be not included in the schema De Ecumenismo. This schema concerns only the internal arrangements, the Ecumene, of the Christian family in which, unfortunately, the Jews have no part. Its inclusion at this point

[30] On 18 July 1870, *Pastor Aeternus* or the Dogmatic Constitution of the Church of Christ was approved by the First Vatican Council. The Constitution dealt with the authority of the Pope.

might seriously harm the image of the Roman Catholic conception of ecumenism, suggesting that it was little more than a gesture of benevolence to all men of goodwill.'

Report No. 100   14th November, 1963

OUR 100TH REPORT

This seems to be an occasion to send a respectful greeting to our distinguished readers. The first report was written on the 19th April 1961, in days when ecumenical relations were very different from what they are now. A lot has happened in three years. In those days Cardinals Ottaviani and Tardini were tyrannising the circles and making the life of the new-born Secretariat for Unity very difficult. Now the Secretariat holds its head high in the Council and Cardinal Ottaviani is at bay, a rather pathetic figure trying in vain to stave off the episcopal hounds.

This assignment continues to be very exacting, including many useful peripheral activities which we have no time to chronicle here. But it is exciting beyond description and involves prolonged and intimate contact with an unbelievable variety of people – of whom the members of the observers' tribunal are among the most interesting.

We should like to take this opportunity of saying that we are very conscious of inadequacies in the literary style etc. of these reports, often from sheer lack of time to correct them. Now that we have a secretary here life is much more satisfactory, but often we have to lay elaborate plans to meet because of the endless engagements. Otherwise notes made rapidly in the Council (from Latin), or at other meetings, have to be left to be transcribed and translated with press bulletins and newspaper reports.

DE ECUMENISMO

The Council will finish with De Episcopis at the end of this week or the beginning of next (Friday 15th or Monday 18th) and will then go over to De Ecumenismo, which is awaited with considerable anticipation.

RELIGIOUS LIBERTY

The Secretariat, after long trials, have got their material on religious liberty past the Theological Commission, and it is going to be included as a last chapter in De Ecumenismo. This seemed to me to be a very inappropriate place for its inclusion, and that it ought to stand by itself. I should have been tempted to object to its inclusion on the same grounds as we quoted in the case of the Jews. The Secretariat said this was the only way in which the subject could be introduced into the Council – otherwise it would be dismissed as 'political'. On consultation with the other observers it was decided to raise no objection.

[. . .]

THE UNIATES

A great French ecumenist, P. Maurice Villain, friend and disciple of Couturier, told me of a dilemma in which the Roman Church now finds itself with regard to its own uniates. These patriarchs make themselves a considerable nuisance in the Council, wishing to be regarded as taking precedence before the cardinals. In a united Church Rome would probably have no objection to this, but what is she to do at the present moment? These patriarchs represent very small communities of ten quite small minorities, yet under Roman ecclesiology they are the rightful successors in the ancient apostolic sees. If they exalt them, they offend the Orthodox, if they disregard them they disturb their own people. But the 'Liberals' regard them as most useful because they are so critical of the Roman pretensions.

64TH GENERAL CONGREGATION, MONDAY 11TH NOVEMBER

Chapter II of the Schema on Bishops and the Government of Dioceses.

Cardinal Spellman made a characteristic contribution, saying that not a few indications led them to believe that here were many inexact ideas being set forth on such questions as the collegiality of the bishops of the Church. The theology they all learned in the seminary taught them that the Pope alone had full power over the entire Church. He did not need the help of others. As far as the Roman Curia was concerned it was only an executive organ of the Holy Father. Consequently it was not up to them to try to reform or correct it. They could only offer suggestions and recommendations.

[. . .]

Cardinal Döpfner, Archbishop of Munich, considered the dominant theme of the present schema should be the idea of the bishop as shepherd and head of his diocese. Good order in a diocese called for only one head. Titular bishops in the Church had their own particular dignity and the constitution should put this in a clearer light. By way of answering Cardinal Ottaviani's strictures he observed that the special point proposed on the collegiality of bishops, as submitted for vote some days ago, was formulated in terms which reproduced, if not the actual words, at least the substance of passages drawn from the schema prepared by the Theological Commission. It would be to no purpose now to obscure what was clear in itself.

[. . .]

At the end of the morning's session it was announced that the Council Fathers would be asked to vote the next day on referring Chapter V of the schema on Bishops etc. to the future commission for the revision of Canon Law. This chapter, dealing with the erection of parishes and the determination of parish boundaries appeared to be much too detailed to be discussed on the council floor.

Report No. 101   14th November, 1963

65TH GENERAL CONGREGATION, TUESDAY, 12TH NOVEMBER

[. . .]

Discussion then continued on Chapter II of the Schema on Bishops, etc. on Coadjutor and Auxiliary Bishops.

Cardinal Suenens, Archbishop of Mechelen-Brussels, said when the preparatory commission began its deliberations the members were almost unanimously opposed to any obligatory retirement age for bishops. After the matter had been thoroughly discussed at many meetings, the opinion became almost unanimously in favour of such legislation. This was a point which needed to be determined by law, since no one could be expected to be an impartial judge in his own case [. . .]. If it were objected that an obligatory retirement age would be a violation of the quasi-marital bond uniting a bishop with his diocese, they might reply that the Council was full of 'divorced bishops', that is bishops who had been transferred from one diocese to another. The supreme law must be salvation of souls. A real precept with binding force was required; a pious exhortation would be next to useless. The decision could not be left in the hands of the bishops themselves, not even of cardinals. Today's needs called for an ability to animate all diocesan activities; the bishop must be the head and the heart of his diocese. This demanded a man's full strength. The accelerated rhythm of modern life called for youthful vigour and a young mind and heart. Old age put a gap between the bishop and the world in which he lived, and also between him and his clergy. In governmental, university, industrial and diplomatic circles a retirement age was mandatory. It was true that the office of bishop was different from a purely human office, but in both cases a man's physical strength remained the same. Consequently the text should make it clear that the obligation extended to all bishops, with the exception of the Roman Pontiff, whose office was perpetual in view of the very welfare of the Church. Retiring bishops should be assured of proper support. The Roman Pontiff would have the power to grant exceptions in individual cases, and the application of this provision to Oriental churches would depend on the special circumstances in which these churches lived and operated. But whatever provision was adopted, it should be a question of law, not a mere recommendation [. . .]

[. . .]

Cardinal McIntyre, Archbishop of Los Angeles, a notorious conservative, said, national episcopal conferences could be accepted if they were on a voluntary basis but were to be deplored if they assumed a strictly juridical character. Authority given to such a body always tended to take on greater expansion. The obligation imposed by national conferences should not be juridical, but voluntary and free. Juridical authority was not necessary to enable a conference to provide for national needs. Wanting to give a national conference juridical character could be interpreted as an attack on the Roman Curia, and thus as an indirect attack on the infallibility of the Pope. This proposal brought clouds to the horizon. No one knew better than the Pope how to provide for the needs of the Church. His natural talents were elevated by supernatural protection which made him the one best qualified to understand problems and find their solutions. Why put strictures on him through the adoption of a juridical character for national conferences? [. . .]

Cardinal Gracias, Archbishop of Bombay, said that there were now some fifty national episcopal conferences in the Church and their number could be expected to grow. They demonstrated the value of organized effort and had made a genuine contribution to the welfare of the Church. The crucial point of this chapter was whether to give these conferences juridical status. It would seem more advisable for the Council not to inject its authority into a question still open to controversy. It was better to allow each national conference to decide for itself the kind of obligation to be imposed on its members, with the approval of the Apostolic See. It would be unwise to impose one iron-clad procedure for all.

Cardinal Ritter, Archbishop of St. Louis, U.S.A., said national conferences were essential for any effective apostolate in the Church. Attributing juridical binding force to the decision of these conferences seemed necessary. They all knew how frequently unanimity was required to achieve a purpose and to provide support for individual bishops, not only in things directly concerned with the salvation of souls, but also with regard to social and moral problems. National conferences with juridical power would promote decentralization because, according to the principle of subsidiarity, when problems were solved on a local level, central authority had no need to intervene. The Council had taught all the bishops the significance of working together for the entire Church and trying to understand the problems of others. National conferences would accomplish this on a small scale. The text was sound and prudent and breathed a universal spirit. It was prudent because it excluded positive moral obligation without intervention by the Holy See. National conferences had nothing contrary to the nature of the episcopate. Thus they did not interpose a new body between the bishops and the Pope.

OBSERVERS' MEETING, TUESDAY 12TH NOVEMBER

De Ecumenismo

Introduction by Professor Thils, Louvain, who asked the Observers to consider how revolutionary the conception and the language was from the Roman Catholic point of view, and to be patient with any insufficiency.

There were three possible interpretations of unity:-
1) Where Peter is, there is the Church,
2) Where the Eucharist is, there is the Church,
3) Where the Spirit is, there is the Church.

It was the baptismal community which proclaimed, for better or for worse, what unity there was. Why then did we refuse to give the name of Church to any baptismal body? The terminology of mysticum corpus. Before 1943 this applied to the whole mystical body – since then it has applied to the Roman Church only.

Ecumenism consisted mainly of a reform in the hope that it would make the Church more acceptable to those who might return to it. Was this a reasonable programme?

Professor Cullmann said the Schema was an ecumenical event of the first order, because it was the first time that we had a definitive text from the Roman point of view. We could all accept the biblical foundations of the first chapter. We even began to accept some of the biblical foundations on which Peter rested, but it was the question of the succession. The schisms which have arisen have had as their cause the allowing of charismata to outgrow their proper limits.

The difference between ecclesiae and communitates ought to be tackled, as unsatisfactory. Where was the limit of vestigia beyond which a community was no longer a church? Did not the act of inviting observers constitute the recognition of a church as such? A beginning should be made from the idea of Koinonia[31] in the hope of reaching a solution, because the doctrine of the vestigial was likely to lead to bankruptcy.

Pastor Roux, Eglise Réformée de France, said it was not Peter who was the bond of unity in the New Testament. Paul in the Epistles was deliberately discouraging the idea. It was rather the preaching of the gospel and the consequent reception of it which was the bond of faith, and therefore the 'stuff' of unity.

Fr. Ahern, Passionist, said that the scripture texts in the Schema should and could be improved upon. The Roman text for baptism should be replaced by the one in Galatians, where the baptised 'put on Christ'.

Mgr. Mathew, Malankarese, deplored the inclusion of the text concerning the Jews on exactly the same grounds as those set forth in the Anglican observations.

DE ECUMENISMO

In discussion about this with responsible members of the Secretariat, we get the impression that the text of the Schema as it stands is the result of a long struggle with conservative elements on the Theological Commission, etc. and represents an optimum of what we can expect. We should therefore prepare ourselves and our public not to be disappointed if certain positions at present occupied are heavily attacked and even lost. Some of the texts (e.g. that on permission for corporate prayer) are deliberately vague, in the hope that they will be able to be given a favourable context later.

---

[31] Communion, i.e. the communion of the saints.

69TH GENERAL CONGREGATION, MONDAY 18TH NOVEMBER[32]

[. . .]

There was a notable atmosphere of expectation as the Council set about discussing the Schema *de Ecumenismo.*

[. . .]

Cardinal Tappouni, Syrian Patriarch of Antioch, said there should be a separate chapter concerning the Orientals, because the problems were so different. The chapter on the Jews was quite out of place.

[. . .]

Cardinal Ruffini, Archbishop of Palermo, said it was misleading to use the word ecumenism in two different senses, as in Ecumenical Council and as in the Ecumenical Movement. This latter was introduced by the Protestants some forty years ago. He agreed with Tappouni that the question of relationships with the East was so different from that of the Protestants. He understood there were 511 sects in Australia. With the Eastern they had almost everything in common, but with the Protestants only baptism and the Bible.

They could have done without the first section because it was all in the *de Ecclesia.* It was often easier to convert a non-Christian than a Protestant. They must remember that many Protestants even support communism, which was death to all religions [. . .]

Cardinal de Arriba y Castro, Archbishop of Tarragona, Spain, said there should be exhortation to the Protestants to stop proselytising. There should be an ecumenical catechism in which people could see both the resemblances and the differences with Protestants. The right to preach to the nations was given only to the one Church, not to all.

Cardinal Bueno y Monreal, Archbishop of Seville, thought this ecumenism was a dangerous equivocation. Both sides were using the term in different senses and even dialogue can give rise to the most dangerous consequences unless it is conducted by expert theologians. The way of Catholic ecumenism should be made clearer, viz. that it is the seeking of a unity which the Catholic Church already possesses by those who don't possess it, and the helping of them by the Church.

---

[32]This report must have been completed several days after it was begun.

Report No. 102   19th November, 1963

66TH GENERAL CONGREGATION, WEDNESDAY, 13TH NOVEMBER

Concerning Chapter III (Episcopal Conferences).

Cardinal Spellman, Archbishop of New York, said there were regional conferences already which did a lot of good work. But it would be a mistake to entrust them with juridical power. What about the Papal Delegate? Would he have a veto?

Cardinal Frings, Archbishop of Cologne, said there had been episcopal conferences for a hundred years centred on Fulda. He described its working, especially in good works for Germany after the last war, and for Latin America. Their greatest importance was not in juridical decisions but in the spirit of cooperation. The schema should not tie conferences down to close procedural rules, which should be flexible. [. . .]

Bishop McDevitt, Auxiliary of Philadelphia, said that although he was entirely in favour of episcopal conferences, and even of giving them juridical authority, they must beware of deducing their authority from the collegiality of the bishops. They must not limit the rights of the individual bishop.

Bishop Amadouni, Exarch for the Armenians in Cyprus, said the permanent patriarchal synod of the Oriental Church was clearly the answer to the problems of the West. But in the East, as often as not, these synods were not national or regional but often united bishops of one rite.

67TH GENERAL CONGREGATION, THURSDAY 14TH NOVEMBER

The discussion on Chapter III and IV of the Schema de Episcopis dragged its length along. The only significant point which attracted our attention was that of the Patriarch who said, rather airily, that of course the necessary degree of decentralisation had already been achieved centuries ago by the system of patriarchates, which the Eastern churches had preserved.
[. . .]

68TH GENERAL CONGREGATION, FRIDAY, 15TH NOVEMBER
[. . .]

Report No. 103   20th November 1963

70TH GENERAL CONGREGATION, TUESDAY 19TH NOVEMBER

Before the general business of the day Cardinal Bea read the introduction to the Schema *de Judaeis*. His main preoccupation seemed to be to disclaim any political incentives in the Schema, presumably in order not to give any offence to the Arab world. He also disclaimed any intention to wish to establish diplomatic relations between the Holy See and Israel. We had been informed that the U.S.A. were very keen on this Schema.

It was interesting to note that the Cardinal was having to contradict arguments (which must still be current in the Church) based on the most literal interpretation of the scriptural condemnation of the Jews by Our Lord, arguments which I remember were used by Hitler to justify his 'solution of the Jewish problem'.

He referred to the wound to some Catholic consciences inflicted by the phenomenon of National Socialism, but omitted any mention of the fact that anti-semitism found a place in Italy as well as in Germany.

Discussion then turned to the Schema de Ecumenismo in general.

Cardinal Léger, Archbishop of Montreal, recalled in several examples the intentions of John XXIII and his present successor for the unity of Christendom. This unity must not be an emotion which will fade. Other communions have a right to some tangible token from us. The remarks about the separated brethren were sketchy and unsatisfactory, but what else could they be? He hoped there wouldn't be lengthy discussion of this.

Cardinal König, Archbishop of Vienna, considered the Schema corresponded to the Pope's intentions for the Council. The different uses of 'ecumenism' should at least be mentioned and resolved. Here they were dealing with Catholic ecumenism only. This should be the title of the first chapter. There should be a distinction made between those who have a valid succession and acknowledge all the sacraments, and those who do not. Perhaps they could then refer to 'communitates ecclesiales'.[33]

Cardinal Rugambwa, Bishop of Bukoba, Tanganyika, said God's revelation of Himself went on outside the Roman Church and they must respect the signs wherever they saw them. They were used to this kind of behaviour in the mission field. They were happy to observe the progress at New Delhi, etc.[34]

His Beatitude Ignatius Peter XVI Batanian, Armenian Patriarch of Silicia, said that as they proceeded in charity they must not lose sight of the truth which was one and indivisible. They must not lose sight of the ultimate goal which was the visible union of all in one faith under one head, the Pope. Unless this was acknowledged as the goal, dialogue was useless. Let the separated brethren see how fortunate they were to have such an infallible source of truth, without which there could be no security. He continued the unbroken succession of those who did not want the Jews to be mentioned in this Schema.

Archbishop Garrone, of Toulouse, said that to forestall error it should be stated at the outset that their ecumenism was based on integral and unshaken faith and on courageous hope. This would make it possible to seek out sincerely mutual understanding, in spite of some disagreements. There were as many elements of ecumenism as there were mysteries of faith. It would be a mistake to see such elements only in some words or some aspects of revealed doctrine, because God's will for unity stood out everywhere in revelation. They had an obligation to practice ecumenical charity, not a vague or soft kind of benevolence, but a genuine charity diffused in their hearts by the Spirit who was given to them [. . .]

Bishop Elchinger, Coadjutor of Strasbourg, said one third of the French Protestants lived in his diocese. For them to be able to approach the Protestants they must undertake a thoroughgoing reformation. They must admit their mistakes in history. The reformers were not rebelling against unity but against false teachers. They should admit that this ecumenical movement was started outside the Roman Church, whereas it should have begun in it. They must put an end to the idea

---

[33]'Ecclesial community'. Within a Roman Catholic understanding this applies to a Christian religious group that does not meet the Roman Catholic definition of a 'Church'. Although the word 'ecclesial' itself means relating to the Church, the Catholic Church applies the term 'Church' only to Christian communities that have true sacraments and hold to the apostolic succession, the priesthood, and the Eucharist.

[34]A reference to the third General Assembly of the World Council of Churches in New Delhi in 1961, at which the Russian Orthodox Church was admitted to the Council.

that 'the faith' was a dead set of propositions to be learnt by heart, but a living source of truth, continually to be revised and reconsidered. The dangers of uniformity were enormous.

Archbishop de Provenchères of Aix, said the Schema set forth the Church as a mystery and a communion, not merely as a juridical society. It showed the problem of Christian unity in positive terms and did well to distinguish between Christian communities having an episcopal structure coming from the Apostles and those which did not. But there was a serious defect in the text. There were three steps to union: 1) charity, 2) dialogue, 3) the internal renewal of the Church. The text treated the first two adequately but not the third. There should be more emphasis on the interior renewal of the Church through the liturgy, the revamping of some ecclesiastical institutions, and even research into theological doctrine.

OBSERVERS' MEETING, TUESDAY, 19TH NOVEMBER

De Ecumenismo

Fr. Thijssen said that the schema was a meditation by a Church on itself. Every Church must be true to itself and must hide nothing. The W.C.C. has said that membership does not compromise ecclesiology. Thus if a Church does not regard other churches as churches, it does not need to say so for the sake of union, or even of ecumenical dialogue. Perhaps we ought to seek some other more suitable word.

About the word 'vestigia'. This means marks of the Church. The word 'additus' in the schema is meant to exclude 'reditus'.[35]

Professor Küppers, Old Catholic, said the Old Catholic Church can talk of the Roman Church as her 'mother church' as no other communion can. There ought to be more explicit reference (even on Roman standards) to the sovereign status of the scriptures as a prelude to dialogue. Then there should be a carefully prepared basis for the use of tradition – particularly, of course, that part of it which was common before the respective separations.

[. . .]

Professor Lindbeck, Lutheran, said there are basic conceptual mistakes in approach. The Roman Church is the sole deposit of truth. All other communities are grouped in a quantitative descending scale. A Church which is corrupt and moribund is regarded as more important than one which is overflowing with the Spirit and zeal just because

---

[35]'Return'.

of the historical accident that it happens to have retained the tactual succession of a valid ministry.

Fr. El-Moharaky, Copt, said the schema fails to offer practical steps towards understanding. Catholic catechisms accuse Copts and Alexandrine Orthodox of being Eatychians, Antiochenes in theology, and say that the Copts were left to the mercies of the Moslems because of their heresy. Roman Catholic theologians could prove their sincerity by reading Coptic sources. If there is real sincerity, proselytism and uniatism should cease. These divisions have seriously hindered the mission of the Church to the Moslem world.

Muslims are children of Abraham, but also to a certain extent heirs of the New Testament. They accept Our Lord as prophet and as Word of God; they have a veneration for our Lady and could almost be called a Christian heresy. Therefore if the Jews are mentioned, the Muslims should also be treated. Better to treat them together outside the Schema.

[. . .]

Professor van Holk, International Association for Liberal Christianity, thought that we should all face the fact that there are many who do not believe in credal formulas or in an institutional Church whose place in Christendom must be admitted. Should not the schema find some place for them?

Canon Pawley, Church of England, drew attention to the fact that the Relatio concerning de Ecumenismo mentioned the drawing up of Directories of regulations for the exercise of ecumenism. But this excellent section contained the suggestion that there should be included notes on how to instruct and to receive converts. It said that this work would not in any way be inconsistent with ecumenism. This would not carry conviction. In England at least the inclusion of such instructions at this point would undermine people's confidence in Roman Catholic intentions. The unfortunate speech of Archbishop Heenan had already shown how necessary it was to keep these ideas apart.

[. . .]

Report No. 104   22nd November, 1963

71ST GENERAL CONGREGATION, WEDNESDAY, 20TH NOVEMBER

[. . .] when the assembly turned its attention to *De Ecumenismo*

Cardinal Meyer, Archbishop of Chicago, expressed his pleasure that the chapters on the Jews and on religious liberty were included. He was the first speaker to do so, all others being against.

Cardinal Bacci of the Curia, the Latin expert, deplored the title. It was not for them to alter the sense of a well-established word by making ecumenism now mean something near inter-confessionalism. He therefore proposed 'The Union of Christians' as a title.

Bishop Jelmini, Apostolic Administrator of Lugano, said that the whole schema should be written round Christ as the Head of the Church. All who were in Christ by baptism in faith were in the Church, schisms or not. He agreed that the Latin Church needed much renewal [. . .]

Archbishop González of Saragossa, Spain, welcomed the schema warmly because of its positive approach and its omission of the usual warnings and condemnations. He wondered if they could go still further. The separated brethren rejected any idea of 'return' because they were convinced that they were in the Church of Christ. On the other hand the Church could not disown herself or her God-given mission. Was any real dialogue possible in these circumstances? Yes, if they were faithful in the service of truth, which did not belong to them but to Christ and the Gospel, and if they were understanding and considerate in their relationships with the separated brethren [. . .]. The question of the Jews should be treated, not here, but in the schema on the presence of the Church in the world.

[. . .]

Archbishop Heenan. The full English text of this speech has already been forwarded. The official Vatican press report showed as follows:-
'This present schema is welcomed with joy by the English hierarchy because it shows us the mind of the Church and gives us guidance for the future. Without this guidance our ecumenical work can make no progress. Some non-Catholics have turned to Catholics outside Britain in search of ecumenical dialogue. They are free to do so, of course, but the principle should also remain that ecumenical dialogue should take place in the country where the interested parties live. One reason for this is that the dialogue should take place against the background of daily life, and the second reason is the desirability of accustoming all Christians to live with each other. In the ecumenical movement we should have regard for the greatness of our common heritage and should forget past injuries in order to allow charity to be in control and to cast out the spirit of dissension. Union will never be achieved through argument but only through virtuous living. The text should indicate clearly the immediate objective of ecumenism, which

is mutual understanding and love amongst those who are united by Baptism but divided by doctrine. Its final aim is the visible union of all Christians in the one Church of Christ. The schema should emphasise both the necessity of ecumenical dialogue and the obligation of the Church of preaching the whole truth. Some suspicious Catholics eye the ecumenical movement with misgivings and would cooperate with other Christians only on the level of charity and sociology. This is not enough. The renewal of the Church requires a true religious dialogue. Genuine interest in the mission of the Church demands that we undertake a fuller and more frequent dialogue with all Christians of whatever denomination.'

THOUGHTS ON ARCHBISHOP HEENAN'S SPEECH

We have had considerable difficulty in making a balanced estimate of this speech. Our first reaction was of its insufficiency in comparison with our own hopes and practice in ecumenism. It certainly falls very far short of what it ought to be. But we have to estimate the value of this declaration against the total absence of Roman Catholic ecumenism in Britain only five years ago and also of the present resistance of large sections of the Roman Catholic hierarchy and people.

Many of those here, on whose opinions we rely, think that we ought to be thankful to have got as far as we have. Heenan has made his hierarchy declare unanimously in favour of ecumenism within a few weeks of his accession, and that (we are credibly informed) against considerable pressure. The Unity Secretariat people here, who have not hesitated to be very critical of the English hierarchy and of Heenan when necessary, were relieved at what he said and thought it might have been much worse, considering what he is up against. Abbot Butler of Downside said openly that he had put his name down to speak (in case Heenan said anything dreadful) and withdrew it with relief when he heard the speech. All this on the credit side.

The 'staging' of the speech itself was most careful. We were provided in the tribune with copies of the Latin and the English before the speech began. Cardinals, the Apostolic Delegate, came beaming into the box immediately after it had finished, to collect our reactions. I tried to be as generous as I could, saying that it was certainly an improvement on the past, though it still fell a long way behind the spirit of the Secretariat and of northern Europe etc. The speech was delivered with much flourish, and when the Archbishop said that the English hierarchy were behind the Schema, there was a certain amount of clapping, which I interpreted as being at least in part the ironic applause of those who thought this declaration overdue. The point about forgetting past injuries is a feeble echo of what the Pope said and an even feebler echo of what we mean and what real ecumenism requires. The *forgetting* of past injuries is useless by itself, and even wrong, if theological, pastoral and other consequences of *forgiving* also are not at the same time worked out to the last letter.

The hope of taking up dialogue in England is one which we should wish to respond to, but is it meant as a hint that we are not expected from that time onwards to treat direct with Rome? In that case, of course, we shall wish to say promptly that, although the *Church of England* will gladly have dialogue with Westminster now that this is possible, the *Anglican Communion* as such will continue to treat with Rome direct. Would it not be worth considering immediately giving an inter-provincial character to Dr. Kelly's Theological Committee (i.e. the one which has met at Selwyn[36] and in Assisi, perhaps by co-opting an American or two in the first instance) fairly soon? I imagine that Heenan will want to direct its activities to Westminster at once, and as long as its membership is exclusively English it will be a little difficult to gainsay him. The Roman Catholic sub-committee of C.F.R. will then be the English Committee for this dialogue. Since it now will have to confront the official committee of the Roman Catholic hierarchy, ought it not to be strengthened with a Bishop as its chairman, etc.? Ought we to be prepared for Heenan to move fast after he gets home? I wonder whether the Archbishop of Canterbury will increasingly have to be careful to distinguish between anything he does or says towards the Roman Catholic hierarchy in England (which perhaps he might do as often as possible through the episcopal chairman of the R.C. Church) and what he says or does in his capacity (whatever that exactly is) in the Anglican Communion? Out here we have continually to uphold the distinction between these two functions.

There are, to my mind, several other points under this head. We hope that the official entry of the Roman hierarchy into the arena isn't meant to shackle the activities of the Roman Catholic religious orders, who have so far been almost the only people who have had anything to say to us. Further, even the English (as distinct from the Anglican) Committee must feel free to talk to the French, Belgian,

---

[36]Selwyn College, Cambridge.

German etc. Catholics in so far as they represent a spirit which is not to be found in official R.C. circles in England.

Report No. 105   22nd November, 1963

72ND GENERAL CONGREGATION, THURSDAY, 21ST NOVEMBER

[. . .]

After several speakers had carried on the discussion on ecumenism in general, the Cardinal Moderator informed the assembly that a standing vote on this point would be taken. The Fathers were overwhelmingly in favour of closing the preliminary debate and passing on to Chapter I. Before opening discussion on Chapter I of the Schema the assembly voted overall approval of the schema independently of Chapters IV and V.

At a later date separate votes will be taken on the overall approval of Chapter IV, on the relationship of Catholics with Jews, and of Chapter V on religious liberty.

Bishop Flores Martin of Barbastro, Spain, said this schema led us into the path of ecumenism which was so dear to Pope John XXIII. This topic must be treated in order to prepare the way of the Lord for cooperation among all men of goodwill. The text should tighten up the logical connection between various parts and should clarify the foundation of ecumenism in the unity of God considered as Creator, Father and Preserver. They shared with their separated Christian brethren in the indelible sacramental character and in spiritual participation in the priesthood of Christ [. . .]. The widest possible latitude should be allowed for participation in non-Catholic religious services in order to avoid the struggles which are all too common among those who should be living together in peace.

Archbishop Florit of Florence considered it unacceptable to say that the Church was built on the foundation of the Apostles and the prophets. This expression gave rise to difficulties and the Council should not leave itself open to the accusation of not knowing its exegesis. It was too optimistic to say that certain elements which were common to the separated brethren and the Roman Catholics were a manifestation of unity. Rather they emphasised division. Prayers said by them and the separated brethren for unity were only externally the same, for they were basically different because of the internal personal intentions of each one. The text had high praise for the separated brethren, but not all of them deserved this praise in the same degree. The treatment of the Jews would be more appropriate in the Schema on the Church. The chapter on religious liberty would be better off in the forthcoming schema on the presence of the Church in the world, since it pertained more to the affirmation of human rights than to ecumenism. When they said that every man had a natural right to the profession and exercise of religion according to his conscience, did they mean to imply that this involved a natural right to diffuse a false religion? Diffusing a false religion was basically wrong, and no one could claim the right to do wrong; all error was against common good. However, this common good could vary according to circumstances and it might at times be better for the common welfare to allow the diffusion of a false religion than to prohibit it publicly and officially.

Archbishop Aramburu of Tucumán, Argentina, thought the schema should [...] map out a little course as a basis for common agreement. Ecumenism should not be treated as a problem but should be elevated to the dignity of a mystery [...]

Archbishop Nicodemo of Bari, Italy, said that this decree was very important, especially Chapter I, because it laid down the conditions necessary for the unity of Christians. It was the task of the Council to give clear and definite principles for ecumenism. Observations could be made on certain expressions used in the text. The schema should give a concrete idea of Catholic ecumenism. Even though this would be in the Vademecum to come later, nevertheless it should also be in the decree.

Bishop Volk of Mainz, Germany, said that Catholic ecumenism must rest on the certainty that only the Catholic Church fulfilled perfectly the promise of Christ to His Church. This presumed the Catholic Church to be really catholic in doctrine and practice. Consequently all Christian truth, all genuine Christian values could find a legitimate place in the Catholic Church. Similarly the Church wanted to recognise and welcome everything Christian. Although promised by Christ catholicity involved their responsibility also. If the Church did not realise this catholicity it would be only one religious group among others and would cease to be genuinely universal. Concrete catholicity was a serious condition of the credibility of the Church and her ecumenical mission.

These two speeches contain the substance of the two main views of the Council, in stark juxtaposition. They are of course quite incompatible.

It would save much time if the vote could be taken at this point. If it were, on this sole issue, I think there is now no doubt that the view of the Bishop of Mainz would prevail. Laus Deo![37]

FUTURE VISITS

I have been thinking about my plans for next year, assuming that the Council will not reassemble until September. Heenan's speech would seem to indicate the importance of keeping up the continuity of this office outside and independent of the Council, and therefore of a visit here in the interim, say in May, on principle [. . .]. The people of the Secretariat say that May would be a good time to come, as there will be meetings of most of the conciliar commissions during that month [. . .]

Report No. 106   26th November, 1963

73RD GENERAL CONGREGATION, FRIDAY, 22ND NOVEMBER

[. . .]

74TH GENERAL CONGREGATION, MONDAY, 25TH NOVEMBER

[. . .]

Continuing the debate on Chapter I of De Ecumenismo

Cardinal Léger, Archbishop of Montreal, said one of the weaknesses of the schema was its manner of presenting unity as a note of the Church. On this point the text was incomplete. Because of undue insistence on unity in the past, the false impression was given that the Church promoted a monolithic unity which entailed excessive uniformity in doctrine, liturgy, etc. In their insistence on unity, they had too often lost sight of the advantages of diversity. When properly understood and promoted, diversity did no harm to unity. Separated non-Catholic churches have their traditions, doctrines and special riches which they understandably want to preserve. They should not neglect to show how this could be done without placing any obstacle in the path of unity based on perfect obedience to the Vicar of Christ. The Schema should also provide them with more effective

---

[37] 'Praise be to God'.

means of providing solutions for their doctrinal differences. Charity and truth must not suffer in their discussions. But they must pursue truth in humility as well as in charity. Since separation became a sad reality, the separated brethren had been engaging in their own doctrinal research. Discrepancies between them and us could not be resolved without joint theological investigation. The Church had known many heresies and schisms. The remedy was not necessarily in authority, but in humble progress in the faith. It was their privilege to have the opportunity to investigate with the separated brethren the unsearchable riches of Christ. Immobilism in doctrine was a serious obstacle in the path of unity. They could usefully recall the words of St. Augustine: 'Seek that you may find and then continue to seek that you may find more'. Genuine Christianity had no room for immobilism.

Cardinal Ritter, Archbishop of St Louis, U.S.A, said it should be pointed out how the unity which was the goal of all ecumenism was a fundamental principle of the ecumenical movement. For this reason the schema should show a real concept of unity. The basic inspiration must be pastoral. They were not only issuing a decree, but were also expected to provide it with effective stimulus for action. The goal to be achieved was the principle of all motion. They had with their separated brethren common desires and common activities. They should present unity not merely as a goal of inestimable value, but in such a way as to show disunion as an evil of equal magnitude. Chapter I presented a concept of unity which only Catholics could recognise. In her present state the Church was far from the realisation of the full perfection which belonged to her by nature. Separation and division in the ranks of Christians was a scandal to the world. The text told them that such divisions retarded the coming of the Kingdom of God. We should, of course, be united in perfect union only when we all shared together in the Lord's table. We should all pray for unity in recognition of one same truth.

Cardinal Bea said there had been much talk in recent days about the 'dangers' of the oecumenical movement. These dangers existed where the question of unity was treated by men who might be inspired by good will, but who were not sufficiently cautious. All inter-faith discussions should be under the supervision of local bishops [. . .]. Directives would come from Rome but must be applied on a local basis. Consequently local Ordinaries and national Episcopal Conferences would be able to take appropriate steps to forestall any possible dangers. It would be useful for regional secretariats to be set up for the promotion of unity in collaboration with the permanent secretariat in Rome. It is claimed that the ecumenical movement will foster a spirit of false irenicism. To obviate this danger, theological dialogue will be placed in the hands only of men qualified by theological knowledge and a deep spirit of devotion to the Church. Who these men were could be better determined by local bishops than by any office in Rome. It was a fact of experience that our separated brethren did not want to be presented with any watered-down version, but wanted only a clear statement of exactly what we teach. As far as the ordinary faithful were concerned it would be the duty of bishops to see that they were well instructed in their faith. It was objected that undue emphasis was placed in the text on what was true in the teaching of the separated brethren, but that there was no full presentation of Catholic truth. It should not be forgotten that the text was not directed to the separated brethren but to their own people. Hence they presumed that they knew their Catholic teaching. It was not their task here to present the whole outline of Catholic doctrine. The Catholics were only too often ignorant of the riches found among the separated brethren. They were to find the 'traces of Christ' and the effects of the gifts of the Holy Spirit in virtue of their baptism and the graces flowing from this Sacrament. If this approach was wrong, then they must criticise every Pope from Leo XIII onwards. No one should find fault with the exhortation to common prayer with the separated brethren. The Holy Office had already approved the common recitation of the Lord's Prayer. All of us pray for that unity for which Christ prayed and bishops should teach their faithful how to do this. All this showed how important it was for all Catholics to understand and appreciate the ecumenical movement.

[. . .]

THE ENGLISH PRESS

We continue to notice Roman Catholic influence on the English press, usually at sub-editor level. I have often helped the *Times* correspondent prepare his statements when they have concerned conciliar affairs. His despatch on Heenan's speech was clearly doctored in Heenan's favour when it appeared next morning. The correspondent reckons there are several Roman Catholics among the sub-editors.

There was a particularly glaring instance in last Sunday's *Sunday Times* (24th November, page 17) in which in the same short article Cardinal Griffin is referred to as the Archbishop of Westminster, but Dr. Stopford[38] as the Anglican Bishop of London. Are we drawing attention to this form of propaganda?

[38]Robert Stopford (1901–1976), Bishop of London, 1961–1973.

Report No. 107   28th November, 1963

75TH GENERAL CONGREGATION, TUESDAY, 26TH NOVEMBER

Some Fathers claimed the right to go on speaking about Chapter I (i.e. they could get five other bishops to support their claim in writing).

Archbishop Manek of Endeh, Indonesia, said that in the Christian communities which came out of the Reformation there were elements which made them real churches, even in an imperfect sense. They accepted the creeds of the first councils and had sacraments, which are the means of grace. They could not deny that the Holy Spirit uses them as a means of salvation. If they possibly could they ought to call them churches, and if they expect dialogue to be effective it ought to proceed on that basis.

Mgr. Kleiner, Abbot General of the Cistercians, said there could be no unity without Mary. Who could heal the divisions in the family better than the Mother?

Bishop Leven, Auxiliary of San Antonio, U.S.A., spoke to all, juncti et seiuncti.[39] His speech was a daring answer to those (particularly in Italy) who spoke disparagingly of work for Ecumenism. There had been charges of infidelity to the Church, to the Pope, to doctrine. But it was not among them that these things were seen. Why don't these Italian prelates look to their own Church affairs? In Italy baptised people fail to go to church and then vote communist; there the Lateran pact makes the Church guilty of conniving at injustice; there you can find ignorance and superstition. Let them educate and train their people. To hear them speak you would think there were no passages in scripture other than those which refer to Peter. They speak as if recognising good in others were to betray one's own faith. [. . .]

OBSERVERS' MEETING, TUESDAY, 26TH NOVEMBER

De Ecumenismo

Professor Schlink asked two questions:
What status has a dogmatic constitution? [. . .]
What is the difference between a constitutio and a decretum? There is not complete agreement between the decretum on Ecumenismo and

---

[39]'Joined and separated'.

the dogmatic constitutio de Ecclesia. Then we hear of a directorium in the de Ecumenismo. That is a practical publication; will it be like an instructio?

Mgr. Willebrands gave a short answer saying that the constitution de Ecclesia is as yet in an unfinished state. A schema is only a draft. The intention at least is the same. If there are any discrepancies it is hoped that they will be ironed out. A directorium is not in any sense a source of dogma, though it ought to correspond, in its dogmatic implications, to all other sources. It is not safe to think of 'degrees' of authority. Generally speaking a decretum is pastoral first, and a constitutio primarily dogmatic.

Professor Witte said a matter is only de fide tenendum[40] if it explicitly says so. Otherwise it is an expression of the magisterium.

Professor Schlink said

When he gets back to Germany and reports to his bishops on Chapter II they will say that this view of ecumenism is without significance for us. The whole schema is written round baptism. There is some difference about the Roman Catholic reaction to Evangelical baptisms when Lutherans, for example, convert to Roman Catholicism. Sometimes they baptise sub conditione,[41] other times not. The doctrine of baptism is different in different regions. But sometimes the Roman Catholics ask different questions,

a) was the baptism in the Trinitarian formula?
b) was the baptism done by the pouring of water?
c) Was the real intention to be baptised?

therefore it is to be hoped that something very precise will be said about the real nature of baptism. There is great difference between the regions, as indeed sometimes between the practice of baptism in the various Landeskirche.

Mgr. Willebrands in answering said that the Secretariat discourages a rigid attitude about this, and also that in the 19th century there were

---

[40] The Extraordinary Magisterium infallibly teaches both de fide credenda (i.e. of the faith to be believed) and de fide tenenda (i.e. of the faith to be held) doctrines through what are called Defining Acts.

[41] Conditional baptism: baptism administered when there is doubt whether a person has already been baptised or whether a former baptism is valid.

German Protestant theologians whose views of baptism were so queer that Roman Catholic bishops naturally became suspicious.

[...]

Dr. Nissiotis, Orthodox, asked in what way the schema expressed the Catholic mind of ecumenism. What is its purpose? It is a document first for Roman Catholic people, catechetical, pedagogical. But in this case should it not have a different title, such as 'the Catholic view of Ecumenism'? We have to be careful that the hoped-for dialogue is not closed before it begins. Although the Orthodox come off better than anyone else, this schema gives no new thought. It is not easy for one Church to describe another. Does the Council realise the difficulty? There can be a certain amount of limited occidental dialogue, but that is about all. As far as it is for the Roman Catholic faithful, it is misleading. As for the Protestant churches, it is outside the possibility of dialogue. The treatment of history is very inadequate. It speaks of events without interpreting them.

[...]

Report No. 108   29th November, 1963

76TH GENERAL CONGREGATION, WEDNESDAY, 27TH NOVEMBER

[...]

Still on *Chapter II* –

Bishop Nuer of Thebes, Egypt, said that association with their separated brethren in prayer could be realised, not only in the recitation of common prayers, as indicated in the schema, but in other ways as well. This was particularly true of the participation of Catholic priests and laity in non-Catholic religious services. The presence of a Catholic priest at an Orthodox funeral, and vice versa, could provide a broadening basis. It hardly made sense, for instance, when two brothers of the same family, one a Catholic and one an Orthodox, were being married on the same day to have the Orthodox priest performing one ceremony with his back turned to the Catholic priest, or to have the Catholic priest do the same with his back turned to the Orthodox. Such procedures would never create goodwill or lead to union. For the same reason Catholics should sometimes be allowed to partake of the Holy Eucharist in a non-Catholic rite, because if they are allowed union with a member of the Mystical Body, they should be allowed to communicate with the Head.

Archbishop Mingo of Monreale, Italy, said there was a great difference between many of their separated brethren and themselves; many of the separated brethren would not admit the primacy or infallibility; others deny the natural law on marriage, and some even doubt the existence of a personal God.

Bishop Necsey, Apostolic Administrator of Nitria, Czechoslovakia, thought a paragraph should be added to Chapter II in order to insist on the necessity of removing obstacles standing in the way of the achievement of union. One of these obstacles was found in the tone of several of the books used for religious instruction. Their catechisms and texts of Church history should be revised in the light of truth and charity. They must avoid whatever could cause animosity or bitterness, never forgetting that the members of *all* churches were men with human sensibilities.

Discussing Chapter III of De Ecumenismo –

[. . .]

Bishop Collin of Digne, France, said the Anglican Church should be given special treatment, just as was done for the Oriental churches.

Bishop Dwyer of Leeds said those who lived in the midst of non-Catholics could be expected to have certain lights on ecumenical questions, which were not available to those who could speak eloquently, but who did not, perhaps, have in their dioceses even one of their separated brethren. We should not be deluded into thinking that a few kind words and a spirit of cordiality would bring on union in the immediate future. We had come a long way from the time when Catholics lived in closed communities. Polemics had waned. But union was still far off. There were differences in faith and in morals. Some, even bishops, (this means Woolwich)[42] did not admit the virgin birth or the fact of the resurrection. While holding the principles of true faith, some did not regard contrary doctrines as being against this same faith. They were unwilling to admit that there were actions intrinsically wrong. Even the Quakers, who were traditionally among the most rigid groups outside the Church, had recently declared themselves favourable to opinions

[42] See p. 38, n. 8, and p. 188, n. 48.

which were in complete contrast with basic morality. A non-Catholic bishop (the Archbishop of Wales[43]) had stated that those outside the Church reject Catholic dogmas, not because these dogmas are not understood, but because they have been understood and are rejected as erroneous. The basic principle of all ecumenism is to take each man exactly as he is. The dialogue must be perfect on both sides. There can be no preliminary accepting of conditions. We must begin with mutual respect and recognise problems, such as the basic one of how to reconcile human liberty with the authority of the Church. Our attitude cannot be that of a mother talking to a prodigal son. We must remember that today the one sheep is in the fold and ninety-nine are out in the desert.

Archbishop Gouyon, Coadjutor of Rennes, said had this schema kept silence on the Oriental churches, this would have been interpreted either as ignorance or as a lack of affection for these churches. If the text was to have its full value it should *forget nothing*. Anglicanism, because of its specific differences from Protestantism, should be given special mention. We should not use the term 'community' which had only a sociological sense, but rather the term 'communion', (koinonia), which was the term used in the early Church.

Bishop Baraniak, Auxiliary of Poznań, Poland, asked how they could promote ecumenism if they paid no attention to the suggestions of our separated brethren. The text speaks of unity as of a simple return of those outside the Church. This was not acceptable. They must study honestly all the difficulties of their separated brethren and with equal honesty propose solutions. Without this our ecumenism was nothing more than a pious desire and our words were as those of one beating the air.
[. . .]

THE APOSTOLIC DELEGATE[44]

When the Delegate was fêted at the English college a few days ago, Archbishop Heenan assured him of the loyalty of English Catholics. The Apostolic Delegate in reply said that he looked forward to working with them, but that they must not be surprised if they found him doing some things to which they were not accustomed – such as accepting invitations to Lambeth if he received them.

---

[43]Edwin Morris (1894–1971), Archbishop of Wales, 1957–1967.
[44]The newly appointed Igino Eugenio Cardinale (see *Dramatis Personae*).

PAPAL AUDIENCE

The Bishop of Ripon and Canon Pawley were received in private audience on the 29th November. They had twenty minutes with his Holiness at the end of a morning in the Council. Rather to their surprise, and slightly to their disappointment, most of the audience was an exchange of courtesies, though they were real courtesies and the Pope spoke very sincerely of his affection for the Anglican Church, saying that it had a real part to play in the work for ecumenism. The Bishop presented bound copies of four of his published works of which the Pope expressed appreciation. While looking into one of the historical books, he showed how conscious he was of the great figures of English church history which had contributed to the good of the universal Church, quoting St. Anselm in particular. Canon Pawley presented a record of Christmas music in Ely cathedral, knowing the Pope's delight in such things. He repeated that we should always feel free to come and see him 'when you wish'. He told us to convey his greeting to the Archbishop of Canterbury, which we hereby do.

Report No. 109   2nd December, 1963

77TH GENERAL CONGREGATION, THURSDAY 28TH NOVEMBER

Still on Chapter II of De Ecumenismo.

Cardinal Frings, Archbishop of Cologne, said that in the Council they had been, so to speak, in the school of the Holy Spirit and all of them had learned much. The world had great hopes of this Council in the field of ecumenism, but they should take care to clarify some points in order to forestall misunderstandings. They should show that the 'one holy' Church was not something to be waited for in the future but that it was of the very nature of the Church founded by Christ. Consequently these notes must be found in the Church now, in expectation of the ultimate glorification of the Church with Christ in the world to come. They should insist on the question of religious schools for the education of their children. This insistence was not prompted by any desire to dominate the minds of the children, but rather by the wish to provide a spiritual centre and atmosphere for the process of education. Other churches had naturally the same right, and recognition of this fact would be a great contribution to tolerance. They should at the same time declare disapproval of mixed marriages. If a non-Catholic feels it is against his conscience to promise to bring up his children in the Catholic faith, he should not be subjected to pressure, but he should give up any idea of marriage in the circumstance. They should declare the validity of mixed marriages contracted in the presence of a non-Catholic minister and should remove the ecclesiastical penalties for such marriages. All this would clear the atmosphere and prepare the way for fruitful ecumenical activity.

This was a surprisingly reactionary statement for one of the 'progressives' of the Council. But he is an old man. Nevertheless he did end up by suggesting the abolition of the Ne Temere decree.[45]

[...]

Archbishop Blanchet, Rector of the Catholic Institute, Paris, said they should not lose sight of the importance of intellectual activity in the work of reconciliation. The faith of their separated brethren could not be reduced to a simple list of propositions which it was enough to refute. They should make serious efforts to understand all their doctrines. They should carefully avoid any feelings of superiority or condescension and should guard against any attitude which might give the impression that accepting the Catholic Church was like abandoning one's mother. They should have great respect for the positive aspects of the faith of their separated brethren. This implied also mutual aid in fraternal service of the truth.

Fr. Reetz, O.S.B., Superior General of the Benedictines of Beuron, Germany, said the experiences of recent years at the Abbey of Beuron had provided an opportunity to see what outsiders like and dislike in the Church. In the monastery there were six priests who were converts to Catholicism. Theologians from the Protestant faculty of the University of Tübingen frequently came to the monastery for a few days of retreat. One of their major complaints was what we might call contorted and acrobatic theology – such as the book, printed with ecclesiastical approbation, arguing for the immaculate conception of St. Joseph and his assumption into heaven. Such theology did not reflect the doctrine of scripture and tradition. Similarly they disliked excessive scholasticism in Roman Catholic theology which was often lacking the biblical touch. They disliked undue juridicism, which exalted the legal element in the Church to the point where it became difficult to understand its relationship with human liberty. Lastly they objected to certain forms of piety which obscured true piety. This was particularly

---

[45] The Ne Temere ('Not rashly') decree of 1907 set down the requirements of the Roman Catholic Church for marriage by members of that Church. The decree adopted a severe and rigid view of mixed marriages and was now widely regarded as inoperable.

true in the field of Marian devotions – such as the rosary of the tears of Mary. The Roman Catholic presentation of the theology of indulgences often seemed to lose sight of the prudent warning of the Council of Trent. On the other hand they admired the liturgy with chant, the marvellous unity of the Church, the monastic life, the celibacy of the clergy, and sacramental confession. On one of the closing days of the Council the opening Mass should be the Votive Mass for Church Unity.

Fr. Capucci, Superior General of the Order of St. Basil, Aleppo, Syria, considered the legislation on participation in non-Catholic religious services should be changed for ecumenical, social, apostolic and pastoral reasons. This would involve no danger of scandal or indifferentism. The invalidity of mixed marriages before non-Catholic ministers should be rescinded. The Council should recognise the right of Patriarchal Synods to dispense from ecclesiastical laws on participation in non-Catholic religious services. Local Ordinaries should have the same right in specific cases.

Archbishop Fares of Catanzaro and Squillace, Italy, said the Octave for Christian Unity should be included officially in the liturgy, with permission for the Votive Mass for Church Unity. The Sunday falling in this Octave could be observed as Church Unity Sunday with solemn services to impress the faithful with their obligation to pray for unity.

Bishop Schoemaker of Purwokerta, Indonesia, said Chapter II spoke of the biblical movement as a pledge and augury of the success of the ecumenical movement. The Council should entrust to a post-Conciliar Commission the preparation of a text of the Vulgate for all Christians. This text should be prepared with the assistance of outstanding scholars and biblical experts from every nation and religious confession. It could be called the 'Vatican Vulgate'. This proposal was once made by Desiderius Erasmus. It would be fitting now for the Council to accept the 'desiderium Desiderii'.[46]

The following speakers continued the discussion on Chapter III.

Archbishop Morcillo of Saragossa, Spain, said the distinction made in the text between the Oriental churches and the Protestant churches of the West was inadequate, because a geographical basis was used for the Orient while chronology was used for the Protestants. This enumeration of groups was lacking in ecumenical sensitivity. It omitted some groups, such as the Old Catholics, and even certain others who had Observers here at the Council. The Anglicans also, for example,

---

[46] 'Desiderius' wish' / 'wish's wish'.

have preserved a wonderful tradition which should not be ignored. The episcopate could serve as an adequate basis for distinction among the churches according to whether they had apostolic succession.

Bishop Malanczuk, Exarch for Ukrainians resident in France, thought the schema should make some mention of non-religious causes of past separations: politics, race, excessive patriotism, the desire to be free of outside influences, mutual ignorance, distrust [. . .]. It should be made clear that union with Rome for Oriental churches would not be made dependent on the suppression of local particular churches [. . .] [. . .]

THE NEXT SESSION

This will be held from 14th September to 20th November 1964. It is taken for granted that there will be at least one more after that.

Report No. 110   4th December, 1963

78TH GENERAL CONGREGATION, FRIDAY 29TH NOVEMBER

[. . .]

Discussion of Chapter III of the schema on ecumenism continued.

Bishop Goody of Bunbury, Australia, said there should be a clear exposition of the Catholic doctrine on the basic truths on which there would have to be complete agreement. One of these points would be the place of a hierarchical priesthood in the Catholic sense, because not infrequently they heard it said that Leo XIII's declaration on the invalidity of Anglican Orders was dictated by political necessity. Other doctrines which should be stressed were the primacy, the integrity of sacramental life and the public cult of the Blessed Virgin. The importance of this stress on clear doctrine came from the fact that if our separated brethren found us voicing nothing but praise and emphasising particularly doctrines on which we already agreed, they would be led to think that union was already achieved. There should, of course, be no harsh polemics, but clarity was indispensable. Where Catholics were in the minority, priests must first be convinced themselves of the ecumenical movement and then teach their people the principles of true ecumenism, urging them to the faithful practice of charity.

Bishop Helmsing of Kansas City – St. Joseph, U.S.A., considered the text as it stood, with its unwillingness to recognise the term 'church' as applicable to non-Catholic communities, would certainly be an obstacle to any effective ecumenical action. Reasons for this would be: (1) ordinary decency and politeness, because in daily life Catholics and non-Catholics alike use the term 'church' to designate such Christian communities. (2) the word 'church' does not have a strictly univocal meaning, but can be used analogically. (3) in the Old Testament when the Northern part of the Kingdom of Israel was cut off by schism it nevertheless continued to belong to the people of God, was moved by the Spirit of God and had prophets. (4) the elements of imperfect union referred to in the text were found not merely in individuals but likewise in these communities considered as groups. Many of them had an admirable sense of the ministry and had also had martyrs. They could not deny them communion in the sense of koinonia. Everyone was expecting a vote on the acceptance of Chapters IV and V as a basis for discussion, even though time would prevent them from being fully discussed on the floor. There was no reason why this vote could not be taken even today.

Bishop Rupp, Monaco, thought that although the statements in the text were not completely without theological foundation, they gave a general impression of superficiality. For instance, nothing was said about devotion to the episcopate which was found in several separated Christian communities. In the Anglican Church, for example, many beautiful and inspiring things were to be found on bishops and their place in the Church. Neither was there sufficient emphasis on the concept of divine transcendence, the idea which meant so much to Karl Barth[47] and which had a real foundation in the Old Testament. This would be a real positive element. While they must hold fast to the entire deposit of revelation, they must nevertheless remember that there was a hierarchy in the importance of revealed truths. Lastly, attention should be drawn to the special providence watching over all men of goodwill living in these communities. Cardinal John Henry Newman[48] stated, after 21 years in the Catholic Church, that the fact that the Anglican Church had for three centuries produced so many holy people and accomplished so much good could be explained only by a special intervention of divine providence. The optimism reflected

---

[47]Karl Barth (1886–1968), the great Swiss Reformed theologian, author of the multi-volumed *Church Dogmatics* and many other studies, whose reputation across the Protestant world was now colossal.

[48]See p. 213, n. 2.

in the text was exaggerated and should be toned down so as to be more realistic.

Bishop Zoghby, Patriarchal Vicar for Melchites in Egypt and the Sudan, said that after nine centuries of separate evolution the Latin Church and the Oriental churches were now recognising their similarities. The difficulty in the past was that effective dialogue was blocked by social, cultural and political considerations. The Oriental churches always opposed the centralisation of Rome, seeing in this a threat of uniformity and a menace to their own particular Christian heritage. Unity of faith was impossible if it meant harm to the traditions of the Oriental Church. But, since they were both apostolic and traditional, real unity between these churches could be achieved. Dialogue must be on a basis of equality. The Oriental churches had the task of promoting this dialogue if they wished, within the Catholic Church, to bear witness to the institutions and traditions of the Orient.

Fr. Hage, Superior General of the Order of St. Basil in Lebanon, said the Council should authorise a mitigation of the prevailing legislation prohibiting participation in non-Catholic religious services. This prohibition causes an increase in dislike and fanaticism against the Church. There was no question of active participation, but only of having a passive part. This could be justified by the moral principle of double effect, or by the other principle which tells us to choose the lesser of two evils. There was no danger to faith, fear of scandal, or danger of indifferentism to be feared from this passive participation in Oriental communities, because the Oriental Church professed no formal error.

COUNCIL OF TRENT

The Pope held a Cappella Papale[49] on Tuesday 3rd December to celebrate the 400th anniversary of the end of the Council of Trent. Most of the Observers abstained from attending, as it was for them more in the nature of a disaster to be mourned. The Bishop of Ripon attended on the grounds that it was a Council function and that he was here as an Observer to observe, not to demonstrate. I took advantage of the fact that I am technically a 'guest' and not an Observer to absent myself in preference for much paperwork.

---

[49]The papal chapel is a solemn function, typically Mass or Vespers, celebrated by the Pope or in his presence, and it takes place, as a rule, in the chapels of the apostolic palaces, basilicas, and churches.

I notice, on looking up the facts, that the Council ended on 4th December 1563 and that on the 2nd and 3rd they rushed through the decrees on Purgatory and Indulgences, for which we give no thanks at all.

[. . .]

A NEW BOOK

There seems to be a book recently published, 'Vatican II – A Struggle of Minds and other Essays', by E.H. Schillebeeckx, O.P.,[50] which has some interesting ideas. One which attracts me (to judge from reviews) is the use of the word 'essentialist' to describe a theologian who believes that divine truth can be and must be essentially contained in a proposition of words, which is therefore incapable of revision. I imagine the antithesis of this truth, which is that truth can never even adequately (let alone finally) be caged inside a proposition is nearer to our way of thinking. The future of this basic idea is presumably very important for ecumenism.

ECUMENICAL DIALOGUE

Cardinal Bea, in his last speech to the Council [. . .] emphasised quite rightly that ecumenical work shall only be undertaken by people who are intellectually qualified to do so. In this he was voicing the fears of many Roman Catholics who are afraid of too much open discussion.

I am interested in the obverse of this idea. There are far too many people, in my experience, on the Roman Catholic side engaged in 'ecumenical' work, who have not had the necessary preparation. There has often been occasion to refer adversely in these reports, e.g. to the FOYER UNITAS in Rome, to its staff and to its leader, Fr. Boyer S.J., whose continued ignorance about the C. of E. needs to be experienced to be believed. I have several times recently been approached by R.C. ecumenical enthusiasts who have asked where I think ecumenical dialogue should begin. They can often be deflated by being asked if they have ever read any Anglican book about the C of E.

---

[50]Edward Schillebeeckx (1914–2009), progressive – and increasingly distinguished – Roman Catholic theologian, much involved in advising the Dutch bishops at the Council. Although never named *peritus* he was theological adviser to Cardinal Alfrink during the Council.

Report No. III   5th December, 1963

79TH AND FINAL GENERAL CONGREGATION OF THE 2ND SESSION, MONDAY 2ND DECEMBER

[. . .]

Cardinal Ruffini, Archbishop of Palermo, obviously filling in time, said that the only real way of ecumenism was the submission of all to Rome.

Bishop Green of Port Elizabeth, S. Africa, said some new attitude should be worked out towards Anglicans and the problems of their orders. Apostolicae Curae[51] should be rethought.

Bishop Muldoon of Sidney, Australia, said the references to Anglicans and Protestants were totally inadequate. If the relevant passage went out to the world as it was, they would demonstrate to the world that they totally misunderstood and misrepresented the Protestant world. There was too little spirit of repentance about the undoubted mistakes which the Catholic Church had already made. Many of the orators who spoke so proudly as if the Church were perfect in all things ought to go to a good confession [. . .]

[. . .]

Bishop Tomášek of Buto, Czechoslovakia, said that if there was to be any hope of reunion between the Orthodox and Rome, there must obviously be as a sine qua non a 'round table' conference of representatives of all bishops of both sides without any question of precedence. This alone was an 'ecumenical' council. Thus the deep psychological barriers would be overcome, and the solution of problems of unity would be in sight.

[. . .]

Dom Christopher Butler agreed with those who agreed that there should be special reference to the Anglican Communion, especially as they are bundled in with the Protestants. This decree should not be something which offends those who claim some continuity with the past. Why not say that they were 'separated in the 16th century'? The paragraph about penitence should be more carefully phrased to show that such penitence was mutual and sincere and that it was to be a starting point for better relations.

---

[51] The papal encyclical of 1896 which declared Anglican Orders 'null and void' and accordingly defined Anglican–Roman Catholic relations unhappily for the next half-century.

Cardinal Bea said that he regretted it had not been possible to examine Chapters IV (Jews) and V (Religious Liberty), but they would discuss them first thing in September next. He asked the fathers to consider them both most carefully and to send in emendations etc. to the Secretary General.

N.B. American publicists are very disappointed that a snap vote was not taken about these two chapters, but we are not. In our view the Americans are being somewhat naïve about this. Freedom, especially in its political context, is a great idol of theirs. Englishmen perhaps see it as one, no doubt the chief, of several political goods. But freedom of conscience for all Christians, but especially for Roman Catholics, is a very complicated problem. Protestants make it the greatest of virtues, because they have had to fight for it. But it is obviously not easy for the Roman Catholics suddenly to turn their backs on centuries of a contrary tradition. Even today it presents problems in detail, apart from the need to reconcile it to the principle of obligation in religion. It is not to be expected that, for example, the Spanish bishops will easily agree in effect that American Protestant fundamentalist sects can go everywhere unmolested and create havoc among their faithful. It is better that this problem should be carefully thought out and stated in a manner which will carry conviction, and also be able to be administered practically. Otherwise there is a danger that the whole chapter will be regarded by the world as a cynical piece of flag-waving.

[...]

CONCLUSION OF 2ND SESSION OF VATICAN COUNCIL, WEDNESDAY 4TH DECEMBER

The 2nd Session of the Council ended with a celebration in St. Peter's and the solemn promulgation of the two items so far completed, the Constitution on the Liturgy and the Decree on the Means of Communication [...]

The discourse of the Pope calls for little comment. It showed approval of the course the Council had taken and expressed the hope that it would continue on these same lines. At one point he said, 'We hope that the third session in the autumn of next year will bring the Council to its completion.' The discourse ended, as will have been widely reported, by the announcement of the Pope's impending visit to the Holy Land.

[...]

POWERS OF THE EPISCOPATE IN THE ENCYCLICAL LETTER PASTORALE MUNDUS

The Pope has recently accorded to the bishops the right of their see and a large number of faculties (40 in all) for which they previously had to refer to the Holy See. This is in line with the present policy of reducing the power of the Curia and increasing that of the bishops. Many of them are so ludicrous as not to be worthy of mention, but we selected the following:

1) To give permission for a priest to say two masses on a week day or three on a Sunday.
2) To give dispensations from fasting for certain cases according to circumstances.
3) To celebrate evening masses.
4) To celebrate Holy Communion outside churches.
5) For sick priests to celebrate sitting in bed.
6) To administer confirmation in cases of necessity.
7) To dispense for a just cause from the impediments of a mixed religion or disparity of cult.
8) To give people in minor orders and lay people, even women, the right to wash the altar linen (believe it or not!)
9) The right to enter for a just cause into the enclosure of a monastery or convent.
10) The right to give people permission to read prohibited books.

[. . .]

Report No. 115   March 25th 1964

MY MOVEMENTS

I propose to return at the beginning of May and shall be on duty there for about three weeks, including doing a job for Bishop Bayne. We shall then take our summer holiday in Italy and return to this country about the 10th of June.

[. . .]

UNIATE CATHOLICS

I never cease to wonder at the 'enlightened' opinions of the prelates of the Uniate churches. I had expected them to be unusually obscurantist because of their proximity to the Orthodox (for the same kind of reason that the English hierarchy are 'sticky'). But such is not the case. I recently read a report of a speech by Archbishop Edelby (Melchite)[52] on the Schema de Ecclesia, in which he said:

> The Western Church is still too clerical in its outlook and behaviour. It starts from a premise different to ours: Christ established Peter as the supreme head – 'a kind of a Roman emperor in a soutane' – then He gave him colleagues and finally subjects, the clergy and the faithful. For us of the Eastern Church it is the other way round: Christ was first of all united to the faithful, to whom the preaching of the Gospels belongs by right; then He gave them apostles, and finally, so that this collegium should remain coherent, he chose a head for them. In contemporary Catholic thought there is as it were a morbid obsession with the primacy of the Pope.

Do we have much traffic with these people? I have made some very good contacts in the Council which I should like to see followed up afterwards.

There is obviously much variety in the ecumenical 'value' of the Uniates. These real Easterns, of ancient lineage, seem to know what it is all about. On the other hand one got the very worst impression of the so-called 'Greek Catholics' in Greece who by the proselytism etc. are one of the principal obstacles to the ecumenical progress.
[. . .]

Report No. 118   6th April, 1964[53]

[. . .]
RETURN TO ROME

I returned on May 4th.

---

[52]Neophytos Edelby (1920–1985), Titular Archbishop of Edessa, 1962–1968.
[53]So dated, but 6th May is clearly meant.

THE FUTURE OF THE COUNCIL

Opinion almost everywhere seems to be divided about the question whether the next session will, or ought to be, the last. Most of our friends in the Secretariat incline to the view that the next session ought to be, but probably won't be, the last.

The Pope has ceased saying with confidence that the next will be the last, and never now says he hopes it will.

Conservatives say that most of what is good is done by Popes anyhow, often after Councils –as at Trent and Vatican I. But they also say that what is good about the Liturgy Schema was all said by Pius XII anyhow. In a recent press interview Cardinal Siri, of Genoa, an extreme right-wing conservative, said:

1. One more session is enough.
2. The Schema on Divine Revelation is important. He hoped nothing would be said to impair the magisterial authority of the Church.
3. The only other schema that really needs treating by the Council is that on the Laity, which has incipient dangers.
4. All other business could as well, and even better, be done by 'ordinary' means.
5. There is no need for statements on the Jews or on Religious Liberty. The church's views on these are clear and well-known.

Others say that the Council must lay down certain principles however long it takes (e.g. the principles of academic liberty already laid down by them in de Revelatione divina,[54] which would never have been stated without a Council) etc.

I feel quite unable to assess the answer to either of these questions. One factor is undoubtedly that people are getting tired of the Council and that it might be advisable to go and develop the ground already won, with the general intention of having another Council within, say, a decade.
[. . .]

THE 2ND SESSION IN RETROSPECT

It is fascinating to observe the recurrent phenomenon of the Roman Church behaving like an oyster with regard to the present irritants in

[54]Dogmatic Constitution on Divine Revelation, *Dei Verbum*, which was solemnly promulgated by Paul VI on 18 November 1965. The Catholic faith is based on divine revelation and this Constitution explains in some detail what the Church believes and teaches with regard to divine revelation, primarily as it is contained in the Bible.

its shell. The latest example of this is represented by several articles I have read on the subject of the Church in the 2nd session. We should describe what happened there as a welcome halting and reversal of trends in Roman ecclesiology which if pursued would have been disastrous. The articles I am thinking of (particularly one by a prominent Italian Jesuit Grassi in a recent *Civiltà Cattolica*[55]) regards the development of Catholic ecclesiology since the Reformation as a necessary progress. In days of error the Church has to become conscious of itself as the societas fidelium.[56] It was at Vatican I (!) that the Church was again able to look at itself as the ineffable mystery. This happy development was continued, of course, in Pius XII's encyclical Mystici Corporis[57] and is now being crowned by the deliberations of the Fathers of Vatican II.

There is no doubt that the indication given by Vatican II that the episcopate is to be regarded as having plenary authority over the Church as a college is not proving easy to reconcile with the full doctrine of the Papacy enunciated at Vatican I, in which the Pope has in himself that full authority derived directly from Christ without reference to the episcopate. To my mind one of the great difficulties about this universal jurisdiction is that if it is to be understood it ought from the first to have been conferred sacramentally by a second consecration. If a man has to be ordained to the priesthood and consecrated to the episcopate a fortiori the assumption of universal jurisdiction over all bishops and the entering in to the position of Vicar of Christ should involve a sacramental grace. If a Cardinal was elected Pope who was only in Priest's (or even Deacon's) orders he was always consecrated bishop after election. But he was Pope from the moment of election. How very difficult it is for the Romans that it was S. Paul who felt wearied by 'that which cometh upon me daily, the care of all the churches'.

There are many hints in reviews that this new conception of collegiality needs much theological reconciliation with existing dogmas. It will be remembered that when, in the Council, the theologians said that they could not accept the principle of collegiality for that reason they were firmly told that the teaching office of the Church lies with the executive and not with the theological department. This all constitutes a pregnant situation for the future. As presumably the Council will be unwilling to negative the Papal decree of Vatican I I hope they may be content to leave some inconsistencies for the future to resolve.

---

[55] Jesuit periodical (see p. 37, n. 6).
[56] 'Society of the faithful'.
[57] Perhaps the most influential encyclical of Pius XII, issued in 1943.

WAYS OF TREATING THE TRUTH

The last sentence of the last item recalls one of the current jokes of the last session, retailed by Abbot Butler, which said that whereas 'Les Russes nient la verité, les Allemands compliquent la verité, les Anglais s'en fichent de la verité, les Espagnols luttent pour la verité, les Italiens la possèdent'.[58]

[...]

THE EVANGELICAL CHURCH IN GERMANY

While in Frankfurt last week I had considerable opportunity to tour churches and various ecclesiastical centres. It was most vexing to find all the Lutheran churches shut, with no evidence of life on their notice boards (except the kind of thing we are accustomed to see on chapel boards in England – Next Sunday 10, Pfarrer[59] X; 6, Pfarrer Y, not even indicating what the service was). The main church of Frankfurt (Niemöller's[60] 'cathedral') was in fact shut when it was advertised to be open.

The Roman churches are all beautifully clean, many of them refurnished simply according to the Liturgical Reform, bristling with notices about activity. And the new architecture of the churches in the suburbs was breath-taking. There was good literature about the Council and its follow-up.

Report No. 119   7th May, 1964

MIXED MARRIAGES

I had a long talk with Willebrands about this matter, continuing our discussion at Ely a few weeks ago. There is no doubt that he has been deeply disturbed by a visit he had from Franklin Clark Fry[61] (I think that is the name – one of the presidents of the World Council of Churches and a Presbyterian from America?). Willebrands said that this man's revelation of the 'complete absence of a theology

---

[58]'The Russians deny the truth, the Germans complicate the truth, the English don't care about the truth, the Spanish struggle with the truth, and the Italians possess it.'

[59]'Pastor'.

[60]Martin Niemöller (1892–1984), Lutheran pastor who came to define the witness of the Confessing Church in the Third Reich before he was imprisoned in 1938. After the War he became a leading light in the ecumenical movement internationally.

[61]See p. 92, n. 64.

of marriage' among Protestants in general made him realise how serious the differences were, and gave him a feeling of hopelessness about any immediate improvement in relationships on that score. Our conversation at Ely turned on my illustrating how we were not to be confused with the general run of Protestants in this, as in many other matters. Willebrands said that Clark Fry denied not only the sacramental character of marriage but the indissoluble nature of it, and even that the contracting parties should have an intention of indissolubility. There is no doubt that there is a serious problem for us all here (i.e. to determine how far it is wise for us to make common cause with the Protestants over this matter until we are quite sure how much common ground we have.) The Bishop of Bristol once warned me that we mustn't be too censorious about indiscipline among Protestants because of the questionable discipline e.g. of P.E.C.U.S.A. But a variety of practice in the treatment of divorce is a different matter from deep differences about the nature of matrimony itself.

Willebrands has often said that the Roman Catholic Church cannot be expected to take the submissions of Protestants seriously until they show some intention to define what they mean by matrimony. He has asked if there is any possibility of us every declaring Holy Matrimony a sacrament. I thought not, because we were anxious to emphasise the importance also of matrimony contracted outside the Church. Were there then no differentiae of Christian Marriage? I said, as to its validity in God's sight, no, if its intention was life-long; but as to its efficacy, Christian marriage obviously profited by the fact that it was deliberately used as a means of grace.

The Anglican definitions are not easy to defend. The language of Art. 25 is deplorable.[62] To begin with, it doesn't even define which of the 5 'ex-sacraments' are 'such as have grown partly of the corrupt following of the Apostles' or which are 'states of life allowed in the Scriptures'. If it is the latter then this meagre language ill accords with the language of the service which describes it as 'an honourable estate instituted by God in the time of man's innocency' and that it is 'consecrated ... to such an excellent mystery that in it is signified and represented the spiritual marriage betwixt Christ and his Church'.

I have never tried to defend Art. 25 and sincerely hope it will one day be superseded. But to the Romans I have constantly said that

---

[62] Article 25 of the 39 Articles of the Church of England, *Of the Sacraments*, retains those two sacraments 'ordained of Christ our Lord in the Gospel ... baptism and the supper of the Lord', the other five being excluded as having 'grown partly of the corrupt following of the Apostles'.

it does not appear to us necessary to define matrimony any further than perhaps to assemble and clarify the principles stated or implied in the Prayer Book. The question whether or not it is a sacrament, or in what sense, would raise more questions than can be answered. The declaration, or absence of declaration, that Holy Matrimony was a sacrament would not alter its sacramental efficacy in any case. The only pastorally urgent question is as to whether the ordinance is regarded as life-long. This is unmistakably clear from the liturgy and has in any case repeatedly been declared dogmatically by the Convocations.

Willebrands finds it difficult to agree that the Roman Church can declare Anglican marriages valid in the absence of a declaration that they are a sacrament. Still less would it be possible to accept the validity of state marriages (I told him of the declaration of life-long contract status exhibited in civil registrars' offices in Britain). This is a strange conservative streak in an otherwise liberal man.

As for the progress of the question in the Council, Willebrands for once seems to be quite uncertain. At the beginning of our last talk about the matter he said he thought it would only come up after the Council in the course of the revision of Canon Law. But when I pressed him about Cardinal Frings' hope to get all 'reasonable' Protestant marriages to be declared valid in the eyes of the Roman Church, he admitted that it might come up under the Schema de Sacramenti, the text of which he had not seen.

I have frequently stressed the point that from the point of view of the 'image' of the Roman Church in the eyes of the contemporary world the whole of the marriage discipline (which is much wider than the question of Mixed Marriages) gives an unsatisfactory impression, both inside the Roman Church and outside. It is commonly said that decisions at the Rota can be bought – this is probably untrue, but it is said [. . .]

Willebrands has several times said, and I have had to agree with him, that if we reckon to object officially to the workings of the Rota we ought to be documenting our objections most carefully. It would be reasonable to forward cases complained about to the Secretary for Christian Unity for information.

Presumably the new Commission on Roman Catholic Relations will set to work on all this. How is it intended to convey to the clergy and church people that the Commission on Roman Catholic Relations is now the body to whom complaints of injustice, malice or misbehaviour should be sent? We obviously can't make a public announcement to that effect. Will the Archbishops perhaps make a statement about the proposed functions of the Commission on Roman Catholic Relations in committee to the convocations? Or what? The Secretariat seems to think it important that we should be documenting our case. I notice that the press hand-out of 8.5.64 refers to 'discussions of theological questions with Roman Catholics' as if they were the only activity of the Commission. Would the public understand theological to mean 'academic' only? Or as excluding practical, liturgical questions? That would be a pity.

[. . .]

THE EVANGELICAL CHURCH OF GERMANY

I had Willebrands and Mgr. Höfer (Counsellor at the West German Embassy, Professor at Paderborn, Member of the Secretariat for Christian Unity, etc.) to dinner recently. The conversation turned on the diversity of the reactions within the Lutheran Church in particular to the Council. Reference has already been made in these reports to the belief that an agreed formula e.g. on Justification could easily be reached, and that controversy be regarded as at an end. But Höfer remarked that although e.g. Schlink has frequently agreed with him on this subject in private conversation there seems to be a hardening of the arteries when he gets home among his Lutheran friends. There is almost on principle a fear among Lutherans of a new reformation, dogmatic or liturgical, if it is thought of in connection with the Vatican Council. They think of themselves as the purest reform, and have great feelings of trust responsibility towards the immutable principles of the Lutheran Reformation.

[. . .]

Report No. 120   11th May, 1964

[. . .]

THE SECRETARIAT AFTER THE COUNCIL

Cardinal Bea and Willebrands take it for granted that my office will continue. For the first time the other day Willebrands said that the Secretariat had been talking about appointing an Anglican specialist from their side who wants to spend half his time in Rome and half in England, or in some other Anglican centre.

[. . .]

Report No. 121   13th May, 1964

[...]

PROTESTANT REACTION TO THE COUNCIL

One of the most articulate and influential of the observers was the Revd. Robert McAfee Brown, Presbyterian, Professor of Dogmatics in some Western University of the U.S.A. He recently summed up his reactions as follows:

a. We now know that ecumenism has definitely taken root in the Roman Church.
b. It is admitted that there must be internal reform of the Roman Church before ecumenism can become effective.
c. The reform of the Liturgy has been on lines entirely pleasing to Protestants.
d. The intention to concentrate on the gospel and the figure of Christ in all issues has been most impressive and encouraging.
e. The Council has shown itself anxious to reform the one-sided version of authority which has tormented the Church since Vatican I and the infallibility decree.
f. The bishops have shown their deep concern for the world outside the Church.
g. The Council has shown a desire to hear what the observers had to say to a degree which would have been thought impossible.
h. The expected majority for a decree on religious liberty is most welcome.

[...]

Report No. 122   19th May, 1964

THE APOSTOLIC DELEGATE

A *bon mot* is reported from Mgr. Heenan who, when asked how the new Apostolic Delegate was getting on, said: 'Oh very well indeed – he's making lots of friends, even among the Catholics.'

ECUMENISM IN BRITAIN

I was told by a member of the Secretariat for Unity (which had a plenary meeting in Italy in April) that Mgr. Heenan had said that he was firmly determined to bring all ecumenical discussion in Britain under the control of the hierarchy. No doubt we are equally determined to exercise our freedom to discuss these matters where and with whom we choose.

THE WEEK OF PRAYER FOR UNITY

The week of prayer for the union of Christians was celebrated in all Italian dioceses from the 18th to the 25th January. It is reported that until two years ago the prayers of the week were 'for the return of the Orthodox, the Anglicans, the Protestants, etc, to the Catholic Church'. Last year faithful Catholics were invited to pray 'for reconciliation to the Holy See of the Orthodox, the Anglicans, etc'. This year the prayer was simply 'for the Orthodox', 'for the Anglicans' etc.
[. . .]

PILGRIMAGES

The pilgrimage and visitor season is now in full swing again. I found myself invited to a party at which the Walsingham enthusiasts were demonstrating a film and proudly showing how 'catholic' life was coming back into the Church of England. The film had been taken and was being shown by a renegade Anglican priest (named Waterhouse) now at the Beda College. The principal lady official at Walsingham was in charge and had invited me to bless the whole issue (I didn't realise until I was there that there was to be a film and a talk). Fortunately I was asked to make a speech also and was able gently to correct the impression that the Church of England as a whole set much store by the revival of this shrine. Fortunately also I knew enough about the sordid end of medieval Walsingham to be able to see it as a means to illustrate the necessity of the Reformation.

One is frequently faced here with the need to discourage keen Anglicans whose conception of progress with Rome is that of showing the Romans how many Roman practices there are going on within the Church of England. In so far as these are also Catholic practices in the wide sense that is obviously to be encouraged. But drawing attention to stale practices, which the Romans want to reform themselves, defeats its own purpose. It was not easy to distinguish between the revival of pilgrimages, which are salutary (provided they are Christocentric) and the unnecessary recrudescence of Marian extravagances. I have already asked Percy Coleman[63] to do what he

---

[63] Frederick Philip 'Percy' Coleman (1911–1998) became General Secretary of the English Church Union in 1955 but left the movement in 1968. A striking figure in the world of

can to circularise among Church Union members the need for caution and common sense in these matters. I wonder if the new Commission[64] might consider sending a memorandum to 'catholic' organisations in England concerning the need to rethink our behaviour under the new conditions which now prevail?

[. . .]

CARDINAL TISSERANT

I had lunch with this remarkable prelate yesterday, one of his many 80th birthday lunches. He has been a Cardinal 26 years, and is Dean of the College. He had just been to America and was full of the World Fair and the 4 more honorary degrees he had collected.

At one point he took me aside and said, 'Is there anything you're burning to ask me?' I said, 'How is the reform of the Curia going on?' He said, 'Bien ça commence. Ce Pape est très courageux, et très "furbo" (an Italian word meaning "cunning, artful") et il fera ce qu'il veut; il y a beaucoup de gens là bas qui ont peur'.[65] The Cardinal again hinted that he would like to be asked to England, but he doesn't think Heenan will ask him. I wonder if Cardinale would?

[. . .]

THE DECREE DE ECUMENISMO

The decree has had a chapter added to it on 'Islam' and on 'non-Christian religions'. I imagine the inclusion of Islam has political reasons, lest it should be thought that the Vatican was especially concerned with the Jews (vis-à-vis the situation in the Middle East).

I imagine this makes it all the more desirable for this section to be removed from the decree and to stand apart.

Anglo-Catholicism, deeply influenced by French Catholicism and Christian socialism, Coleman was enthusiastic about the new Vatican council.

[64] It is not clear to which commission Pawley is referring here.

[65] 'It is going well. The Pope is very brave and very cunning and he can do as he wishes; there are many people over there who are afraid.'

Report No. 123   9th June, 1964

THE OBISPO SUPREMO OF THE PHILIPPINES

You ask for further details of Bishop de los Reyes' visit to Cardinal Bea. The O.S. did most of the talking, with the Cardinal a very interested listener. There is no doubt that the Cardinal was very impressed with the O.S.'s discourse. The O.S. spoke with much animation and emotion, which was never excessive, but most telling. Incidentally, in his humility (which is impressive) he had asked me a number of questions about what I thought he ought to say, but at the interview, although he adopted my few suggestions, it was clear that his mind (and heart) were already full of a considerable number of things.

After the introductory courtesies the Cardinal apologised that he hadn't visited the Philippines and said that he had read about the circumstances of the origin of the P.I.C.[66] The O.S. then took the floor and said, with a great smile, that he hoped it had been an unprejudiced account. He said that had he (Cardinal Bea) lived through the circumstances of political, social and moral degradation of the Church in the Philippines he too would have had no alternative but to rebuild the Church on new foundations. Perhaps he would have been Obispo Supremo (laughter).

He then went on to extol Pope John XXIII and Cardinal Bea himself in a very touching and humble way. They were real patterns of the kind of church leader the world needed – all this with quite a display of knowledge as to what they had said and done in detail. Having thus prepared the ground he stopped abruptly and said: 'Your Eminence, there is something which needs doing in our Saviour's name in the Philippines which I think you can do for us. It is this. The friendly spirit of Pope John and yourself must reach our islands at all cost, and soon. As I stand beneath our Saviour's image (pointing to the crucifix) I can honestly say that I have never spoken unkindly of or behaved unkindly towards Roman Catholics. And I have always encouraged my clergy and people to imitate this example. But I'm afraid your Cardinal Santos (R.C. Archbishop of Manila, P.I.) could not say the same! (Much laughter) We are a humble people and we don't ask to be made much of – we just ask that other Christians shall be kind to us. Can you not soften Cardinal Santos? (Laughter again.) I am President of the Council of Churches in the P.I. and

---

[66] Philippine Independent Church, or Aglipayan Church, which separated from Rome in 1902.

I have often asked Cardinal Santos if he will send observers to our meetings so that we can act together on social questions, which are very pressing in our islands. He does not even answer my letters. I know that many of his clergy and people would want things to be different.'

Cardinal Bea was evidently very pleased with all this and promised that he would act. The interview ended with the O.S. promising to send the Cardinal copies of their liturgy, Canon Law etc.

All this takes on new interest in view of the reports that the Pope is to visit the Philippines next spring. This has been in the Italian newspapers, and the Secretariat are unable to confirm or deny it: they think it likely. The occasion is said to be the 400th anniversary of the evangelisation of the islands by (?Spanish) missionaries. It is certainly the only predominantly Christian country in Asia, and the fact that this would be his first visit to an Asiatic nation as such would be justified on that score (the visit to Bombay will be a visit to an Eucharistic Congress, not to India). If the Pope does go to Manila, we must try to arrange that he receives the O.S.

FAMILY PLANNING

Cardinal Ottaviani has made a speech criticising the action of such as Cardinal Suenens and Archbishop Heenan in speaking on the above subject (particularly about the 'pill') before the Holy Office or the Council have pronounced.

Heenan at least had no alternative, with his Czech (?) doctor at his heels. It is unusual, and perhaps not a bad thing for his public image, to find Heenan being bracketed with the liberals by the Holy Office.
[. . .]

THE POPE AND BUSINESS EXECUTIVES

The professional organisation of Big Business Executives in Italy (U.C.I.D.) has been having its annual conference in Rome. At its annual banquet Cardinal Siri of Genoa was the principal speaker. His speech, which was most acceptable, was on a theme which I can remember hearing from more than one conservative Anglican prelate in the days when the Welfare State was coming to birth, that too much material prosperity is not good for the soul, and that God helps those who help themselves [. . .]

The executives were subsequently received by the Pope, and were offered very different pabulum. This speech was a sure step in the self-commitment of the present Pope, entirely to be admired. He said that in interpreting the gospel for the political and economic needs of nations in successive generations the Church was always in difficulty. It was not her business to make executive decisions or detailed programmes. That was for them (his audience). The Church's function was to call industrial leaders back to the gospel principles in so far as and when they seemed to be in danger of forgetting or transgressing them. Any form of political or economic theory which entailed for the fulfilment of its programme the control of one class of society by another, was mistaken. Thus capitalism in its 19th century form and 'the present successors of Manchester liberalism'[67] were outworn. The religious and moral rights of individual men were to be woven into the industrial pattern at every stage. They (his audience) were under a heavy obligation to see that while the capitalist system prevailed it should be made to pass rapidly out of its primitive stage (that of the profit motive alone). Atheistic materialism was by no means the preserve of communism, and could be seen at work as well in many parts of capitalist society. Where it was allowed to run riot it just played havoc with society and left the politicians to clear up the resultant mess. He was bound to say that he favoured gradual evolution to drastic revolution; but social evolution must now be accelerated if it was to keep pace with the needs of man. The system of free initiative could only satisfy man's needs if it was guided by men who had the common good, rather than their own profit, as their aim, by people who had a spiritual conception of the dignity of individual man.

This line of talk sounds very much 'redder' in Italy than it would do in Britain, where we are accustomed to Christian sociology. It gives the lie to the American view that this Pope is a disguised conservative playing a skilful hand. Incidentally the American allegation (Report 119) that Capovilla, the left wing chaplain of John XXIII, had been 'kicked upstairs' is quite untrue. He is still in service with Paul VI, and probably helped to write the speech now reported.

[67]The school of free-trade economics inspired by Adam Smith and David Hume, and later developed by Richard Cobden and John Bright, who campaigned against the Corn Laws in Britain in the 1840s.

WILLEBRANDS TO BE A BISHOP

Mgr. Willebrands has been nominated titular Bishop of Mauritia (?) which I believe is a heap of sand in the hinterland of Morocco, in partibus gentium.[68]

This gives him a seat in the Council and upgrades the status of the Secretariat of which he will continue to be Secretary. It can be regarded as a pat on the back for the ecumenical department. It would be too much to interpret it as a step in grooming Willebrands for Cardinal Bea's post, though it would be acceptable if it were. Perhaps it is part of the reform of the Curia, presaging the elevation of the Secretariat to the status of a congregation.

[...]

Report No. 124   19th June, 1964

RETURN

I return to Ely on July 13th and shall be there, off and on, until the middle of September.

[...]

AUDIENCE WITH THE POPE

I had another private audience, quite alone, with the Pope, the day before I came away. This now seems to be a well-established privilege. I had asked the Chaplain-in-course whom I know best to advise as to whether it would be judicious to ask each time, or whether it would be over-playing the former acquaintance, and he said that the Holy Father was quite pleased to see me each time. This could prove useful in emergency.

This time the Pope immediately got down to the question of when the Archbishop was coming to see him. I said that as far as I knew, although the Archbishop was looking forward very much to a visit, he had not been thinking of coming before the Council was over. There would clearly then be much to discuss, particularly the form which 'dialogue' would take. The Pope said he did not think he need necessarily wait till then if he wished to come before. The Ecumenism decree would

---

[68] 'In areas of the people'. A bishop of this class is invested with his office but has no stated charge or diocese.

probably be decided upon at the next session and that alone would give much to talk about. But it would be more convenient if the Archbishop came outside a council session. He told me to say that although he could not repay the Archbishop's call in London he would certainly repay it in Rome. I have since wondered if the Archbishop would go as the Primate of All England (in which case he would presumably stay with our Minister to the Holy See) or as the head of the Anglican Communion, in which case what would he do? Incidentally my American hosts (the lay vestrymen, at least) never cease to remind me that Archbishop Fisher didn't visit them when in Rome. They very much hope this can be remedied in any subsequent visitation. Perhaps if the Archbishop intended to have an 'omnium gatherum' service in Rome it might be held at the American church next time.

I promised to convey the Pope's invitation to the Archbishop [. . .]. He spoke briefly about the Council and said that although its progress was getting slower, for obvious reasons, he hoped it wasn't thought that enthusiasm was flagging. I said that we were very satisfied with what had happened so far. We wanted progress to be sure, so that reforms passed at the Council would really be effected afterwards. But we hoped that nevertheless he felt that the need for progress towards unity was very urgent. He agreed.

I said that the condition of the Church in Italy, and the consequent effects on the political situation, seemed very disturbing. The Pope said that it was very difficult for him to attempt to give any lead in Italian politics without being misunderstood. Did he feel the same abut Spain? He said he hoped that the publicists would realise that when he spoke e.g. to U.C.I.D.[69] his remarks could be interpreted as applying to other spheres as well. When he said that Christians must always support policies which tried to solve the problems of the world by voluntary rather than compulsive methods that could be taken to apply to Spain as well. Christian sociology must always be kaleidoscopic. (This I interpreted to mean that it was never wedded to any 'school of thought' or political party, it drew the best ideas from them all and showed their relationship to religious principles). I said that that had always been the Anglican tradition.

I presented the Pope with the latest record of Easter music from Ely Cathedral, and he enquired about the details of the services. He presented me with a copy of his speeches in Palestine, I having previously expressed our admiration for the enterprise.

[69] See Report 123, pp. 299–300.

He asked me to convey his greetings to the Archbishop and to tell him that he looked forward with great anticipation to his visit.
[. . .]

MINISTER TO THE HOLY SEE

The First Secretary to the Legation, Donald Cape, who is of course an R.C. went out of his way before I left to ask me if there was anything we could do to ensure a good appointment in succession to Sir Peter when the time came. They had just had an inspection by an F.O.[70] inspector to whom he had expressed the hope that Sir Peter's successor would be a man who would be able to understand the ecumenical issues etc. The F.O. was not obliged to appoint a Christian, though perhaps it would be invidious for them not to do so. There had been in the past 'shaky' churchmen. The F.O. inspector had said that of course they couldn't be guided merely by a man's religious suitability. The field was always small, and usually consisted of officials who were entitled to a quiet job.

Report No. 125   3rd July, 1964

[. . .]
BIRTH CONTROL

In a recent speech the Pope referred to this question for the first time. He said:

'The Church recognises its many aspects, that is today the many competences, among which primarily are that of husband and wife, their freedom, their consciences, their love and duty. But the Church must also affirm its own aspect, that is, God's law interpreted by the Church, and the Church must proclaim this law of God in the light of scientific, social and psychological truths which lately have had new and ample studies and documentation. It will be necessary to look carefully in the face of the theoretical and practical development of the question. And this is what the Church is actually doing.

We will therefore soon put forth the conclusions in the forms which will be considered more adequate for the object dealt with than the target to be achieved.'
[. . .]

---

[70] Foreign Office (more properly Foreign and Commonwealth Office).

THE THIRD SESSION AND AFTER,
SEPTEMBER–DECEMBER 1964

Commentary: September–November 1964 – the third period of the Council

The Council reopened on 14 September 1964 and the Pope concelebrated mass with twenty-four others from nineteen different countries. The next day the Council returned to the revised text of *Lumen Gentium*. The bishops confirmed the Church as a 'divine mystery' going beyond comprehension and therefore it could not be precisely defined. The document now stressed the important role of local and provincial councils throughout history and held up the model bishop as one who collaborated with the priests and the laity. Although the bishop was still in charge, the document stressed the horizontal dimension of the relationship between bishop, priest, and layman.[1]

Regarding religious freedom and the Jews, De Smedt argued that the early Church did not oppose religious freedom as it was fundamental to the faith. The right to religious liberty is a natural right of the individual human to civil liberty. The right is neither a moral licence to adhere to error nor a right to error.

Of the other documents considered, *Nostra Aetate* (Declaration on the Relation of the Church to Non-Christian Religions) led Asian bishops to query why the attitude had only changed to the Jews but not to Muslims and other Asian religions. According to *Dei Verbum* (Dogmatic Constitution on Divine Revelation), scripture was now regarded as the primary source of revelation and the *Magisterium* was not above the word of God but served it. All teaching must have a basis in divine revelation. The schema for *De Apostolatu Laicorum* (Decree on the Apostolate of the Laity) was introduced by the President of the Commission on the Apostolate of the Laity,

---

[1] John O'Malley, *What Happened at Vatican II* (Cambridge, MA, and London, 2008), p. 211.

Cardinal Fernando Cento, who stressed that the Commission had been established by John XXIII, which showed the regard for the laity. Rather than regarding the laity as being in the Church, they were the Church.

Probably the most important new discussion centred on *Gaudium et Spes* (The Pastoral Constitution on the Church in the Modern World). This document addressed the whole of humanity and not just the sons of the Church, as the aspirations of humanity were also those of the Church. It was the only Vatican II document which was addressed to people outside the Church. Every type of discrimination – whether based on sex, race, colour, social condition, language, or religion – was to be overcome and eradicated as it was contrary to the intention of God. The Council recognized that fundamental rights were not yet universally honoured. Unlike Pius IX's *Syllabus of Errors*, which had condemned the modern world and had been instrumental in Church teaching since 1864, *Gaudium et Spes* actually regarded the world positively and addressed specific problems such as world peace and matters of justice.

The Pastoral Constitution avoided using the traditional terms of primary and secondary reasons for marriage (procreation, the overcoming of sexual urges, and the expression of love between two people). This was an explosive topic exacerbated by the invention of the contraceptive pill. Although John XXIII had set up a Birth Control Commission in 1963, the Council was informed that it was not to discuss the issue as it was the preserve of the Papal Commission. However, it proved predictably difficult to avoid as it was also relevant in terms of population growth in the developing world. The issue of birth control remained under the auspices of the Papal Commission and in 1968 *Humanae Vitae* was propagated by Paul VI.

Optatam Totius (Decree on Priestly Training) stressed that the responsibility of priestly training would rest with the local episcopal conferences, although the Holy See retained final approval. The decree also prioritized the spiritual formation of the seminarians and gave primacy to scripture. Finally, the Council was due to vote on *Dignitatis Humanae* (Declaration on Religious Freedom), with votes being taken on individual chapters. The text was therefore treated as an improved text. Some Fathers, however, found that the text had been reworked so extensively that it was essentially a new text and should be treated as such. It was therefore to the great consternation of many of the bishops present when it was decided that the vote on the schema would be postponed until the following year.

Report No. 127   8th September, 1964

RETURN TO ROME

I shall return on September 19th, late for the third session of the Council, which begins on Sept. 14th.
[. . .]

HEENAN ON MIXED MARRIAGES

This is the department of our negotiations in which 'timeo Romanos et dona ferentes'.[2] There have been quite a lot of cases in which apparently liberal attitudes have been taken by Romans. E.g. a ceremony in which the Anglican priest (in S. Louis, U.S.A.) was allowed to assist in a mixed marriage in an R.C. Church, in Cardinal Ritter's diocese. But my French *Informations Catholiques* says that the 'Anglican party had given the necessary assurances about the upbringing of children'. So this was again only really a 'farewell service'. I do not think we should show much satisfaction about the promises not being signed; and the verbal promise can be equally offensive. Can the observers please have some guidance about what attitude they should take about this?

THE SCHEMATA

I have asked that copies of the Schemata be sent to Lambeth for the use of the Archbishop and his advisers. I hope they will have arrived
[. . .]

DE ECCLESIA

I have still not had time to study these schemata carefully, but this schema in general follows the line mapped out for it by the 2nd session. The main points I have noted so far are:

a. the Petrine texts, the primacy, universal jurisdiction etc. remain intact.
b. certain jurisdiction is delegated to national episcopal conferences.
c. the 'collegial' magisterium of the bishops 'under Peter' is asserted.
d. the One, Holy, Catholic and Apostolic Church of the creeds is identified still with the Roman Catholic Church.

---

[2] '[One should] beware of Romans bearing gifts'. This is presumably a pun on the phrase from *The Aeneid*, Book II, line 49: 'Timeo Danaos et dona ferentes' ('beware of Greeks bearing gifts').

e. Baptism confers status, though not full membership, as before. But whereas in the second draft this relationship was defined as 'quaedam communio', this now reads 'vera quaedam communio'.[3]

f. the married diaconate is very guardedly stated. I do not think the Council will be satisfied with the text, and will wish to be more open.

DE ECUMENISMO

The main change here is in our status, to that of a communitas ecclesialis in which there are certain (though not all the) 'vestigia' of the Church. Among those so described 'praeeminet Communio Anglican'!! How much good that compliment will do us among the Protestant brethren could be a matter for conjecture. The section on future dialogue admits that they must enter it 'par cum pari'[4] and seems to make possible considerable degrees of common prayer, study and social action – as much, at least, as it will take all concerned decades to implement effectively.

[...]

The section on the reformation and its consequences is again much improved upon in comparison with the former draft, and represents an immense triumph for Cardinal Bea, even though of course it doesn't go as far as we should like it to do. It talks of the 'ecclesiae et Communitates ecclesiales ... quae vel in gravissimo illo rerum discrimine, quod in Occidente iam ab exeunte medio aevo initium sumpsit, vel posterioribus temporibus ab Apostolica Sede Romana separate sunt'.[5] I can't think who the ecclesiae can be, except the Old Catholics.

A new and pregnant phrase is 'Baptismus igitur vinculum unitatis *sacramentale* constituit vigens inter omnes qui per illud regnerati sunt.'[6]

The material on the Jews and the non-Christian world, on which I have commented in a previous report, is set out in two Declarations. I still wish these two could be separated from Ecumenism altogether.

---

[3] This passage from *Lumen Gentium*, ch. 15, reads 'Accedit orationum aliorumque beneficiorum spiritualium communion; imo vera quaedam in Spiritu Sancto coniunctio' ('They also share with us in prayer and other spiritual benefits; likewise we can say that in some real way they are joined with us in the Holy Spirit').

[4] Peer to peer.

[5] 'Churches and ecclesiastical communities ... which separated from the Apostolic See of Rome during that most serious crisis which began in the West towards the end of the middle ages or during later periods.'

[6] 'Baptism therefore constitutes a bond of sacramental unity which is active between all who are ruled/governed by it.'

THE FUTURE

It is likely that the Ecumenism decree will be promulgated during this session, before Christmas. I hope that the Church as a whole will be able to 'buy up the opportunity' which this occasion will offer. Anglicans will need to be carefully led in this matter. It is becoming difficult for me now, after such close familiarity with the dramatis personae, to imagine the perspective of it all as seen from the point of view of the average parishioner at home, who will only have newspaper reports of it all. It will not be difficult for ill-disposed Anglican prophets to show from the published documents that all the old barriers are still there, undestroyed; and so to evaluate the Council as a failure. It therefore seems to me that considerable efforts should be made to show that not only do paper documents represent an immense advance in comparison with their predecessors but behind them lies the great struggle, which still goes on. Our friends in the Roman Church have won much ground, more than we thought they would, against a deep and sinister conspiracy of powerful, politically-minded reactionaries. Our favourable and understanding reception of the results of the Council will help our friends to continue the struggle. We also have a duty to educate the largely uncomprehending Protestant world (including some of the W.C.C. 'Curia').

[. . .]

Report No. 128   18th September, 1964

OPENING OF THE THIRD SESSION OF THE VATICAN COUNCIL, MONDAY 14TH SEPTEMBER.

The allocation was considerably shorter than that which marked the opening of the Second session on the 29th September, 1963, perhaps because the Pope has so recently (in his Encyclical, Ecclesiam Suam[7]) dealt at great length with many of the issues confronting the Council. Also in spirit it seemed nearer the Encyclical than the speech of last year. It even reminded one of the speech he delivered in November, 1963, on the occasion of his enthronement at St. John Lateran. There was, that is, a heavy and not easily explicable emphasis on the Roman primacy.

[7]Promulgated 6 August 1964.

For reasons which may or may not be obvious, the Pope chose to speak of only one subject: episcopal collegiality and the relation of the episcopate to the Holy See. His praise of the character and office of bishops was great, but always carefully set within the context of the Roman primacy and the definitions of Vatican I. The closer attention one pays to the text the more difficult it is to say precisely how he would like Vatican II to define episcopal collegiality. Whatever the finally approved wording of the Schema de Ecclesia may be, it seems certain that the Pope's words will prove patient of an interpretation consonant with that wording. There is at least something in the allocution to suit every variety of opinion. [. . .]

If the content of the allocution struck a tone rather more reserved than that of last year, so did the actual delivery. It was only in the final paragraphs that the Pope's voice and manner displayed great feeling: that is, in his words addressed directly to the Observers. There can be no doubt whatever of the depth of the feeling which lay behind those words. Yet once again there was a careful 'balance'. The reiteration of the word 'churches' and the phrase 'pluralism in practice' were notable; but they were followed by an invitation 'to enter into the fullness of truth and charity which, as an unmerited blessing but a formidable responsibility, Christ has charged Us to preserve.'
[. . .]

From the point of view of Anglican–Roman Catholic relations and dialogue it may ultimately be no disservice that the question of the primacy has been so carefully elaborated in this allocution. At some stage it has to appear and this allocution gives at least some indication of how far (or how little) the present Pope is prepared to go in the *aggiornamento* of the central Roman claim.
[. . .]

Report No. 129   18th September, 1964

80TH GENERAL CONGREGATION, TUESDAY 15TH SEPTEMBER.

Cardinal Tisserant, Dean of the Sacred College and chairman of the Council Presidency, began the morning's work by thanking the Fathers for the work they have already accomplished for the success of the Council and drew their attention to the importance of their task. He said there was a desire among many of the bishops that this should be the concluding session of the Council, and he asked them to keep to the point and not to waste time. He ended by reminding them of their obligation of secrecy and regretted that certain imprudent interviews had been given during the last session.

Cardinal Agagianian greeted the Council in the name of all the Moderators and said there was much to be discussed and voted on, but that neither the nature of the work nor the amount would become tiring if the task was undertaken in the spirit of love of God and dedication to the interest of the Church. The Council must aim at concluding its deliberations as soon as possible, but without prejudice to full freedom of speech.

Archbishop Felici drew attention to the rules concerning the Periti as defined by the Commission of Coordination in the name of the Pope on the 28th December 1963, and as follows:

1) The Periti must reply with all science, prudence and objectivity to the questions which the Commissions put before them for examination.

2) They were not to try and influence votes, to give interviews or to put forward publically their personal ideas about the Council.

3) They were to abstain from criticising the Council and from giving news about the activities of the Commissions, remembering that it was for this reason that the Pope had decreed that the work of the Council should be secret.

[...]

OBSERVERS' MEETING, TUESDAY 15TH SEPTEMBER.

[...]

Professor Müller of Louvain spoke about Chapters 7 and 8 of *de Ecclesia* on eschatology and on the Blessed Virgin, and in particular pointed out the extreme difficulty which the theologians had incurred in reaching an agreed text in the case of Chapter 8, because of the wide divergence in views on the Marian question. The discussion which followed was completely given over to Chapter 7, for lack of time, but the next meeting will be devoted to Chapter 8.

Fr. Scrima, representing the Ecumenical Patriarch, and Fa. Borovoj pointed out the difficulties which much of the text would create for the Eastern Church. This was eschatology understood in a purely Latin and Western sense.

Prof. Skydsgaard said that he found, much to his surprise, that the actual world that we live in, and all its sufferings and so on, were completely absent from the chapter. In this picture of eschatology there was no sense of the world in which we live.

Prof. Müller, in his reply to all the Observers, seemed very clearly not prepared to defend the existing text, but simply said how it had arisen and what the difficulties for Latin theologians of divergent views were. All his replies were noticeably ironic [*possibly* 'irenic'].

Report No. 130   19th September, 1964

81ST GENERAL CONGREGATION, 16TH SEPTEMBER.

[. . .]

Cardinal Wyszynski, Archbishop of Warsaw, said the bishops of Poland had presented to the Pope a request for official acknowledgement of the spiritual maternity of Mary for all men. They wanted the Council to proclaim Mary the 'Mother of the Church'. Mary's universal motherhood was a salient point of the Church's teaching on her. This declaration should be a solemn public act entrusting the Church to the Virgin Mary for the protection of morality, furthering the mission of the Church, promoting the unity of the human race, and working for the cause of peace. The Bishops of Brazil and Belgium had presented similar petitions. Cardinal Wyzsynski considered this chapter should be chapter 2 to emphasize Mary's relationship with the mystery of the Church.

Cardinal Léger, Archbishop of Montreal, thought this year's text was an improvement over last year's, especially with regard to the use of scripture. They must not lose sight of the necessity of renewing doctrine and preaching on Mary. They should use accurate, clear and sober words in describing Mary's vocation. Preachers sometimes indulged in hyperbole and exaggerations. This turned many away, because people today were more attracted by sobriety than exaggeration. They needed more precision in their description of the relationship between Mary and the human race. They should avoid everything not required by strict doctrine, even though it may be commonly used by preachers. They should weigh carefully all their expression with regard to their origin and meaning. The term Mediatrix appeared late in Church literature and was open to the objection that it ran counter to the teaching of St. Paul. In its present context it was acceptable, but because this context was not always at hand, it seemed advisable to avoid the title in the Schema. The text spoke out against Marian abuses, but offered nothing positive to assist in correcting possible deficiencies.

Cardinal Döpfner, Archbishop of Munich, considered the chapter provided a solid and accepted explanation of doctrine. Not too much should be said about Mary as Mediatrix, as this could give rise to controversy. There should be a treatment of the general foundation for the special role of the texts as a reply to objections against the teaching here presented. The expression in which Mary, in her immaculate conception, was 'redeemed in a more sublime fashion' should be modified, so as to indicate that she received a more sublime share in the fruits of redemption. The former could cause some misunderstanding, if the cause of Mary's redemption was thought to be different from that of the human race.

Cardinal Silva Henríquez, Archbishop of Santiago, said that, despite certain defects, the text was well balanced. The doctrinal foundation of the chapter was Mary's divine maternity [. . .]. The chapter was commendable for its insistence on the sole mediation of Christ. Many people talked too much of the mediation of Mary and not enough of that of Christ. This sometimes caused scandal among the faithful and also among those outside the Church.

Cardinal Bea said it should not be forgotten that criticism of this chapter dealt only with the appropriateness of the text in view of the interest of the Church. There was no question of anyone's personal devotion to the Virgin Mary. The chapter was basically acceptable, but it failed to keep the promise not to enter into theological controversies. It was not enough merely to give general warnings against 'whatever might cause abuse', practical directives should be given. In several places the doctrine needed to be more precise to obviate misunderstanding. The text needed to be broadly revised in order to get more solid arguments and to avoid controversial discussions.
[. . .]

82ND GENERAL CONGREGATION, THURSDAY 17TH SEPTEMBER.

[. . .]

Cardinal Suenens, Archbishop of Brussels, continuing the discussion on Chapter 8, said the text had two defects. Firstly, there was not enough stress on Mary's spiritual maternity in the Church today. She appeared rather as a figure belonging to the past, whose present activity was hardly noticed. The text was too prudent and too timid.

There was not sufficient emphasis on the profound association which linked Mary with the work of Christ. It was good to concentrate on Christo-centrism, but not if this involved the danger of being anti-Marian. Secondly, nothing in the text showed the connection between Mary's spiritual maternity and the apostolate. Historically Christ was born of the Holy Spirit and of the Virgin Mary. Mystically speaking Christ was born and grows in the same way, i.e. through the Holy Spirit and through the Virgin Mary. The apostolate, which aimed to communicate the life of Christ to the world, was intimately related to Mary's spiritual activity. Marian piety should be made to stand out in bolder relief.

Archbishop Gawlina, Titular Archbishop of Madytus, considered devotion to Mary no obstacle, but rather a stimulus, to unity. It marked out a path of unity between the Church and their separated brethren. It was a bridge to ecumenism because real unity and authentic ecumenism were founded on charity. The separated brethren in the Oriental Church had deep and tender devotion to Mary. Even the founder of Protestantism composed several devotional works on the Mother of God [. . .]. Even in the Soviet Union visitors had been struck by the deep devotion of the faithful to Mary. This could be a bridge between the Orthodox and the Roman Catholics. Because Mary leads to Christ she acts ecumenically.
[. . .]

Bishop Arceo of Cuernevaca, Mexico, thought the Council should agree on a text which would eliminate any danger of their seeming divided before the world. The doctrine presented in the schema was traditional. The title 'Mother of the Church' was foreign to the traditions of the Oriental Church and too recent to have a place in a Council declaration. Leo XIII was the first Pope to use it. St. Pius X cautiously referred to Mary as the 'Mother of the members of the mystical body'. Pius XII was equally careful. John XXIII used the title. Paul VI had always used it conditionally. If the Church were their mother, as they were accustomed to regard her, then Mary, as the Mother of the Church, would really be their grandmother. She would also be the Mother of the angels because St. Thomas maintained that the angels were part of the Church. The simple fact that they did not use the title would not imply any condemnation of it, but would only mean that the time was not regarded as ripe for its use. The Mexican bishops asked for a definition of Mary's motherhood of all men, not of her spiritual maternity over the Church. Mary, a traditional sign of unity in the Church, could not be turned into a sign of division.
[. . .]

Report No. 131   22nd September, 1964

83RD GENERAL CONGREGATION, FRIDAY 18TH SEPTEMBER

In spite of the discussion on Chapter 8 of de Ecclesia having been concluded the day before, it was announced that three Fathers had obtained the necessary 70 signatures from other Fathers to enable them to return to the discussion of the B.V.M.

Cardinal Frings, Archbishop of Cologne, began by saying that the chapter did not contain anything against the truth or that could offend the legitimate demands of the separated brethren. It represented a middle way which all could take. It was necessary for the vote on the chapter to bring together the divergent views and to arrive at a practical compromise. Everyone must be prepared to sacrifice something of his personal opinion.

Cardinal Alfrink, Archbishop of Utrecht, speaking on behalf of 124 Fathers (and he said he could have obtained the signatures of many more, if time had permitted) said there had been confusion in the debate between Marian devotion and doctrine. It was for the Council to set forth the faith of the Church and not the opinions of theologians and the faithful. If one spoke of Marian devotion, the terms maximalism or minimalism were appropriate. If one spoke of faith it was another thing, it had to be the truth. The title Mediatrix was not appropriate to explain the doctrine of Mary's spiritual maternity. When applied to the Blessed Virgin the term was essentially different to when it was used for the unique mediation of Christ. For this reason Cardinal Alfrink preferred that the chapter should not mention a title which caused confusion among Catholics and astonishment and scandal among non-Catholics.
[. . .]

84TH GENERAL CONGREGATION, MONDAY 21ST SEPTEMBER

Bishop Franić of Split, Yugoslavia, a very reactionary consultor of the Holy Office, read a speech from certain members of the Theological Commission, against the amendments of Chapter 3 (on the Episcopate) of de Ecclesia. On the question of sacramentality of the Episcopate, he said, the Schema touched on a question historically complex and obscure, not to say theologically debatable. The majority of theologians upheld that the Episcopate was a sacrament which conferred a distinct category. The Fathers who held the opposite opinion were few, but a certain number of them had asked that the matter should not be defined, because it was too complex. On the subject of collegiality, the text expressed satisfactorily the supreme authority of the Pope, but if the bishops received through consecration the power to co-govern the whole Church, with the Pope and under the Pope, how could these two facts be reconciled? The supreme power of the Pope must inevitably be reduced.

[. . .]

The whole thing was interesting as it showed how clearly the conservatives regarded the revised Schema as inconsistent with previous teaching. In particular it would be contrary to the teaching of Vatican I concerning the universal jurisdiction of the Pope. The allowing of a married diaconate also would be the first stop [*sic*] to the abandoning of the celibacy of the priesthood. It had already been advocated as such by certain Catholic professors. There was evidently to be a headlong collision on these points. [. . .]

Cardinal König of Vienna and *Bishop Parente of the Holy Office* between them argued that there was no such collision between the two Councils, because the potestas under concern was in any case that of Christ, and was indivisible.

We (the Anglican observers) are nevertheless of the opinion that there is a real contradiction here (and of course are glad of it). Similarly, we agree with the conservatives that the married diaconate could easily be the edge of a slippery slope. It seems to us to be very significant that the Council, after frequent monition, applauded Parente. This man *was* one of the stickiest members of the Holy Office, who had been converted on the matter of collegiality during the Council. When I asked the second in command of the Secretariat who had converted him, he said 'Spiritus Sanctus Dominus, quis renovabit faciem terrae'![8]

Cardinal Léger, Archbishop of Montreal, continuing the discussion on *De Pastorali Munere Episcoporum*[9] said a new approach was necessary in the bishop's method of teaching and governing. It was important for them to understand men as they were. Things were different today from what they were a generation ago. People were technically minded and they had new attitudes towards religion and authority. They were critical and they would accept only what was true and genuine. They objected to paternalism in the hierarchy or clergy and had new ideas of obedience, maintaining their personal responsibility. Bishops and clergy must speak so as to be heard and understood, and the so-called

[8]'The Holy Spirit as the Lord, who shall renew the face of the earth.'
[9]'On the functions of bishops in the church'.

ecclesiastical language, which was archaic and cut off from modern reality, might be one of the reasons why their voices were crying in the wilderness. Their language should be humble, especially in fields in which they had no particular competence. There must be contacts between the bishops, priests and the faithful. Too often they knew nothing of the living conditions of their flock. There was also room for reform in dress, titles and other details.
[. . .]

FUTURE OF THE COUNCIL

There is a notable tendency to expedite the business of the Council, and strong rumours are running that this may be the last session. Archbishop Heenan said that they might postpone the fourth session for two or three years, but that is regarded as a guess. There is no doubt in my mind that the main business will be completed by November. The text of the Schema on the Church in the present world has been issued. On the whole it is a series of wide balanced pronouncements on general themes (what else can it be?) rather on the lines of the less exciting Church Assembly reports. One gets the impression that the best thing would be to get it hurried through as soon as possible (it is bound to be regarded as 'tame' by the press) so that all concerned can settle down to living it out. It might cause great debate in detail, but we shall see.

Report No. 132   23rd September, 1964

85TH GENERAL CONGREGATION, TUESDAY 22ND SEPTEMBER

[. . .]
Today's votes were of the greatest importance. Vote No. 8, for example, established that episcopal consecration gave a bishop all the powers he needed for the exercise of his office, though he could not exercise them except in communion with the Pope and other bishops. This is said to be an advance on the present position. The notes on the passage say that the Orthodox exercise these powers de facto. When I asked for explanation, I was told that the position of Orthodox prelates in Catholic eyes is that they exercise jurisdiction with the *tacit* permission of the Pope. When I referred to our position I was told that, if at some future time the validity of Anglican orders were established, the same would be true of us. Ergo, if the Archbishop of Canterbury's

orders were valid, his canonical position would be that he would be exercising his episcopate with the implicit consent of the Pope!!

Vote No. 10 established the position of collegiality by declaring that Peter, with the eleven, formed the college.

When the whole Schema has been voted in detail, it will then be voted on as a whole. It must then, of course, get its two thirds majority. It is said that Maximos IV of Antioch has submitted a number of 'modi', complaining that the language of the Schema is still too juridical, too pompous and too Latin.

OBSERVERS' MEETING, TUESDAY 22ND SEPTEMBER

Fr. Benoit, O.P., École Biblique, Jerusalem
De B.V.M.
The Old Testament
The themes of the Daughter of Sion, Jerusalem, etc. The town is a feminine personification, an allegory of the marriage of Jehovah with his people. The Bride, sometimes unfaithful, often punished, but always loved, invited to return – before the Exile. After the exile the emphasis is on the redemption of the unfortunate [...] Isaiah 41. Then she appears to be going to be the mother of the Messiah, the Emmanuel.

There are many references also to the daughter of Sion as Virgin. Isaiah 62, 63. The return of Israel, Jeremiah 31. The 70[10] introduces the translation of the word parthenos. Rejoicing introduced in the later prophets. IV Ezra has much material. Some texts from Qumran preserve the idea of the mother of the Messiah.

The New Testament
St. Luke is clearly and deliberately giving us the connecting thread in the birth narratives. Isaiah 14 etc. The Annunciation exploits it. The obvious connection of the Magnificat with the Song of Hannah and the idea of the Church as the community of the poor. The words of Simeon at the presentation, cf. Ezekiel 14.17. The same sword which will cleave the heart of Mary.

In the marriage at Cana we see Mary in face of the disciples. John entrusted with the care of Mary and vice versa. All her life Mary had formed Jesus, and her whole existence was dedicated to the accomplishment of this. The woman of Apocalypse 12 is deliberately

---

[10] This is presumably a reference to the Septuagint, which uses the Greek word *parthenos* (translated 'virgin').

meant as the completion of the Church and Mary. Mary as a type of the Church.

Prof. Quanbeck, Lutheran, U.S.A., said that his Church tried to do justice to the place of Mary. They appreciated the aim of Chapter 8 to try and compromise. Gen. 3.15 should not be used, nor Micah 5, 2–3. The tendency to 'psychologise' the text should be resisted, as at Cana and in John 19. The chapter should not proceed from allegory and devotion to dogmatic assertion – that was quite another thing. There was a total difference in the use of language.

Gr. Willebrands remarked that much of this was in the line of Cardinal Bea's intervention.

Fr. Benoit distinguished between 'interpretation by accommodation' and the 'interpretation by unwinding of a revelation'. This must be by comparison with the whole context of revelation. i.e. it was sometimes legitimate to read back meanings which were not understood until later.

Prof. Cullmann agreed that Mary was an instrument chosen in the 'history of salvation', but there were other, many other, such instruments, e.g. Abraham, the Apostles. Mary indeed 'longe antecellit',[11] but only as a question of degree. All these instruments had been chosen, elected and were therefore blessed within that history. There was no 'Abrahamology' or 'Paulology'. The faith of Mary is undoubtedly there in the narratives. The schema was too rapid about the life of Jesus. Did the faith of Mary never fail, Luke 2.41, 'The parents understood not . . .'. In Mark 3, 21, those about him came to take him away because he was beside himself. Jesus' answer is very uncomfortable.

Fr. Benoit thought that Mary's particular relation to the incarnate body put her in a totally different relationship. He drew a distinction between 'lack of comprehension of faith' and 'lack of faith'.

Fr. Scrima, Representative of the Ecumenical Patriarch, said the main problems were not really biblical, but psychological. Typology was an effort to draw out the spiritual meaning of Holy Scripture. The place of the

---

[11] 'Far surpasses'. The full section in *Lumen Gentium* is as follows: 'The Virgin Mary, who at the message of the angel received the Word of God in her heart and in her body and gave Life to the world, is acknowledged and honoured as being truly the Mother of God and Mother of the Redeemer. Redeemed by reason of the merits of her Son and united to Him by a close and indissoluble tie, she is endowed with the high office and dignity of being the Mother of the Son of God, by which account she is also the beloved daughter of the Father and the temple of the Holy Spirit. Because of this gift of sublime grace she far surpasses all creatures, both in heaven and on earth.'

B.V.M. in the mystery was to give its context to Christology and Pneumatology. The Theotokos was present also at Pentecost, with the Church, at the completion of Christology. The B.V.M. was a type of the Church and of man, because she knew all suffering. Was it the intention that this great source of devotion and inspiration should disappear from the Christian scene, or that she should pull us back to unity in Christ? There is ontological necessity for some doctrine and some devotion.

Prof. Schlink, Evangelical Church in Germany, said the Reformation churches had much in common with the Roman Catholic Church, not only the body of Christ born from Mary, but the act of faith. The proposed chapter 8 was indeed a blow for the 'maximalists', but it by no means avoided the difficulties of Protestant objectors. Mark 3, 31–5 was a most impressive text for those who opposed Mariological tendencies. Mary was included among those whose faith was inadequate, and there was no confession of faith parallel to that of St. Peter.

Mary was not simply a model in the spiritual sense, but in her we are united through her with the company of the apostles. The greater exploitation of this relationship was a possibility for future understanding. But was the title of Mediatrix, unexplained, an opening for future dogmatic definition? Mediator was one of the titles of Jesus which was applied to him alone, and therefore should only be used of him if the meaning of it was made crystal clear. The introduction of this title in the Council would be an ecumenical catastrophe. They had hoped that the insertion of this chapter meant that it would be shown how Mary was a member of the Church. On the contrary, every effort seemed to have been made to emphasise the difference between her and the Church. This now seemed to be almost the crown of the Schema.

Fr. Benoit admitted that the first tradition hadn't much to say about Mary, for naturally the force and weight of the Resurrection etc. at first crowded out everything else.

Prof. Nissiotis said that the Orthodox were proud of their Mariology, and brought Mariology to the West, but they were shocked by the recent Roman mania of doctrinal definition. All this was due to a total lack of Pneumatology. Was this mania a substitute for the Holy Spirit? Much of Fr. Benoit's exegesis attributed to Mary the energies of the Holy Spirit, due to this vacuum. The role of Mary was not that of mediatrix redemptionis, but mediatrix intercessionis, in the centre of the Church. The mosaic of Daphne was the true type of Mary praying in the Church. The Roman Catholic Church will spoil this picture at her peril. In doing so she will injure unity.

This meeting was altogether one of the most moving I have ever attended. The Orthodox marshalled their arguments most skilfully and swept the board. This seems to me to epitomise the work of the Council at its best. All was in good humour, and the confrontation was direct and effective. The best thing since 1054.

Willebrands and *Benoit* tried to answer and failed to do so effectively, in my judgment. Willebrands said that Mediatrix intercessionis would equally lead to a doctrine of mediation if it were used that way. To which Nissiotis countered that that was only one more argument for not having the title in the Schema anyhow.

Report No. 133   25th September, 1964

[...]
86TH GENERAL CONGREGATION, WEDNESDAY 23RD SEPTEMBER

Cardinal Ruffini, Archbishop of Palermo, who is normally spoken of as a 'Fascist', opening the debate on *Religious Liberty*, said that it was only the truth which should be free. What association was there, then, between error and liberty? What was to become of the Concordats (e.g. in Italy, Spain, etc.) if there were religious freedom for all? The text said that a government should not favour one form of religion over another. That too undermined concordats. He ended by drawing attention to a passage forbidding Roman Catholics to impose their religion by force, and asked whether it was right that they should be given this instruction, when in many countries Roman Catholics were being persecuted for their faith.

Cardinal Léger, Archbishop of Montreal, considered the text acceptable because it safeguarded the rights both of individuals and of groups. It answered the patient expectation of those who were suffering everywhere for their religion. It provided a foundation for dialogue with the separated brethren. The text was prudent in its warning against relativism and indifferentism. But it needed to be clarified on two points. On the subject of religious liberty, what the text said was, strictly speaking, applicable only to believers. It must, however, be applicable to all men without exemption, even those who do not believe. They must affirm the freedom of religion of those who wish to profess no religion at all. As for the foundation of religious liberty, it was inexact to put it in following the will of God or corresponding to man's divine vocation. This presupposed God, and some will not accept God. This foundation should be put in the highest exercise of human reason. Anything against religious liberty was also against man and his reason.

[. . .]

Cardinal Meyer, Archbishop of Chicago, said the declaration should be accepted because it was in line with the declaration of modern Popes, especially of John XXIII. It was necessary for the following reasons: 1) Men wanted from the Church a proclamation of religious liberty because their common experience had shown that, where the state dominated religion, civic welfare was generally harmed, whereas, where religious freedom was enjoyed, civic welfare flourished. 2) This confirmation of religious liberty by the Council would point the way to civil governments and show them how to act. 3) It would show that true religion was not in external acceptance but consisted chiefly in the conscious and full acceptance of the will of the Creator. 4) It would aid the Apostolate by making clear that religion was best promoted by interior conviction. 5) It was necessary to insure fruitful dialogue with the separated brethren. They must give to others what they claimed for themselves. The importance of this declaration was so far-reaching that, if the Council were not to approve it, nothing else which it might do would satisfy the expectations of men.

Cardinal Henríquez, Archbishop of Santiago, Chile, thought the text was much better than that presented in 1963. It was acceptable because it was not a chapter but a distinct declaration. It was correct in declaring the incompetence of civil authorities in religious matters. He approved of the statement that the doctrine given was traditional in the Church. The declaration would have extreme importance, not only for Christians, but for all men. In Latin America especially it would dissipate certain opportunist ideas, according to which the stand on religious liberty would vary as to whether the Church was in the majority or the minority. The declaration would have a special impact on the work of evangelism. The peoples of Latin America need a new Christianisation. [. . .]

Cardinal Ottaviani said there were some exaggerations in the text as, for example, where it stated that, even though he be in error, a man was worthy of honour. A man in error deserved charity and kindness, but it was not clear how he was entitled to honour. The declaration forgot many elements which were beyond the field of ecumenism, and it did not pay sufficient attention to non-Christian religions. Attention must be paid not to natural rights but also to supernatural rights. Those professing a revealed religion had rights over those coming from the natural law. They must profess and defend their Catholic faith no matter what the consequences. How many prisons had been sanctified by confessors of the faith. Religious liberty could exist only in dependence on the Divine Law. It was not true that the state was incompetent to choose a religion. If this were so, they would have to suppress all the concordats made by the Holy See. This would mean the suppression of the many benefits which these concordats had produced, such as the protection of marriage and religious education in the concordat with Italy. It was not lawful to admit freedom to spread a religion when this might harm the unity of a Catholic nation and culminate in weakening it. [. . .]

This speech by the head of the reactionaries was delivered with a consummate oratory. He is the only speaker who really *speaks* Latin.

The six votes of the morning were of the greatest importance, and were one of the turning-points of the Council:

Vote 13.   The order of bishops, succeeding the college of the Apostles in magisterium and pastoral government, in union with its Head, is likewise a subject of supreme and full power over the universal Church, but this power may never be exercised independently of the Roman Pontiff - - - Very large majority.

Vote 14.   The power of binding and loosing given to Peter personally was also given to the College of the Apostles in union with its Head - - - Very large majority.

Vote 15.   With due respect for the primacy and authority of its Head, Bishops exercise their own power for the welfare of the faithful and even the whole Church through the help of the Holy Spirit - - - Large majority, Non placet 152.

Vote 16.   This supreme power is exercised in Ecumenical Council. Only the Roman pontiff can invoke, preside over and confirm Councils. There can be no Ecumenical Council not confirmed, or at least accepted, by the successor of Peter - - - Large majority.

Vote 17.   This same collegial power in union with the Pope can be exercised by Bishops throughout the world, provided the Head of the College calls them to collegial action or at least approves their unified action freely - - - Large majority, non placet 204.

Vote 18.   The collegial union of the bishops is reflected in their relationships with their particular churches and with the universal Church. Individual bishops represent their churches and all of them together with the Pope represent the entire Church in the bond of peace, love and unity - - - Large majority.

THE OBSERVERS' AUDIENCE

This has not yet taken place, it is said because of the departure of Cardinal Bea and Willebrands to Greece. When the Standing Committee of the Observers (of which I am a member) met to decide who should reply to the Pope's address it was easily decided that the Ecumenical Patriarch's representative should do it. It is very satisfactory how readily the Protestants accept the general leadership of the Orthodox. We of course encourage this as over against any hegemony of the W.C.C.

[. . .]

Report No. 134   28th September, 1964

87TH GENERAL CONGREGATION, THURSDAY 24TH SEPTEMBER

[. . .]

The following speakers continued the discussion on the text of the *Declaration on Religious Liberty*. Considering the urgent nature of the subject, the speeches were on the whole insipid, and only a few of them are here recorded.

Cardinal König, Archbishop of Vienna, said that, although he considered the declaration acceptable as it stood, it should not keep silent about the tragic fact that there were nations who enjoyed no religious freedom. Some governments today were militantly atheistic, while others granted religious freedom only when this could be distorted into meaning the suppression of all religion. The Council should find a way to speak out in the name of all men in order to arouse the conscience of the world and to prevent those deplorable situations where atheism had all the privileges and religion had no rights.

Cardinal Browne of the Theological Commission, said that the declaration could not be approved in its present form, a form which was not even necessary for the peace and unity of the peoples of the world. It put the foundation of religious liberty in the rights of the human conscience. But it was evident that social rights, based on an individual conscience which was erroneous, could not be equated with rights flowing from an individual conscience which was right.

Archbishop Parente, Assessor of the S.C. of the Holy Office, thought the text could not be approved as it stood. It prefers the rights of man, his liberty and his conscience to the rights of God. There was no clear distinction between the objective and subjective aspects of truth and error, nor was there a forthright admission of the mission of the Church. Much of the text was open to equivocation. They should be concerned about the probable reactions among various governments and learned circles. The declaration spoke of protecting followers of every religion in the name of liberty of conscience. It seemed to forget the duty of the Church to preach the truth with prudence and charity. It was an unfortunate suggestion [. . .]

Bishop López Ortiz of Tui-Vigo, Spain, considered that the passage declaring a state incompetent to judge the truth regarding religion should be deleted from the text, because of its false and harmful consequences. It insinuated that no government could declare itself Catholic if it so wished. When a government made such a declaration it was not passing judgment on truth concerning religion, but solemnly manifesting its obedience to the Divine Law [. . .]. When the citizens of a nation, with practical unanimity, profess the true religion, then the state should act accordingly.

Bishop Pohlschneider of Aachen, Germany, said this declaration was a truly historical document which would serve the good cause of peace on earth. It needed to be supplemented, however, by a reference to freedom of education. [. . .]

Bishop Primeau of Manchester, New Hampshire, said they should distinguish between religious liberty which is internal and personal and religious liberty which is external and social. In present day parlance the first was called liberty of conscience, and the second was known as freedom of worship. There was a commonly accepted bond between the two. They must beware of the false concept of man which would make him first an individual and then social. Man was essentially social [. . .]. Because of this, it was unlawful to recognise a man's right to freedom of conscience while restricting him in his freedom of worship. Both freedoms were equally essential and pertained to the integrity and dignity of the human person [. . .]
[. . .]
Archbishop Dubois of Besançon, France, thought the text was too philosophical and too juridical. It should be given a tone more in keeping with the spirit of scripture and tradition. Everyone must be regarded as a man, as a member of human society and as an object of

the love of Christ. It was for these reasons that St Augustine addressed a heretical bishop as 'honourable brother'. Our Lord commended religious liberty, as could be seen in the passages comparing the Apostles to light and salt, comparisons which excluded coercion. Many other texts of scripture could be used to illustrate this point.

88TH GENERAL CONGREGATION, FRIDAY 25TH SEPTEMBER

[. . .]

Cardinal Roberti, President of the Commission for the reform of the Curia, continuing the debate on religious liberty, said a clear distinction must be made between freedom of conscience and freedom of consciences. This distinction was dear to Pius XII. The Church could not admit freedom of conscience because that would be contradicting herself. Freedom of conscience was too often understood as conferring on someone the right of free, personal choice even when confronted with the law of God. But the Church could admit freedom of consciences, because this implied freedom from all external coercion in the belief and exercise of religion.

Archbishop Hurley of Durban, S. Africa, said it was completely unlawful to impose on anyone the rejection of a religious belief as a condition for sharing in the benefits of civic life. No religious group could be subordinated to the political ends of the state. Nevertheless, since the classical argument for the union of Church and State was the obligation of the state to make a social profession of religion, this argument could influence many people in the opposite direction from that intended. The weakness in this argument was that it ascribed to the state the obligation to provide for social worship, whereas this was an obligation only of the Church. The Church would be more effective in the discharge of its mission when it worked with its own resources and did not have to depend on the support of the state.

Archbishop Alter of Cincinnati, U.S.A., said they were not speaking of the declaration of religious freedom in every possible sense, but only in the right of every human being to be free from force in his worship of God. They did not affirm the right of anyone to teach error or to do harm. No one had such rights before God. They were claiming only freedom from social coercion. It would promote the cause of peace and harmony if the Council issued a clear declaration on this point, especially in those areas where the Church was living in a pluralistic society. Catholics had been accused of inconsistency and even insincerity, and of shifting their stand on religious liberty according to whether they were in the majority or minority. The text should therefore forestall any repetitions of these doubts and suspicions. They should affirm the absolute incompetence of public officials to judge religious matters, and should reiterate their obligation to use all appropriate means to ensure the free practice of religion with safety to the individual. Matters as sacred as this could not be left merely to the majority vote of citizens.

Bishop Lucey of Cork, said liberty of conscience was not to be understood as a personal moral right, but as a human right. It could be called a negative right, as it entitled us not to be interfered with in the practice of religion. [. . .] There was a universal obligation to respect good faith, no matter where it was found. There were even atheists in good faith. A man's personal acts of religion were always acceptable to God, but this gave him no right to interfere with the acts of religion of others.

After this, *Cardinal Suenens* proposed to the Fathers a standing vote on the closing of the debate on Religious Liberty. A vast majority declared themselves favourable. The Moderator reminded the assembly that the debate could be continued by those who could secure the support of at least 70 others.

[. . .]

Report No. 135   30th September, 1964

88TH GENERAL CONGREGATION, FRIDAY 25TH SEPTEMBER (CONTINUED)

Cardinal Bea began his Relatio on the Declaration on Jews and Non-Christians by remarking on the vast interest it had aroused. There was practically no other schema on which so much had been written. This showed how the world was looking to the Church for approval or rejection of this schema, and the judgement of many on the whole Council would be based solely on this. The Church must follow the example of Christ and the Apostles in their love for the Jewish people. The crucial point of this entire discussion was the question of 'deicide', i.e. whether, and in what way, the death of Christ could be said to be the fault of the Jewish people as such. It was wrong to say that this was the chief reason for anti-semitism, since there were many other reasons such as religion, politics and psychological, social and economic prejudices. It was a historical fact that the culpability for the death of Christ had at times been laid on the entire Jewish people with the result that they were often despised and persecuted.

The leaders of the Sanhedrin in Jerusalem, although not democratically elected, were regarded as the legitimate authority of the people. But were the leaders of the Jewish people fully aware of the Divinity of Christ to the extent that they could be said to be deicides? St. Peter and St. Paul indicated that the death sentence was the result of ignorance. Could the entire Jewish people of that time be said to be responsible? [. . .] Anyway there were no grounds for attributing to the Jewish people of today any responsibility for the death of Christ.

The second part of the Declaration dealt with non-Christian religions, with explicit mention of the Moslems. This was of special importance as even non-Christian religions today were troubled by practical irreligiosity or even militant atheism. It was agreed to stress three points: 1) God is the Father of all men and they are His children. 2) All men are brothers. 3) All discrimination, violence and persecution of national or racial origin is to be condemned.

Many felt that the present Declaration on the Jews was out of place in the schema on ecumenism, which should, strictly speaking, deal with the promotion of Christian unity. On the other hand there was a close connection between all Christians and the chosen people of the Old Testament. A compromise has been reached and the subject has been treated in a separate document connected with the schema on ecumenism.

It must be realised that they were dealing only with religion, and were in no way touching on politics. There was no question of Zionism but only of the followers of the law of Moses, wherever they may be. The purpose of this Declaration was for the Church to imitate the charity of Christ and the Apostles and to consider how God worked out her salvation and what great benefits He conferred on the Chosen People. This renovation of the Church was of such importance that it justified the risk of being accused of pursuing political ends.
[. . .]

ENTERTAINMENT: BELGIUM

We received Cardinal Suenens and Bishop De Smedt of Bruges to dinner. This was very easy, these two being among the most relaxed of all the Council Fathers. Even so, the Cardinal seemed unfamiliar with the relationship between the C. of E. and P.E.C.U.S.A. and was interested to pick up information about the latter. He referred with pleasure to the Archbishop's visit to Belgium and hoped it would be repeated. We said we valued contact with Belgium, especially at Louvain. When I said that Belgium was nearer to Cambridge than some parts of England (in mileage) they both laughed heartily and obviously knew what was intended. The letter said openly that of course the English hierarchy was sticky but that it was getting better. [. . .]

ENTERTAINMENT: CANADA

We received Cardinal Léger of Montreal, Bishop Pocock (assistant to Cardinal McGuigan, Archbishop of Toronto) and a very young-looking man called de Roo, Bishop of Victoria, B[ritish].C[olumbia] [. . .]

Fairweather knew the first two of our guests very well already. The Cardinal, he said, had a real intense interest in Ecumenism. That certainly appeared from the number of questions he asked. We discussed religious liberty and Canadian nationalism: the Cardinal was obviously against it, but saw no reason for anxiety about the Queen's visit.[12]

They said that there was now a tension in the Council, on lines which cut across the usual alignment of conservative and liberal, about the duration and the prospect of a fourth session. There was considerable dissatisfaction about the text of the Church in the World. Liberals said it would be better to put out nothing than this, or that they should prolong the Council indefinitely until some adequate text was presented. The conservatives are divided between those who want to send the bishops home as soon as they can, so that they can get down to the business of 'bossing' the Church again, and those who want to elaborate the text on the B.V.M. and get the slightly reactionary text on This World on to infallible paper.
[. . .]

OBSERVERS' AUDIENCE, 29TH SEPTEMBER

We had the routine audience, this time in the Sistine Chapel, so that the long wait was a sheer joy. Cardinal Bea made a formal introduction, saying how appropriate it was that this meeting should be happening so soon after the 'gracious gesture' scil.[13] of St. Andrew's head.[14] The principal observer of the Patriarch (Archimandrite Rodopoulos) added that, although the head was indeed a gracious

---

[12]The Queen visited Canada on 5–13 October 1964.
[13]'To wit'.
[14]The relic had been presented to the Greek Church as a gesture of goodwill during the previous session of the council.

gesture, they should not forget that there were formidable obstacles [. . .]. The Pope nodded appreciatively.

In his answer the Pope announced his intention of suggesting the foundation of an interconfessional institute for the study of theological problems, the first of which should be the 'history of salvation'.

In the presentations afterwards the Pope spent a flatteringly disproportionate time with me saying, 'so you are abandoning us' and '. . . but you mustn't, for you are civis Romanus now'.[15] I didn't explain at length on plans about the future, but will do so at a private audience later.

We were all presented with a specially bound copy of the New Testament with Greek on one page and the Vulgate on the other.

Report No. 136   1st October, 1964

89TH GENERAL CONGREGATION, MONDAY 28TH SEPTEMBER

[. . .]

Having secured the signatures of at least 70 other bishops, four prelates were authorised to continue the discussion on religious liberty, of whom four we quote only the speech of:

Archbishop Heenan of Westminster who drew attention to the 16th century bitter battle between Protestants and Catholics in England. He said that religious liberty was soon banished and the number of martyrs was evidence of the ferocity of the persecution. In all honesty, though, it must be admitted that, when a Catholic queen occupies [*sic*] the throne, Protestants suffered a similar fate. By the end of the century Protestantism had triumphed and [the] Church of the early centuries had almost ceased to exist. Great Britain could in no sense be described as Catholic today. The Church of England is the established Church and the Queen is its head. The general mentality of the country was Christian in the sense that babies were usually baptised, couples generally preferred to be married in the Church and almost all were given Christian burial. It was true that many professed no religion; nevertheless, religion was honoured both publicly and in private. The State made substantial contribution for Church schools and paid

---

[15] 'A Roman citizen'.

full salaries to all teachers, lay or religious. Catholic schools were granted the same rights as the Church of England schools. Everyone recognised that liberty and equality of treatment for all was the only way to obtain peaceful civic relations. He praised and unreservedly approved the declaration of religious freedom. Because the world was small, what happened in one state could have repercussion all over the world. Some feared the danger of allowing the propagation of error. This was a genuine fear because no one could feel happy at the prospect of the young or ignorant being led into error. But against the contempt for all restraint, they must safeguard liberty. Freedom must be defended at all costs. Experience showed that any state interference in religious matters had always been harmful. The external practice of religion should be subject only to those restrictions which were absolutely necessary to safeguard public order. The text did well to base this right on something more positive than tolerance and the common good. This pastoral doctrine should not omit some doctrinal considerations, because they should give some indication of the methods used to reach their conclusions.

Archbishop Heenan was announced as 'Archbishop of Westminster in France'. The beginning of this speech [...] we found very unacceptable. It was contentious, inaccurate and provocative. It introduced, quite unnecessarily, an inadequate reference to the Reformation. In a discussion on religious liberty it seemed to us quite inexcusable to refer to the severities of persecution in Queen Elizabeth's reign without acknowledging what was the obvious cause of them, viz. the knowledge that the Pope was encouraging a naval and military expedition against the freedom of these islands. It therefore behoves no one to refer to these unhappy days except in the spirit of Pope Paul VI, who said: 'In this great cauldron of human history many severe things were done of which we are all together culpable.'

It seemed strange to us, moreover, that the Vice-President of the Secretariat for Union should provoke us by the bland and misleading statement that 'the Queen is Head (of the Ecclesia Anglicana)'. The only Head of any Church, we would hope, is Jesus Christ. The honorific title of the Queen of England only runs in the provinces of Canterbury and York: and even then it does not in practice impinge upon the liberties of the Church to anything like the degree voluntarily assumed in the Roman Catholic Church, e.g. in Spain.

If Archbishop Heenan has wanted to illustrate any of the evils of religious intolerance he could have done so better from the state of affairs in Italy at the present moment, where the Roman Catholic Church is in league with the State for the suppression of religious liberty. (Ask the Waldensians).

The discussion then returned to the attitude of the Church towards Jews and other non-Christians.

Cardinal Liénart of Lille thought the text [. . .] was acceptable in its treatment of the common patrimony of Christians and Jews. Nevertheless, more stress should be put upon the statement that the Jewish people were not to be regarded as reprobate. St. Peter and St. Paul never regarded the Jews as a rejected people, so neither can we.

Cardinal Ruffini of Palermo, commended the praises of the Jewish people. It hardly seemed necessary to insist that Christians should have love for Jews. Many incidents in the last war were eloquent proof of this, and the Grand Rabbi of Rome had felt obliged to express thanks publicly for asylum granted by the Holy See. It would also be in order to urge Jews to love Christians, particularly Catholics, and to desist from offensive practices which have taken place in the past. It was known that most Jews followed the Talmudic text which inculcated contempt for all who were not Jews. It was well known that Jews supported Free Masonry, which was hostile to the Church and which had been outlawed to members of the Roman Catholic Church under pain of excommunication. Why was there no mention in the text of redemption through Christ also for Jews? The text hardly mentioned non-Christians except Moslems. There were in the world as many Buddhists and Hindus as Moslems, and they were no further removed than the Moslems from basic Christian teaching.

Cardinal Léger, Archbishop of Montreal, said the importance of the declaration on Jews and other non-Christians was that it was an act of a renewed Church. [. . .] Reference to the Jewish origin of Jesus, Mary and the Apostles should be made more clear. They should explain why they condemned hatred of the Jews, i.e., not only because they were men, but because they were specially related to us. They should declare that past persecution of Jews came from false philosophies and wrong interpretation of Christian doctrine. The text was too ambiguous [. . .]

Cardinal Cushing of Boston said their declaration about the Jews and love for the sons of Abraham must be more clear and positive, less timid and more charitable. In a word it must manifest Christ. The text must rule out any special culpability for the death of Christ which would be made to affect later generations [. . .]. They must proclaim to the world in this sacred assembly that there was no logical or historical reason which could justify the iniquity, the hatred or the persecution of our Jewish brethren. It may well be true that not many voices of this kind were lifted in the past, but at least they could be lifted now.

[. . .]

Cardinal Meyer, Archbishop of Chicago, said the importance of this declaration had been stressed by many and it should be accepted with our whole hearts [. . .]. It was enough to say that the Church deplored the persecution of Jews merely because it condemned injustice to all men. There should be explicit mention of the special bonds uniting us to the Jews, as in the previous text [. . .]. The text should make it very clear that the Church took a vigorous stand against any and all discrimination of nation or race, etc. This should be set forth with greater clarity.

[. . .]

Report No. 137   2nd October, 1964

90TH GENERAL CONGREGATION, TUESDAY 29TH SEPTEMBER.

[. . .]

The discussion was continued on the declaration on the Jews.

[. . .]

Archbishop Heenan said it was not surprising that the Jews had received the new version of this declaration without enthusiasm. It was natural that they should ask why certain changes had been made as there was a subtle difference in tone and spirit in the new version. The wording of the document now before the Council was not precisely the wording given it by the Secretariat of Christian Unity. The reasons were not clear, but it was safe to say that there was no desire to make the approach less warm or generous. The change may have been made by men inexperienced in ecumenism. There have been unpleasant reactions to the 'conversion' which seems to be the reason for quoting St. Paul to the Romans. But conversion was not in the context of ecumenism (!), which aims to lead people only to examine each other's beliefs. Its goal was not victories but mutual understanding and esteem. Nonetheless, their hope was for the return of all the brethren of Christ to the one fold. The fact that this quotation had been taken badly by the Jews was sufficient reason for eliminating it. Unless a change is made in the mention of deicide the obvious conclusion will be that, after a year's reflection, the Council Fathers have decided that the Jewish people are culpable. The Council should proclaim that the Jewish people are not guilty. It would certainly be unjust if all the Christians in Europe were judged guilty of the death of millions of Jews in Germany and Poland. It was no less unjust to condemn the whole Jewish people for the death of Christ.

We were pleased to hear Archbishop Heenan disconnecting conversions from ecumenism. This represents a step forward.

[. . .]

We wished that the Moderator would feel able to silence speakers for insufferable repetition of what had already been said.

Report No. 138   5th October, 1964

91ST GENERAL CONGREGATION, WEDNESDAY 30TH SEPTEMBER.

[. . .]

Bishop Wright of Pittsburgh, Pennsylvania, presented the Relation on Chapter 4 of de Ecclesia. He pointed out that the discussion in the previous session seemed to revolve around three main points: (1) many thought the idea of the layman, as presented in the text, was too negative; (2) Some felt the text was insufficient and even inexact in its presentation of the accepted Catholic doctrine on the hierarchical constitution of the Church; (3) Others wanted more explanation of the concept of royal priesthood and of the role of the laity in the Church, especially concerning the consecration of the world.

The Commission had endeavoured to express its idea of the laity in more positive terms [. . .]. With regard to the second point, the Commission had tried to steer a middle course between confusion between the laity and ordained ministries and such a distinction and separation as would offend against the basic unity of the Body of Christ [. . .]

Consequently the content of the introduction had been developed on a broader base, although nothing really new had been added. The text now spoke more explicitly of the dignity of the laity as members of the people of God, but the amendments were really only of secondary importance. The Schema now presented an explicit proposition of the

way in which the laity were to exercise their apostolate in the Christian life, and recognised a closer cooperation between some members of the laity and the apostolate of the hierarchy.
[. . .]

A start was then made on the revised text of *de Divina Revelatione*. The minority report was presented to begin with by:

Bishop Franić of Split, Yugoslavia, who indicated that the basic problem of the disagreement in the Commission was over the relationship of Scripture and Tradition, i.e. could tradition be said to have a wider scope than scripture in such a way that certain doctrines could be held in virtue of tradition alone, even though they were not based on scripture. He then outlined the views of the minority of the Commission. He felt that the schema would be basically defective unless a clear stand were taken on this important point.

The first argument tried to show how the adoption of the position on the wider scope of tradition would be of great ecumenical value in relations with the Orthodox churches. The Protestant brethren also wanted to have a sincere and open statement on this question. They should not be deceived with a silence aimed at hiding disagreement, as this would not be genuine charity.
[. . .]

This kind of minority report is one of the most interesting features of the Council. We agree on his main contention that the report represents a serious departure from the doctrines of the Council of Trent, though we are of course glad of this. [. . .]

Report No. 139   6th October, 1964

92ND GENERAL CONGREGATION, THURSDAY 1ST OCTOBER.

The Council discussed the *Schema de Divina Revelatione*.

Cardinal Léger, Archbishop of Montreal, said it was wise to avoid any solemn conciliar pronouncements on the difficult problem of one or two founts of Revelation. The schema should stress the transcendence of the Apostolic deposit transmitted to us through scripture and tradition. Divine Revelation transcends the entire life of the Church and all the acts of the Magisterium. In the strict sense only Revelation is the Word of God. It was right that the Church should turn to Revelation as the source of inspiration for her renovation. It would be advisable for all of them to make a careful examination of conscience, as there was no doubt that there had been exaggerations on the importance of the Magisterium. On the subject of Revelation and Magisterium there should be a clear distinction between the teaching of the Apostles and that of their successors. The Apostles were direct eye witnesses of the events they described, and they were direct preachers of Revelation, and so in this way they were different. They must realise that there had been at times certain indiscretions in insistence on infallibility. This set up a wall between the Roman Catholic Church and their separated brethren. They should distinguish between the infallibility which is strictly speaking proper to Revelation and that which is proper to the Magisterium of the Church.

[. . .]

Cardinal Browne of the Theological Commission made a reactionary statement and said that the text unfortunately omitted all mention of the role of theologians in furthering the evolution of the teaching of Tradition. There was a wrong emphasis on deeds instead of words. It should be stated that Revelation was contained in words and deeds, because words were the principle means of expressing thought. Tradition did not grow and the substantial content of Scripture was always the same. Certain expressions should be clarified to prevent modern error on the priority of 'religious experience'.

[. . .]

Archbishop Attipetty of Verapoly, India, said the deliberate avoidance by the Theological Commission of the touchy question of the objective content of Tradition could not be defended. They were dealing with two contradictory things, i.e. whether Tradition alone without scripture was the fount of Revelation. One opinion holds as a dogma of faith that Tradition alone is a source of Revelation. If this were now contradicted it would mean that what has up to now been proclaimed as dogma would be declared false. Recent studies had shown that the mind of the Council of Trent on this point had prevailed in the Church in the intervening centuries. If no stand were taken on this the Church would be open to ridicule, as though she had been hitherto teaching a false doctrine. The dogmas like the Assumption, which was based on Tradition, would also appear ridiculous. Nothing was more dangerous than to allow ecumenical preoccupations to harm the integrity of the faith. Nothing could justify silence. Therefore, if the Council was unable to reach agreement on this, the Pope should be asked to decide in virtue of his supreme Magisterium. (A surprisingly reactionary statement from India).

[. . .]

THE UGANDA MARTYRS[16]

We now know that our Archbishop of Uganda has accepted the Secretariat's invitation to be present in St. Peter's on the 18th October for the canonisation of the martyrs, at which the Pope will mention the Anglican martyrs in his speech. This is another unprecedented encounter.

Report No. 140 6th October, 1964

93RD GENERAL CONGREGATION, FRIDAY 2ND OCTOBER.

The debate was continued on the schema *de Divina Revelatione* and the main speakers were:

Archbishop Beras of Santo Domingo, Dom. Republic, (as an example of a really reactionary approach) said that if there were any desire to avoid discussion of the question of the objective content of Revelation, the whole question could be postponed. This suggestion was not prompted by any doubt of the truth, but merely of the opportuneness of making a definitive statement at the present time. Was it not for Ecumenical Councils to decide and confirm what had been traditional doctrine in the Church? It seemed necessary to proclaim the doctrine of Vatican I, which stated that not all truths were contained in scripture, some were made known to the Apostles and transmitted by them to us. Such a stand was of great importance with regard to the three basic Marian dogmas of Perpetual Virginity, the Immaculate Conception and the Assumption [. . .]

Bishop Alba Palacios of Tehuantepec, Mexico, suggested the title should be changed to 'Divine Tradition' instead of 'Sacred Tradition' in order to show that there was not sufficient emphasis on preaching as the chief means of transmitting the Word of God, an idea which frequently recurs in the Epistles of St. Paul. There was nothing wrong in the acceptance of teaching which was not based on St. Thomas. Pope Pius XII issued an Apostolic constitution clarifying the matter of the

---

[16]Christians of both Roman Catholic and Anglican churches were killed by King Mwanga of Buganda in 1885–1887. The twenty-two Roman Catholics were canonized by Paul VI on 18 October 1964. One of the first Christians to die was Bishop James Hannington, the first Anglican bishop of East Africa. That the Anglicans were publicly acknowledged at the same time was regarded as a significant step forward in ecumenical understanding.

Sacrament of Orders, even though St. Thomas had held a different opinion.

Very Rev. Christopher Butler, Abbot President of the English Congregation of the order of St. Benedict, said that it would seem that the text used the term 'tradition' in two different senses. In the first it includes scripture, but in the second sense the text speaks of the 'relationships between scripture and tradition', thus giving us to understand that tradition is different from scripture. The Theological Commission had no doubts as to the teaching of the Council of Trent on tradition. In judging the statements made by the ordinary Magisterium of the Church distinction must be made between words used and the intention behind the words. It should not be forgotten that at the time of Trent exegesis was more static than dynamic, whereas today it was essentially dynamic, thus enabling them to see more in scripture than was possible for previous generations. Magisterium never had any intention to declare deficiency in scripture. Since any definition by the Council would be seriously misunderstood, the matter was plainly not mature for final decision.

[. . .]

OBSERVERS' MEETING, FRIDAY 2ND OCTOBER.

Religious Liberty

I asked for clarification of Archbishop Heenan's position with regard to the place of proselytism in the scheme of things. In the Schema de Ecumenismo he had asked for the insertion of a section declaring that the work of 'reconciliation' was not ruled out by the Schema. Yet in the declaration on the Jews he had said that there was no connection at all between proselytism and ecumenism.

I said that the world would judge the whole Schema and its declarations by the practical outcome of them. It would therefore expect:

a) Suggestions concerning the revision of some of the Concordats now in existence in which the R.C. Church is compromised because liberty of others is restricted thereby.
b) Suggestions concerning the running of ecumenical institutes so that they will under no circumstances be suspected of proselytising activities.
c) Positive directions for the guidance of people working in the mission field both with regard to the preservation of the rights and liberties of the Roman Church, and also with regard to the rights and correct treatment of others working in the same area.

Willebrands said that the Secretariat would welcome suggestions for the Directorium on Ecumenism and for the practical working out of the Declaration on Religious Liberty.

94TH GENERAL CONGREGATION, MONDAY 5TH OCTOBER.

Archbishop Martin of Rouen, presented the Relatio on *Chapter 1 of de Ecumenismo* and said that the expression 'restoration of unity' with which the schema now opened should be a source of satisfaction to the separated brethren. The doctrine outlined in the schema was closely connected with the teaching of the constitution *de Ecclesia*. [. . .]

Report No. 141   7th October, 1964

95TH GENERAL CONGREGATION, 6TH OCTOBER.

[. . .]

Bishop Helmsing of Kansas City, U. S. A., presented the Relatio on *Chapter 2 of the Schema de Ecumenismo*. He said that Chapter 1 had dealt with the general nature of the ecumenical movement and that Chapter 2 showed the connection between this movement and the life of individual pastors and faithful. To bring about this conversion of heart, it would be useful, even necessary, to pray for unity sometimes in brotherly association with Orthodox and Protestant Christians. [. . .]

96TH GENERAL CONGREGATION, WEDNESDAY 7TH OCTOBER.

[. . .]

The Secretariat was happy to accede to the wishes of many Fathers who asked for a degree of latitude in the legislation on participation in non-Catholic services. A general ruling on this point had been made part of the text. The approval of this text would mark the beginning of a new era in the history of the Church and lead all Christians to the primitive and genuine unity of the Church of Christ.

Archbishop Heenan presented the Relatio on Part 2 of Chapter 3 dealing with separated churches and ecclesial communities in the West. The title of this second part had been changed in order to make it more objective. The groups which had arisen as a result of separation in the West were not merely agglomerations of individual Christians, but were made up of genuine ecclesial character. It was intended to include all those who called themselves Christians. There was no intention to go into the disputed question of what was required for a Christian community, theologically speaking, to be called a Church. There was now no reference in the text to Christian communities which arose 'since the 16th Century', but only to communities 'separated in the West'.

A new method of presentation had been adopted. There was no attempt to provide a description of definition of other communities but only to set down four points which must be accepted in these communities: 1) belief in Christ; 2) study of the sacred books; 3) sacramental life; 4) life with Christ. These were common to all Christians and served as a foundation for dialogue with the separated brethren. As a part of this dialogue there was an indication of those doctrines on which there was disagreement. This tempered and well-balanced presentation aimed at satisfying the worries of those Fathers who were concerned about avoiding either any semblance of proselytism or any danger of indifferentism.

The conclusion in Article 24 was to be regarded as the conclusion of all three chapters, not only of this present part. The article provided a brief indication of the general principles underlying all ecumenical activity, namely fidelity to the Catholic faith taught by the Church and fidelity to the inspiration of the Holy Spirit, who was moving all Christians towards the unity willed by Christ. These principles showed the pastoral and ecumenical aim of the Council as formulated by John XXIII and continued by Paul VI.

The entire world was awaiting the outcome of this vote. The separated brethren united with Roman Catholics in Christian hope and prayer and wanted to collaborate in an ever-increasing degree. Even men with no religion would examine the statements on Christian unity very carefully. Here there was an opportunity to demonstrate that today, no less than in Apostolic times, Christians were recognised by their brotherly love.
[...]

Bishop Hengsbach of Essen presented the *Relatio* on the Schema on *the Apostolate of the Laity*. He explained that the text had been completely revised.
[...]

The schema considers four main fields of the Apostolate: 1) the family, 2) ecclesial communities, i.e. the parish, the diocese and the universal Church, 3) the special milieu of the laity, and 4) organisations with open membership. The family is considered as a subject of the Apostolate, because it is there that the faithful first come into contact with the Apostolate. In ecclesial communities the order of procedure goes from the parish to the diocese. There is greater insistence on inter-parochial collaboration because of the pastoral needs of modern cities and rural areas which sometimes also go beyond national barriers. It is recommended that there should be scientific studies of these situations and careful examination of how these social structures could be rearranged according to the teaching of the Gospel. Only very general principles can be given for inter-parochial and international activities. There are two distinct objects in the Apostolate of the Laity, i.e. the conversion of men and their progress towards God, and the Christianisation of the temporal power.

The text deals with various degrees of the dependence of the lay apostolate on the hierarchy and concludes with a recommendation of collaboration with other Christians and with non-Christians.

Finally an invitation was issued to the laity to participate through the hierarchy in bringing about the one mission of Christ in His Church and to adapt this in the future to the needs of the time.

Cardinal Ritter, Archbishop of St. Louis, Missouri, began the discussion of the Apostolate of the Laity by saying that the schema seemed to contain everything necessary for the present day needs [. . .]. The weaknesses were juridicism, treatment of points which should be left to the revision of Canon Law and discussion of the relationship of the laity with the hierarchy. The text should also not give special praise to Catholic Action (there is a growing crisis about this in the Roman Catholic Church). There should be a distinction between different forms of the Apostolate of the Laity according to their mutual relationship and not their relationships with the hierarchy.

Bishop De Roo of Victoria, Canada, said that the text as it stood would be a great disappointment for the laity. It failed to lay down the essential principles of the Lay Apostolate and did not give any indication of the real character or spirit of their vocation. St. Paul, on many occasions, called the attention to the vocation of individual Christians to apostolic activity. This must be realised in the Church [. . .]. If the Apostolate of the hierarchy was ever completely separated from the lay apostolate then the hierarchy could not really fulfil their mission.
[. . .]
Bishop Sani of Denpasar, Indonesia, thought the schema needed to be written in language more adapted to the laity. It did not explain what a 'temporal order' was nor did it say how its restoration was one of

the activities of the lay apostolate. The faithful must be taught that this apostolate was not something distinct from their daily life, it was their daily life [. . .]

[. . .]

Archbishop Maccari of Mondovi, Italy, thought the entire schema should be completely revised before it was approved. It failed to come up to the expectations of either the Church or the world. One of the reasons why the text was disappointing was its insufficient treatment of Catholic Action. The general apostolate was praised warmly but the special apostolate of Catholic Action was almost belittled. The text made a compromise on Catholic Action and, what was still more grave, what had been the hitherto accepted notion of Catholic Action in the Church. This was dangerous because the enemies of the Church were legion today and the Church should not be lulled into a sense of false security and induced to lay down the arms of prudence. (This last is given as an example of a really reactionary speech). The bishop conceived Catholic Action as a totally submissive action group, which of course solidly favours the Christian Democrat party).

Report No. 142   13th October, 1964

97TH GENERAL CONGREGATION, THURSDAY 8TH OCTOBER.

[. . .]

The Council then continued the discussion on the *Apostolate of the Laity*.

Archbishop d'Souza of Bhopal, India, (one of the bishops whom we dined on the 5th October) said the inspiration to implement the decisions of the Council could only come from the Holy Spirit. Consequently they should see to it that the text contained nothing which might hamper the workings of the Spirit. When they realised that they must treat laymen as adults, it was amazing to read in the text that 'nothing is to be done without the bishop'. This phrase could open the door to untold abuses and repressions of initiative. The People of God was not a totalitarian state where everything was run from the top. The hierarchy must assure the laity that they recognised that they could count on collaboration. [. . .] They must show that they were genuinely ready to de-clericalise their outlook and treat the laity as brothers. The hierarchy should not take upon themselves the laity's responsibilities, but should leave them to do those things which they can do better. For example why should representatives of the Church

in international organisations always be priests? Laymen could be used in many different offices in the Curia. They also could be employed in the diplomatic service of the Holy See and could even be appointed Nuncios in some cases. There were countless examples at all levels of Church life. Vain would be their talk of promoting the preaching of the Gospel unless they had a radical reorganisation of their way of thinking. The text should say what needed to be reorganised. There was no hope for the apostolate of the laity if they were always to remain under the thumb of clerics. There would be mistakes and difficulties, but one of the facts of life was that there was no growth without crises. The schema opened up a new era and a new spirit.
[...]

Bishop Leven, Auxiliary of San Antonio, Texas, was happy that for the first time the laity were being discussed in a positive way in an Ecumenical Council. This showed that the Church was not merely juridical but the living spirit of Christ. The lay apostolate was not a concession made to the faithful, but their right. Every Christian had the cause of Christ at heart and this was the apostolate of Christians, the majority of whom were laymen. The hierarchy could direct this apostolate but must not forbid it or hem it in with such restrictions as to make it meaningless. They needed real dialogue between bishops and the laity, and this was impossible if the laity were expected only to listen. The schema was too timid and hesitant [...]. This was most important for areas where the laity were educated and were ready to give their time and efforts to the cause of the Church. Little would be gained if a bishop consulted only a few people, especially if these few were only his doctor and his housekeeper. It was desirable that every diocese should have a kind of diocesan senate, perhaps modelled on the one suggested for the Pope. This would make it possible for the bishop to maintain contact with different trends in his diocese and consider all reasonable suggestions. There might be problems because fanatics and crackpots were to be found everywhere, but still they must be prepared to take chances, because the movement towards the lay apostolate was one of the signs of our times.

Bishop Tenhumberg, Auxiliary of Münster, Germany, said the apostolate of the laity was necessary for more than just extrinsic reasons. References to the 'canonical mandate' for the exercise of the apostolate sounded like a residue of clericalism. The commission would do well to consult with authoritative members of the laity in order to perfect the final version of the schema. *The laity should be represented in ecclesiastical curias.* The idea of the apostolate had for too long been restricted to the hierarchy. The theological aspects of the apostolate should be used as a guide for the apostolic training of the laity, so as to give them a clear idea of their proper place in the Church. The final version of the text should take care to avoid schoolroom language.

THE POPE: SPECIAL AUDIENCES

I have now had three audiences within a fortnight! The first was the normal Observers' collective audience, already reported. The second was the occasion of a pilgrimage of Fr. Curtis, who had already been to a general audience. The Holy Father got to know that there were 'amici del Canonico Pawley' in town and requested that I brought them to a private audience, which I did. We tacked on a pilgrimage led by the Bishop of Huron[17] which happened to be around.

The Pope was very affable indeed, and said it was always a special pleasure to greet Anglicans. I introduced Fr. Curtis C.R.[18] as a 'veterano dell'Ecumenismo', as indeed he is. Fr. Curtis then presented the Holy Father with a copy of his new book on l'Abbe Couturier,[19] which the Pope received. He said, 'I always read English books when they are given to me'.

THE POPE: PRIVATE AUDIENCE

The third audience was at my request through the private access I have through Dom. Pasquale Macchi whom I have known for some time, who is now his principal private secretary. The audience came the day after the previous one. It took place at the end of a working morning.

My object in going in was to make sure the Holy Father understood what was in the minds of the Observers concerning his proposed response to the suggestion of an ecumenical institute (see my letter of 6th October to the Archbishop). All the Observers were unanimously of the opinion that this should not be made to appear a Papal enterprise, still less a Papal institution, to which the rest of us are summoned. I said that the Orthodox and the Protestants were more touchy than we were about it all. But we agreed in thinking that the Pope would be well advised to call a meeting of representatives of heads of churches as soon as possible and not to allow the scheme to mature before presenting the rest of us with a fait accompli.

---

[17] From the Anglican Church of Canada.

[18] Community of the Resurrection, an Anglican Order founded in Pusey House, Oxford, in 1882.

[19] Paul Couturier (1881–1953), priest and inspirational French ecumenist; creator of the annual Week of Prayer for Christian Unity.

He said it was impossible to commit the Roman Catholic Church to a round table conference on these matters. We did not know one another well enough for that. I said that there was a danger of the thing foundering if he didn't.

The Pope said there was the difficulty of who would pay, who would be the governing body of the institute etc., who would decide who should be the students, where the building should be located.

I said that the question had come up in the W.C.C. at the beginning, but is simply solved by the allocation of proportionate expenses to the participants. Similarly a representative meeting could appoint an executive committee to decide the other questions.

He said he saw our point, and thanked me for drawing his attention to it. He was sensitive to the whole position and would do his best to avoid wrong appearances. At the same time he said quite firmly that he could not let go of control. He was going to propose the institute should be under the Catholic Universities' Organisation.

I said with considerable deference that even that might be misunderstood. Could not they be his representatives? He said we were not to worry: there would be no attempt to 'capture' the enterprise, still less to exploit. I said we should never suppose of him (emphasis on the last two words). He smiled. I hoped I hadn't spoken out of turn. He said 'No', he was glad to know indirectly what was going on. He was of course also getting reports through the Secretariat. But he was always pleased to hear what the Anglicans thought – they were very sane!
[...]

We then spoke of the Council, and when he asked for my impressions I took the liberty of saying I would like to communicate something which was the common talk of many of the bishops and of the observers. That was that much now depended on 'whether the Holy Father gave us the *senate of bishops* we have so clearly said we want'. He smiled the smile he always smiles when he doesn't want to talk about something and said something to the effect that we must wait and see. I didn't of course expect him to discuss this, but was glad to have made the point.

We exchanged some personal information and he invited me to come again as often as I liked. This certainly is now a very useful link. He repeated that he wanted to see the Archbishop of Canterbury as soon as convenient. I explained the matter of the Archbishop's two tours next spring.

'CONCILIUM LATERANENSE'

The bishops (and observers) spend so much time now in the aisles and coffee-bars of St. Peter's that this assembly is normally called by the above name. It is almost always more useful than the Council itself. We make endless interesting and profitable contacts there.

Report No. 143   14th October, 1964

98TH GENERAL CONGREGATION, FRIDAY 9TH OCTOBER.

Discussion continued on the *Apostolate of the Laity*.

[. . .]

Archbishop Kozlowiecki of Lusaka, N. Rhodesia, said the description of the apostolate was inaccurate, narrow-minded and one-sided, as though it were to be reduced to mere activity or preaching the Gospel. In this sense the laity would have no apostolate except as helpers for the hierarchy. But if they looked beyond this and realised that work, suffering, sacrifices and prayer were part of the apostolate, then the laity would be true apostles aiding the hierarchy. The text should omit the exhortation to the laity to build up their piety through parochial liturgy, because it was not the Council's job to dictate to the Holy Spirit how He should inspire the laity. The description of the apostolate in the text was so narrow that it only covered activities which came under the direction of the hierarchy. The Council had much to say about religious liberty for all men and, in the same spirit, they should not be too quick to limit the liberty of their own laity.

Bishop Carter of Sault Ste. Marie, Canada, said the schema still needed to be completely rewritten. It lacked unity because everything contained in the longer version had been compressed leaving a collection and the commission had realised that it was absurd for a group of ecclesiastics alone to study the apostolate of the laity. But when a group of lay experts had been called in the work of the commission was almost finished and therefore their contribution was hardly noticeable. The schema did not come up to the expectations of the faithful. They were supposed to be working for dialogue, but in fact the text only spoke to the hierarchy.

[. . .]

Bishop Rastouil of Limoges thought the schema was not clear enough about the powers, the rights and the duties of the laity. It should be insisted upon that the basis of the Lay Apostolate was the share on the

priesthood of Christ through baptism and confirmation. It must never be forgotten that the whole Church was one of a sacerdotal nature. It was regrettable that they had not yet succeeded in working out an adequate theology of the sacrament of confirmation. (!) (Shall we send them a copy of the 'Theology of Christian Initiation'?)[20]
[...]

THE DECLARATION ON THE JEWS AND RELIGIOUS LIBERTY

The Secretariat for Union has apparently had a strong push from the conservatives to persuade it to deal with the above [...]. This is undoubtedly in response to heavy pressure from the Middle East. The Rome papers said that the two declarations are 'in danger': this in our view is an exaggeration. We (the Observers) seem to be agreed that we are not happy about the statement on the present situation of the Jews in regard to the Covenants (it being in any case unnecessary to define it); and that we should be glad that the declaration is out of the context of Ecumenism. (Dr. Kelly's[21] opinion to the contrary notwithstanding).

We were told today by 'authoritative sources' that this attempt to force the issue has failed. A group of cardinals wrote protesting to the Pope against this interference. The Pope has intervened in favour of letting the Council run its course and against an attempt by the 'old guard' to stifle it. This piece of news has given great pleasure in the Council. It has at once shown up the weakness of the old Italian 'dead-beats' and the reliability of the Pope's rule.

PROF. HANS KÜNG

We had dinner in the company of this remarkable young man the other day. He is still very impatient indeed about the progress of the Council. He thinks the appointment of the 'Senate' will be the decisive move. With six appointments, if they were the right men, he said, the Pope could change the face of the Church.

Mgr. Höfer, who was also present, said that even Pius XII had invited bishops to nominate suitable young men for service in the Curia. But all were agreed that the lower offices should all be filled by specially trained laymen (equivalent to a Civil Service) and that bishops from

---

[20]The report of the Theological Commission of the Church of England, published in 1948.
[21]Dr J.N.D. Kelly (1909–1997), Principal of St Edmund's Hall, Oxford, 1951–1973; eminent scholar of biblical and patristic studies.

important sees elsewhere should be called in (without previous 'curial' experience) to direct the main policy (cf. the Cabinet Ministers).

Report No. 144	16th October, 1964

99TH GENERAL CONGREGATION, MONDAY 12TH OCTOBER

Cardinal Liénart, Bishop of Lille, continuing the discussion on the Apostolate of the Laity, said that it was right to stress that the apostolate did not exclusively belong to the clergy. The laity participated in the apostolate through baptism and confirmation. The text should emphasise the importance of giving them real responsibility.
[...]

Bishop Padín, Auxiliary of Rio de Janiero, (This speech illustrates how unexpectedly liberal thought comes out of quarters which were normally supposed to be entirely reactionary) said the laity must have its proper share on all the work of the Church in under-developed nations. The text should show the great diversity of fields of the apostolate [...]. Their policy should be to open doors, not to close them, and they should make every effort to avoid putting things into categories. Some people criticised the privilege of using the name 'Catholic Action', but had they been called from all over the world merely to discuss names? [...] Similarly there should be no such name as 'Holy Office', because all ecclesiastical offices were holy [...]. The passage dealing with the future secretariat of the lay apostolate was too clerical. The laity should not merely be invited to 'cooperate' but should be summoned to positions of direct responsibility.

Archbishop Heenan thought the schema was not merely opportune but most necessary for the Church of today, when the place of laymen in the life of the Church had completely changed. Gone were the days when the vast majority of the laity were uneducated [...]. The faithful today were sometimes more learned than the priests [...]. The laity may have a vast knowledge of secular things, but they still needed careful spiritual training which only theology and asceticism could give them. The work of the lay apostolate was sacred and delicate as it was concerned with the salvation of souls. Those who wished to be lay apostles must put themselves humbly in the hands of their priests for training [...]. The enemies of the Church do their utmost to create divisions between the clergy and the laity. The apostolate of the laity should not be thought of as being in opposition to the apostolate of the clergy. The authors of the schema should be commended for their efforts to bring the clergy and laity together and unite their respective apostolates [. . .]. The proposed secretariat for the lay apostolate was bound to fail unless the laity were fully consulted, in fact most of the members should be chosen from the laity [. . .]. Let the laity be 'doers of the word and not hearers only'. The people chosen for this work should be those who have taken the lead in the lay apostolate and others who are not connected with any organisation. They should not send to Rome only old gentlemen loaded down with ecclesiastical honours. They should send young men and women who had to earn their daily bread. They must show their devoted laymen that they have the full confidence of the hierarchy.

(This is a good speech. But I am informed it does not represent a conversion: Heenan has always been enlightened by the laity.)

The president called for a standing vote on the closure of the debate on the lay apostolate, and this was carried by an overwhelming majority. [. . .]

Report No. 145.   19th October, 1964

101ST GENERAL CONGREGATION, WEDNESDAY 14TH OCTOBER.

Discussion continued on *Priests*:

Bishop Bánk, Auxiliary Bishop-elect from Hungary, drew attention to the need for proper support for priests. The world was waiting for new laws adapted to present circumstances and expected more deeds than words. It could not be denied that the clergy sometimes disregarded encyclicals of the Pope, especially when these concerned salaries for people who help them, and the fact that these people should not be overworked. Vatican I was called the Council of the Pope. Vatican II was said to be the Council of the Bishops. Vatican III will be the Council of Priests. It would be advisable to assure younger clergy that an assignment was not indefinite, but that they could expect periodical promotion. The present system of stole fees could be reorganised and, in a parish, all these fees should be added together and then distributed equally at the end of the year.

Archbishop Baldassarri of Ravenna, Italy, thought it right that the Council should put the Episcopate in its proper light, but it was not right for the bishops to treat their chief helpers, the priests, in a second-rate way. He wanted the schema to be completely revised. After the excellent speech made by the lay auditor it would be perfectly in order to ask that the Council should be addressed by an experienced parish priest. The text should take care to use the words 'sacerdos' and 'presbyter' in the right sense. It should not be forgotten that they were not synonymous in the early Church. The Council could lay down general principle[s] and leave practical details to the national episcopal conferences. They should not be less considerate in their treatment of priests than they were in that of bishops and the laity.

Bishop Sánchez-Moreno Lira, Auxiliary of Chiclayo, Peru, said there was a great need for priests today. They must first endeavour to break down the wall of separation which tended to cut them off from the people, for it was their duty to go out in search of the sheep. Secondly, priests must have a fuller knowledge of present pastoral needs. Doctors tried to keep up with developments in medicine and, as doctors of souls, priests must do the same. Lastly, there should be no more mobility and specialisation in the organisation of priests, so that they may be more readily available.

Archbishop Gomes dos Santos of Goiânia, Brazil, said it was no use hiding the fact that the schema was a big disappointment. After all that had been said about bishops and laity a few propositions on the priesthood were almost an insult [...]. He proposed that a new text should be drawn up and submitted at the 4th session of the Council. The priesthood was too important to be discussed in haste.

Bishop Garaygordóbil, Prelate Nullius of Los Rios, Ecuador, said the pastoral work of the Church depended on the bishops, who in turn, could only work through their priests. Priests needed to be protected against 'arbitrariness' of their bishops, who were neither confirmed in grace nor infallible [...]. In every diocese a representative board of priests should be set up as consultants.

Bishop González Martín of Astorga, Spain, thought something similar to the second novitiate for the religious would be of great value to the secular clergy, giving a period of spiritual renewal after some time spent in the ministry. Great attention should be paid to the distribution of clergy, perhaps through national or international seminaries. It was unbelievable that in a country like Spain between one and two thousand candidates were turned away from seminaries every year because they were not needed in their home diocese, while many other dioceses were having great difficulty in providing the minimum number of priests required.

Bishop Corripio Ahumada of Tampico, Mexico, was anxious for unity to be safeguarded in the Church among priests. They should do away with the many financial inequalities resulting from the benefice system [...]. All priests would be provided with social security and health insurance. A good way of doing this would be to set up a common fund in each diocese to provide for the needs of all.

THE UGANDA MARTYRS

No doubt this matter has had full treatment in the British press, in spite of the elections, Khrushchev and the Chinese atomic bomb; than all of which it is probably more significant in the long run. The Archbishop of Uganda was ceremoniously received, royally entertained, given a prominent place in the basilica. The Pope received him in private audience immediately afterwards. He was entertained to a reception by all the R.C. bishops in Africa.

In his speech at the canonisation the Pope said, among other things:

'Uganda est un champ d'apostolat missionaire, qui accueillit comme premiers messagers de l'Evangelie des anglicanes, venus d'Angleterre, auxquels se joignirent, deux ans plus tard, des missionaires catholiques de langue française, les Pères Blancs ...

'Et nous ne voulons pas oublier non plus les autres qui, appurtenant à la confession anglicane, ont affronté la mort pour le nom du Christ.'[22]

Report No. 146.   20th October, 1964

102ND GENERAL CONGREGATION, THURSDAY 15TH OCTOBER.

Continuing the discussion on *Priests*:

Cardinal Alfrink of Utrecht said the text was not up to the expectations of the priests. It did not give a clear image of either the priest or the priesthood, and it left out, or only treated superficially, many

[22]'Uganda is a field of apostolic mission that welcomed Anglicans, from England, as the first bearers of the Gospel, to whom were joined, two years later, French-speaking Catholic missionaries, the Pères Blancs [official name, Missionnaires d'Afrique]. ... And we do not want to forget all the others who, subscribing to the Anglican confession, have confronted death in the name of Christ.'

problems in a priest's life. The apostolate required new thinking on the mission of priests and should be adjusted to the needs of modern times. The discussion of celibacy was of great importance and the Council could not afford only to mention this matter in passing, as it was receiving widespread publicity which had almost created a crisis on this important point of Church discipline. Celibacy should be presented in a more biblical light, with fuller explanation from tradition. Many felt the schema could not be published as it stood without the risk of great disappointment. It was hoped that a new text would be satisfactory and a source of greater consolation for priests in their difficulties.

The discussion was then closed.

[. . .]

Discussion on the Oriental Churches:

Cardinal König of Vienna, opening the debate, said the text should be revised so as to be more in harmony with the schema on ecumenism. The treatment of the Patriarchs should be based on the schema on the pastoral duties of bishops. The discipline of the sacraments was either common to the universal Church or was peculiar to the Oriental Patriarchs. If the former, then it was out of place here. If the latter it should come under legislation of the particular rites.

His Beatitude Stephanos I Sidarousa, Coptic Patriarch of Alexandria considered the schema generally acceptable. Nevertheless many Orientals would have preferred it to come under the schema on the Church for, although the Oriental churches had different rites, they were not, strictly speaking, separate churches. It would be preferable to leave freedom of choice of rite to those within the Catholic Church. Steps should have been taken soon to restore the ancient rites and privileges of Patriarchs [. . .]

His Beatitude Maximos IV Saigh, Melchite Patriarch of Antioch, thought the present text was a real improvement on the previous one and the Commission should be congratulated. It was not, however, satisfactory in every detail. The weakest chapter was the one on Patriarchs, and this was absolutely inadmissible. It misinterpreted history and did not prepare the way for the future. It was absolutely wrong to say that the Patriarchs were a purely Oriental institution. The first Patriarch of the Catholic Church was the Bishop of Rome [. . .]. It was no use to shower Patriarchs with praise and reverence in the text and then reduce them to the position of subordinates, obliging them for many administrative details to apply to the Roman Curia. They have their own Synods and should have freedom of action. That this outlook had guided the preparation of the schema was evident from the building, when the text stated that the Catholic Church wished to show its affection and esteem for the 'Oriental churches', thus implying that they were not Catholic. Steps should be taken to restore the Patriarchs to their previous dignity. Steps should also be taken to eliminate the honorary Patriarchs in the West.

[. . .]

DIRECTORIUM

We have been invited to present suggestions about material for inclusion in the above, and are compiling some. We have as headings so far:

1. Ecumenical institutes (especially in view of item 3, Report No. 147 on Trier et alia). The nature and purpose of these need to be carefully defined. It should be entirely objective and should abjure proselytism.
2. Definition of powers of united prayer, drawing the bonds as wide as possible.
3. Exhortation against provocative literature.
4. (eventually) Something about the ecumenical context of mixed marriages.

[. . .]

Report No. 147   21st October, 1964

103RD GENERAL CONGREGATION, FRIDAY 16TH OCTOBER.

[. . .]

Discussion continued on the *Oriental Churches*:

Cardinal de Barros Camâra, Archbishop of Rio de Janeiro, said the Council should avoid giving the impression that it was concerned with those of the Oriental faith who actually lived in the East. There were millions of them living in other countries and among Latin Catholics. In Brazil alone there were members of eight Oriental rites. Those who were converted to the Catholic Church should, as in the present legislation, be given freedom to choose their rite, although they should be encouraged to keep their original rite [. . .]

His Beatitude Alberto Gori, Latin Patriarch of Jerusalem, thought that the passage which insists on converted Orientals retaining their original rite, but says that when in difficulty they should appeal to the Holy

See, was hardly likely to provide the right answer [. . .]. It was ironical that a convert wishing to change rites should have to appeal to the authority of Rome, which he had always been taught to distrust [. . .]
[. . .]

Archbishop Ghattas of Thebes, Egypt, considered the schema needed revision, firstly because the Oriental churches were not just appendages to the Catholic Church but an integral part of it. They should therefore be included in the Schema de Ecclesia [. . .]

Archbishop Zoghby, Patriarchal Vicar for Melchites in Egypt, raised two points: Firstly, the patriarchal system, as canonised by early ecumenical councils, was in force also in the West for many centuries. It was gradually supplanted, but Latin patriarchs were set up in various Oriental sees. They were generally regarded as intruders and shadows of the Pope and their presence was a constant source of friction. There must be some new thinking on the validity of the patriarchal system for the Church of the West today. Secondly, until Vatican I the primacy of the Pope, which was the chief source of division between East and West, was regarded in the East only as a canonical structure. The decision to proclaim the infallibility of the Pope as a dogma of faith was taken by a Council at which representatives from the Orient were conspicuously absent (!). When the Orientals broke with Rome they attached no special theological value to the primacy, neither did they consider they were separating from the universal Church of Christ, but only from the Latin Church. The text should be revised so as to eliminate a false vision of the Church.
[. . .]

Report No. 148   22nd October, 1964

104TH GENERAL CONGREGATION, MONDAY 19TH OCTOBER.

[. . .]

The debate was then continued on *Oriental Churches*:
[. . .]

Archbishop Tawil, Melchite Patriarchal Vicar of Damascus, said the Church wanted to have dialogue with all those who believed in Christ. To do this they must change many things in their way of thinking and acting. This schema should be in harmony with the schema on Ecumenism. It should not be forgotten that the Latin Church was also a 'particular church'. The Latin Church had been governed by the patriarchal system for over 1,000 years. It was strange that the text, while mentioning the great Patriarchates of the Oriental Church, failed to list their names. One might wonder what was the value of the Latin Patriarchate in Jerusalem [. . .]. For the Orientals it was the last word in Latinisation of the Orient. The Council should remedy these situations and a post-conciliar commission should be set up to work out the details.

[. . .]

Abbot Hoeck, President of the Bavarian Congregation of the Order of St. Benedict, said the most important thing in the Oriental churches was the patriarchal structure of the Church. This was also most important for ecumenism [. . .]. The system should be re-established. In any discussion about unity the great churches of the East immediately ask what their place will be in the Catholic Church. Will they be subordinated to the Roman Curia, and will they take second place after the College of Cardinals? For 1,000 years the churches of the East enjoyed full freedom when choosing their patriarchs and bishops, and in organising their liturgy and canon law. The right of intervention by Rome was always recognised, but seldom carried out. Any attempt to restore unity with the Orthodox churches must be on the understanding that this unity will be based on the same principles as existed before the break [. . .]. This question cannot be discussed, much less decided, by a council which is predominantly Latin.

Report No. 149   22nd October, 1964

105TH GENERAL CONGREGATION, TUESDAY 20TH OCTOBER.

[. . .]

Discussion began on the: SCHEMA ON THE CHURCH IN THE MODERN WORLD:

Bishop Guano of Livorno presented the Relatio and said that, while the bishops had been busy in Rome with the renewal of the Church, their brethren throughout the world had been living their own lives. They were concerned with the problem of daily bread, with their own dignity and with the peace and unity of the world. Often they paid no attention to the Church, but all the same, if for no other reason than custom, they felt there was something superhuman in the Church and that from it could come some world which would be of importance and serve their interests. Therefore they ask the Church what she thinks about men, culture and civilisation, and the worries and desires of men. They want to know if the Church is ready to help them and to fulfil the hopes of the world.

The schema was different from the others because it had nothing to do with the usual matters of Church renewal, sacramental and liturgical life etc. It dealt with the burning problems of today. The Church wanted men to speak to her about their problems and to learn from her what Christians can and must do to help solve the great crises of the world. In this the Church would only speak in her own light and about the problems as they were related to her mission, which was to preach Christ and to lead men to God through Christ.

It would be as well to remember that the work of this sub-commission benefited greatly from consultation with competent laymen.

The answers of the Church take up the chief questions posed by materialism [. . .] or atheistic communism. These problems will be discussed instructively in order to provide answers and to make Christians immune from subsequent evil influences.

Cardinal Liénart of Lille welcomed this important topic which for the first time was being dealt with in an Ecumenical Council. The text was acceptable in substance, but not in form. It exhorted Christians to come to the assistance of the world, but if they were to have dialogue between the Church and the world it was not enough to exhort only Christians. The world carried on its life in the natural order, which with the supernatural orders was the work of God [. . .]. It would help to declare the Church's esteem for worldly life and to show how helpful this could be on the level of personal, family and social life. All this should be said before indulging in any exhortations.

Cardinal Spellman [. . .] said this schema epitomised all the hope of the Council. It was good, clear and sincere. The Commission had done an admirable piece of work, and any modifications should be carefully made so as not to weaken the text. The Council's aim in this schema was to listen and to be listened to, as they tried to help the whole human race.

Cardinal Ruffini of Palermo said the text was weakened by many repetitions. In some parts the meaning was doubtful and could even be offensive. There was such stress on the Church's humanitarian mission that the main mission of procuring eternal salvation was almost obscured. Some passages dealing with ecumenism seemed to go too far [. . .]. The schema needed to be completely revised so that it was based on the encyclicals and other declarations of modern Popes, beginning with Leo XIII.

The cardinal was called to order by the Moderator, Cardinal Döpfner, for speaking on particular points rather than on general principles. Cardinal Ruffini was evidently very cross about this. He usually only speaks when Cardinal Agagianian is in the chair, as he is too scared of him to do such a thing.

[. . .]

Cardinal Döpfner of Munich considered the text acceptable as a basis for discussion. In the first three chapters the theological matter should be made clearer, briefer and give even more meaning. A clearer concept should be given of the 'world' and of the 'service' to be given by the Church to the world. More attention should be paid to atheism and those whom Christianity had not reached, lest it be thought that the text was only meant for Christians. Any quotations from scripture should be given modern exegesis, and all arguments in the schema should be based on scripture. For this schema and for that on the Apostolate of the Laity the commissions should have all the time required for careful work. (Liberal members often speak in favour of prolongation of the Council).

[. . .]

Report No. 150   23rd October, 1964

107TH GENERAL CONGREGATION, THURSDAY 22ND OCTOBER.

[. . .]

Discussion of the Schema on THE CHURCH IN THE MODERN WORLD then continued.

Archbishop Heenan said it would be ungracious not to praise the efforts of the Commission, but nevertheless the schema was quite unworthy of a General Council of the Church. If they were to speak at all they must do so in down-to-earth terms for all the world had been waiting for the Council's advice on many grave problems. It would be better to say nothing than to produce a set of platitudes. They had spent a lot of time discussing such things as the sources of revelation, and the theologians naturally regarded this as a highly important topic, but to the citizens of the world, whether Catholic or non-Catholic, it was far less important than the problems of the world. If they now rushed through a debate on world hunger, nuclear war and family life they would become the laughing-stock of the world and people would wonder what they meant when they called this a pastoral Council.

The schema was going to dash the hopes of everyone. It was more like a sermon than a document of the Council. They had been given the schema with certain supplements, but even read with the supplements it remained obscure; read on its own it was dangerous and could prove harmful. They had been told to debate the schema and pass over the rest without comment, but if they failed to scrutinise both documents with great care, the mind of the Council would have to be interpreted to the world by specialists who had helped the Commission to draw up the schema, and God forbid that this should happen.

Between the sessions of the Council the Church had suffered a great deal from the writings and speeches of some of the periti. They were few in number but they cared nothing for the ordinary teaching authority of bishops, nor even for that of the Pope. It was idle to show them a papal encyclical in which a point of doctrine was laid down. They would immediately reply that a Pope was not infallible when writing an encyclical. It really did not seem worth while for the Pope to write any more encyclical letters, since they could no longer be quoted in support of the faith. They must protect the teaching of the Church. There was no point in talking about a college of bishops if specialists contradicted what they said. Until now it had not been the doctrine of the Church that the theologians admitted to the Council were infallible. The theories of one or two must not be mistaken for a general agreement among theologians.

Perhaps the Commission had no chance of success for they had been denied the help of experts who really knew their subjects. When dealing with problems of social life it was necessary to consult those who knew and live in the world. It was useless to seek advice only from those who had spent their lives in monasteries, seminaries or universities [. . .]. If they were looking for examples of this they need only study the section on matrimony. Everyone knew that doctors were trying to produce a satisfactory contraceptive pill. This was to be the panacea to solve all sexual problems between husbands and wives. Meanwhile, it was said, married couples and they alone must decide what was right and wrong. Everyone must be his own judge, but the couple act according to the teaching of the Church. This was precisely what people wanted to be told – what was now the teaching of the Church? The schema said some practical solutions had made their appearance and more were to come. This was no way for a document of the Church to be written [. . .]. It was said that learned men and married couples must work out with theologians ways of understanding more thoroughly the mysteries of nature, but this should be done before and not after the schema was drawn up. The Archbishop proposed that a new Commission should be set up including members of the laity and priests with long pastoral experience and that a fourth and final session of the Council should meet in three or four years to discuss these social problems. It was a scandal to rush the debate now that they had at last come to really pastoral problems.

(There is no doubt that the part of the speech concerning the periti was a 'brick' of the first order and was taken very badly by the Council. Almost every speaker since, for a whole day, has gone out of his way to be gracious to the periti. I had some time with Archbishop Heenan last evening and he was aware himself that all was not well. He is still disturbed about the episode of his former 'brick' about the 'pill' in England.[23] It is said that these remarks were chiefly intended for Haering[24] who, it will be remembered, was the peritus involved in the other case. Two jokes were current this morning, one saying that Heenan was chasing a 'red Haering' and the other that he had an attack of 'peritonitis'.)

Bishop Stimpfle of Augsburg, Germany, said one of the gravest problems of our age was atheism which had wrecked churches, imprisoned and killed bishops and priests and tried to replace religion with the pseudo-religion of materialism. They could not possibly leave this out when dealing with the modern world. If they were silent they would be called blind watchmen and watchdogs who knew not how to bark. They must open dialogue with militant atheism, not to condemn it but to preach the truth in Christ [. . .]

Bishop Soares de Resende of Beira, Mozambique, said the term 'world' had different meanings in the Old Testament, in St. John, in classical authors and among the people at large. Why therefore speak of

---

[23] As the first part of the Report shows, Cardinal Heenan voiced a very critical attitude to the work and presence of the *periti* at the Council and many of the bishops present took offence at this open hostility towards the *periti*. In May 1964 Heenan had, in the name of the bishops of England and Wales, issued a statement saying that contraception was not a question to be debated as it was against the law of God. Two years later he made waves in England owing to his opposition to the use of contraception and his emphasis that the voices of the bishops were hushed mainly as a result of the universal confusion. He also appeared on television, on *Frost on Friday* in 1968, discussing contraception, particularly the pill.

[24] Bernard Häring (1912–1991), German Roman Catholic theologian and Redemptorist priest. He served as *peritus* at Vatican II and was involved in preparing the constitution *Gaudium et Spes.*

the modern 'world' when it refused to provide solutions of social and economic problems. The laity should be encouraged to take an active part in politics. Genuine poverty would help the Church. If she presented herself not merely as the Church of the poor, but as a poor Church, she could begin to claim more attention. This depended on all the Church. They could begin with the garments the bishops wore. Why did they need all this dignity and all this show?

Archbishop Hurley of Durban thought the main defect of the schema was that it was composed before its purpose was clearly determined. The solutions it provided were too theoretical for very practical problems. There were apparent contradictions and obscurities in the text. It was first necessary to show the value of the world in its proper light and in relation to man's final end [. . .]. All members of the Church must cooperate with all men to find practical solutions to the world's problems. A small group of Periti should be instructed – there are still some good ones left – to work out precisely what the schema intended to accomplish.
[. . .]
Archbishop Beck of Liverpool said the schema might well be the second most important of the Council. With de Ecclesia it was the base of the 'aggiornamento' so much desired by John XXIII [. . .]. It was their duty to offer practical and moral guidance with great compassion, but at the same time affirming the moral law. The desire for brevity must not prevent definitive teaching. The Church must avoid appearing as no more than a welfare institution [. . .]. Their difficulty today was not faith without works, but rather works without faith. The Church must try to make men better, not merely better off. The Council must emphasise that man and all creation had no meaning without eternity and a final destiny beyond this life. Man had no fulfilment except in God through Jesus Christ.
[. . .]

Report No. 151.   27th October, 1964

108TH GENERAL CONGREGATION, FRIDAY 23RD OCTOBER

[. . .]
After warmly praising the work of the periti (this was clearly a criticism of Archbishop Heenan), the General Secretary asked the Commission who were revising texts already discussed in the Council to make every

effort to finish so that some of them may be ready for approval before this session adjourns.

Discussion then continued on THE CHURCH IN THE MODERN WORLD:

Archbishop Tchidimbo of Conakry, Guinea, said that it was understandable that the writers of the schema could not work out a synthesis of so many varying problems. Nevertheless it was disappointing that the text was apparently intended more for Europe and America than for Africa. It had nothing to say on such crucial problems as underdevelopment, colonisation and racial discrimination. The schema failed to consider man collectively at a time when socialism was being preached widely in Africa. It was not enough just to speak of poverty. The Church would not really be poor unless bishops and all the sons of the Church started on the road to socialisation [. . .]
[. . .]
Abbot Reetz, Superior General of the Benedictines at Beuron, said he only undertook to speak with fear and trembling having heard it said the day before that monks could not be expected to know anything about the world (another 'dig' at Heenan) [. . .]. How could it be said that monks knew nothing of the world when the next day the Pope was going to proclaim a monk patron of Europe [. . .]. It should be explained what was meant by 'world' [. . .]

Bishop de Vet of Breda, Holland, wanted a special chapter added to the schema on atheistic communism. The Church could not ignore communism and, in defence of the truth, it should be exposed as an accumulation of all heresies. The world should be warned that there was always persecution where communism was in power [. . .]. Such a declaration would console the victims of communism. This subject should be treated openly, clearly and completely.

After a number of desultory speeches the Moderators called for a vote closing the debate on the schema in general, and this was agreed by an overwhelming majority. A second vote followed by secret ballot on whether the text was acceptable as a basis for discussion, and whether the discussion should move on to individual chapters. The results were as follows: Placet 1,579; non placet 296.

Bishop Guano of Livorno summed up in the name of the Commission. He wanted to make it clear that a good number of laity and scholars had been consulted when the schema was being drawn up. Priests with pastoral experience and some bishops were also consulted, but nevertheless the ultimate responsibility rested with the bishops alone. All the speeches will be carefully sifted, but it must not be forgotten that the Council could not go into too much detail, especially on some important points. The Pope had made it known that some of these questions were being carefully examined by experts and that he reserved the final judgement for himself. The Council had accepted the schema with varying degrees of enthusiasm and, as far as he could make out, only one bishop had damned the whole text to eternal fire – without including the periti. The Commission would begin revising the text at once, but it would not be possible to produce the final version during this session. They may all the same possibly be able to prepare pronouncements on such important topics as world peace, hunger, poverty and atheism.

[. . .]

Report No. 152   30th October, 1964

109TH GENERAL CONGREGATION, MONDAY 26TH OCTOBER.

Discussion continued on the INTRODUCTION and CHAPTER I of the SCHEMA on THE CHURCH IN THE MODERN WORLD: [. . .]

Bishop Guerra, Auxiliary of Madrid, considered the Church must learn how to judge efforts made by Marxism to interpret all religion as a denial of human nature. This idea pervaded a large part of present day culture. It should be made clear that aspiration to God was not a denial of human dignity, but a dynamic expression of one's perfection. They should be very careful not to seem to describe Christianity as an ideological system.

Archbishop Pogacnik, Apostolic Administrator of Ljubljana, thought the schema could be improved by stating clearly what the mind of the Church was and what she did for those living in misery. Among the 'signs of the times' special emphasis needed to be put on atheism, from which the Church had already suffered so much [. . .]. Atheism must be fought with constant prayer and fruitful penance, also the promotion of social justice. Pastoral letters were useless unless they were followed by practical results. It was well known that some government officials read 'Mater et Magistra' before many bishops.

Discussion then passed to CHAPTERS II and III:

Bishop La Ravoire Morrow of Krishnagar, India, said the Church in the West seems to have become far too juridical. Many people could not understand how God could be expected to damn an individual to hell for eternity for such a thing as eating meat on Friday, and thus put him on a level with an adulterous atheist. There was no proportion between the deed and the punishment. The mentality behind such legislation seemed more legal than religious and made the Church a laughing-stock for many. It was well known that rules did not produce the desired effect, but only dulled the moral sense of the faithful. People did not generally need to be forced. Insistence on this kind of thing made real dialogue impossible.

Bishop Cule of Mostar, Yugoslavia, said that if Christians led no better lives than those who had not faith, then all their preaching was pointless. It would be as well if the Church avoided acquiring special status from civil authorities. Lacordiare once said that the Church ran a greater risk from a government which was too well disposed towards it than from one which was hostile. It would be useful to organise a special centre for the co-ordination of Catholic activities.
[...]

Bishop Spülbeck of Meissen said the Church must recognise that she received much help from the world. Her relations with science were often archaic and they must be open-minded in their contacts with scientists. How could they explain the influence of Fr. Teilhard de Chardin?[25] They knew he was a pious priest and scientists told them that they felt he was close to them because he spoke their language. Some people would have condemned him as an enemy, as though they were afraid of seeing concord between religion and science. This would be a repetition of the history of Galileo. Disagreement between science and faith had been caused not so much by bad will as by lack of understanding. Religious scepticism was growing among students today and could easily lead them into the attitude which would enable them to maintain a spirit of comradeship in intellectual research without harm to the principles of faith.

Bishop Klepacz of Łódź, Poland, said the glorification of science in modern times had led to a genuine apotheosis of man and, they

---

[25] Teilhard de Chardin (1881–1955), French Jesuit and philosopher, whose thought had in important areas diverged from the teachings of the Roman Catholic Church. Some of his work had been condemned in the 1950 encyclical, *Humani Generis,* but by the time of the Vatican Council he was attracting more sympathetic interest across the Church.

might almost say, the construction of a new tower of Babel. There were conflicting trends of exaggerated optimism and nihilistic pessimism. The Church must fight against both these destructive tendencies.

Archbishop Golland Trinidade of Botucatu, Brazil, said that in the Council the General Secretary often addressed the bishops as 'Illustrissimi Domini'.[26] This was exactly what they were when they went to St. Peter's clothed in garments which were quite foreign to the world in which they lived. They gave the impression of being rich although they were not. They, who were supposed to be fathers, appeared to be separating themselves from their children. Why would it not be possible in the next session to go to the Council dressed in black? Their clothes would then open the way to a centre of dialogue, i.e. somewhere where anyone would be welcome who wanted to talk either for or against the Church. This would really mean opening themselves to the world.

Bishop Fourrey of Belley, France, thought the doctrine of poverty in the schema was true but that it was presented in a tone of exhortation and not based on countries and races. The malediction of the rich was as applicable to rich nations as to rich individuals. The schema said nothing at all about collective poverty – individual poverty was not enough. Usury should be condemned in all its forms, and by this it was meant exploitation of want for purposes of gain [. . .]

Towards the end of the morning there were so many bishops in the aisles and in the bars that the session was brought to an end abruptly. [. . .]

Report No. 153.   4th November, 1964

110TH GENERAL CONGREGATION, TUESDAY 27TH OCTOBER.

The debate continued on CHAPTERS II and III of the SCHEMA ON THE CHURCH IN THE MODERN WORLD:

Cardinal Caggiano, Archbishop of Buenos Aires, said that if everyone had his due we should not have the vast armies of unemployed. The condition

---

[26] Illustrious gentlemen.

of the proletariat all over the world would gradually be improved. Hence, the importance of proclaiming the Church's doctrine on justice. (It was interesting that even this reactionary Cardinal felt he had to speak up for social justice).

[...]

Bishop Kuharić, Auxiliary of Zagreb, Yugoslavia, thought the Council should make a declaration about the relation between science and religion. In countries under an atheistic regime the Church was constantly being called the enemy of progress and science. They should show how many men had become eminent scholars without losing their faith. In many countries abortion was permitted by law. Perhaps many people did not realise that more deaths have been caused this way than by many wars. The schema should declare the inviolability of human life within the mother's body.

OBSERVERS' MEETING, TUESDAY 27TH OCTOBER.

[...]

SCHEMA 13 on THE CHURCH IN THE MODERN WORLD.

[...]

Canon Pawley, on behalf of the Anglican Observers, submitted a statement suggesting that the Church's description of itself in the Schema should be more modest. The Church (particularly the Roman Catholic Church in Italy) has a very bad record in resisting new knowledge and social improvement. In the minds of many it was equivalent to reaction. The Church has a right to hope that this era had come to an end, if there were any hope of making contact with the modern world.

Dr. Vilmos Vajta, Lutheran, hoped that the Christian doctrine of history would be more clearly stated.

[...]

Bro. Max Thurian, sub-editor of Taizé, hoped that the Schema would be divided into two parts, the first saying what the world meant to the Church. There were two conceptions of the world even in the Schema. What was the Church's doctrine of nature?

Professor Thomas, Presbyterian, suggested that the paragraphs on social justice were addressed exclusively to the management classes, and should be expanded to cover the duties and responsibilities of the 'working' classes as well.

[...]

111TH GENERAL CONGREGATION, WEDNESDAY 28TH OCTOBER.

Cardinal Agagianian, Moderator, announced that there would be no public discussion on certain points in CHAPTER IV of the CHURCH IN THE MODERN WORLD. This was to prevent possible misunderstanding and misinterpretation outside the Council. All were, however, urged to present their observations.

Bishop Wright of Pittsburgh, U. S. A., presented the report of the Commission on Chapter IV. He said it was not for them to find clever answer to all problems. That would take years. But they must make every effort to apply the ancient wisdom of the Church to the new conditions harassing the human conscience today. The Church did not pronounce the last word on these problems, only the first word of dialogue. It would be a mistake to ask too much of a schema which had no precedent in council history, but which was full of hope for the future. He assured the Council that a commission had already been set up to receive observations from every source, particularly from 'the third part' of the world. A report would then be sent to the Plenary Mixed Commission.

Discussion began on the INDIVIDUAL PARTS of CHAPTER IV:

Archbishop Athaide of Agra, India, said it could not be denied that slavery existed even now in the world. Men were being bought and sold and deprived of rights. They were often, through apartheid, made the victims of discrimination because of the colour of their skin. The Council should make a positive stand, as all men expected liberation from this new slavery. This was not a request for a condemnation of peoples or nations, only an appeal to arouse the conscience of the world. They should praise those who had made efforts in this direction. Among them were Mahatma Ghandi, who had devoted his entire life to bettering the lot of some 60 million outcasts. A great example had also been given by John Kennedy, and there were many other examples among laity and clergy. In a private audience recently given to Martin Luther King, the Pope had encouraged him in his peaceful crusade for racial equality and praised him for his policy of peaceful resistance. The faithful must be urged to collaborate against all discrimination.

Archbishop O'Boyle of Washington wanted a new section [...] to deal strongly with the problems of racial discrimination, which was found all over the world in various forms. What the text said was good, but the importance of the subject called for separate treatment. The problem was not merely sociological but moral and religious. The condemnation of racial discrimination must be given a theological foundation, for only in this way could it be effective.

Bishop Coderre of St. Jean, Canada, thought the schema should stress the role of women, which had previously been obscured by the wrong idea of the basic inferiority of the female sex. Full civil rights for women was one of the signs of the times of which the Council must take note. The Council must invite men to help women to attain their proper place in the Church. God made man and woman equal with equal responsibilities towards the life of the Church.

Bishop de la Chanonie of Clermont, France, said the Council should take up the special problem of the evangelisation of children who were handicapped physically, psychologically, morally or socially. In France they amounted to almost one fourth of all adolescents, numbering nearly 3 million, and in other countries the proportion was still greater. The Church called herself the Church of the poor and these children were the poorest of all. Despite their affliction they had a right to fulfil their human vocation.

Archbishop Malula of Léopoldville, Congo, said the principles of respect for human dignity should be the basis of ethics. The schema showed this, but only in passing. They should insist on this respect because it was the truth. Such crimes as racial discrimination and slavery of women came from the basic disregard of this fundamental principle. No one outside Africa could grasp the full impact of the canonisation of the Uganda martyrs. This was proof to Africa that the gates of heaven were open to all men no matter what their colour. Tribalism in Africa was racism on a minor scale. It affected Christians, causing hatred and fear and must be declared a serious sin against charity. Another serious problem in Africa was the proper understanding of the role of women. Here the Church could make a definitive contribution.

112TH GENERAL CONGREGATION, THURSDAY 29TH OCTOBER.

[...]
Discussion then continued on Articles 19 and 20 of the Schema on the CHURCH IN THE MODERN WORLD:

Bishop Stimpfle of Augsburg, Germany, said the schema urged the faithful to change social conditions when they were contrary to Christian principles, but this raised a difficulty. They knew that slavery existed in the time of Christ but neither Christ nor the Apostles opposed it [...]. Full liberty came from faith and obedience to truth. The attitude of the early Christians towards slavery changed the approach of the faithful, and this new way of thinking spread bringing about the gradual elimination of slavery. They must stress the importance of liberty in education. Full liberty must be allowed in scientific research. Those in administrative positions must leave a great deal of liberty to their subordinates because the suppression of liberty would cause more harm than the abuse of liberty.

Bishop Frotz, Auxiliary of Cologne, said that modern women expected to be accepted as equal to men in intellectual and cultural life. Just as the Church once failed to appreciate the problem of labour, today she faced a new problem arising from the changed position of women in modern society. The Church was not yet aware of the world-wide implications of this problem. The spiritual and religious interests of woman must be fostered so that she may apply her special gifts to the Church apostolate. Women should be accepted as grown up daughters of the Church, not just as children. In the liturgy they should be addressed directly as 'sisters' and not just submerged in 'fratres'. The relationship of clergy and women should be adjusted to the recognition of women as images of God. Women everywhere would then see the Church as the guardian of their dignity and their talents would be used to a greater extent to the benefit of society as a whole. (It was surprising that this speech came from a German bishop).

Cardinal Feltin, Archbishop of Paris [...] said that in the statements contained in Article 25 on the burning issue of world peace, the world was expecting the Council to be as forthright as John XXIII had been in 'Pacem in Terris'.[27] Public opinion expected a definitive condemnation of war, especially modern war with all its terrifying aspects. The text said sufficient to outlaw what had been called the A.B.C. weapons, i.e. atomic, bacteriological and chemical instruments of war. The Church must speak out because peace was something not merely to be talked about, but to be realised [...]. Emerging nations especially must be taught how to assure their growth in peace. International organisations such as the U.N. must be encouraged and strengthened. Peace must become part of their ordinary pastoral work.

---

[27] Encyclical promulgated by John XXIII, 11 April 1963.

If not the international situation could only become worse as a result of the last century's divorce from moral principles. Peace must also be introduced into their missionary activities. A commission could be set up to follow the progress of studies taken up in this schema and in the supplement. They must spare no effort to get the Catholic world moving and working for peace.

Archbishop Dearden of Detroit, in the name of the Commission, presented a report on Article 21 on DIGNITY OF MARRIAGE AND FAMILY LIFE. He reminded the Council not to expect in this brief statement a full discussion of the nature and sanctity of marriage. The text provided only a synthesis of doctrine to enable Christians to achieve a better understanding of the dignity and sanctity of their marriage. On the fecundity of marriage the schema laid down the principle of conscious and generous pro-creation. This basic question could not be omitted from the discussion. The schema stated that married couples may follow their conscience as to the number of children, under the influence of true love and being rightly informed. When it came to the question of which methods were to be used to reach this end of limiting the number of children, the methods must be judged according to the doctrine and the mind of the Church. Being obliged to judge did not mean that married people were free to use every means. The text left no room for subjectivism. Both the schema and the supplement had deliberately avoided any direct discussion of 'the pill', because the Pope had reserved judgement on this important point for himself. Besides it was an intricate question which certainly could not be settled in any Council discussion.

The following then spoke [. . .]

Cardinal Ruffini of Palermo, thought the very serious problem dealt with in this article was not presented with sufficient clarity or caution. The text almost omitted any mention of the nobility of Christian marriage [. . .]. The unity and the indissolubility of marriage must be safeguarded at all costs. The teaching of the Church on marriage was of prime importance and it would be difficult to defend their stand on many points without it. The text stated that if in particular cases married couples had sufficiently serious reasons to limit the number of their children, they must still manifest their tender love towards each other, but the text failed to explain how this love could be expressed, because Catholic teaching had always maintained that in these circumstances the use of marriage was unlawful!! To say that the final decision on a problem of this importance was left to the individual concerned opened the door to all kinds of abuses. St. Augustine had some very harsh passages on certain aspects of conjugal life in his own time and this showed us that our own age was not so different. In 1930 Pope Pius XI gave the Church his encyclical 'Casti Connubii', and Pius XII's allocution to midwives some years later provided all the principles needed for the solution of this problem.[28] It was to be hoped that in the revision of the text the Commission would follow this authentic Magisterium. (This extremely reactionary view was much disapproved by our liberal friends).

Cardinal Léger of Montreal said the article took up grave problems for which, as yet, no satisfactory answers had been provided. Confessors had been confronted very frequently with the doubts and uncertainties of Catholic husbands and wives that the Church would be accused of opportunism in undertaking such a study. This revision had been provoked by the worries of the faithful and its only scope was to protect the sanctity of marriage. Some people thought that the difficulties might have arisen from inadequate explanations in theological manuals on the ends of marriage, explanations not based on scripture but dictated by undue pessimism. The text did well to avoid the old terminology of the 'primary' and 'secondary' aims of marriage. The principle of marital fecundity was well expressed when it was stated that this must be governed by prudence and generosity. Parenthood must always be regarded as a participation in creation. Fecundity must be looked upon in the light of the married state, not in connection with each individual act. The text should state that human conjugal love involved both soul and body, was something good in itself, and had its own characteristics and laws. They should give clear principles, avoiding that fear of conjugal love which had pervaded so many moral tracts. They must not forget that husband and wife had promised each other mutual help. In marriage they were not only procreators but persons. It was not sufficient merely to state the ends of marriage, more attention must be paid to the purpose of individual acts. This would only put into the principles what had long been accepted in the teaching of the Church, especially in its teaching on the lawfulness of conjugal love in spite of sterility. With this done on the level of principles, moralists, physicians and psychologists would be able to take care of further details.

---

[28] In 1930 the Lambeth Conference approved the use of birth control in limited circumstances. Later that year Pius XI's encyclical *Casti Connubii* (*On Christian marriage* or *On chastity in marriage*) explored the meaning of Christian marriage and emphasized its threefold purpose, borrowed from St Augustine: to produce offspring, to grow in conjugal faith, and to show benefit from the sacrament. Contraception and abortion are identified as posing a threat to the Catholic understanding of marriage. In *The Allocution to Midwives* of 1951, Pius XII reaffirmed the sanctity of life and upheld the views expressed in *Casti Connubii* regarding birth control and abortion.

Cardinal Suenens, Archbishop of Brussels, said the Council must be courageous in facing up to the pastoral demands for an objective study of the theology of marriage. There were reasons for thinking that their outlook had become too one-sided. Their insistence on the command 'to increase and multiply' might have caused them to forget that this was not the only text in scripture and that the other passage, saying that husband and wife 'become two in one flesh' was also contained in Revelation and thus equally divine in origin [. . .]. It was true that the Church could not abandon a doctrine which had been accepted and which clearly came from Revelation. But there was nothing to prevent the Church from making a thorough inquiry to see if all sides of a problem had been sufficiently explored. Modern science might well have much to say in this connection and they should keep a ready ear. The Council should take care to avoid a new 'Galileo' case. One such episode in the history of the Church was quite enough! There were no grounds for being afraid. The Holy Father had set up his commission to study this all-important problem, and the commission should be made up of men of all ranks and walks of life so as to represent the entire people of God. It would be advisable for the means of the members of this commission to be made available to the public.

Maximos IV Saigh, Melchite Patriarch of Antioch, said they needed courage to face up to the problems of the hour in the love of Christ and souls. This was an urgent problem and at the root of a grave crisis of Catholic conscience. There [was] the question of a break between the doctrine of the Church and the contrary practice of the majority of Christian couples. The authority of the Church was called into question and they must have courage to approach the solution without prejudice. The position of the Church should be revised in accordance with modern theological, medical, psychological and social science. In marriage the development of personality and its integration into the creative plan of God were all one [. . .]. Is the physical rectitude of an act the only criterion of morality without considering the moral, conjugal and family climate and prudence, which must be the basic rule of all human activity. The Church proclaims the law of God in the light of social, scientific and psychological truths brought to light in modern times [. . .]. The duty of the Church was to educate the moral sense of her children, not just to surround them with a series of rules which they should observe blindly. They should open their eyes and be practical. See things as they are, not as they would like them to be. Otherwise they ran the risk of speaking in the desert. The future of the Church's mission in the world was at stake.

Report No. 155 10th November, 1964

113TH GENERAL CONGREGATION, FRIDAY 30TH OCTOBER.

[...]
The debate continued on Article 21 (Marriage and the Family) on THE CHURCH IN THE MODERN WORLD:

Cardinal Alfrink, Archbishop of Utrecht, said all priests in the ministry were well aware of the marital problems of those faithful who came for advice. These difficulties were often the cause of people leaving the Church and the spiritual struggle which they involved could eventually weaken even the human values of conjugal life. A sociological analysis could do nothing for the moral aspect of an act. There was no room for situation ethics [...]. With the increasing knowledge of the difference between biological and human sexuality many moral questions were arising. The Church could not afford to rush into a solution. She must guard the purity of divine law and at the same time safeguard human values. Only when she was quite certain would she be in a position to obligate or liberate the conscience of the faithful. Modern scientific progress raised many moral problems. To keep pace with these there should be a standing commission in the Church to study the evolution of various problems with moral judgements referring to modern discoveries and research lagging behind.

Cardinal Ottaviani, President of the Theological Commission, did not approve of the freedom given to married couples in the schema to decide for themselves the number of their children. They should not forget the command in scripture to 'increase and multiply'. This did not contradict the other text which spoke of husband and wife being 'two in one flesh'. Freedom such as that proposed by the schema was unheard of in the past [...]. The Council should not think of approving the proposal in the schema. The text insinuated that the Church had erred in the past of a grave moral problem and any such insinuation was completely out of order. (We have become used to reaction from Cardinals Ottaviani and Browne).

Cardinal Browne said no aspect of the grave problems confronting Catholic married couples should be neglected. They had doctrine on marriage from the Magisterium of the Church and from contributions of theologians. The primary purpose of marriage was the procreation and education of children [...]. There were three goods in marriage: procreation, mutual fidelity and holiness of the sacrament. The conjugal act must conform to nature. It remained lawful in sterile periods. All this could be found in Leo XIII, Pius XI, and Pius XII.

There would always be difficulties which must be solved by scientific discoveries, not theological discussion. The Church must wait for the result of modern research. If the Holy Father wanted the cooperation of the Council in this matter, a commission would have to be formed for this purpose.

Archbishop Urtasun of Avignon, said there was nothing in the schema on divorce which had become such a plague in modern life, especially since the war [. . .]. Protecting the sanctity of marriage and the family was one of the most sacred missions of the Council. [. . .] [. . .]

Bishop Nkongolo of Bakwanga, Congo, thought they could be happy about what the schema said on the dignity of marriage and the sanctity of the family. All this would contribute to an enlightened idea of woman and her role in life. The big problems of marriage in Africa were the lack of free consent and polygamy. The girl had to obey the will of the head of the family and this was in direct violation of personal freedom of choice. The schema should mention the basic simple requirements for valid marriage and should insist on its unity and indissolubility. This would help to counteract polygamy which was making inroads even in Christian communities.

Bishop Fiordelli of Prato, Italy, wanted something said about the problem of abortion. The schema should also mention 'responsible fatherhood' [. . .] [. . .]

Report No. 156   11th November, 1964

114TH GENERAL CONGREGATION, WEDNESDAY 4TH NOVEMBER.
[. . .]

Report No. 157   12th November, 1964

115TH GENERAL CONGREGATION, THURSDAY 5TH NOVEMBER.
[. . .]
Discussion then continued on article 23 of Schema 13 – the CHURCH IN THE MODERN WORLD:
[. . .]

Archbishop Zoungrana of Ouagadougou, Upper Volta, said the Council could not afford to ignore the Third World. Inequalities among nations were growing from day to day. The population would double before the year 2000 in all the poorer areas of the world. Poorer countries could not progress like richer nations because of poor land, lack of environment, lack of education, etc. Ideologies and politics could never forge the bonds of true friendship and only such friendship could assure development in equality. More stress should be put on the overall economic situation of the world. Competent *periti* should be asked to revise Article 23 so as not to neglect the essential question of the Third World. It would be tragic to disappoint the expectations of those in need.

Mr. James Norris, Lay Auditor, President of the International Catholic Commission on Emigration presented the report of the Committee on Article 24 of Schema 13 (World POVERTY):

In the last decade, the problem of poverty had taken on a new shape and become more urgent. The poor differed today because modern science had helped to create a single economy, an inter-dependent neighbourhood, but one largely lacking solidarity, compassion and human obligation.
[...]

Cardinal Frings of Cologne said that to emphasise the Church as the mother of the poor episcopal conferences should organise agencies for the relief of misery everywhere. These agencies should aim at helping others to help themselves. Besides relief they should provide schools for agriculture and domestic science, etc
[...]

Bishop Rupp of Monaco said much of this article was expressed in verbose and turgid style, calling for patience and alertness in the reader. They should denounce Christian nations who close their doors to immigrants from poor countries. They should insist on Christian solidarity while remembering that the term 'Christian' was today often so watered down as to lose all significance. They should attack not only evils but the roots of evils. The Council should aim at direct contact with the youth of the world. The style of the text was too prudent, too diplomatic, too political and, in a word, too feminine to achieve its purpose. If it were not made more direct it would not only not save the world, but would do harm to itself.

Report No. 158   13th November, 1964

116TH GENERAL CONGREGATION, FRIDAY 6TH NOVEMBER.

The Pope assisted at the Mass and afterwards took his place at the President's table.

The Pope addressed the Council saying that it had been his intention since the beginning of the session to come and take part in a meeting of the Council. He had purposely chosen the day of the opening of the discussion of the schema on the missions because he wanted to emphasise the seriousness and vastness of this important subject. The Church was increasingly aware of her divine mandate to preach to all people. The Council would show new ways of achieving this mission and would stimulate the zeal and generosity of the clergy and faithful. [. . .]

The debate was then opened on the schema on THE MISSIONARY ACTIVITY OF THE CHURCH:

Cardinal Léger of Montreal said there was throughout the Church a longing for new impetus to missionary activity. It was the very essence of the Church. [. . .] There was great hope for the beginning of dialogue with non-Christians. For centuries the Church had been afraid of anything of this kind but now she could go ahead. The schema had much to say on the meeting of various cultures, but it was almost silent on the meeting of religions. This was very important in the mission field. It was good to see that the text favoured collaboration between religious institutes and between them and the bishops, for this was necessary to prevent wasted effort. But the schema did not have enough to say about it. If they could succeed in interesting all bishops of the universal needs of the Church, this would be a practical application of episcopal collegiality. The Central Mission Board proposed by the schema would ensure collective activity, but its relationship with Propaganda Fide was not clearly defined. It should be part of the Sacred Congregation. This would provide an opportunity for local churches to become better acquainted with the needs of the whole Church.
[. . .]

Cardinal Bea said there was no doubt that the Council must be source of a new mission drive throughout the Church. Missionary activity was one of the Church's essential roles and the renewal of zeal was necessary to the very nature of the Church [. . .]

Report No. 159.   13th November, 1964

117TH GENERAL CONGREGATION, SATURDAY 7TH NOVEMBER.

[...]
The debate was continued on the schema on the MISSIONS:

Cardinal Frings of Cologne said that the missionary aspect of the Church's mission was so important that it could not be compressed into a few propositions. It should be elaborated on from both the theological and practical points of view and should not be brought up for discussion until the fourth session of the Council. They needed a more profound theology of the missionary character of the Church [...]
[...]
Bishop Lamont of Umtali, S. Rhodesia, said the schema provided only frustration for missionaries. It contained no fire, no inspiration. The glorious missionary tradition of the Church had been reduced to a few dry and miserable propositions. [...] It would be realised that missionary work was essential when they recalled that four-fifths of the world did not know Christ [...]

Bishop Massa of Nanyang, China, said that many Chinese had been kept from the faith not because of the demands of conversion, as their national traditions conformed in many ways to Christian teaching, but because becoming a Christian meant abandoning largely one's culture [...]
[...]
A number of desultory speeches during the morning expressed dissatisfaction with the Schema without stating very precisely what they expected it to say. It was not clear to us what exactly it could say, or whether a Council document on Missions was necessary at all.

118TH GENERAL CONGREGATION, MONDAY 9TH NOVEMBER.

[...]
Discussion of the Schema on THE MISSIONARY ACTIVITY OF THE CHURCH then continued:
[...]
Archbishop Zoghby, Patriarchal Vicar for the Melchites in Egypt, thought it might seem strange for an Oriental bishop to speak about missions, for Oriental churches had been forced by historical events to abandon almost entirely the missionary work, to which they had been so devoted previously. But the schema paid no attention to what the Oriental

fathers regarded as the mystique of the missions [. . .]. Missionaries should not try to impose on people a pre-fabricated Christ, but should let people receive and, so to speak, reincarnate Christ in the light of their own culture. This Christ would be all things to all men. The missions were also regarded as an effusion of the pastoral mystery perpetuated in the Church through the Eucharist.
[. . .]

Discussion was then resumed on article 24 of the Schema on THE CHURCH IN THE MODERN WORLD:

The Very Rev. Gerard Mahon, Superior General of the Missionary Society of St. Joseph of Mill Hill,[29] (This man, as head of the Mill Hill Fathers, seems to be quite influential. He is certainly very friendly, very liberal, and very critical of the R.C. hierarchy in Great Britain. As he lives in London I suggest that his acquaintance be cultivated). He said the Council was proclaiming for the first time the necessity of social justice on an international level. The difference existing today between nations was no less than those formerly existing between social classes. It was staggering to recall that 35 million people die of hunger every year and that 400 million of the world's people go regularly hungry [. . .]. Socio-economic activity was part of the mission of the Church. It could be carried on effectively by missionaries who knew their people and the circumstances in which they lived. Missionaries could collaborate with the international organisations.
[. . .]

Discussion then went on to article 25 on WORLD PEACE:

Cardinal Alfrink, Archbishop of Utrecht, wanted the Council to be no less forthright than John XXIII in his *Pacem in Terris.*[30] The encyclical was more positive in its treatment of the reduction of armaments. The Council should denounce the world race for armaments, as in the encyclical, which proposed reciprocal and simultaneous renunciation of arms with guarantees of sincerity. The statement on the unlawfulness of nuclear warfare should be clarified because, as it stood, it could give the impression that only 'dirty bombs' with uncontrollable consequences were prohibited. Modern research had produced a 'clean bomb', but the text should include this also. They should spare no efforts to bring about world disarmament.

Bishop Ancel, Auxiliary of Lyons, said it had already been pointed out that the text was contradictory. While recognising the legitimacy of

---

[29]Gerald Mahon (1922–1992), Auxiliary Bishop of Westminster, 1970–1992; attended the last three sessions of the Council.

[30]See p. 368, n. 27.

defensive war it declared nuclear war unlawful in any respect. This was the same as saying there was no lawful defence against nuclear attack.

Report No. 160.   16th November, 1964

119TH GENERAL CONGREGATION, TUESDAY 10TH NOVEMBER.

Discussion continued on the concluding articles of the Schema on THE CHURCH IN THE MODERN WORLD:

Maximos IV Saigh, Melchite Patriarch of Antioch, said the entire human race was living in dread of a nuclear war. The world raised its voice in a heart-rending plea and with crises of anguish and despair. The Council should do everything possible to ward off this threat [. . .]

Bishop Hannan, Auxiliary of Washington, said the Schema was wrong when it stated that 'all nations without exception have been derelict in their duty of promoting world peace'. Such a statement was offensive to some nations and to some genuinely great leaders. Their task was to avoid war and to defend national and personal freedom.

Archbishop Beck of Liverpool [. . .] Great clarity and precision were called for in dealing with the use of nuclear weapons from which the problem of peace and war derived its gravity and urgency. The Council must maintain the traditional doctrine that indiscriminate destruction with killing of the innocent was murder and thus evil. The text should not fail to mention biological and chemical warfare. They should make it clear that this Schema was not a universal condemnation of nuclear weapons. In a just war of defence there could be legitimate targets for nuclear weapons. Therefore the Council should not condemn these weapons outright as necessarily evil. They must remember the responsibility for the use of nuclear weapons rested with those lives and property of citizens, and even more the spiritual and cultural values which were the inheritance of a people or nation. It was a matter of fact that at times peace could be assured only by 'the balance of terror', through the deterrent of nuclear weapons against unjust aggression. Governments should not be condemned if they maintained world peace in this way. To turn the other cheek was a counsel of individual perfection but was not applicable to governments which had a grave duty to defend their citizens.

The rest of the debate on this section followed a very desultory course and came to a tame conclusion.
[. . .]

Report No. 161.   17th November, 1964

120TH GENERAL CONGREGATION, WEDNESDAY 11TH NOVEMBER.
[. . .]

Report No. 162.   18th November, 1964

121ST GENERAL CONGREGATION, THURSDAY 12TH NOVEMBER.

[. . .]

The Council then went on to the Schema on TRAINING FOR THE MINISTRY.

Cardinal Meyer, Archbishop of Chicago, thought the schema contained good points. He welcomed the proposal that national episcopal conferences should draw up programmes for seminaries and have them approved by the Holy See. This would help to adapt seminaries to pastoral needs. But the text did not make clear what should be common to all seminary programmes and what could and should be different.

Archbishop Colombo of Milan (the Pope's successor) said that it had often been stated that seminary training today lacked unity and failed to produce mature candidates for the priesthood. The schema appeared to answer this charge effectively and well. The unity which would follow from the application of these principles would prevent disorganisation [. . .]. Other studies, as well as theology, should be organised in the same way [. . .]. The schema also gave a remedy for lack of maturity. It said that men were to be trained with regard to sound psychology. It showed ways of making the training personal and not mechanical. By giving bishops power to interrupt studies for a period of spiritual training or for an opportunity to resolve doubts and anxieties, the schema helped to insure that men would not be ordained without full awareness of what they were doing [. . .]

N.B. This speech was regarded as very revolutionary. It was not easy to get a clear picture of the issues as seen from the R.C. angle (as distinct from what we would like to happen). There is undoubtedly a great tension pro or contra scholastic philosophy, also about more 'liberal' syllabuses, and about the excessively monastic pattern of seminaries.

122ND GENERAL CONGREGATION, SATURDAY 14TH NOVEMBER.

[. . .]
Discussion then continued on the schema on TRAINING FOR THE MINISTRY:
[. . .]

Cardinal Léger, Archbishop of Montreal, said more stress should be put on the spiritual, intellectual and pastoral needs of the clergy. The new text on the whole answered the needs of the times. With regard to philosophical training the term 'perennial philosophy' is ill chosen. It was ambiguous. Did it mean scholastic philosophy? But there were several scholastic philosophies. The term was in conflict with the basic nature of philosophical inquiry because philosophy was interested not in what authors had said, but in what things were. Besides it would be a mistake to impose the system of scholastic philosophy on non-western minds. The task of the Council was not to provide a philosophical system but to give general directives. The text had done well not to insist unduly on St. Thomas in theological training. It would be unwise to rest theology on one teacher [. . .]. Dialogue with the Middle Ages was not dialogue with today [. . .]. The schema should state that moral theology should be brought closer to dogma and scripture. Thus the way would be prepared for a new evangelical dynamism coming from the Council.
[. . .]

Archbishop Staffa, Secretary of the Congregation of Seminaries and Universities, (a notorious reactionary) said that the text should insist on fidelity to the doctrine of St. Thomas. Although they must always be in favour of progress they must not forget that there could be no progress when what was new was separated from what was true. Progress in truth must be integrated in truth already known. St. Thomas had understood truth and proclaimed it better than men, leading them to progress, and this was his place in the intellectual tradition of the Church [. . .]. The doctrine of St. Thomas in philosophy and theology must be wholly safeguarded.

Cardinal Suenens regretted that the general structure of seminaries today was based in many ways on religious houses. Such an atmosphere was

unsuited to the secular clergy and did not give them the spirituality which they needed [. . .]. They needed practical pastoral training in leadership in order to be able to give life to the apostolate. Those who were called by God to live and work in the world could not be trained outside the world.
[. . .]

Report No. 163   19th November, 1964

123RD GENERAL CONGREGATION, MONDAY 16TH NOVEMBER.

[. . .]

The debate continued on SEMINARY TRAINING:

Cardinal Bacci said the importance of the study of philosophies in seminaries was obvious. There were grounds for concern about some of the remarks made in the Council on Saturday about the place to be given to St. Thomas in the studies of the seminaries. No one wanted to throw St. Thomas out completely. Too many popes had praised him since the 13th Century [. . .]

Bishop Komba, Auxiliary of Peramiho, Tanganyika [. . .] The Council should decree that seminary studies should be closely coordinated with those provided by state authorities, lest priests complete their training without gaining the diplomas and degrees which may eventually be required for the proper discharge of their apostolic duties.

Bishop Añoveros of Cádiz y Ceuta, Spain, said the most important thing in seminaries was well trained superiors and directors [. . .]

Bishop Weber of Strasbourg said that, in reorganising seminaries, there were two extremes to be avoided. The first was a spirit of iconoclasm with regard to the work of the Council of Trent and its implementation by St. Charles Borromeo in Italy and also by St. Vincent de Paul, St. John Eudes and M. Olier in France. The second was inflexibility with regard to the needs of modern times. The text satisfactorily combined the old and the new, and the greater freedom allowed to national conferences of bishops was particularly welcome.

Bishop Escuín, Coadjutor of Malaga, said seminarians must be trained in pastoral work. They should only be ordained after two years practical experience following their theological studies. This period could be spent living with priests and gaining practical experience, doing social work and they would gain much by living with the poor during their vacations.

124TH GENERAL CONGREGATION, TUESDAY 17TH NOVEMBER.

[. . .]

The debate then continued on SEMINARY TRAINING, the speakers having obtained the necessary 70 signatures:

Archbishop Garrone of Toulouse commended the article which suggested that much authority or seminary training should be in the hands of the national episcopal conferences. The number of these conferences would make it more than ever necessary for the central office in Rome to coordinate all these relatively autonomous groups. The Sacred Congregation in charge must be modernised so that it would be able to meet the needs of the times and keep up with scientific progress. It should be capable of clearly understanding the problems of individual nations. Until now its attitude had been too negative and detached. It should maintain close contact with the Congregation responsible for priests, so that it should have first hand knowledge of the problems for which priests should be prepared [. . .]

General approval was then given to the Schema.

Bishop Daem of Antwerp presented the Schema on CHRISTIAN EDUCATION. He said that nations of the world were making great efforts about education and the Council was aware of its duty to make some declaration on the mission of the Church in the field of education [. . .]. Much of Christian education took place outside schools, e.g. in the family. Because it covered such a vast field the commission thought it best to refrain from discussing details and to leave them to a post-Conciliar commission which would be able to make a thorough study and then produce its conclusions. The declaration looked at the universal problem of education. The Commission was well aware of the immense necessity of education in the world today [. . .]. The fact must be faced that there were countless young people in the world today who received little or no education.

On the juridical side of the educational problem the Commission felt, in view of present circumstances, that it was opportune to recall the duties and primary rights of education [. . .]. Therefore the text recalled the inalienable rights of parents and the Church to educate and teach their children and to set up schools, observing also what was required by civil society for the common welfare. It stressed the

rights of children to education and the right of parents to send their children to schools of their choice according to their conscience. Lastly it mentions the duty of civil society, without prejudice to its own rights, to help parents to carry out this duty.
[. . .]

Report No. 164.   24th November, 1964

125TH GENERAL CONGREGATION, WEDNESDAY 18TH NOVEMBER.

The Pope assisted at the opening mass which was celebrated in the Armenian rite by the (R.C.) Armenian Patriarch of Cilicia.[31] The mass marked the opening of the 50th anniversary year of the near extermination of 1,500,000 Armenians which took place in 1915 during World War I. All those present were asked to add their prayers for the Armenian people.

We took occasion to express regret (with which the Secretariat agreed) that no mention was made of the existence of what we should call the 'real' Armenians, from whom these are only a Roman schism. And there was an Armenian bishop (Sarkissian) in the box.
[. . .]

126TH GENERAL CONGREGATION, THURSDAY 19TH NOVEMBER.

[. . .]
The DECLARATION ON RELIGIOUS LIBERTY then came up for consideration. There had been a rather grizzly pre-history to its appearance in the Council. The reactionary 'old guard' had evidently been obstructing, blocking and amending the text during the previous months. The American bishops, on the other hand, were hysterically anxious not to return to the United States without having achieved it. The text was actually delivered to the Fathers on Tuesday 17th November. On Wednesday, the 18th, the conservatives petitioned the Presidents to say that there was not time to discuss this matter this session. (There had been considerable additions to and changes in the text). This was clearly a manoeuvre but the Presidents (who are old Pope John's nominees) agreed to it. I reluctantly feel that at this stage

---

[31] Ignatius Bedros XVI Batanian (1899–1979), Patriarch of Cilicia, 1962–1976.

they were right. A large number of bishops surged out of their places and held an indignant meeting in the transept as a result of which a letter with 800 signatures was sent to the Pope. The Pope felt unable to over-rule the Presidents. But the whole thing was evidently a piece of 'dirty work' behind the scenes which was much resented.

Bishop Smedt of Bruges presented the report on the DECLARATION ON RELIGIOUS LIBERTY. He was greeted with tumultuous applause. He gave a resumé of the dates of the progress of the printing to show how the whole thing had been held up. The applause was most moving. Bishops stood and shouted, while the old Italian cardinals looked glum. Cardinal Cicognani, the Secretary of State, is now voted Public Enemy No. 1. The Curia have done themselves much harm by this episode.

Bishop De Smedt said that the objections raised against the previous text fell into two categories. First there were those who admitted the doctrine but felt that certain arguments were not convincing, that the method of procedure was faulty or that certain expressions were not clear or imprudent. On the other hand there were those who felt in conscience unable to admit the doctrine itself. Their objections would be answered later. It was necessary to keep to the point at issue. The declaration did not touch directly on the juridical question of the relationship between Church and State, nor were there any explicit inquiry [*sic*] into the theological problem of the right and mission of the Church to preach the gospel. Neither was there any discussion of the moral doctrine by which a Christian must be guided in his contacts with non-Christians, which demanded the virtue of tolerance. On all these points the doctrine of the Church must be faithfully observed. The schema dealt with the religious liberty which is owed to a human being in the juridical organisation of society and the state. Modern communications were such that there was nowhere in the world an island of Catholics cut off from all others. In our pluralistic society men of good will would want to observe or restore religious peace. They want the Church to state what she thinks about the way secular life is organised. They have set up, or want to set up a mode of life in which no man or no religious community could be coerced in religion. Was such a mode of life lawful or necessary? That was the question. The declaration answered that in religious matters no human should be made the victim of coercion by others. Religious liberty was necessary to human dignity. Religion was above the competence of the state. The state must recognise and defend the free exercise of religion by all its citizens.

On the other hand an individual could not claim unlimited rights in the external manifestation of his religion. It was difficult to find formulas which public authority could not abuse, but the principle was there. There were two aspects. The first was moral: in the external exercise of his liberty no one might violate the rights of others nor fail in his duties towards others. The second aspect was juridical: no one might exercise his religion in such a way as to cause a great and inadmissible disturbance of public order. According to the accepted opinion of jurists and political scientists, the competence of the state in this matter is restricted to the protection of public order. Three things are necessary for public order: public peace, the proper observance of public morality, and harmony among citizens in the exercise of their rights. Religion must be immune from government intervention unless it contravenes the penal laws of the state.

Does the affirmation of religious liberty contradict the rights of the Church? The Church has her authority from Christ. But what is better or more dignified for the Church than to carry out her mission freely and independently. The religious liberty under discussion demands that no one should be subject to violence in order to be made to accept the faith and that the Church herself should be free of violence in society and in the state.

Religious liberty did not prevent the Catholic Church from having a privileged status in a state where Catholics were in the majority. If such a status was granted, this did not prevent other religious communities from enjoying genuine religious liberty. This privileged status was not in opposition to religious liberty, provided that non-Catholics were not subjected to force. Religious liberty was an outstanding benefit and necessary in order that faith in modern society should make deep and solid progress. The confidence of the Church of Christ was not to rest on secular power. In her difficulties and problems she should not seek refuge in the arms of public authority. To the man of the modern world, the Church must show herself personal and free. Her most effective witness to the truth of the Gospel would be in proving that she puts her confidence in the power of truth itself. Their protection was to be found in God and in the strength of their faithful. The Church would ultimately win over all men of goodwill, not by violence or political means, but through the arms of justice and the power of God.

At the conclusion of this report Bishop De Smedt was applauded for several minutes.

Cardinal Masella, President of the Commission on the Discipline of the Sacraments, made the first presentation of the Schema on the SACRAMENT of MATRIMONY. He said the Preparatory Commission had presented its findings on the following items:

matrimonial impediments, mixed marriages, matrimonial consent, the form of the celebration of marriage, the basic principles which should govern a re-organisation of the handling of marriage cases. A chapter had been added on the preparation of couples for marriage and on pastoral concern for their conjugal happiness. The present text dealt only with the Sacrament of Matrimony under its disciplinary aspects. Doctrinal and moral questions were handled by the Moral Commission.

Archbishop Schneider of Bamberg, Germany, presented the report of the Commission. He explained that the present form of the Schema was the result of directives received from higher authority (!) This document was intended to list the various points on which it was necessary or advisable to adapt matrimonial legislation to the needs of the times. The Commission also offered its suggestions for the reorganisation of future matrimonial legislation. Many Fathers had complained the world was expecting something from the Council about this. However the Commission on the Discipline of the Sacraments was of the opinion that this subject was beyond its competence, as it pertained to faith and morals and not to the discipline of the sacrament of matrimony.

Cardinal Gilroy, Archbishop of Sydney, praised the schema for its practical suggestions, all of which aimed at preventing frequent invalid marriages. In addition he suggested that the impediment of disparity of worship should be, not diriment,[32] but only impediment. This would always pre-suppose that no danger of perversion of the Catholic party was involved, in which case the marriage would be forbidden by divine law itself. The Council should insist even more strongly than it did in the schema on dissuading Catholics from contracting mixed marriages, but in such a way that, except for the danger of perversion, these marriages would not be absolutely forbidden. As far as the 'promises' were concerned, it would help to acquire moral certainty that they would be fulfilled if they were to be made before the local pastor. This should be the case even in the new form of promises proposed in the document. Provided a marriage had taken place in conformity to civil law and the parties could produce a legal document testifying to the marriage, it was proposed that the Church should recognise such a marriage even for Catholics as being valid, though unlawful. Clandestine marriages should be strictly forbidden. Those who transgressed the law of the Church regarding marriage should not be admitted to the sacraments until they had taken steps to rectify

[32] An impediment that renders a marriage altogether invalid, unless a dispensation is granted by the Church, which is possible only in certain cases.

the situation. In the case of mixed marriage, Nuptual Mass should not be prescribed but only permitted. It would be helpful to make a new definition of the impediment of mixed religion so as to make it applicable to marriage with a non-baptised person also. All these points should be discussed in the fourth session of the Council.

SECOND VATICAN COUNCIL – THE THIRD SESSION ENDS[33]

There can be no doubt that the machinery of the Council of the Roman Catholic Church is among the most cumbrous yet devised by men. Slow and archaic, it is ill adapted to the needs of the modern world. Yet it does at least give expression to the fact that the Church is concerned with all her parts and members. Even so it is still not totally representative, because neither priests nor laity are able to send delegates.

Since our last despatch in October a number of Schemas, considerably shortened in comparison with their original form, have come up and gone through the laborious process of discussion in general, discussion in particular, reference back, voting on amendments, and then (only some of them) final voting. The course of these debates has been

---

[33] Pawley's analysis was sent direct to Archbishop Ramsey with this covering letter (in Lambeth Palace Library, London, Ramsey Papers, vol. 65 (1964), fo. 191):

Your Grace,

I felt I ought to write a personal note about the Pope's speech at the closing of this session. I have only just returned from St. Peter's and have not had much time to sort it all out. All the Observers, absolutely *all*, are very disappointed, our friends in the Secretariat are puzzled and annoyed, but all the 'old gang' in the Vatican are exultant.

My interpretation (subject to later thought and consultation with others) is as follows. The Council as a whole has been a severe disappointment to the old guard Roman Catholics who have run the Church from here for centuries. The Pope has 'let them down' by agreeing to collegiality, to ecumenism (can you think what a bitter pill this is?) and to the severe blows dealt to the Blessed Virgin Mary in de Ecclesia. There is no doubt that he has been appealed to on all sides to modify these decrees and has refused. So the good captain of the ship, to save the boat rocking too much, has put in a little weight on the other side, to comfort them, and to keep the balance. And I suppose we don't mind her being called Mother of the Church, do we, now that we know officially (ex cathedra) this morning that Church has a subordinatum munus [subordinate function]? All is not lost. Am I right?

With respect.

I am, Your Grace,

Yours sincerely,

Bernard Pawley

continually interrupted by votes about other Schemas in various states of completion, so that at times it has been difficult to remember where one is. Nevertheless, through all this process, the Lord's work of the renewal of the Church has gone steadily on, and our report must be mainly of pleasure and thanksgiving for what has happened. New ideas have continued to find expression. The forces of renewal, doing their uphill battle against dull conservatism and entrenched authority, have been given grace to win the day.

The chief feature of the session has been the final voting on the Schema de Ecclesia and de Ecumenismo, which were publicly promulgated by the Pope at the closing ceremony. These two decrees will undoubtedly stand as the principal work of the Council, and as such should be a matter of considerable thanksgiving. As we have said in a previous report, there is no 'let up' on the traditional dogmas concerning the Papacy, but they are set in a new and more biblical context. Taken in conjunction with the Schema on 'The Pastoral Function of Bishops' they give a more democratic conception to the papal office. The resultant situation is that here is a new version of an old problem which is at least now able to be discussed on grounds which are intelligible. It is sometimes disconcerting to read reports of Protestant leaders minimising and depreciating the work of the Vatican Council on the grounds that the central obstacles still remain. To be fair one must remember that many other confessions are 'saddled' with doctrinal statements which are embarrassing to them and which they have done nothing as yet to revise (Does not the Presbyterian Westminster Confession describe the Pope as Anti-Christ – are we therefore to hold aloof from them because of this?[34]). One other welcome feature of the Decree on the Church is its treatment of the Blessed Virgin Mary, in which again, although previous doctrines are not retracted, yet a definite halt is called to Mariological exaggerations and a real attempt is made to state the Church's attitude to her in terms of references in Scripture. She is described as having only a 'subordinate role' in the work of salvation. Although she is described by the title mediatrix, it is explained that every priest is a mediator of grace when he ministers the sacraments and every layman when he forgives his neighbour or does a work of mercy. With this type of explanation there will be many who will feel there has been a real effort to bring Mariological devotion (very dear indeed to the piety of Roman Catholics) to a point

[34] Westminster Confession (of 1647), Chapter 25, paragraph VI: 'There is no other head of the Church but the Lord Jesus Christ. Nor can the pope of Rome, in any sense, be head thereof: but is that Antichrist, that man of sin, and son of perdition, that exalteth himself, in the Church, against Christ and all that is called God.'

at which it ceases to be offensive and could from now on be a matter of rational discussion.

The decree on Ecumenism we have also referred to in these reports. It has undergone a certain amount of emendation in detail. Here again, although the ecclesiology behind it is not such as entirely to please the World Council of Churches [*underlined and* 'satisfy non-Roman Catholics' *added*] it represents an unbelievable step forward in these relationships. It recognises, for example, the full 'church status' of the Orthodox, and realises that the Anglican Church has a special place to play [*sic*] in the future of ecumenism. All Christians are in some sense members of the Church by baptism, and future discussions will therefore be recognised as taking place 'within the Church'. It leaves to local[,] national or regional conferences of bishops the task of deciding how far and in what way the practice of ecumenism shall find expression in common devotion, in exploratory discussion and in social action. It ushers in a future full of promise. Our Archbishop's Commission on Roman Catholic Relations, which for some time has been enjoying semi-official discussions with Roman Catholics on the continent of Europe, will look forward to exploiting to the full in England the opportunities offered by the new decree.

Discussions have taken place during this session also on the following Schemata or 'Sets of Propositions':

1) on the *Apostolate of the Laity*. In this, as in almost all other discussions, there was a tug-of-war between the 'new thought' of the liberal bishops and the dead conservatism of those who are still satisfied with things as they are. Archbishop d'Souza of Bhopal, India, for example, was heard to say: 'When we realise that we must treat laymen as adults, it is amazing to read in the text that "nothing is to be done without the bishop". This phrase could open the door to untold abuses and repressions of initiative. The People of God is not a totalitarian state where everything is run from the top. We must show that we are genuinely ready to de-clericalise our outlook and treat the laity as brothers. The hierarchy should not take upon themselves the laity's responsibilities, but should leave them to do those things which they can do better. For example, why should representatives of the Church at international organisations always be priests? Laymen could be used in many offices in the Curia. They could also be employed in the diplomatic service of the Holy See and could even be appointed Nuncios in some cases.' And Bishop Leven of S. Antonio, Texas, said, 'This is most important for areas where the laity are educated and are ready to give their time and effort to the cause of the Church. Little will be gained if a bishop consults only a few people, especially if

these few are only his doctor and his housekeeper. It is desirable that every diocese should have a kind of diocesan senate.' [Mr Goyder[35] – *deleted*] Some may be dissatisfied with the rate of progress of synodical government in the Church of England, but he will sympathise with the efforts of some of the Roman Catholic bishops to rescue their Church from total clerical domination. It was in the course of this debate that Mr. Patrick Keegan,[36] an Irishman, was invited to address the Council. He exemplifies in his own person the concern of progressive Roman Catholics to pursue 'Christian action'. He is President of the World Movement of Christian Workers.[37] It will be remembered that Mr. Woodcock[38] and Sir Leslie [*sic*] Carron,[39] two most prominent Trades Union leaders, are Roman Catholics.

2) The discussion on the *Priesthood* was desultory in the extreme and the Schema was eventually rejected for rewriting.

3) A Schema on *Oriental Churches* (i.e. the eastern churches in communion with Rome) was criticised from many sides. It did not do adequate justice to the Orthodox churches, and seemed somewhat preoccupied with the question of the reception of converts. The central authority in Rome dealing with these churches should be representative, consisting largely of Orientals, instead of having a predominantly Latin and therefore juristic approach to most questions. Maximos IV, Melchite Patriarch of Antioch, that giant of the Council, wanted a 'new deal' and [a good deal of – *deleted*] more autonomy for the ancient catholic office of Patriarch. The hope was expressed that the Latin Patriarchate of Jerusalem would be suppressed.[40]

4) The Schema on the *Church in the Modern World* was one which had been long awaited. Its main themes were to be the Church in relation to modern culture, to hunger and poverty, to atheism and to marriage and population problems. It is impossible to analyse the wide

[35] George Goyder, chief administrator of the Church Assembly of the Church of England under Archbishops Fisher and Ramsey.

[36] This contribution by Patrick Keegan was judged by some to be the first occasion on which an ecumenical council had been addressed by a layman since Constantine spoke to the Council of Nicaea in 325.

[37] Based in Belgium, the World Movement of Christian Workers was in the process of formation during this period. It would be formally established in 1966.

[38] George Woodcock (1904–1979), General Secretary of the Trades Union Congress, 1960–1969.

[39] Sir William Carron (1902–1969), President of the Amalgamated Engineering Union, 1956–1957.

[40] Pope Pius IX had re-established a resident Latin Patriarch of Jerusalem in 1847. Between 1949 and 1970 the position was held by Alberto Gori.

range of these debates. In our view it attempted too much, and raised too sanguine expectations. The usual pattern of debate emerged, progressive against conservative. Some reminded the Council of the Church's agelong resistance to modern knowledge (Galileo and all that) and suggested that she should be careful not to be too closely wedded to any particular culture lest she become ossified in it. She had spent the whole of the 19th century denouncing the enlightenment and was now in the 20th having to catch up with it. The sad history of Fr. Teilhard de Chardin and the modern state of the Index were evidence that all was not well. Illiteracy in Latin America (the largest of the 'civilised' world) was said to have been fostered by the Church. Archbishop Heenan of Westminster contributed to the part of the debate concerning population control, but earned the disapproval of the Council by an attack on the 'Periti' or specialist theologians. The Pope had given notice that he intended to keep to himself the regulation of the text concerning birth-control, but there was evident in the general debate a desire to move away from the [kant – *deleted*] blank[et] prohibitions which have so far characterised Roman Catholic legislation on the matter to something more positive and pastoral. The section on world peace went over the ground which is normally covered by the Church Assembly, or every other responsible Christian body, totally condemning war as a means of arbitration, yet unable to agree to a total unilateral disarmament as a duty incumbent on any Christian nation. Strong declarations were made against world poverty and hunger and in a dramatic moment the Pope offered his ceremonial tiara to be sold and given to the poor. The Schema was eventually withdrawn for revision in the light of the debate.

In the last few days the bishops rushed breathlessly through a number of minor Schemas.

5) On *Missions*. Here the Council asked for more representative international control of missions and for the liberation of the Church in new areas from European culture.

6) On *Religious* (it was revealed that there were 2,000,000 of them in the world). Here a strong appeal was made that they should be brought up-to-date both in devotion and in habits of life and that a greater distinction in type of spirituality should be allowed between the contemplative and active orders.

7) On *Seminaries*. In the debate the issue was broadly whether the education of ordinands should continue to be exclusive and universally based on indoctrination in Thomistic philosophy, or whether it should be opened up to the new insights of contemporary knowledge and thought-forms.

8) On *Christian Education*. Here Archbishop Beck of Liverpool pleaded the right of the parent to be able to educate a child in a school of his own choice, according to the tenets of his own conscience; though he did not touch the corresponding question as to whether the State had a right to protect the child from excessive indoctrination.

9) On the last two days of the Council attention was turned to the Schema on the *Sacrament of Matrimony*. There of course the whole world was waiting to see what would be said about Mixed Marriages. The text shows some improvement on the situation as we now know it, dispensing with the extraction of a promise from the non-Roman party and allowing the Roman party to promise 'as far as possible' to ensure the Catholic education of the children. To our great disappointment Archbishop Heenan of Westminster showed himself against even these small concessions (saying he represented the whole hierarchy of Britain), though we gathered that most of his fellow bishops in the rest of the world are against him.

The last two days witnessed a drama of the greatest moment. The long-awaited declaration on Religious liberty, which had been delayed, blocked and modified so often by the conservative members of the Curia, was produced as a printed text in its final form on the Tuesday of the last week, in the hope that it would be voted [on] in one of the last days. But the Council of Presidents decided that the Council fathers had not enough time to digest the revised text. This created an uproar in the Council of dramatic proportions, and it was clear that the overwhelming majority of the bishops was against them. The Pope felt unable to overrule the Presidents, and promised that this should be the first item on the agenda of the next session. But let it be remembered that it was Pope John's ten presidents and not Pope Paul's four moderators who did the overruling. The American bishops in particular will find it difficult to face their fellow countrymen with this disappointment. Our reaction was not quite so violent. After so many centuries of error in this matter, it does not seem to us to be of great moment if the declaration of the official [commission – *deleted*] conversion of the Roman Church is delayed by a few months.

This rather shabby episode sent the bishops away in a bad humour, but it merely serves to emphasise that the 'liberals' in the Council will win in the end and that what the Roman Church needs above all things is a new set of high officials who will help, rather than impede, the present Pope in his intentions for the renewal of the Church. That might be a theme of prayer when we intercede, as we frequently should, for our brethren of the Roman obedience.

Report No. 165.   24th November, 1964

127TH GENERAL CONGREGATION, FRIDAY 20TH NOVEMBER.

Discussion was continued on the suggestion for MATRIMONIAL LEGISLATION:

Cardinal Ruffini, Archbishop of Palermo, praised much of the text such as those parts on the preparation of couples for marriage, the reduction of the number of impediments and the streamlining of marriage cases. It was not correct to use the term 'sacred' except in a broad sense for marriage before the time of Christ, since marriage became sacred because of its sacramental character. The respective roles of the Church and the State in marriage should be clearly shown, and it should be pointed out that the State was only competent in the purely civil side of marriage. It might be advisable to abrogate the excommunication now in Canon Law for Catholics who attempted marriage before non-Catholic ministers, but if this were done the text should formulate a stringent prohibition against such an act. (This represents a great concession on the part of this extremely reactionary Cardinal). The proposal to regard as valid for Catholics a marriage contracted contrary to the leave of the Church before a civil magistrate or a non-Catholic minister was something which at first sight seemed to be well nigh unthinkable.

Cardinal Monreal, Archbishop of Seville, said marriage should be considered not only as a sacrament but also as a duty of nature. More stress should be placed on the indissolubility under all its aspects. Such questions as the prohibited degrees of consanguinity should be left to the National Episcopal Conferences. The impediment of Orders should relate only to the priestly ordination and not to be applied to sub-diaconate and diaconate. The same should be true for solemn vows. With regard to mixed marriages, disparity of worship should affect only the lawfulness of the marriage. Marriage contracted before a civil magistrate or a minister should be regarded as valid, but the parties should remain outside ecclesiastical communion until they repented and made their peace with the Church.

Cardinal Döpfner, Archbishop of Munich, said the present text was in harmony with the doctrine on the Church and the decree on Ecumenism. Since the question of mixed marriages was extremely urgent and the Code of Canon Law could not be revised for at least some years, the Council should ask the Pope to take immediate steps to implement the legislation proposed in this schema.

Cardinal Ritter, Archbishop of St. Louis, Missouri, considered that the text moved prudently and wisely between the extremes of inflexible retention and complete relaxation of the form. The problem of clandestine marriages which preoccupied the Council of Trent no longer existed. Nevertheless there was a new problem, namely the high incidence of early and hasty marriages with the probability of divorce. This was a reason for retaining the form of marriage for the liturgy [. . .]

Bishop Fearns, Auxiliary of New York, said that whatever may be the merits of the legislation proposed in the schema it should certainly not be imposed indiscriminately on all nations. Many bishops were sincerely convinced that this new legislation would be very harmful in the United States. In any case the bishops should have had more time to prepare their pastors for such a drastic modification of the Church's law on marriage. It would be advisable to convoke a meeting of pastors, especially those coming from pluralistic countries to discuss the problems involved. Many felt that this change of legislation would do immense spiritual harm, at least in many quarters of the Church. [. . .]

Bishop Renard of Versailles said that not infrequently priests were confronted with the problem of baptised Catholics requesting Catholic marriage even though they had become lax in their religious practice or had abandoned it completely. Often they were completely ignorant of the sacramental character of marriage. In handling these situations there were two extremes. Some priests simply refused to admit such couples to marriage before the Church, while other priests, for fear of alienating them completely, admitted them to marriage with little or no preparation. To avoid such abuses the Council should issues some pastoral directives on the practical preparation of young couples for marriage, especially in such cases as described above. The Ordinary should be able to permit marriage without any sacred rite whatever, simply in the presence of a priest and two witnesses, whenever a sacred rite might be an occasion of offense. (This seemed an interesting reaction by a French bishop to what is in effect our situation in England. We got malicious joy from knowing that Heenan had to listen to it. Could we not have a joint study group with the French about 'the Administration of Matrimony in a post-Christian society'?)
[. . .]

Archbishop Heenan, in the name of the hierarchy of England and Wales, welcomed the proposals for the future celebration of mixed marriages. Too often the ceremonies for such marriages were so stripped of solemnity and joys as to seem more like a funeral than a wedding. No blessing of the ring, no candles or flowers and – what makes the bride burst into tears – no organ. If the Church granted a dispensation she could do so graciously, magnanimously and in an open-handed way. Let the Church show herself a real mother not only for the Catholic but also for the non-Catholic. Mixed marriages must be looked at realistically. Frequently the non-Catholic partner in England was not a church goer of any kind. Only rarely had he found non-Catholic partners in a mixed marriage to be really active members of any religious community. In such cases the promise to raise the children as Catholic rarely caused difficulty. If the non-Catholic could not with a good conscience promise that the children would be brought up as Catholics there should be no attempt of coercion. It was sufficient for him not to object to the promise being made by the Catholic party. This promise should be without any conditional clause. The words 'so far as I can' were unnecessary because obviously no one was ever bound to the impossible. But the words could be misinterpreted as meaning that the non-Catholic party had no obligation to put up any fight for the children's Catholic education and that for the sake of peace they might be allowed to abandon the faith. Such a conclusion would hardly harmonise with the pastoral goals of the Council. (This was regarded as a reactionary speech by members of the Secretariat, with considerable distaste).

[. . .]

Cardinal Bea presented the Declaration on the RELATIONSHIP OF THE CHURCH WITH NON-CHRISTIAN RELIGIONS. He observed that they could apply to the declaration the biblical comparison of the grain of mustard seed. It was first intended as a brief declaration on the Church and the Jewish people. But in the course of time the little seed had become almost a tree in which many birds were finding nests. That was to say in which all non-Christian religions were finding their proper place. The Council Presidency, the Coordinating Commission and the Moderators were all agreed that this declaration should be closely linked with the schema de Ecclesia. Nevertheless, in order not to interfere with the logical development [of the] Constitution or to complicate the voting and promulgation of this constitution, it was decided to add it at the end of the dogmatic decree as an appendix. This had the added advantage of putting in a clear light the exclusively religious character of the declaration against any unwarranted political interpretation. It also increased the importance of the declaration because it was added to a dogmatic constitution, even though its purpose was not strictly dogmatic, but pastoral.

In judging the necessity of this declaration they must remember that it was of great importance that the Church, the Christian world and world public opinion should have their attention drawn to the problems set forth in this declaration. The importance and extreme value of the declaration was in the fruits to be hoped for. For the first time in Conciliar history principles dealing with non-Christians were set forth in solemn form. The Church had a serious obligation to initiate dialogue with the one billion men who knew not Christ or his work of redemption. It was the task of the Church to help them to obtain a full share of the riches of Christ.

The following votes were taken:

Decree on Ecumenism (Approval of the entire document): placet 2,054; non placet 64; placet j.m.[41] 6; null 5. (Enormous applause.)
Decree on Catholic Oriental Churches: (Approval of the entire text): placet 1,964; non placet 135; placet j.m. 1; null 4.
Declaration on the Relationship of the Church with non-Catholic Religions (Approval of the whole text): placet 1,651; non placet 99; placet j.m. 242; null 4.

The Council was then asked to vote on the following propositions: Is it agreeable that the schema of the suggestions on matrimonial legislation along with all the observations made by the Council Fathers be transmitted at once to the Pope in order that he may make immediate provision through the competent offices?: placet 1,592; non placet 427; J.M.T.N. 2; null 3.

Report No. 166.   25th November, 1964

FINAL PUBLIC SESSION, SATURDAY 21ST NOVEMBER.

This began with a concelebration by the Pope with fourteen other bishops who had Marian sanctuaries in their diocese (including Northampton because of Walsingham). The liturgical occasion was the Presentation (?) of the B.V.M.

The three decrees:
  DE ECCLESIA
  DE ECUMENISMO and
  DE ECCLESIIS ORIENTALIBUS CATHOLICIS

[41] 'Placet juxta modem', a vote or expression of assent but with changes.

were voted and solemnly promulgated by the Pope, the first two with prolonged applause. This event is undoubtedly a milestone in Church history. It represents a commendable effort on the part of the Roman Church to make the best of the situation which has resulted from the disastrous definition of 1870. It confirms the picture we have constantly drawn (in season, out of season) of the present Pope as a friend in the long run of reform and enlightenment.

The Pope's discourse began by emphasising that these decrees represented not new teaching, but only explanations of what always had been. It reiterated that the new teaching about the bishop in no way compromised the position of the Pope as at Vatican I. But it did hint that he was going to call on the bishops extensively for help in the future.

The rest of the speech was given over to an amazing blast of Mariology which left the Observers quite dumbfounded. He declared the B.V.M. 'Mater Ecclesiae', a title which had been rejected for inclusion in the Schema by the Theological Commission. He said he would send a golden rose to Fatima etc. etc.[42] It all seemed for the moment quite disconcerting. The Marian fanatics rose and cheered loudly, while the Observers sat glum and despondent.

The whole thing was quite amazing. Many of the Protestant Observers left the Council reckoning to be totally disillusioned. I personally feared the effects which the speech might have on the Press, causing them to caricature the Pope even further as a disappointment etc. But my own reaction was to rally fairly quickly to the assessment of the situation which I ventured to send to the Archbishop by express letter immediately afterwards, to try to counteract any possible false impressions which the press reports might give. Later consultations, both on the Roman side and with the reliable organs of publicity, confirm the general interpretation given in the letter. *Vide* particularly the excellent despatch of the *Times* correspondent 'Vatican pressure on the Pope' of 22nd November. (I have had continuous and happy association with Peter Nichols,[43] the correspondent in question, which my successor will certainly also enjoy. Nichols' despatches on ecclesiastical questions are first-rate. He has the confidence of some of

---

[42]The Golden Rose is a gold imitation of a spray of roses which is blessed on the fourth day of Lent as a sign of spiritual joy and of future good works brought forth by the Church. When Paul VI closed the third session of the Council he announced that he was sending the Golden Rose to Portugal in the near future to honour the Sanctuary of Our Lady of Fatima.

[43]Peter Nichols (1928–1989) had become Italian correspondent for *The Times* in 1957. He was a distinguished writer and author of *The Pope's Divisions* (London, 1983).

the most reactionary elements in the Curia, as well as understanding and sympathising with the 'liberal' view.)

The main outlines of the situation now seem to me to be:-

1. The progress of the Council, particularly the votes of the Third Session, had been a bitter disappointment for the conservatives.

2. Sinister pressure groups have urged the Pope not to promulgate either de Ecclesia or de Ecumenismo. He has resolutely refused to yield to this pressure.

3. Accusations have been levelled at him, therefore, of 'letting down the Church' and 'betraying the faith'.

4. As a good captain of the ship he has tried to steady her in a stormy hour by giving some comfort to the conservatives. Their most tender spot is the B.V.M., and Chapter 5 of de Ecclesia is bitter for them. He therefore concentrated on that.

5. The 'rose of gold for Fatima' is apparently a sop to the Portuguese, who are cross with the Pope for favouring India by the proposed visit to Bombay, India having swamped the Portuguese territories of Goa.

6. The episode of the delay in the Declaration on Religious Liberty had already been reported (report No. 164) but it is all part of the same situation. Someone observed that it were better that this should be delayed than that on the Jews etc.

7. It is said that the Pope forced one or two amendments on the Secretariat for Unity in the Ecumenism Schema, all but one of which were acceptable. The one difficult one was a change in a passage describing us as those who 'Spiritum Sanctum invocantes in ipsis Sacris Scripturis Deum inveniunt quasi sibi loquentem in Christo'.[44] The word 'inveniunt' was replaced by 'inquirunt', i.e. we seek truth, but do not find it. But perhaps we cannot expect the Roman Church to admit that we find truth, or else their position is clean gone. Or perhaps it could have been allowed to be translated 'are finding', which would have saved face.

8. The Italian elections were due to happen the day following the speech. I don't know the political situation intimately enough to be sure, but it is just possible the Pope might feel he had to

[44]'Invoking the Holy Spirit, find God speaking to them in Christ through the sacred scriptures'.

make a symbolic gesture to the right. In any case the Communists eventually registered slight gains.

The general picture, therefore, of the Council emerges as progressive and a matter for thanksgiving, and of the Pope as having run true to our expectations of him. It is much more important, in the long run, that the decrees on the Church and Ecumenism should have been steered through almost unanimously than that the Declaration on Religious Liberty should have been rushed through now rather than at the next session. The Pope has been heavily pulled in two directions. He has encouraged the tendency of the left and dealt a strong blow at the right. It is up to us, in my opinion, in public communications, to show that we appreciate this and to encourage him to continue this tendency in the future.

ARCHBISHOP HEENAN'S SPEECH ON MIXED MARRIAGES.

[. . .]. The Observers took objection to the description of all non-Roman Catholic Christians in England as 'so-called church-going Protestants'. The Bishop of Ripon thought that the Archbishop of Canterbury's attention ought to have been drawn to this. I am inclined to think that we might ignore it in the interests of making him live up to the one or two liberal phrases in the speech. But it created a bad impression on the whole. I am afraid Heenan had not emerged well from the Council.

Report No. 167. 30th November, 1964.

FAREWELL BY SECRETARIAT FOR UNITY

My wife and I were asked to dinner by Mgr. Willebrands on Thursday 26th November in the 'Columbus' Hotel. We were very much touched on arrival to find that the whole staff of the Secretariat were there (about 12 people), and that this was a dinner given in our honour. In the course of the speech of goodwill and thanks I was interested to note that Mgr. Willebrands repeated twice that the Anglicans *tried to understand* what was going on in the Roman Church and to evaluate it pragmatically. And he referred to 'good humour' etc. There is no doubt that the first thing they look for in any mission is sympathy. I suppose this could denigrate into complacency and too easy acquiescence. But I think they have appreciated our sympathetic handling of the situation (which would come naturally to most Anglicans) in contrast to the rather unselfcritical dogmatic reactions of e.g. the Lutherans. Willebrands stressed that Archbishop Fisher's response to John XXIII's overtures had had a quite observable influence on the progress of the preparations for the Council.

Two positions emerged in the general conversation. One was the confirmation (by Schmidt, Cardinal Bea's private secretary) of the rumour that Cardinal Suenens had fallen out of favour since his speech on the Church in the Modern World and that Cardinals Roberti and Browne were now seeing a lot of the Pope. This was regarded by all as a pity. The other concerned the Lutherans. Mgr. Höfer said there was a great debate going on among the Lutherans as to whether there was such a thing as a 'Lutheran Church' or not. Many of them (including Prof. Schlink) thought there was not. There was not a universally accepted statement of belief; there was no uniform pattern of ministry; there was no executive authenticity with the World Lutheran Federation. In Germany, the home country, the Lutherans were yoked with Reformed in the Evangelische Kirche Deutschlands. In Sweden there was an episcopal state Church etc [. . .]

The rumour was strong that the Council would resume in May. I have had no other confirmation of this date, and it seems unlikely on general grounds.

CARDINAL BEA

I took leave of the Cardinal on November 27th. He was very friendly and asked to be remembered to the Archbishop of Canterbury. He said he would welcome my successor. When he asked how I though the job would develop I said I hoped it would lead to the establishment of an Anglican Institute in some form, and he agreed that that would be desirable. He said that the third session had been memorable for the votes on the two great documents. He thought the acceptance of the declaration about the Jews etc. also very significant because

a. It had been done uphill against constant attrition;
b. Not even the political pressure in the middle East had been able to stop it;
c. It formed a healthy rejoinder to the influence of such things as the Hochhuth play;[45]

---

[45] Rolf Hochhuth's play *Der Stellvertreter* had been premiered in 1963. It accused Pius XII of passivity in the face of the Holocaust.

d. It had been rescued from its improper place at the tail of the Decree on Ecumenism.

He said we (particularly my successor) must be vigilant to follow up the detailed development of the situation on de Ecumenismo. There will be those who will try to torpedo its application in detail.

THE POPE

I had a final audience with the Pope on November 28th. This was very remarkable, because he had invited me to bring all the family, which I did, having warned him that I could not be responsible for what Felicity (aged 3) and Matthew (aged 2) might say or do. He replied that he was quite used to his great nephews and nieces, some of whom had made havoc in the Vatican Palace, a few weeks previously. In the event nothing disastrous happened, and the whole thing was a success. The children were slightly more impressed, naturally, with the Swiss Guards than with the clergyman in the white cassock.

I had an audience alone first. His Holiness enquired about the Archbishop of Canterbury's health and plans (I had previously mentioned His Grace's projected journeys in 1965). I was able to explain our hopes about the future of church union in Nigeria. The Pope asked how these new 'united' churches would stand in relation to Canterbury. Did I think this would be the general pattern of reunion schemes in other parts of the world? He hoped that the Archbishop's visit to Rome would not be long delayed. I thought it might happen in 1965 if a date could be found free of the Council and of the Archbishop's journeys.

The Pope was complimentary about my mission and regretted that it had ended. He asked about Findlow[46] without my prompting and said he would receive him as he had received me. He hoped that I should still be associated with the work. I should always be welcome to visit him, or write or send material for his reading or to ask questions. I thanked him and said that I could have wished for answers to some questions in the last week of the Council. He smiled and said 'There were difficulties, but all is well now'. I said that it was not always easy to report objectively what was really going on. He smiled again and asked what I had reported about the last days. I told him. His face went serious and he said 'Bene, bene', with some emphasis. 'I think Anglicans often understand what is going on among us better than

---

[46]The Revd Canon John Findlow, Pawley's successor; a leading figure in the future of Anglican–Roman Catholic relations. He died in 1970.

anyone else. They have a hierarchy, they believe in the Church. I have clear principles on which I act in times of difficulty. I must act in faith. I must show that I understand the aspirations of the two sides when they disagree, that I love them personally, that I respect their institutions and ways of thinking. As captain of the ship I have to keep her on a steady course' (I had already used this metaphor in a despatch to the Archbishop concerning the Pope's actions). 'So you bring all along with you. I am not going to act in a hurry. We have made great strides, but we have made them together (meaning that the new documents, through not being rushed, had had an almost unanimous vote). It is better for me to go ahead slowly and carry everyone with me than to hurry along and cause dissensions. Especially when I speak in public I must show that I love all my sheep, like a good shepherd'.

All this confirmed the diagnosis of the 'crisis' at the end of the 3rd session previously adopted in these reports. This line of talk gave me the opening I wanted for presenting my C.I.C.[47] booklet. I said that we were often faced with the same situation viewed from our angle. When we spoke or wrote we had to assure our doubtful brethren that we were not compromising our position, and so could attempt to bring them along with us. I had written very frankly in a spirit which was totally friendly and I hoped he would find it so. The Pope again said 'Bene, bene', and added 'we must all speak with frankness, thus you get further in the long run'.

This interview was one of the most satisfactory I have had, offering immediate opportunities for exchange at quite a deep level, without wasting time on courtesies. It was a return to the old Milan days.

My wife and children were afterwards presented. The audience resulted in a pair of photographs which will be a great pride in the future.

[47] Church Information Council.

THE COUNCIL AFTER PAWLEY

September–December 1965: The fourth and concluding period of the Council

Paul VI made two surprising announcements during his opening speech at the fourth and concluding period of the Council: he would create a Synod of Bishops (but reaffirmed that their role was only an advisory one) and he would visit the United Nations during this period to proclaim the Council message of love, peace, and justice.

Dignitatis Humanae (Declaration on Religious Freedom)

The schema was approved by 90% of the bishops. It was a ground-breaking declaration as it advocated that the principle of religious liberty should be treated as a civil right and that governments should protect this right. It also acknowledged that the Church's previous stance on the issue might not have been just. It further declared that the right to religious freedom has its foundation in the very dignity of the human person, this dignity being known through the revealed Word of God and by reason itself.

The Council accepted the Decree on Revelation and the Decree on the Laity, the Pope signed all the remaining documents, and the final approval was accepted by the bishops. On 8 December 1965 the Council was declared concluded.

SELECTIVE BIBLIOGRAPHY

Unpublished sources

Lambeth Palace Library, correspondence, 1960–1964, CGR CR 22–24, Relations with the Vatican, Anglican Liaison, Canon Pawley

Canterbury Cathedral Archives, GB 054 U114, Papers of Bernard Clinton Pawley

History and general accounts of Vatican II

Alberigo, Guiseppe, *A Brief History of Vatican II* (Maryknoll, NY, 2006); first published as *Breve storia del concilio Vaticano II* (Bologna, 2005)

———— (ed.), *History of Vatican II*, 5 vols, English version edited by Joseph A. Komonchak (Maryknoll, NY, 1995–2006)

————, J.P. Jossua, and Joseph A. Komonchak (eds), *The Reception of Vatican II* (Washington, DC, 1987)

Anderson, Floyd, *Council Daybook, Vatican II*, 3 vols (Washington, DC, 1966)

Faggioli, Massimo, *Vatican II: the battle for meaning* (New York and Mahwah, NJ, 2012)

Gaillardetz, Richard R. and Catherine A. Clifford, *Keys to the Council: unlocking the teaching of Vatican II* (Collegeville, MN, 2012)

Hastings, Adrian (ed.), *A Concise Guide to the Documents of the Second Vatican Council*, 2 vols (London, 1968–1969)

Hünermann, Peter and Bernd Jochen Hilberath (eds), *Herders theologischer Kommentar zum Zweiten Vatikanischen Konzil*, 5 vols (Freiburg, 2004–2006)

Kaufmann, Franz-Xaver and Arnold Zingerle (eds), *Vatikanum II und Modernisierung: historische, theologische und soziologische Perspektiven* (Paderborn, 1996)

McEnroy, Carmen, *Guests in Their Own House: the women of Vatican II* (New York, 1996)

O'Malley, John W., *What Happened at Vatican II* (Cambridge, MA, 2008)

Rush, Ormond, *Still Interpreting Vatican II: some hermeneutical principles* (New York and Mahwah, NJ, 2004)

Stacpoole, Alberic (ed.), *Vatican II by Those Who Were There* (London, 1986)

Reception of Vatican II

Bischof, Franz Xaver (ed.), *Das Zweite Vatikanische Konzil (1962–1965): Stand und Perspektiven der kirchenhistorischen Forschung im deutschsprachigen Raum* (Stuttgart, 2012)

Cassidy, Edward, *Ecumenism and Interreligious Dialogue: Unitatis Redintegratio, Nostra Aetate* (New York and Mahwah, NJ, 2005)

Heft, James L. and John O'Malley, *After Vatican II: trajectories and hermeneutics* (Grand Rapids, MI, 2012)

O'Collins, Gerald, *Living Vatican II: the 21st council for the 21st century* (New York and Mahwah, NJ, 2006)

Ratzinger, Joseph, *Theological Highlights of Vatican II*, translated by Henry Traub, SJ, Gerard C. Thormann, and Wener Barzel (New York, 1966); reprinted with an introduction by Thomas P. Rausch (New York and Mahwah, NJ, 2009)

Roman Catholic–Anglican relations

Amand de Mendietta, E., *Rome and Canterbury* (London, 1962)

Barlow, Bernard, *'A Brother Knocking at the Door': the Malines conversations 1921–1925* (Norwich, 1996)

Bell, G.K.A., *Randall Davidson, Archbishop of Canterbury*, 3rd edn (London, 1952)

Bliss, Frederick, *Anglicans in Rome: a history* (Norwich, 2006)

Carpenter, Edward, *Archbishop Fisher: his life and times* (Norwich, 1991)

Catholicism To-Day: letters to the Editor reprinted from The Times with a special article and a leading article (London, 1949)

Chadwick, Owen, *Michael Ramsey: a life* (Oxford, 1990)

Chandler, Andrew and David Hein, *Archbishop Fisher, 1945–1961: Church, state and world* (Farnham, 2012)

Creighton, Louise, *Life and Letters of Mandell Creighton* (London, 1905)

Dix, Gregory, *The Question of Anglican Orders* (London, 1944)

Fallows, W.G., *Mandell Creighton and the English Church* (London, 1964)

Frere, Walter, *Recollections of Malines* (London, 1935)

Gore, Charles, *Order and Unity* (London, 1909)

Grant, Frederick C., *Rome and Reunion* (Oxford and New York, 1965)

Hagerty, James, *Cardinal Hinsley: Priest and Patriot* (London, 2008)

——— *Cardinal John Carmel Heenan: priest of the people, prince of the Church* (London, 2012)

Halifax, Charles Lindley, *Leo XIII and Anglican Orders* (London, 1912)

Hastings, Adrian, *A History of English Christianity, 1920–2000* (London, 2001)

Hebblethwaite, Peter, *John XXIII: Pope of the Council* (London, 1984)

——— *Paul VI: the first modern Pope* (London, 1993)

Heenan, John C., *Cardinal Hinsley* (London, 1944)

——— *A Crown of Thorns: an autobiography, 1951–1963* (London, 1974)

——— *Not the Whole Truth* (London, 1974)

Jasper, R.C.D., *George Bell, Bishop of Chichester* (London, 1967)

Lockhart, J.G., *Charles Lindley Viscount Halifax*, 2 vols (London, 1935–1936)

Manktelow, Michael, *John Moorman: Anglican, Franciscan, Independent* (Norwich, 1999)

Mathew, David, *Catholicism in England: the portrait of a minority: its culture and tradition*, 3rd edn (London, 1955)

Moormann, John, *Vatican II Observed: an Anglican impression of Vatican II* (London, 1967)

Pawley, Bernard C., *An Anglican View of the Vatican Council* (New York, 1962)

——— (ed.), *The Second Vatican Council: studies by eight Anglican Observers* (London, 1967)

——— and Margaret Pawley, *Rome and Canterbury Through Four Centuries: a study of the relations between the Church of Rome and Anglican Churches, 1530–1981* (London and Oxford, 1974; revised edn 1981)

Prestige, G.L., *The Life of Charles Gore: a great Englishman* (London, 1935)

Ramsey, A.M., *Rome and Canterbury: a public lecture in Dublin* (London, 1967)

Sykes, Norman, *William Wake, Archbishop of Canterbury, 1657–1737*, 2 vols (Cambridge, 1957)

INDEX

Bishops and archbishops are of the Roman Catholic Church unless otherwise noted (except for the Archbishops of Canterbury).